murach's
Java
servlets and
JSP

Andrea Steelman
Joel Murach

 MIKE MURACH & ASSOCIATES, INC.

3484 W. Gettysburg, Suite 101 • Fresno, CA 93722-7801
www.murach.com • murachbooks@murach.com

Authors:	Andrea Steelman
	Joel Murach
Cover Design:	Zylka Design
Production:	Tom Murach

Books in the Murach series

Murach's Beginning Java 2
Murach's Java Servlets and JSP

Murach's SQL for SQL Server
Murach's Beginning Visual Basic .NET
Murach's VB.NET Database Programming with ADO.NET
Murach's ASP.NET Web Programming with VB.NET

Murach's Structured COBOL
Murach's OS/390 and z/OS JCL
Murach's CICS for the COBOL Programmer
Murach's CICS Desk Reference

Printed in the United States of America

10 9 8 7 6 5 4 3 2
ISBN: 1-890774-18-9

Contents

Introduction   xi

Section 1   Introduction to servlet and JSP programming

Chapter 1   An introduction to web programming   3
Chapter 2   How to install and use Tomcat   29
Chapter 3   A crash course in HTML   61

Section 2   The essence of servlet and JSP programming

Chapter 4   How to develop JavaServer Pages   101
Chapter 5   How to develop servlets   141
Chapter 6   How to structure a web application   167
Chapter 7   How to work with sessions and cookies   203
Chapter 8   How to create and use JavaBeans   243
Chapter 9   How to work with custom JSP tags   267

Section 3   The essential database skills

Chapter 10   How to use MySQL to work with a database   307
Chapter 11   How to use Java to work with a database   333

Section 4   Advanced servlet and JSP skills

Chapter 12   How to use JavaMail to send email   375
Chapter 13   How to use SSL to work with a secure connection   397
Chapter 14   How to restrict access to a web resource   417
Chapter 15   How to work with HTTP requests and responses   437
Chapter 16   How to work with XML   465
Chapter 17   An introduction to Enterprise JavaBeans   503

Section 5   The Music Store web site

Chapter 18   An introduction to the Music Store web site   523
Chapter 19   The Download application   545
Chapter 20   The Shopping Cart application   557
Chapter 21   The Admin application   579

Appendixes

Appendix A   How to install the software and applications for this book   599
Index   614

Expanded contents

Section 1 Introduction to servlet and JSP programming

Chapter 1 An introduction to web programming with Java

An introduction to web applications **4**
A typical web application 4
The components of a web application 6
How static web pages work 8
How dynamic web pages work 10

An introduction to Java web programming **12**
The components of a Java web application 12
An introduction to JavaServer Pages 14
An introduction to servlets 16
How to combine servlets and JSPs in a web application 16

An introduction to Java web development **18**
Three platforms for developing servlets and JSPs 18
The architecture for servlet and JSP applications 20
Tools for writing servlets and JSPs 22
Tools for deploying servlets and JSPs 24

Chapter 2 How to install and use Tomcat

How to install and configure Tomcat **30**
How to install Tomcat on your own PC 30
A summary of Tomcat's directories and files 32
How to set the JAVA_HOME environment variable 34
How to change the memory settings for Tomcat's batch files 36
How to turn on servlet reloading 38

How to use Tomcat **40**
How to start and stop Tomcat 40
How to view a web page 42
How to view a directory listing 44

A quick guide to troubleshooting **46**
Two common Tomcat problems and how to solve them 46
How to change the port that's used by Tomcat 48

How to deploy and run a web application **50**
How to deploy a web application 50
How to view and run a web application 50
A summary of the directories and files for a web application 52
An introduction to the web.xml file for a web application 54
A summary of the directories and files for the book applications 56

Chapter 3 A crash course in HTML

An introduction to HTML **62**
Tools for working with HTML 62
An HTML document 64

How to code and view an HTML page **66**
How to code an HTML document 66
Where and how to save an HTML document 68
How to view an HTML page 70

More skills for coding HTML documents **72**
How to code links to other HTML pages 72
How to code tables 74
Attributes for working with table tags 76
How to include images in an HTML page 78
How to use a style sheet 80
How to code HTML forms **82**
How to code a form 82
How to code text boxes, password boxes, and hidden fields 84
How to code buttons 86
How to code check boxes and radio buttons 88
How to code combo boxes and list boxes 90
How to code text areas 92
How to set the tab order of controls 94

Section 2 The essence of servlet and JSP programming

Chapter 4 How to develop JavaServer Pages

The Email List application **102**
The user interface for the application 102
The code for the HTML page that calls the JSP 104
The code for the JSP 106
How to create a JSP **108**
How to code scriptlets and expressions 108
How to use the methods of the request object 110
Where and how to save a JSP 112
How to request a JSP 114
When to use the Get and Post methods 116
How to use regular Java classes with JSPs **118**
The code for the User and UserIO classes 118
Where and how to save and compile regular Java classes 120
A JSP that uses the User and UserIO classes 122
How to use three more types of JSP tags **124**
How to import classes 124
How to code comments in a JSP 126
How to declare instance variables and methods 128
A JSP that imports classes and declares instance variables 130
How to work with JSP errors **132**
How to debug JSP errors 132
How to use a custom error page 134
When and how to view the servlet that's generated for a JSP 136

Chapter 5 How to develop servlets

The Email List application **142**
The user interface for the application 142
The code for the EmailServlet class 144
How to create a servlet **146**
How to code a servlet 146
How to save and compile a servlet 148
How to request a servlet 150

Other skills for working with servlets **152**

The methods of a servlet 152

How to code instance variables.. 154

How to code thread-safe servlets 156

How to debug servlets **158**

Common servlet problems 158

How to print debugging data to the console 160

How to write debugging data to a log file 162

Chapter 6   How to structure a web application

The Email List application **168**

The code for the servlet... 168

The code for the JSP 170

How to structure servlets and JSPs **172**

An introduction to the Model 1 architecture 172

An introduction to the Model-View-Controller pattern 174

How to forward and redirect requests and responses 176

How to validate data on the client **178**

An HTML page that uses JavaScript to validate data 178

A dialog box that displays a validation message.. 180

How to validate data on the server **182**

A servlet that validates data 182

A JSP that displays a data validation message 184

How to include code from a file in a JSP **186**

A JSP that includes code from other files 186

How to include a file in a JSP 188

How to work with the web.xml file **190**

An introduction to the web.xml file 190

How to set initialization parameters 192

How to get initialization parameters 194

How to implement servlet mapping 196

How to implement custom error handling 198

Chapter 7   How to work with sessions and cookies

An introduction to session tracking **204**

Why session tracking is difficult with HTTP 204

How session tracking works in Java 204

An application that needs session tracking... 206

How to work with sessions **208**

How to set and get session attributes 208

More methods of the session object 210

How to enable or disable cookies 212

How to use URL encoding to track sessions without cookies 214

How to work with cookies **216**

An introduction to cookies 216

How to create and use cookies 218

How to view and delete cookies 220

Four methods for working with cookies 222

A utility class for working with cookies 224

How to work with URL rewriting and hidden fields **226**

How to use URL rewriting to pass parameters.. 226

How to use hidden fields to pass parameters... 228

The Download application 230
The user interface 230
The file structure 230
The code for the JSPs and servlets 230

Chapter 8 How to create and use JavaBeans

An introduction to JavaBeans 244
How to code a JavaBean 244
A JSP that uses a JavaBean 246

How to code JSP tags for JavaBeans 248
How to code the useBean tag 248
How to code the getProperty and setProperty tags 250
How to set the properties of a bean from request parameters 252
How to set non-string data types in a bean 254
How to use interface and abstract class types with beans 256

The Email List application with beans 258
The application when the MVC pattern is used 258
The application when Model 1 architecture is used 262

Chapter 9 How to work with custom JSP tags

How to code a custom tag that doesn't have a body 268
The JSP 268
The TLD tags 270
The tag handler class 272

How to code a custom tag that has a body 274
The JSP 274
The TLD tags 276
The tag handler class 276

How to code a custom tag that has attributes 278
The JSP 278
The TLD tags 280
The tag handler class 282

How to code a custom tag that reiterates its body 284
The JSP 284
The TLD tags 286
The tag handler class 286

How to work with scripting variables 290
An introduction to scripting variables 290
The TEI class 292

Classes, methods, and fields for working with custom tags 294
Methods and fields of the TagSupport class 294
Methods and fields of the PageContext class 296
Methods and fields of the BodyTagSupport class 298
Methods and fields of the BodyContent class 300

Section 3 The essential database skills

Chapter 10 How to use MySQL to work with a database

An introduction to MySQL **308**
What MySQL provides 308
What MySQL doesn't provide 308
Two ways to interact with MySQL 310
How to start and stop the MySQL database server 312

How to work with the mysql program **314**
How to start and stop the mysql program 314
How to create, select, and delete a database 316
How to create and delete a table 318
How to insert or load data into a table 320
How to configure the mysql program 322

The SQL statements for data manipulation **324**
How to select data from a single table 324
How to select data from multiple tables 326
How to insert, update, and delete data 328

Chapter 11 How to use Java to work with a database

How to work with JDBC **334**
How to obtain and install a database driver 334
How to connect to a database 336
How to return a result set and move the cursor through it 338
How to retrieve data from a result set 340
How to insert, update, and delete data 342
How to work with prepared statements 344

The SQL Gateway application **346**
The user interface 346
The code for the JSP 348
The code for the servlet 350
The code for the utility class 354

How to work with connection pooling **356**
How connection pooling works 356
How to install a connection pool 358
How to customize a connection pool 358
How to use a connection pool 360

The Email List application **362**
The user interface 362
The code for the JSP 362
The code for the servlet 364
The code for the UserDB class 366

Section 4 Advanced servlet and JSP skills

Chapter 12 How to use JavaMail to send email

An introduction to the JavaMail API **376**
How email works 376
Protocols for working with email 376
How to install the JavaMail API 378
Code that uses the JavaMail API to send an email message 380

How to create and send an email message 382
How to create a mail session 382
How to create a message 384
How to address a message 386
How to send a message 388
How to send an email message from a servlet 390
A helper class that can be used to send a message 390
A servlet that uses a helper class to send a message 392

Chapter 13   How to use SSL to work with a secure connection

An introduction to SSL 398
How SSL works 398
How TLS works 398
When to use a secure connection 398
How SSL authentication works 400
How to obtain a digital secure certificate 402
How to configure a testing environment for SSL 404
How to install the JSSE API 404
How to create a certificate for testing 406
How to enable SSL in Tomcat 406
How to test a local SSL connection 408
How to work with a secure connection 410
How to request a secure connection 410
A page that uses a secure connection 412
How to return to a regular HTTP connection 412
How to switch from a local system to an Internet server 412

Chapter 14   How to restrict access to a web resource

An introduction to authentication 418
How container-managed authentication works 418
Three types of authentication 420
How to restrict access to web resources 422
How to create a security constraint 422
How to implement the JDBC realm 424
How to create the tables for the JDBC realm 426
How to use basic authentication 428
The login dialog box 428
The XML tags 428
How to use form-based authentication 430
The login page 430
The XML tags 430
The code for the login page 432

Chapter 15   How to work with HTTP requests and responses

An introduction to HTTP 438
An HTTP request and response 438
Common MIME types 440
Common HTTP request headers 442
Common HTTP status codes 444
Common HTTP response headers 446
How to work with the request 448
How to get request headers 448
How to display all request headers 450

The request headers for the IE and Netscape browsers 452

How to work with the response **454**
How to set status codes 454
How to set response headers 454

Practical skills for working with HTTP **456**
How to return a tab-delimited file as an Excel spreadsheet 456
How to control caching 456
How to encode the response with GZIP compression 458
How to require the File Download dialog box 460

Chapter 16   How to work with XML

An introduction to XML **466**
An XML document 466
Common uses of XML 466
XML declarations and comments 468
XML elements 468
XML attributes 470
An introduction to DTDs 472
An introduction to XML APIs 474

How to work with DOM **476**
The DOM tree 476
Interfaces for working with the DOM tree 478
How to create an empty DOM tree 480
How to add nodes to a DOM tree 482
How to write a DOM tree to a file 484
How to read a DOM tree from a file 486
How to read the nodes of a DOM tree 488
How to add, update, and delete nodes 490

The Email List application **492**
The code for the XMLUtil class 492
The code for the UserXML class 494
The code for the EmailServlet class 496

How to return an XML document via HTTP **498**
The code for the XMLServlet class 498
The XML document displayed in a browser 498

Chapter 17   An introduction to Enterprise JavaBeans

How Enterprise JavaBeans work **504**
The components of a web application that uses EJBs 504
What EJBs can provide 506
The pros and cons of EJBs 506
Typical EJB developer roles 506

How to implement EJBs **510**
How to implement an entity bean 510
How to code the remote and home interfaces 512
How to code the bean implementation class 514
How to implement BMP 516
How to access an EJB in an application 518

Introduction

Ever since the late 1990s when Java servlets and JavaServer Pages (JSPs) came into widespread use, web site developers have been switching from CGI scripting languages to servlets and JSPs. As a result, there has been tremendous growth in the use of servlets and JSPs. Although this trend has slowed somewhat with the bursting of the dot-com bubble, there's little doubt that servlet and JSP technology is here to stay.

From the start, though, servlets and JSPs have been a training problem because web programming with them requires so many different skills and so much conceptual background. That's why it's been so hard to organize and teach these skills and concepts in a single book or course. But now, by reading just this book, you can master all the skills that you need for developing e-commerce applications. And to prove that, this book's CD includes a complete e-commerce web site that uses just the skills that are presented in this book.

Why you'll learn faster and better with this book

When we started writing this book, we knew we had to take a new approach if we wanted to teach you everything you need to know in a way that's faster and better than the other books. Here, then, are a few of the ways in which our book differs from the others:

- Chapter 3 of this book provides a crash course in HTML. Since this is essential background for the use of JSPs, this means you won't have to use a second book to figure out how HTML works.

- Three of the early chapters (4 through 6) show you how JSPs work, how servlets work, and how to use the Model 2 architecture to get the most from JSPs and servlets. From that point on, you'll learn to use servlets when they're appropriate for the task at hand and JSPs when they're appropriate. As a result, you won't waste your time learning how to use servlets for tasks that should be handled by JSPs, or vice versa.

- This book shows you how to work with a specific servlet and JSP engine (Tomcat) and a specific database server (MySQL). That way, you learn the coding details for these popular products, which helps you get the most from them. At the same time, though, you learn the principles that apply to all servlet and JSP engines and all database servers.

- To make it easy for you to learn on your own, the CD that comes with this book provides all of the software that you need including Java, Tomcat, and MySQL. It also provides all of the examples and applications that are presented in this book so you can run them on your own PC.

- Like all of our books, this one includes hundreds of examples that range from the simple to the complex. That way, you can quickly see how a feature works from the simple examples, but you'll also see how the feature is used in more complex, real-world examples.

- Like most of our books, this one has exercises at the end of each chapter that help you practice what you've learned. They also encourage you to experiment and challenge you to apply what you've learned in new ways.

- If you page through this book, you'll see that all of the information is presented in "paired pages," with the essential syntax, guidelines, and examples on the right page and the perspective and extra explanation on the left page. This helps you learn faster by reading less...and this is the ideal reference format when you need to refresh your memory about how to do something.

What you'll learn in this book

- In section 1, you'll learn the concepts and terms that you need for working with web applications. You'll learn how to install and use Tomcat, the software that lets you use servlets and JSPs for web applications. And you'll learn how to use HTML, which is essential to the use of JSPs. When you're done, you'll be ready to learn how to code and run servlets and JSPs.

- In section 2, you'll learn the skills for creating servlets and JSPs that you'll need for almost every application. These chapters move from the simple to the complex as they show you how to work with JSPs, servlets, the Model 2 architecture, sessions, cookies, JavaBeans, and custom JSP tags.

- In section 3, you'll learn how to use servlets and JSPs to work with a database. Since MySQL is a popular open-source database that works well with Java and is commonly used for web applications, this section presents the details for working with MySQL. However, these principles can be applied to the use of any database.

- In section 4, you'll learn the advanced servlet and JSP skills that you will need for certain types of web applications. This includes the use of JavaMail, SSL, security, HTTP, XML, and EJBs. Since the chapters in this section have been designed to work independently of each other, you can read them in any order you want. This makes it easy for you to learn new skills whenever you need them.

- To complete your Java web programming skills, section 5 presents an e-commerce web site that puts the skills presented in the first four sections into context. Once you understand how this web site works, you will have all the skills you need for creating your own web applications. Then, you can use the code that's on the CD that comes with this book as a starting point for your own web applications.

Who this book is for

If you have basic Java skills, the kind you get from a beginning Java course, you're ready for this book. Those basics should include the use of inheritance and interfaces with Java classes, the use of vectors and strings, and the use of text files.

If you're new to Java or you don't have a complete set of these basic skills, you can get up to speed quickly by reading *Murach's Beginning Java 2*. In particular, you can read chapters 1 through 10 to learn the basics of Java programming including the use of vectors and strings, and you can read chapters 16 and 17 to learn how to work with text files. If you do that, you'll have the prerequisite skills for developing servlets and JSPs, and you'll have a book you can refer to whenever you need to refresh your memory about the basics.

Everything you need is on the CD

To make it easy for you to learn on your own, the CD that comes with this book provides all the software that you need, including:

- The Tomcat servlet and JSP engine, which lets you run servlets and JSPs on your own PC.

- The Java SDK (Software Development Kit) that contains the Java compiler and runtime environment that you need for developing servlets.

- The MySQL database software, a MySQL driver, and a Java class that implements a connection pool. This software lets you create servlets and JSPs that use a MySQL database.

- The SQL scripts for the databases. You can run these scripts to create the databases that are used by the applications in this book.

- Trial versions of the TextPad and HomeSite text editors. That way, you can use TextPad to work with Java classes such as servlets, and you can use HomeSite to work with HTML and JSP documents.

- The source code for all of the examples and applications presented in this book. That way, you can test this code on your own PC and modify it to see how the changes work.

To help you install these components, chapter 2 shows you how to install Tomcat, and appendix A shows you how to install the rest.

Support materials for trainers and instructors

To make it easy to run a course that's based on this book, a complete set of instructor's materials is available on CD. These materials include solutions to the exercises in this book, student projects, solutions to the student projects, tests, answers, and PowerPoint slides. Taken together, this book, its CD, and these instructional materials make a powerful teaching package.

To download a sample of the instructor's materials and to find out how to get the Instructor's CD, please go to our web site at www.murach.com and click on the Instructors link. Or, if you prefer, you can get more information by calling Karen at 1-800-221-5528 or by e-mailing her at karen@murach.com.

Please let us know how this book works for you

When we started this book, our goal was to teach you how to develop real-world web applications with Java servlets and JSPs as quickly and easily as possible. In particular, we wanted to make it a lot easier for you to learn Java web programming than it was for us. Now, we hope that we've succeeded. If you have any comments, you can email us at murachbooks@murach.com.

So thanks for buying this book. Thanks for reading it. And good luck with your web programming.

Andrea Steelman
January 2, 2003

Joel Murach
January 2, 2003

Section 1

Introduction to servlet and JSP programming

The three chapters in this section provide the background information that you need for writing servlets and JavaServer Pages (JSPs). In chapter 1, you'll learn what web programming is and how servlets and JSPs work. In chapter 2, you'll learn how to install and use the Tomcat software for running servlets and JSPs on your own PC. And in chapter 3, you'll learn how to develop the HTML documents that pass data to the servlets and JSPs of a web application.

1

An introduction to web programming with Java

This chapter introduces you to the concepts and terms that you need for working with servlets and JavaServer Pages (JSPs) as you create web applications. In particular, this chapter introduces you to the software that you'll be working with.

An introduction to web applications 4
A typical web application 4
The components of a web application 6
How static web pages work 8
How dynamic web pages work 10
An introduction to Java web programming 12
The components of a Java web application 12
An introduction to JavaServer Pages 14
An introduction to servlets 16
How to combine servlets and JSPs in a web application 16
An introduction to Java web development 18
Three platforms for developing servlets and JSPs 18
The architecture for servlet and JSP applications 20
Tools for writing servlets and JSPs 22
Tools for deploying servlets and JSPs 24
Perspective 26

An introduction to web applications

A *web application* is a set of web pages that are generated in response to user requests. The Internet has many different types of web applications, such as search engines, online stores, auctions, news sites, discussion groups, and games.

A typical web application

Figure 1-1 shows the first two pages of the shopping cart application that's available from *www.murach.com*. Here, the first page presents some information about our beginning Java book. This page contains two buttons: a View Cart button and an Add To Cart button. When you click the Add To Cart button, the web application adds the book to your cart and displays the second page in this figure, which shows all of the items in your cart.

The second page lets you change the quantity for an item or remove an item from the cart. It also lets you continue shopping or begin the checkout process. In this book, you'll learn all the skills you need to create a shopping cart application like this one.

If you take a closer look at these web pages, you can learn a little bit about how this application works. For the first page, the Address box of the browser shows an address that has an htm extension. This means that the page was rendered from an HTML document.

In contrast, the Address box for the second page shows the address of a servlet named ShoppingServlet that's stored in the murach.ordering package. This means that the HTML code for this page was generated by the servlet. After the servlet address, you can see a question mark and one parameter named productCode that has a value of "java". This is the parameter that was passed from the first page. You'll learn how this navigation from page to page works in chapter 3.

The first page of a shopping cart application

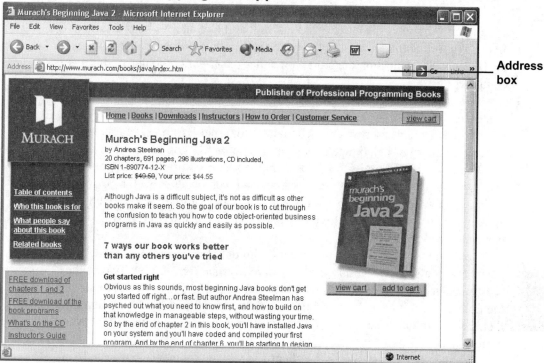

Address box

The second page of a shopping cart application

Figure 1-1   A typical web application

The components of a web application

Figure 1-2 shows the basic components that make up a web application. Because a web application is a type of *client/server application*, the components of a web application are stored on either the *client* computer or the *server* computer.

To access a web application, you use a *web browser* that runs on a client computer. It is the browser that converts HTML code to the user interface. The most widely used web browser is Microsoft's Internet Explorer, and the most popular alternative is Netscape's Navigator (commonly known as Netscape).

The web application itself is stored on the server computer. This computer runs *web server* software that enables it to send web pages to web browsers. Although there are many web servers, the most popular one for Java web applications is the Apache Software Foundation's *Apache HTTP Server*, which is usually just called *Apache*.

Because most web applications work with data that's stored in a database, most servers also run a *database management system* (or *DBMS*). Two of the most popular for Java development are *Oracle* and *MySQL*. Note, however, that the DBMS doesn't have to run on the same server as the web server software. In fact, a separate database server is often used to improve an application's overall performance.

Although this figure shows the client and server computers connected via the Internet, this isn't the only way a client can connect to a server in a web application. If the client and the server are on the same *Local Area Network*, or *LAN*, they function as an *intranet*. Since an intranet uses the same protocols as the Internet, a web application works the same on an intranet as it does on the Internet.

Components of a web application

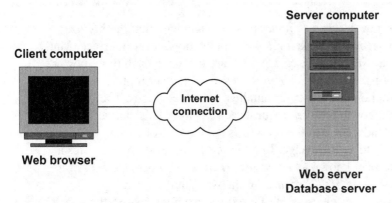

Description

- Web applications are a type of *client/server application*. In a client/server application, a user at a *client* computer accesses an application at a *server* computer. For a web application, the client and server computers are connected via the Internet or an intranet.

- In a web application, the user works with a *web browser* at the client computer. The web browser provides the user interface for the application. The most commonly used web browser is Microsoft's Internet Explorer, but other web browsers such as Netscape's Navigator are also in use.

- A web application runs on the server computer under the control of *web server* software. For servlet and JSP applications, the *Apache* server is the most widely used web server.

- For most web applications, the server computer also runs a *database management system* (*DBMS*). For servlet and JSP applications, *Oracle* and *MySQL* are two of the most popular database management systems.

Figure 1-2   The components of a web application

How static web pages work

HTML, or *Hypertext Markup Language*, is the language that the browser converts to the web pages that make up a web application's user interface. Many of these web pages are *static web pages*, which are the same each time they are viewed. In other words, they don't change in response to user input.

Figure 1-3 shows how a web server handles static web pages. The process begins when a user at a web browser requests a web page. This can occur when the user enters a web address into the browser's Address box or when the user clicks a link that leads to another page. In either case, the web browser uses a standard Internet protocol known as *Hypertext Transfer Protocol*, or *HTTP*, to send a request known as an *HTTP request* to the web site's server.

When the web server receives an HTTP request from a browser, the server retrieves the requested HTML file from disk and sends the file back to the browser in the form of an *HTTP response*. The HTTP response includes the HTML document that the user requested along with any other resources specified by the HTML code such as graphics files.

When the browser receives the HTTP response, it formats and displays the HTML document. Then, the user can view the content. If the user requests another page, either by clicking a link or typing another web address in the browser's Address box, the process begins again.

How a web server processes static web pages

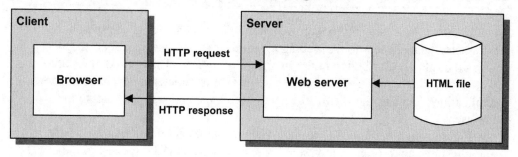

Description

- *Hypertext Markup Language*, or *HTML*, is the language that the web browser converts into the web pages of a web application.

- A *static web page* is an HTML document that's stored in a file and does not change in response to user input. Static web pages have a filename with an extension of .htm or .html.

- *Hypertext Transfer Protocol*, or *HTTP*, is the protocol that web browsers and web servers use to communicate.

- A web browser requests a page from a web server by sending the server a message known as an *HTTP request*. For a static web page, the HTTP request includes the name of the HTML file that's requested.

- A web server replies to an HTTP request by sending a message known as an *HTTP response* back to the browser. For a static web page, the HTTP response includes the HTML document.

Figure 1-3   How static web pages work

How dynamic web pages work

In contrast to a static web page, a *dynamic web page* changes based on the parameters that are sent to the web application from another page. For instance, when the Add To Cart button in the first page in figure 1-1 is clicked, the static web page calls the web application and sends one parameter to it. Then, the web application generates the HTML for a new web page and sends it back to the browser.

Figure 1-4 shows how this works. When a user enters data into a web page and clicks the appropriate button, the browser sends an HTTP request to the server. This request contains the address of the next web page along with any data entered by the user. Then, when the web server receives this request and determines that it is a request for a dynamic web page, it passes the request back to the web application.

When the web application receives the request, it processes the data that the user entered and generates an HTML document. Next, it sends that document to the web server, which sends the document back to the browser in the form of an HTTP response. Then, the browser displays the HTML document that's included in the response so the process can start over again.

How a web server processes dynamic web pages

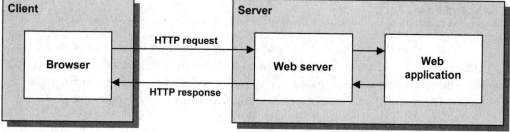

Description

- A *dynamic web page* is an HTML document that's generated by a web application. Often, the web page changes according to parameters that are sent to the web application by the web browser.

- When a web server receives a request for a dynamic web page, the server passes the request to the web application. Then, the application generates a response, which is usually an HTML document, and returns it to the web server. The web server, in turn, wraps the generated HTML document in an HTTP response and sends it back to the browser.

- The browser doesn't know or care whether the HTML was retrieved from a static HTML file or was dynamically generated by the web application. Either way, the browser displays the HTML document that is returned.

Figure 1-4   How dynamic web pages work

An introduction to Java web programming

In the early days of Java, Java received much attention for its ability to create *applets*, which are Java applications that can be downloaded from a web site and run within a web browser. However, once Microsoft's Internet Explorer stopped supporting new versions of Java, applets lost much of their appeal. As a result, many developers switched their attention to *servlets* and *JavaServer Pages*, or *JSPs*. These technologies allow developers to write Java web applications that run on the server.

The components of a Java web application

Figure 1-5 shows the primary software components for a Java web application. By now, you should understand why the server must run web server software. To run a Java application, though, the server must also run a software product known as a *servlet and JSP engine*, or *servlet and JSP container*. This software allows a web server to run servlets and JSPs.

Sun's *Java 2 Platform, Enterprise Edition*, or *J2EE*, specifies how a servlet and JSP engine should interact with a web server. Since this specification is available to all developers, most modern web servers support any servlet and JSP engine that implements this specification. In addition, all servlet and JSP engines should work similarly. In theory, this makes servlet and JSP code portable between servlet and JSP engines and web servers. In practice, though, you may need to make some modifications to your code when switching servlet and JSP engines or web servers.

Tomcat is a free, open-source servlet and JSP engine that was developed by the Jakarta project at the Apache Software Foundation. This engine is the official reference implementation of the servlet and JSP specification set forth by Sun, and it's one of the most popular servlet and JSP engines. In the next chapter, you'll learn how to install and use Tomcat on your own PC.

For a servlet and JSP engine to work properly, the engine must be able to access Java's *Software Development Kit*, or *SDK*, that comes as part of the *Java 2 Platform, Standard Edition*, or *J2SE*. The SDK contains the Java compiler and the core classes for working with Java. It also contains the *Java Runtime Environment*, or *JRE*, that you need for running the Java classes. Since this book assumes that you already have some Java experience, you should already be familiar with the SDK and the JRE.

Many large websites also use a Java technology known as *Enterprise JavaBeans*, or *EJBs*. To use EJBs, the server must run an additional piece of software known as an *EJB server*, or *EJB container*. Although there are some benefits to using EJBs, they're more difficult to use when you're first learning how to code Java web applications. That's why this book focuses on developing web applications without using EJBs. In chapter 17, though, you'll get an introduction to EJBs.

The components of a Java web application

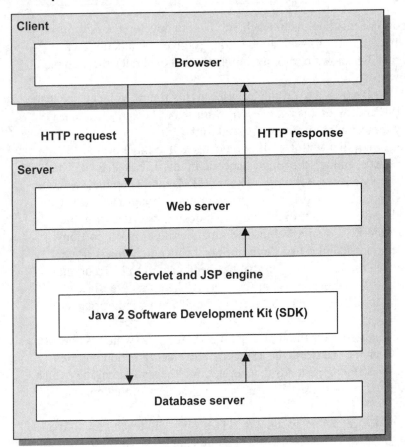

Description

- Java web applications consist of JavaServer Pages and servlets. You'll learn more about them in the next two figures.

- A *servlet and JSP engine*, or *servlet and JSP container*, is the software that allows the web server to work with servlets and JSPs.

- The *Java 2 Platform, Enterprise Edition*, or *J2EE*, specifies how web servers can interact with servlet and JSP engines. *Tomcat* is one of the most popular servlet and JSP engines. It was developed by the Jakarta project at the Apache Software Foundation.

- For a servlet and JSP engine to work, it must have access to Java's *Software Development Kit*, or *SDK*, which comes as part of the *Java 2 Platform, Standard Edition*, or *J2SE*. Among other things, the SDK contains the Java classes, the Java compiler, and a *Java Runtime Environment*, or *JRE*.

- Java web applications that use *Enterprise JavaBeans*, or *EJBs*, require an additional server component known as an *EJB server*, or *EJB container*. For more information about working with EJBs, see chapter 17.

Figure 1-5   The components of a Java web application

An introduction to JavaServer Pages

One of the goals of this book is to teach you how to develop the *JavaServer Pages*, or *JSPs*, that are part of a web application. To give you a better idea of what they are, figure 1-6 shows part of a simple JSP that generates the web page shown in the browser.

If you look at the Address box of the browser in this figure, you can see that the address of a JSP ends with a jsp extension. After that, you can see a question mark followed by the parameters that are passed to the JSP.

If you're already familiar with HTML, you can see that most of this JSP consists of HTML code. In fact, the only Java code in this JSP is shaded. That's why JSPs are relatively easy to write if you know HTML and keep the Java to a minimum. If a JSP requires extensive Java programming, though, it's easier to write the Java code with a servlet. In practice, web designers often write the HTML portions of the JSPs, while web programmers write the Java portions.

In case you're interested, the first three lines of Java code in this JSP get three parameters from the request object that has been passed to it. To do that, the code uses the getParameter method of the object. Then, the three Java expressions that are used later in the JSP refer to the String variables that store the parameters.

When a JSP is requested for the first time, the *JSP engine* (which is part of the servlet and JSP engine) converts the JSP code into a servlet and compiles the servlet. Then, the JSP engine loads that servlet into the servlet engine, which runs it. For subsequent requests, the JSP engine runs the servlet that corresponds to the JSP.

In chapter 3, you'll get a crash course in HTML that will teach you all the HTML you need to know for writing JSPs. Then, in chapter 4, you'll learn how to combine HTML code with Java code as you write JSPs. When you're done with those chapters, you'll know how to write significant JSPs of your own.

A web page that's returned from a JSP

Partial code for the JSP

```
<head>
  <title>Chapter 4 - Email List application</title>
</head>
<body>
<%
  String firstName = request.getParameter("firstName");
  String lastName = request.getParameter("lastName");
  String emailAddress = request.getParameter("emailAddress");
%>
<h1>Thanks for joining our email list</h1>
<p>Here is the information that you entered:</p>
  <table cellspacing="5" cellpadding="5" border="1">
    <tr>
      <td align="right">First name:</td>
      <td><%= firstName %></td>
    </tr>
    <tr>
      <td align="right">Last name:</td>
      <td><%= lastName %></td>
    </tr>
    <tr>
      <td align="right">Email address:</td>
      <td><%= emailAddress %></td>
    </tr>
  </table>
```

Description

- A *JavaServer Page*, or *JSP*, consists of Java code that is embedded within HTML code. This makes it easy to write the HTML portion of a JSP, but harder to write the Java code.

- When a JSP is first requested, the JSP engine translates it into a servlet and compiles it. Then, the servlet is run by the servlet engine.

- In chapter 3, you'll learn how to create HTML documents. In chapter 4, you'll learn how to create JSPs.

Figure 1-6   An introduction to JavaServer Pages

An introduction to servlets

A second goal of this book is to teach you how to develop the *servlets* that are part of a Java web application. To give you a better idea of what they are, figure 1-7 shows part of a servlet that generates the same web page as the JSP in figure 1-6.

In contrast to the JSP, the servlet is a Java class that runs on a server and does the processing for the dynamic web pages of a web application. That's why servlets for a web application are written by web programmers, not web designers. After the processing is done, the servlet returns HTML code to the browser by using the println method of an out object. Note, however, that this makes it more difficult to code the HTML.

In case you're interested, each servlet for a web application is a Java class that extends (or inherits) the HttpServlet class. Then, each servlet can override the doGet method of the inherited class, which receives both a request and a response object from the web server, and the servlet can get the parameters that have been passed to it by using the getParameter method of the request object. After that, the servlet can do whatever processing is required by using normal Java code.

In chapter 5, you'll get the details on how servlets work. When you complete that chapter, you'll be able to write significant servlets of our own. But as you'll learn next, the real trick as you develop Java web applications is to use a combination of servlets and JSPs so you get the benefits of both.

How to combine servlets and JSPs in a web application

As you have seen, servlets are actually Java classes so it makes sense to use them for the processing requirements of the web pages in an application. Similarly, JSPs are primarily HTML code so it makes sense to use them for the design of the web pages in an application. But how can you do that in an efficient way?

The solution is for a servlet to do the processing for each web page, and then forward the request and response objects to the JSP for the page. That way, the servlet does all the processing, and the JSP does all of the HTML. With this approach, the JSP requires a minimum of embedded Java code. And that means that the web designer can write the JSPs with little or no help from the Java programmer, and the Java programmer can write the servlets without worrying about the HTML.

In chapter 6, you'll learn how to use this approach for developing web applications. You'll also learn how to use the Model-Controller-View pattern to structure your applications so they're easy to manage and maintain. When you finish that chapter, you'll know how to develop Java web applications in a thoroughly professional manner.

Partial code for a servlet that works the same as the JSP in figure 1-6

```
public class EmailServlet extends HttpServlet{

    public void doGet(HttpServletRequest request,
                      HttpServletResponse response)
                      throws IOException, ServletException{

        response.setContentType("text/html");
        PrintWriter out = response.getWriter();

        String firstName = request.getParameter("firstName");
        String lastName = request.getParameter("lastName");
        String emailAddress = request.getParameter("emailAddress");

        out.println(
          "<html>\n"
        + "<head>\n"
        + "  <title>Chapter 5 - Email List application</title>\n"
        + "</head>\n"
        + "<body>\n"
        + "<h1>Thanks for joining our email list</h1>\n"
        + "<p>Here is the information that you entered:</p>\n"
        + "  <table cellspacing=\"5\" cellpadding=\"5\" border=\"1\">\n"
        + "  <tr><td align=\"right\">First name:</td>\n"
        + "      <td>" + firstName + "</td>\n"
        + "  </tr>\n"
        + "  <tr><td align=\"right\">Last name:</td>\n"
        + "      <td>" + lastName + "</td>\n"
        + "  </tr>\n"
        + "  <tr><td align=\"right\">Email address:</td>\n"
        + "      <td>" + emailAddress + "</td>\n"
        + "  </tr>\n"
        + "  </table>\n"
        + "</html>);
```

Description

- A *servlet* is a Java class that runs on a server. Although servlets are commonly used for web applications, they can also be used for other types of applications like mail or FTP server applications.

- A servlet for a web application extends the HttpServlet class. This makes it easy for a Java programmer to write the code for the processing that a web page requires. Once a servlet is compiled, it can be run by the servlet engine.

- To return HTML code to the browser, a servlet uses the println method of an out object. This makes it more difficult to write the HTML portion of the code.

- To get the best results from servlets and JSPs, you use a combination of the two as you develop web pages. In particular, you use servlets for the processing that's required by the pages, and JSPs for the HTML that's required by the pages.

- In chapter 5, you'll learn how to create servlets. And in chapter 6, you'll learn how to structure and code your web pages so they take advantage of the best features of both servlets and JSPs.

Figure 1-7   An introduction to servlets

An introduction to Java web development

This topic introduces you to servlet and JSP development. In particular, it presents some of the hardware and software options that you have as you develop web applications.

Three platforms for developing servlets and JSPs

Figure 1-8 shows the three types of platforms that you can use for developing servlets and JSPs. First, you can use a single PC. Second, you can use a Local Area Network (or LAN). Third, you can use the Internet.

When you use a single PC, you of course need to install all of the required software on that PC. That includes the Java SDK, the web server software, the servlet and JSP engine, and the database management system. To make this easy for you, the CD for this book includes everything that you need. In particular, it includes Tomcat, which functions as both a web server and a servlet and JSP engine. It also includes MySQL, which is a DBMS. In the next chapter, you'll learn how to install Tomcat, and you can learn how to install the other components in appendix A.

When you work on a LAN, you can use the same software components, but you divide them between client and server. To compile and run servlets on the server, the server requires the Java SDK, a combined web server and servlet and JSP engine like Tomcat, and a DBMS like MySQL. To compile servlets on a client, the client requires the Java SDK and the servlet.jar file, which contains all of the classes required for servlet development in a compressed format. This JAR file comes with Tomcat, but you can also download it for free from the Sun web site. When you run a web application on a LAN like this, it functions as an intranet.

When you work over the Internet, you use the same general components as you do when you work over an intranet. To improve performance, though, you normally have a separate web server like Apache in addition to a servlet and JSP engine like Tomcat. If necessary, you can also improve the performance of an intranet application by using Apache as the web server.

Since the SDK, Apache, Tomcat, and MySQL can be run by most operating systems, Java web developers aren't tied to a specific operating system. In fact, the Windows operating system is commonly used for both the client and server computers during development. But when the applications are ready for use, they are often deployed on a Unix or Solaris server.

Stand-alone development

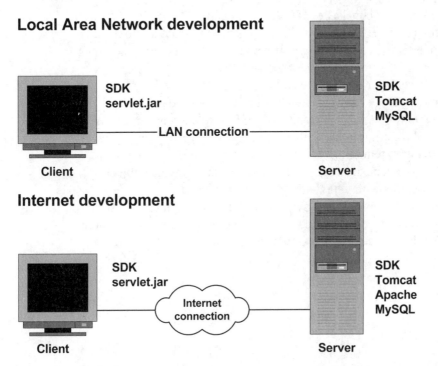

Description

- When you develop web applications, you can work on platforms at three levels.
- If you want to develop web applications on your own PC, you need to install the Java SDK, a web server, a servlet and JSP engine, and a DBMS. To make that easy for you, the CD that comes with this book includes everything you need including the MySQL DBMS and Tomcat 4.0, which functions as both a web server and a servlet and JSP engine.
- If you're working in a small group on a Local Area Network (LAN), the server can run Tomcat as both the web server and the servlet and JSP engine, and MySQL as the DBMS. Then, the client just needs the Java SDK and the servlet.jar file, which isn't part of the SDK. When you run web applications on a LAN, it functions as an intranet.
- If you're working in a group over the Internet, you normally use a product like Apache as the web server and a product like Tomcat as just the servlet and JSP engine. Otherwise, this works the same as when you're working over a LAN.

Figure 1-8   Three platforms for developing servlets and JSPs

The architecture for servlet and JSP applications

Figure 1-9 shows the architecture for a typical web application that uses servlets and JSPs. This architecture uses three layers: (1) the *presentation layer*, or *user interface layer*, (2) the *business rules layer*, and (3) the *data access layer*. In theory, the programmer tries to keep these layers as separate and independent as possible. In practice, though, these layers are often interrelated, and that's especially true for the business and data access layers.

The presentation layer consists of HTML pages and JSPs. Typically, a web designer will work on the HTML stored in these pages to create the look and feel of the user interface. Later, a Java programmer may need to edit these pages so they work properly with the servlets of the application.

The business rules layer uses servlets to control the flow of the application. These servlets may call other Java classes to store or retrieve data from a database, and they may forward the results to a JSP or to another servlet. Within the business layer, Java programmers often use a special type of Java class known as a *JavaBean* to temporarily store and process data. A JavaBean is typically used to define a business object such as a User or Invoice object.

The data layer works with data that's stored on the server's disk. For a serious web application, this data is usually stored in a relational database. However, this data can also be stored in text files and binary files. In addition, the data for an application can be stored in a special type of file that uses *Extensible Markup Language*, or *XML*. You'll learn more about working with XML in chapter 16.

The architecture for a typical Java web application

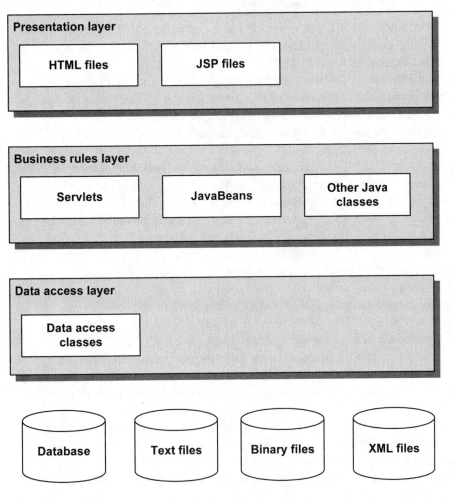

Description

- The *presentation layer* for a typical Java web application consists of HTML pages and JSPs.
- The *business rules layer* for a typical Java web application consists of servlets. These servlets may call other Java classes including a special type of Java class known as a *JavaBean*. Chapter 8 will show how to work with JavaBeans.
- The *data access layer* for a typical Java web application consists of classes that read and write data that's stored on the server's disk drive.
- For a serious web application, the data is usually stored in a relational database. However, it may also be stored in binary files, in text files, or in *Extensible Markup Language* (or *XML*) files. Chapter 16 will show how to work with XML.

Figure 1-9   The architecture for servlet and JSP applications

Tools for writing servlets and JSPs

When you write servlets, you normally use a text editor that's designed for entering, editing, compiling, and testing Java classes because that can save you a considerable amount of time. In figure 1-10, for example, you can see an editor named TextPad that is being used to edit a servlet. In case you don't already have an editor like this on your PC, a trial version of TextPad is included on the CD that comes with this book and appendix A shows how to install it. Then, if you decide that you want to use TextPad beyond the trial period, you can pay the fee of about $27, which we think is a bargain.

When you write JSPs, you can use a text editor like TextPad, but you can also use an editor that is designed specifically for working with HTML and JSPs. One of these editors is Macromedia's HomeSite, which is shown in this figure as it's used to edit a JSP. Here again, a trial version is included on the CD in case you want to experiment with it, and appendix A shows how to install it. Then, if you decide to use this software beyond the trial period, you can pay the required fee of about $85 to register your copy.

Although this figure doesn't show one, you can also use an *Integrated Development Environment*, or *IDE*, for developing servlets and JSPs. For instance, Sun ONE Studio 4.0 and Macromedia's JRUN Studio 4 are two IDEs that are designed for developing servlets and JSPs. As a result, they not only provide custom text editors, but also visual tools for designing and debugging servlets and JSPs. Similarly, Macromedia's Dreamweaver is an IDE that has special features for developing HTML documents and JSPs, but not for developing servlets.

Because IDEs can help you work more productively, professional programmers often use them. However, IDEs also have their own learning curves. That's why it's probably best to use a text editor like TextPad while you learn the skills presented in this book. Then, when you're done, you'll be ready to take full advantage of an IDE.

TextPad with the code for a servlet

HomeSite with the code for a JSP

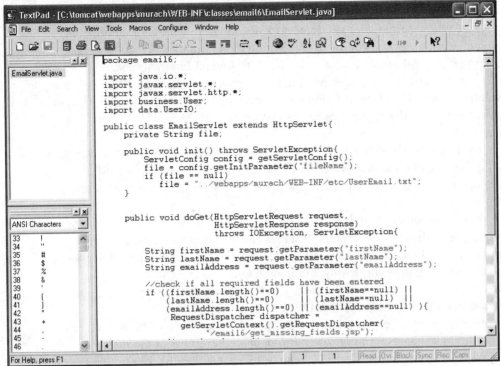

Figure 1-10   Tools for writing servlets and JSPs

Tools for deploying servlets and JSPs

Once you've tested your servlets and JSPs on your own PC or an intranet, you may want to deploy your web application on the Internet. To do that, you need to get a *web host*. One way to do that is to find an *Internet service provider*, or *ISP*, that provides web hosting that supports servlets and JSPs. If you read the text for the ISP on the web page shown in figure 1-11, for example, you can see that this ISP supports servlets and JSPs starting at just $24.99 per month.

If you search the web, you'll be able to find many other ISPs and web hosts. Just make sure that the one you choose not only supports servlet and JSP development, but also the database management system that your application requires.

When you select a web host, you get an *IP address* like 64.71.179.86 that uniquely identifies your web site (IP stands for Internet Protocol). Then, you can get a *domain name* like *www.murach.com* from a company named VeriSign. To go to the web page for getting a domain name, you can enter *www.netsol.com* or *www.verisign.com*. Until you get your domain name, you can use the IP address to access your site.

After you get a web host, you need to transfer your files to the web server. To do that, you can use *File Transfer Protocol*, or *FTP*. One of the most popular programs for doing that is CuteFTP, which is illustrated in this figure. It lets you upload files from your computer to your web server and download files from your web server to your computer.

An ISP that provides web hosting that supports servlets and JSPs

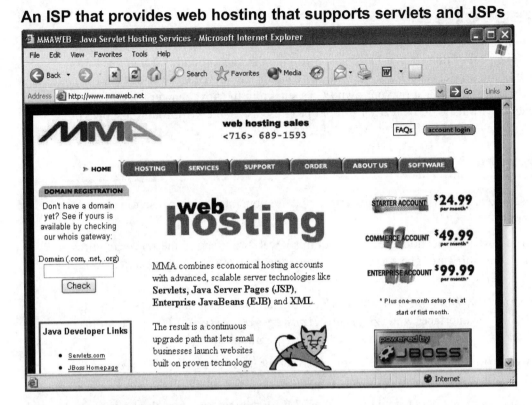

The CuteFTP program

Figure 1-11   Tools for deploying servlets and JSPs

Perspective

The goal of this chapter has been to provide the background that you need for developing servlets and JSPs. Now, if this chapter has succeeded, you should be ready to install Tomcat on your own PC as shown in the next chapter. Once you've done that, you should be ready for rapid progress as chapters 3 through 5 show you how to develop HTML documents, JSPs, and servlets.

Summary

- A *web application* is a set of web pages that are generated in response to user requests.

- To run a web application, the *client* requires a web browser and the *server* requires *web server* software. The server may also require a *database management system*, or *DBMS*.

- *Hypertext Markup Language*, or *HTML*, is the language that the browser converts into the user interface, while *Hypertext Transfer Protocol* (or *HTTP*) is the protocol that web browsers and web servers use to communicate.

- A web browser requests a page from a web server by sending an *HTTP request*. A web server replies by sending an *HTTP response* back to the browser.

- A *static web page* is generated from an HTML document that doesn't change, while a *dynamic web page* is generated by a web application based on the parameters that are included in the HTTP request.

- To run Java web applications, the server requires the Java 2 *Software Development Kit*, or *SDK*, plus a *servlet and JSP engine* like Tomcat.

- A *JavaServer Page*, or *JSP*, consists of HTML with embedded Java code. When it is requested, it is converted into a servlet and compiled by the JSP engine. Then, it is run by the servlet engine.

- A *servlet* is a Java class that runs on a server. For web applications, a servlet extends the HttpServlet class. To pass HTML back to the browser, it uses the println method of the out object.

- When you develop a Java web application, you can use servlets for the processing that's required and JSPs for the page design.

- You can develop servlets and JSPs on your own PC, on a network that functions as an *intranet*, and on the Internet. When you use the Internet, you usually use a web server that's separate from the servlet and JSP engine.

- As you develop a Java web application, you try to divide its classes into three layers: *presentation*, *business rules*, and *data access*. This makes it easier to manage and maintain the application.

Terms

web application	Tomcat
client/server application	Software Development Kit (SDK)
client	Java 2 Platform, Standard Edition (J2SE)
server	Java Runtime Environment (JRE)
web browser	Enterprise JavaBean (EJB)
web server	EJB server
Apache	EJB container
database management system (DBMS)	JavaServer Page (JSP)
MySQL	servlet
local area network (LAN)	presentation layer
intranet	user interface layer
Hypertext Markup Language (HTML)	business rules layer
static web page	data access layer
Hypertext Transfer Protocol (HTTP)	JavaBean
HTTP request	Extensible Markup Language (XML)
HTTP response	Integrated Development Environment
dynamic web page	(IDE)
applet	web host
servlet and JSP engine	Internet Service Provider (ISP)
servlet and JSP container	IP address
Java 2 Platform, Enterprise Edition	domain name
(J2EE)	File Transfer Protocol (FTP)

Objectives

- Name the software component that is required on the client of any Internet application, and name the two software components that are usually required on the server of any Internet application.

- Distinguish between HTML and HTTP.

- Distinguish between static web pages and dynamic web pages.

- Describe the extra software components that are required for developing servlet and JSP applications.

- In general terms, distinguish between the code for a servlet and a JSP. Then, explain why you use both servlets and JSPs in a Java web application.

- Describe the three types of platforms that can be used for developing web applications.

- List the software components that you need for running servlets and JSPs on your own PC.

- Distinguish between an intranet application and an Internet application.

- List the three layers of a typical Java web application.

Self-study questions

If you're using this book for a course, the tests will be based on the objectives. In other words, the tests try to determine whether you can do what the objectives call for. For this chapter, then, you should be able to answer questions like the ones that follow.

1. What software is required on the clients of an Internet application?

2. What two software components are usually required on the server of any Internet application?

3. What's the difference between HTML and HTTP?

4. What's the difference between static and dynamic web pages?

5. What other software components are required on the server for a Java web application?

6. What is the major coding difference between JSPs and servlets?

7. Why are both servlets and JSPs used in a Java web application?

8. List the three types of platforms that can be used for developing Java web applications?

9. What software do you need for developing servlets and JSPs on your own PC?

10. What's the difference between an intranet and an Internet application?

11. Name the three layers of a Java web application.

2

How to install and use Tomcat

As you learned in the last chapter, Tomcat can be used as both the web server and the servlet and JSP engine for web applications. Now, in this chapter, you'll learn how to install and use Tomcat on your own PC. Along the way, you should take the time to install Tomcat.

Before you start this chapter, we recommend that you install the other software that's on the book's CD as summarized in appendix A. If you've used our Beginning Java 2 book to get started with Java, most of this software should already be installed. Once you have all of it installed, including Tomcat, you'll be ready to start developing servlets and JSPs on your own PC.

If you're going to work in a client/server environment, of course, the web server and the servlet and JSP engine may already be installed on the server. In that case, you won't need to install it on your client computer. If, on the other hand, you're the one who is supposed to install Tomcat on the server, the procedure is similar to the one in this chapter, and you can get the extra information that you need from one of the text files that's described in this chapter.

How to install and configure Tomcat 30
How to install Tomcat on your own PC 30
A summary of Tomcat's directories and files 32
How to set the JAVA_HOME environment variable 34
How to change the memory settings for Tomcat's batch files 36
How to turn on servlet reloading 38

How to use Tomcat 40
How to start and stop Tomcat 40
How to view a web page 42
How to view a directory listing 44

A quick guide to troubleshooting 46
Two common Tomcat problems and how to solve them 46
How to change the port that's used by Tomcat... 48

How to deploy and run a web application 50
How to deploy a web application 50
How to view and run a web application 50
A summary of the directories and files for a web application 52
An introduction to the web.xml file for a web application 54
A summary of the directories and files for the book applications 56

Perspective 58

How to install and configure Tomcat

Although this topic shows how to install and configure Tomcat on a Windows system, similar concepts apply to all operating systems. As a result, if you're using another operating system, you may be able to get the installation done by following the procedures in this topic. Otherwise, you can go to the Tomcat web site to get information about installing Tomcat on your system.

How to install Tomcat on your own PC

Figure 2-1 shows how to install version 4.0 of Tomcat. If you're using Windows, the easiest way to install it is to use the CD that comes with this book. After you navigate to the Tomcat 4.0 directory on the CD, you use a zip program like WinZip to extract the files from the zip file named Jakarta-Tomcat-4.0.1.

The other alternative is to download the current version of Tomcat from the Tomcat web site. However, since the Apache Software Foundation is continually updating this web site, the procedure in this figure may be out of date by the time you read this. As a result, you may have to do some searching to find the current version of Tomcat.

After you've installed Tomcat, its top-level directory is jakarta-tomcat-4.0.X. This can be referred to as the *Tomcat home directory*. To make it easier to refer to this directory later on, we recommend that you change its name to tomcat. This is the second last step in both of the procedures in this figure.

The last step in both procedures is to copy (not move) the servlet.jar file that's in the tomcat\common\lib directory to the jre\lib\ext directory for the Java SDK. That way, the servlet classes that come with Tomcat are available to the SDK. Although you could get the same result by adding the tomcat\common\lib directory to the classpath of your system, copying the files is a better way to do this.

Since this book was designed to work with Tomcat 4.0, we recommend that you install Tomcat 4.0 from the CD that comes with this book. However, the applications presented in this book will also run under newer versions of Tomcat, such as Tomcat 4.1 and 5.0. Unfortunately, this requires some additional configuration. For directions on how to configure newer versions of Tomcat so they work with the applications presented in this book, please visit this page on our web site:

www.murach.com/books/jsps/questions.htm

The Apache web site address

```
www.apache.org
```

How to install Tomcat from the CD that comes with the book

1. Put the CD that comes with this book into your CD drive, and navigate to the Tomcat 4.0 directory.
2. Use a zip program such as WinZip to extract the files from the zip file named jakarta-tomcat-4.0.1. If you don't have WinZip, you can get it free from *www.winzip.com*.
3. If necessary, move the jakarta-tomcat directory to the C drive.
4. Rename the jakarta-tomcat directory to tomcat.
5. Copy the servlet.jar file from the C:\tomcat\common\lib directory to the C:\j2sdk1.4.0\jre\lib\ext directory.

How to download and install Tomcat from the Apache web site

1. Go to the Apache web site (*www.apache.org*).
2. Navigate to the Apache Projects heading and click on the Jakarta link.
3. Navigate to the SubProjects heading and click on the Tomcat link.
4. Navigate to the Download heading and select the Binaries link.
5. Navigate to the Release Builds heading and select the most recent version of Tomcat.
6. Select the bin directory link and download the jakarta-tomcat-4.0.X zip file.
7. Save the zip file to your hard disk.
8. Use a zip program such as WinZip to extract the files from the zip file. If you don't have WinZip, you can get it free from *www.winzip.com*.
9. If necessary, move the jakarta-tomcat directory to your C drive.
10. Rename the jakarta-tomcat directory to tomcat.
11. Copy the servlet.jar file from the C:\tomcat\common\lib directory to the C:\j2sdk1.4.0\jre\lib\ext directory.

Description

*   The directory that holds the files for Tomcat is known as the *Tomcat home directory*. By default, this directory is jakarta-tomcat-4.0.X. However, to save yourself typing, we recommend that you rename this directory to tomcat.
*   The servlet.jar file contains the Java classes that you need for developing servlets. By copying this JAR file from the tomcat subdirectory to the SDK subdirectory, you make the classes available to the SDK.
*   This figure shows how to install Tomcat 4.0, which is included on the CD that comes with this book. For instructions on how to install and configure versions of Tomcat that are newer than Tomcat 4.0, such as Tomcat 4.1 or 5.0, visit our web site (*www.murach.com*), go to the main page for this book, and click on the FAQs link.

Figure 2-1   How to install Tomcat on your own PC

A summary of Tomcat's directories and files

Figure 2-2 shows the directories and files for the Tomcat home directory, which has been changed to c:\tomcat. By default, this directory has nine subdirectories. Of these, the most important are the bin, conf, log, webapps, and work directories.

The bin directory holds the binary files that let you start and stop Tomcat. You'll learn how to do that later in this chapter.

The webapps directory contains some servlet and JSP applications that come with Tomcat. You can run these applications to make sure Tomcat has been installed properly. Later, when you develop your own web applications, you will store them under this directory.

The conf directory contains some XML files that you may need to edit as you configure Tomcat, while the log directory contains text files that Tomcat uses to log its operations. You can open these XML and log files in a text editor to learn more about how Tomcat works.

The work directory is used by Tomcat to store the servlet files that the JSP engine creates. In chapter 4, you'll learn how to view these files in a text editor to help debug your code.

In the Tomcat home directory, you can also find two text files. The readme text file contains some general information about Tomcat. The running text file contains more information about installing, starting, and stopping Tomcat. Although most of this information is presented in this chapter, you can check the running file if you encounter any problems installing and running Tomcat. In particular, this file includes directions for Unix users, and it includes directions for how to install Tomcat on a server so it can be shared by multiple users across a network.

The file structure of Tomcat

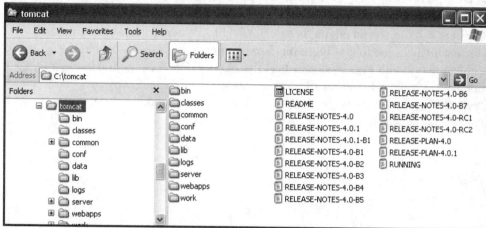

The subdirectories of Tomcat

Directory	Description
bin	The binary executables and scripts
classes	Unpacked classes that are available to all web applications
common	Classes available to internal and web applications
conf	Configuration files
lib	JAR files that contain classes that are available to all web applications
logs	Log files
server	Internal classes
webapps	Web applications
work	Temporary files and directories for Tomcat

The files of Tomcat

File	Description
readme.txt	General information about Tomcat
running.txt	Instructions for installing, starting, and stopping Tomcat

Description

- Since Tomcat is an open-source project, developers who work on Tomcat can download the source distribution for Tomcat, modify the source code, and build Tomcat from the source code. That's why you'll find directions for how to build Tomcat on the Tomcat website.

- Developers who develop web applications only need to download the binary for Tomcat distribution and install it as described in this chapter.

- To make the classes within a JAR file available to Tomcat so you can run an application that uses them, you can put the JAR file in Tomcat's common\lib directory.

Figure 2-2   A summary of Tomcat's directories and files

How to set the JAVA_HOME environment variable

In Tomcat 4, the servlet engine is named Catalina. When Tomcat starts, it runs the catalina.bat file to configure this servlet engine. For the servlet engine to be able to work with Java, your must set the JAVA_HOME environment variable stored in the catalina.bat file so it points to the SDK that's installed on your system. Figure 2-3 shows how. Once you set this environment variable, Tomcat will know which version of Java to use.

The catalina batch file opened for editing

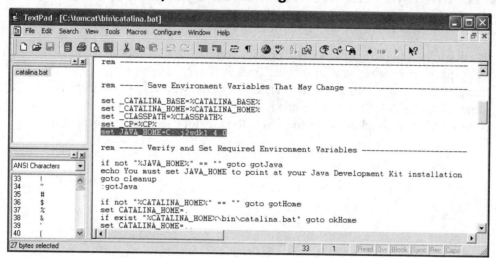

How to set the JAVA_HOME environment variable

1. Use a text editor like Notepad or TextPad to open the catalina.bat file located in the c:\tomcat\bin directory. One way to do that is right-click on the name of the file in the Windows Explorer and choose Edit.

2. Scroll down to the section named "Save Environment Variables That May Change."

3. After the last Set command, enter "set JAVA_HOME=c:\j2sdk1.4.0" where c:\j2sdk1.4.0 is the directory that contains the SDK that's installed on your system. When you enter this command, don't put spaces around the equal sign.

4. Save your changes to the catalina.bat file.

5. If necessary, stop and restart Tomcat.

Figure 2-3　How to set the JAVA_HOME environment variable

How to change the memory settings for Tomcat's batch files

If you're using Windows 95, 98, or ME, you may get an "out of environment space" error when you try to start Tomcat. To solve this problem, you can change the memory settings for the batch files that start and stop Tomcat as shown in figure 2-4. On the other hand, if you're using Unix or Windows NT, 2000, or XP, you shouldn't need to change the memory settings for these batch files.

The Properties dialog box for the startup batch file

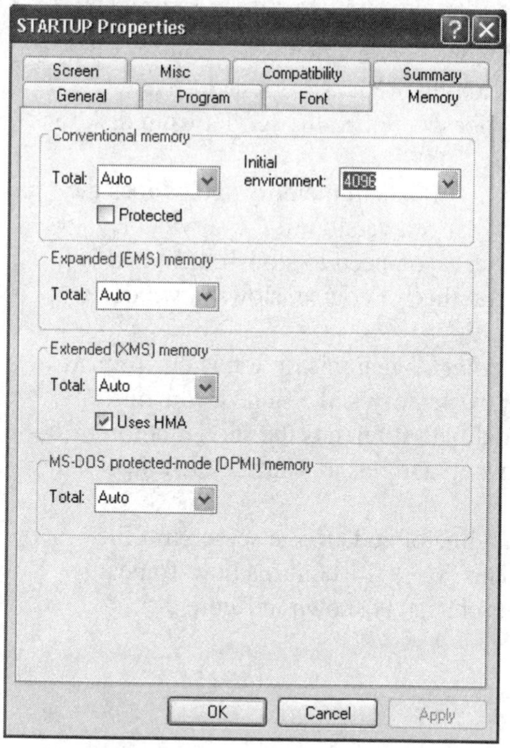

How to change memory settings for the startup batch file

1. Start the Windows Explorer and navigate to the bin directory of Tomcat (c:\tomcat\bin if you changed the directory name as suggested in figure 2-1).
2. Right-click on the startup batch file and select the Properties option.
3. From the Properties dialog box, select the Memory tab.
4. Change the Initial Environment option from Auto to 4096.
5. Click on the OK button.

How to change memory settings for the shutdown batch file

• Follow the steps shown above, substituting shutdown for startup.

Figure 2-4   How to change the memory settings for Tomcat's batch files

How to turn on servlet reloading

As Tomcat runs, its servlet engine loads the servlets that users request from disk into internal memory. Then, if there's another request for one of the servlets that's already in memory, Tomcat doesn't reload the servlet from disk to memory. It uses the one that's in memory.

But what if you change one of the servlets that's in memory? How does the servlet engine know that it should use the changed version of the servlet? By default, it doesn't. As a result, to test a servlet, you need to stop Tomcat and restart it each time you change a servlet. But this, of course, slows down development.

The solution is to turn on *servlet reloading*. When this option is on, Tomcat checks to make sure the requested servlet in memory is the same as the one on disk. Then, if the one on disk has been modified, it reloads the servlet before it runs it. This means that you don't have to stop and restart Tomcat each time you change a servlet.

To turn servlet reloading on, you add a line of code to the server.xml file that's stored in Tomcat's conf directory. This XML file controls how Tomcat is configured. The procedure for making this change is shown in figure 2-5.

The server.xml file

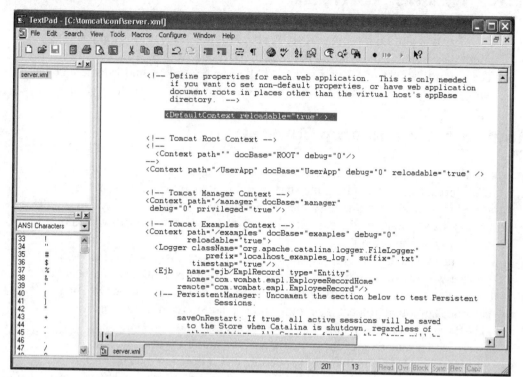

How to turn on servlet reloading

1. Use the Windows Explorer to navigate to Tomcat's conf directory and open the server.xml file in a text editor.
2. Scroll down to the comment shown above and insert the following statement below it:

   `<DefaultContext reloadable="true"/>`
3. Save the changes to the server.xml file
4. If necessary, stop and restart Tomcat.

Description

- If *servlet reloading* isn't on, which is the default setting, you have to stop and restart Tomcat each time that you change one of the classes that's in memory.

- If you turn servlet reloading on, Tomcat checks the modification dates of the classes in memory and automatically reloads the ones that have changed so you don't have to stop and restart Tomcat each time a class changes. Although this is useful in development, it can cause performance problems in a production environment.

- The server.xml file is an XML file that controls how the Tomcat engine is configured. Tomcat reads this file every time it starts to configure itself. You can use a text editor to edit this file. Then, you can stop and restart Tomcat to put the changes into effect.

Figure 2-5   How to turn on servlet reloading

How to use Tomcat

Now that you know how to install and configure Tomcat, this topic shows you how to use it. First, you'll learn how to start and stop the Tomcat engine. Then, you'll learn how to view some HTML pages, servlets, and JSPs that come with Tomcat. This shows that Tomcat is installed correctly on your system.

How to start and stop Tomcat

Figure 2-6 shows how to start and stop Tomcat. To do that, you open up a DOS prompt window and run the startup and shutdown batch files that are stored in Tomcat's bin directory. Before you do that, though, you need to use the cd command to change the current directory to tomcat\bin so DOS will know where to find the batch files.

When you start Tomcat, several message lines are displayed in the DOS prompt window including two that show the current classpath and the Java home directory. Then, Tomcat displays a console in a second window. This console shows that Tomcat is running and is ready to receive requests for HTML pages, servlets, and JSPs.

If servlet reloading is on, you only need to start Tomcat at the start of a development session, and you only need to shut it down at the end of the session. If servlet reloading isn't on, though, you need to stop and restart Java every time you want to test a newly compiled class. As a result, you'll want to leave the DOS prompt window open so you can easily start and stop Tomcat.

If you're using Unix, you can use a procedure that's similar to the one in this figure to start and stop Tomcat. After you start a Unix command prompt, you use the cd command to change the current working directory to Tomcat's bin directory. When using Unix, though, you use front slashes in the directory path instead of the backslashes that are required by DOS. Then, to start and stop Tomcat, you use the startup.sh and shutdown.sh commands.

When you start Tomcat for the first time, you test whether you've done the installation and configuration properly. If you haven't, one or more messages will be displayed, which should help you figure out what you did wrong. For some operating systems, though, getting everything to work right can be tedious and painstaking.

In particular, for some versions of Windows 95 and 98, we've received "out of environment space" messages, even though we've done the procedures in figure 2-4 correctly. Our solution to this problem is given in this figure, which is just another way to set the environment space variables.

DOS commands for starting Tomcat

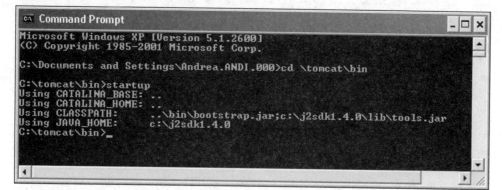

The console that Tomcat displays when it's running

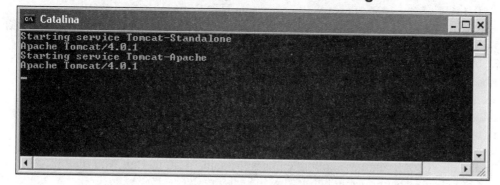

How to use the DOS Prompt window to start and stop Tomcat

1. Open a DOS Prompt window and use the cd command to change the current directory to Tomcat's bin directory.

2. To start Tomcat, type "startup" and press the Enter key. To stop Tomcat, type "shutdown" and press the Enter key.

What to do if Tomcat doesn't start because it's "out of environment space"

- First, make sure that you did the procedures in figure 2-4 correctly. If you did and you're using Windows 95 or 98, you can then set these variables this way: (1) click on the Title bar of the DOS Prompt window; (2) select Properties from the shortcut menu; (3) click on the Memory tab; and (4) change the Initial environment setting to 4096. After you close and reopen the DOS Prompt window, this should fix the problem.

Figure 2-6   How to start and stop Tomcat

How to view a web page

On most systems, you can view an HTML document without using a web server. To do that, you can use the Windows Explorer to navigate to the HTML file for the page and double-click on it. This opens up your web browser, which displays the HTML document. Another way to view an HTML document is to open up your web browser and enter the path and filename for the HTML file.

To view a web page that's generated by a JSP or servlet, though, you need to use HTTP to request the web page through Tomcat as shown in figure 2-7. After you start Tomcat and your browser, you enter a *Uniform Resource Locator*, or *URL*, in the browser. Then, Tomcat finds the servlet for the page that you've requested, runs the servlet to generate the HTML for the page, and sends the HTML back to your browser.

The Address box of the Internet Explorer browser that's shown in this figure contains a typical URL. This URL requests an HTML page that's part of a web application. Here, the URL begins with the *protocol*, which is Hypertext Transfer Protocol, or HTTP. The protocol is followed by a colon and two slashes.

After the protocol, the URL must specify the *host*, which is the server that's hosting the web application. To specify the local system, you can use the localhost keyword. To specify another computer, though, you usually use an address that includes the domain name like *www.murach.com*. The alternative is to use a specific IP address like 64.71.179.86, but you rarely have to do that.

After the host, the URL must specify the *port*. By default, the port for Tomcat is 8080. If another application uses the same port, though, you may need to change that port number as shown in figure 2-10.

After the port, you specify the *path* and the *filename* of the resource. In this example, the web browser has requested the index.html file that's stored in Tomcat's examples/servlets directory. Please note here that front slashes are used to separate the components of a path in a URL, although backslashes are used to separate them in a DOS path.

If you display the page shown in this figure and read it, you'll see that it lets you run several of the servlet examples that come with Tomcat. To make sure that the Tomcat servlet engine is installed properly on your system, you can run some of them. If, for example, you scroll down to the Hello World application and click on the Execute link, the application should use a servlet to display the words "Hello World" in your browser. This shows that your servlet engine is working properly.

Similarly, if you display the index page for the examples\jsp directory, you'll see a page that lets you run several of the JSP examples that come with Tomcat. To make sure that the JSP engine is configured properly, you can run some of these examples.

A web browser that displays a web page

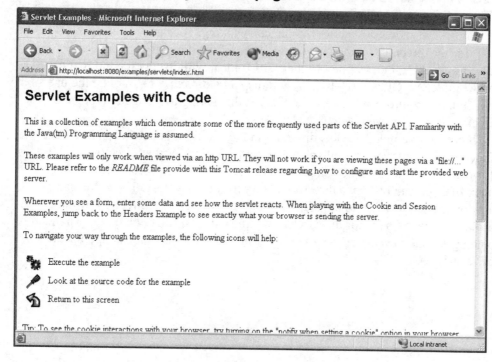

The components of an HTTP URL

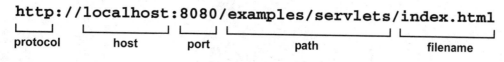

How to view a web page via an HTTP URL

1. Start Tomcat.
2. Start your web browser.
3. In the Address text box (for the Internet Explorer) or Location text box (for Netscape), type a URL and press Enter.

Description

- You can use the syntax shown above to specify a *Uniform Resource Locator*, or *URL*.
- When Tomcat is running on your local machine, you can use the "localhost" keyword to specify the host machine.
- The default port for Tomcat is 8080. If another application is already using this port, you can change the default port as shown in figure 2-10.

Figure 2-7   How to view a web page via an HTTP URL

How to view a directory listing

Figure 2-8 shows how to view a directory listing. To start, you enter the URL for the directory into your browser. Then, if the directory contains a file named index.htm, index.html, or index.jsp, Tomcat will display the index file for the directory. Otherwise, Tomcat will display a directory listing like the one shown in this figure. You can use the links in this listing to navigate to other directory listings or web pages.

Since the examples\servlets directory in the last figure contains an index file named index.html, you can't display a directory listing for that directory. However, since the examples directory shown in this figure doesn't contain an index file, you can display a directory listing for this directory. Then, you can click on the servlets link to navigate to the examples\servlets directory, which displays the index page for the servlet examples, or you can click on the jsp link to navigate to the examples\jsp directory, which displays the index page for the JSP examples.

A web browser that displays a directory listing

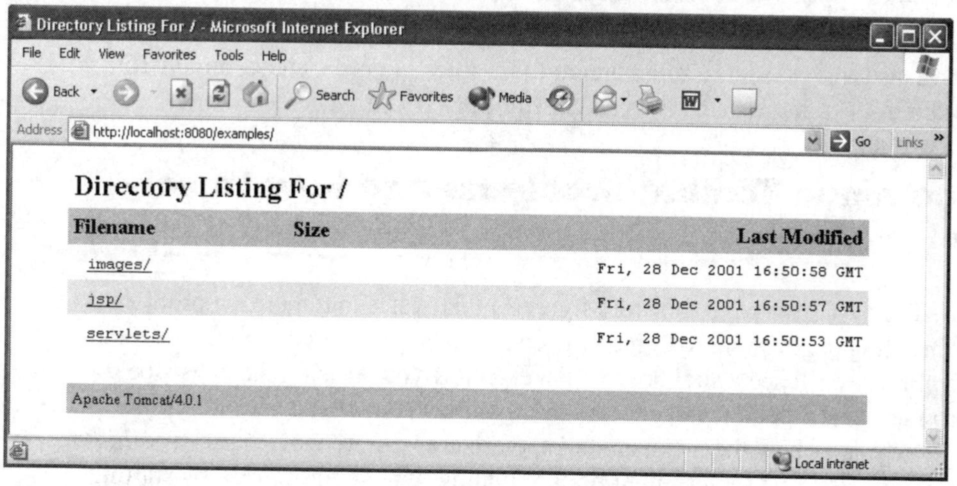
Directory Listing For / - Microsoft Internet Explorer
File Edit View Favorites Tools Help
Back Search Favorites Media
Address http://localhost:8080/examples/
Go Links
Directory Listing For /
Filename Size Last Modified
images/ Fri, 28 Dec 2001 16:50:58 GMT
jsp/ Fri, 28 Dec 2001 16:50:57 GMT
servlets/ Fri, 28 Dec 2001 16:50:53 GMT
Apache Tomcat/4.0.1
Local intranet

Description

- If a URL specifies a directory but not a filename, most web servers will automatically display any file within that directory named index.htm, index.html, or index.jsp. However, if that directory doesn't contain an index file, most web servers will display a directory listing like the one shown above.
- To navigate to the examples\servlets or examples\jsp directories from this web page, you can click on one of the links.

Figure 2-8 How to view a directory listing via an HTTP URL

A quick guide to troubleshooting

This topic presents a quick guide to troubleshooting some common Tomcat problems. For more help, you can consult the Apache web site.

Two common Tomcat problems and how to solve them

The first error page shown in figure 2-9 indicates that there's a problem connecting the browser to Tomcat. If you're using a different version of Internet Explorer, you'll see a similar error page. And if you're using the Netscape browser, you'll get a message that says that the browser can't locate the server.

No matter how the message looks, there are two probable causes for this problem. First, the server might not be running, which you can fix by starting Tomcat. Second, you may have entered the URL incorrectly, which you can fix by making sure that the URL points to a valid web server. In this example, the user didn't enter the port correctly, which is a common problem.

If neither of these approaches solves the problem, it may be because another web server or process is trying to use the same port as Tomcat. If so, you'll need to change the port used by Tomcat as shown in the next figure.

The second error page in this figure shows that the browser has successfully connected to the server, but the server can't find the page requested by the browser. This is the default error page that Tomcat uses for this problem. If you're running Tomcat on a local Windows machine, you can use the Windows Explorer to make sure the directory in the URL really exists.

Since it's a common practice to substitute a custom error page for the default error page, the error page that you get when you encounter a 404 error might look different than the one in this figure. Later in this book, you'll learn how to create your own custom error page and how to configure Tomcat to display that page when it encounters various types of errors.

The Internet Explorer's error page

Tomcat's default 404 error page

Description

- If the browser displays a message like the first error page, the HTTP request isn't connecting with a web server. To solve this problem, make sure that the Tomcat engine is running, and make sure that you've entered a valid URL.

- If the browser displays a Tomcat error page like the second error page, Tomcat is receiving the HTTP request, but it can't find the requested resource. To solve this problem, make sure that you've entered the path and filename of the URL correctly.

- The second error page is the default 404 error page that's returned by Tomcat when it can't find the requested resource. However, it's possible to configure Tomcat so it displays a custom error page instead of the default error page.

Figure 2-9   How to solve common Tomcat problems

How to change the port that's used by Tomcat

By default, Tomcat uses port 8080 as shown throughout this chapter. However, if you have a port conflict with another application, you may need to change that port as shown in figure 2-10. Here again, you modify the server.xml file that's stored in Tomcat's conf directory. In particular, you replace all instances of 8080 with another four-digit number that's greater than 1024.

After you save the server.xml file and stop and restart the server, the new port should take effect. If, for example, you change from port 8080 to 1979 as shown in this figure, you can access the directory listing for Tomcat's examples by entering this URL:

```
http://localhost:1979/examples
```

Because port 80 is the default port for most browsers, another alternative is to change the port from 8080 to 80. Then, you don't have to enter the port number in your URLs as in this example:

```
http://localhost/examples
```

Since this can save some typing, you may want to try this. However, if this causes a port conflict, you will have to change to another port.

The server.xml file

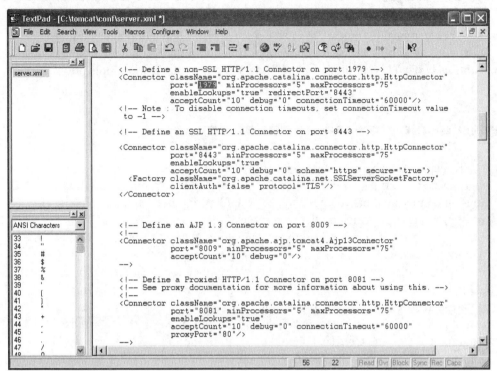

How to change the port that's used by Tomcat

1. Use the Windows Explorer to navigate to Tomcat's conf directory and open the server.xml file in a text editor.

2. Replace all instances of the current port, which is 8080 by default, to a four-digit number that's greater than 1024 or to 80. To do this, you may want to use the Find and Replace feature of your text editor.

3. Save the changes to the server.xml file.

4. Stop and restart Tomcat.

Description

*   If you have a port conflict with another application, you can change the default port from 8080 to a four-digit number that's greater than 1024.

*   If you don't enter a port when you specify a URL, your browser will use port 80. As a result, if you change Tomcat's default port from 8080 to 80, you don't need to enter a port when entering a URL in the browser. Then, assuming that there isn't a port conflict, you can view a web page by entering a URL like this:

```
http://localhost/examples/servlets
```

Figure 2-10   How to change the port that's used by Tomcat

How to deploy and run a web application

Once you install Tomcat, you can deploy a web application and run it. To start, you can deploy the web applications that are included on the CD that comes with this book. This should help you understand how J2EE web applications are structured.

How to deploy a web application

To deploy a web application, you copy the files for the web application to the appropriate directories on the web server. To deploy a web application that's running on the Internet, you need to use an FTP program to upload your files to the appropriate directories on the web server. But to deploy a web application that's running on an intranet or on your own computer, you can use a tool like the Windows Explorer to copy the files to the appropriate directories.

Figure 2-11 shows how to install the web applications that are included on the CD that comes with this book. These web applications include the examples that are presented in each chapter, plus an online music store application that's presented in the last four chapters of this book. To start, you run the Install.exe program that's on the CD. That should copy all of the files for the web applications to the c:\murach\webapps directory on your hard drive. Then, to install the web applications in the appropriate directories for Tomcat, you copy (not move) the murach and musicStore directories from the c:\murach\webapps directory to Tomcat's webapps directory.

How to view and run a web application

Once you've copied the files for a web application to the appropriate directory, you can view and run the pages for the web application by entering a URL that points to a web page or by clicking on a link that points to a web page. In this figure, the URL points to the index page for the murach directory that's stored in Tomcat's webapps directory. Then, each link on this web page points to a web application that's used in one of the chapters of this book.

Since you will probably want to visit this page often as you work through this book, you may want to use your web browser to bookmark this page. Then, you'll be able to access this page without having to type the complete URL each time.

The index page for the webapps\murach directory

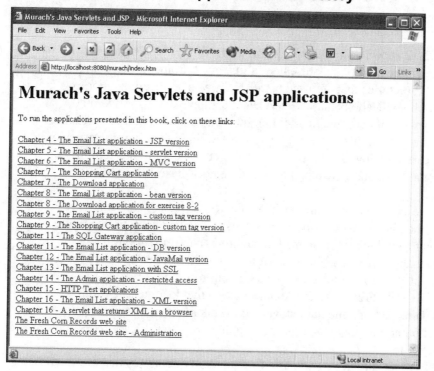

How to install the web applications that are on the book's CD

1. From the root directory of the CD, double-click on the file named Install.exe and respond to the dialog boxes that follow. This will install the source code and test files in the c:\murach\webapps directory.

2. Copy the c:\murach\webapps\murach directory and all its subdirectories to c:\tomcat\webapps.

3. Copy the c:\murach\webapps\musicStore directory and all its subdirectories to c:\tomcat\webapps.

How to view and run the web applications that are on the book's CD

*   To view the index page for all applications stored under the murach directory, start Tomcat and access http://localhost:8080/murach from your browser. Then, click on the link for the application that you want to run.

*   To view the index page for the musicStore directory, start Tomcat and access http://localhost:8080/musicStore from your browser. This will display the index page for the Music Store application that's presented in this book.

Note

*   Appendix A presents the procedures that you need for installing all of the components that the CD contains. Once you install these components, including the murach and music databases, all of the web applications for the book should work.

Figure 2-11   How to install and run the book applications

A summary of the directories and files for a web application

Figure 2-12 shows a simplified version of the directory structure for the Music Store application that's presented in this book. Some of these directories are standard directories that are used by all J2EE web applications. For example, all web applications that use servlets must have the WEB-INF and WEB-INF\classes directories. In addition, though, some of the directories are defined by the programmer to help structure the web application. In particular, the admin, cart, and download directories are used to contain the Administration, Shopping Cart, and Download applications that make up the Music Store application.

To start, each web application must have a root directory that can be referred to as the *document root directory*, or just *document root*. In this figure, the document root directory is named musicStore, and it is subordinate to Tomcat's webapps directory. Then, all of the other directories and files for the application must be subordinate to this document root.

The WEB-INF directory that's subordinate to the document root directory usually contains just one file named web.xml. This file is used to configure the servlets and other components of the web application. You'll learn more about it in the next figure.

The WEB-INF directory also has a few standard directories that are subordinate to it. In particular, the WEB-INF\classes directory contains the servlets and other Java classes for the application that aren't compressed into JAR files. These are typically the classes that you write. In contrast, the WEB-INF\lib directory contains the JAR files for the application, and the JAR files that apply to all the applications that Tomcat is running must be stored in the webapps\common\lib directory. In case you need to refresh your memory, a *JAR file* contains a group of classes in a compressed format.

To organize the classes that you create for the application, you can store them in *packages*. In that case, you need to create one subdirectory for each package. For example, the application in this figure uses five packages: admin, business, cart, data, and download. Three of these packages contain servlets that work with the HTML and JSP files for the application while the other two contain the Java classes that provide the business objects and data access objects for the web application.

Besides the standard WEB-INF subdirectories, the Music Store application uses the WEB-INF\etc directory to store all of the data files that it uses. Since the WEB-INF directory and its subdirectories aren't web accessible, this prevents users from accessing these files with a web browser.

As you progress through this book, you'll learn how to use some other standard directories to deploy web applications. For example, if you use custom tags, you'll need to include the WEB-INF\tlds directory. For now, though, this figure should give you a general idea of what it takes to deploy a web application.

The directory structure for a web application named musicStore

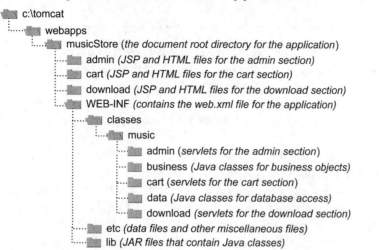

c:\tomcat
  webapps
    musicStore *(the document root directory for the application)*
      admin *(JSP and HTML files for the admin section)*
      cart *(JSP and HTML files for the cart section)*
      download *(JSP and HTML files for the download section)*
      WEB-INF *(contains the web.xml file for the application)*
        classes
          music
            admin *(servlets for the admin section)*
            business *(Java classes for business objects)*
            cart *(servlets for the cart section)*
            data *(Java classes for database access)*
            download *(servlets for the download section)*
        etc *(data files and other miscellaneous files)*
        lib *(JAR files that contain Java classes)*

A summary of the directories and files for a web application

Directory	Description
document root	The *document root directory* is the root directory for a web application. This directory typically contains the index file for the application. In addition, this directory or its subdirectories contain the HTML and JSP files for the application.
\WEB-INF	This directory contains a file named web.xml. It can be used to configure the servlets and other components that make up the application.
\WEB-INF\classes	This directory and its subdirectories contain the servlets and other Java classes for your application that aren't compressed into JAR files. If you're using Java packages, each package must be stored in a subdirectory that has the same name as the package.
\WEB-INF\lib	This directory contains any JAR files that contain Java classes that are needed by this web application, but not by other web applications.

Description

- A Java web application is a hierarchy of directories and files in a standard layout defined by the J2EE specification. This means that each Tomcat web application must use the four directories summarized above.

- To organize your Java class files, you can store them in *packages*. A package of classes must be stored within a subdirectory of the WEB-INF\classes directory.

- If you need to make classes within a JAR file available to more than one web application, you can put the JAR file in Tomcat's webapps\common\lib directory. If you need to make classes within a JAR file available to a single web application, you can put them in the WEB-INF\lib directory for that application.

- You can use the WEB-INF\etc directory to store any files that you don't want users to be able to access. For example, you can store any files that store data for the application in this directory.

Figure 2-12   A summary of the directories and files for a web application

An introduction to the web.xml file for a web application

Figure 2-13 introduces you to the web.xml file that is known as the *deployment descriptor*. This file is used to configure a web application, and this figure should give you a general idea of what the web.xml file can do for an application. At the minimum, this file must contain the shaded code. This code defines the type of XML that's being used and the type of J2EE standards that the web.xml file follows.

Typically, though, a web.xml file contains some additional code that's used to configure the web application. In this figure, for example, the XML tags within the Servlet tags specify an alias and some initialization parameters for a servlet. In particular, they specify an alias for the EmailServlet that's stored in the email package so it can be accessed by the name EmailResponse. And they specify an initialization parameter that says to use the UserEmail.txt file for a parameter named filename.

As you progress through this book, you'll learn some specifics for working with a web.xml file. In chapter 6, for example, you'll learn how to use a web.xml file to work with servlet aliases, servlet mapping, initialization parameters, and custom error pages. And in chapter 14, you'll learn how to use the web.xml file to restrict access to the pages within a web application.

A web.xml file

```
<?xml version="1.0" encoding="ISO-8859-1"?>

<!DOCTYPE web-app
    PUBLIC "-//Sun Microsystems, Inc.//DTD Web Application 2.2//EN"
    "http://java.sun.com/j2ee/dtds/web-app_2_2.dtd">

<web-app>

  <servlet>
    <servlet-name>EmailResponse</servlet-name>
    <servlet-class>email.EmailServlet</servlet-class>
    <init-param>
      <param-name>filename</param-name>
      <param-value>UserEmail.txt</param-value>
    </init-param>
  </servlet>

</web-app>
```

What the web.xml file can do

- Provide an alias for a servlet class so you can call a servlet using a different name.
- Enable servlet mapping so you can call a servlet using any URL or URL pattern.
- Define initialization parameters for a servlet or the entire application.
- Define error pages for an entire application.
- Provide security constraints to restrict access to certain web pages and servlets.

Description

- Every web application requires a web.xml file in the WEB-INF directory. This file is known as the *deployment descriptor* for the web application. At the minimum, this file must contain the information that's highlighted above.
- Throughout this book, you'll learn how to manipulate the web.xml file to implement the tasks described above.

Figure 2-13   An introduction to the web.xml file for an application

A summary of the directories and files for the book applications

In figure 2-12, you saw the directory structure for a web application. Now, in figure 2-14, you can see the directory structure for the many small applications that are used to illustrate the skills presented in chapters 3 through 16. Once you understand this structure, it will be easy for you to find the parts of these applications that you want to review.

In this case, the document root directory is the murach directory. Then, for each chapter, the JSP and HTML files are stored in a subdirectory like murach\email6, and the servlet classes are stored in a subdirectory of the classes directory like WEB-INF\classes\email6.

Beyond that, the classes that can be used by any of the chapter applications are stored in packages in subdirectories like classes\business, classes\data, and classes\util. The data files that can be used by all the applications are stored in the WEB-INF\etc directory. And the JAR file for the MySQL database driver is stored in the WEB-INF\lib.

Please note that the directory structure in this figure doesn't include all of the directories. But with this as background, you should be able to find any of the files that you install from this book's CD.

The directory structure for the book applications

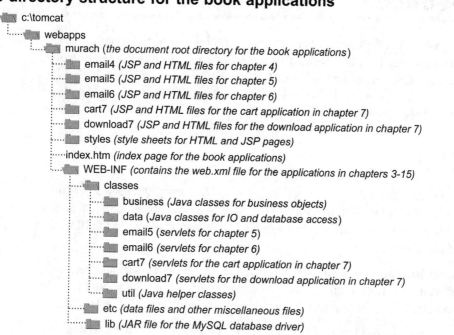

- c:\tomcat
  - webapps
    - murach *(the document root directory for the book applications)*
      - email4 *(JSP and HTML files for chapter 4)*
      - email5 *(JSP and HTML files for chapter 5)*
      - email6 *(JSP and HTML files for chapter 6)*
      - cart7 *(JSP and HTML files for the cart application in chapter 7)*
      - download7 *(JSP and HTML files for the download application in chapter 7)*
      - styles *(style sheets for HTML and JSP pages)*
      - index.htm *(index page for the book applications)*
      - WEB-INF *(contains the web.xml file for the applications in chapters 3-15)*
        - classes
          - business *(Java classes for business objects)*
          - data *(Java classes for IO and database access)*
          - email5 *(servlets for chapter 5)*
          - email6 *(servlets for chapter 6)*
          - cart7 *(servlets for the cart application in chapter 7)*
          - download7 *(servlets for the download application in chapter 7)*
          - util *(Java helper classes)*
        - etc *(data files and other miscellaneous files)*
        - lib *(JAR file for the MySQL database driver)*

Description

- In chapters 3 through 16, you'll learn how to develop the web applications that you install from this book's CD. Unlike the Music Store application that's summarized in figure 2-13, these applications are short applications that are designed to illustrate the skills presented in each chapter.

- The document root directory for all of these applications is webapps\murach. And the index file that provides links to these applications is in the murach directory.

- The HTML documents, JSPs, and servlets for each of these applications are stored in specific directories. For instance, the HTML and JSPs for the chapter 6 application are stored in the murach\email6 directory, and the servlet classes for this chapter are stored in the murach\WEB-INF\classes\email6 directory.

- Files that aren't specific to a chapter are stored in subdirectories of the murach directory.

- Java classes that are available to all applications are stored in separate packages in the WEB-INF/classes directory.

- Although the directory structure above doesn't include all of the directories for the book applications, you can view the complete structure after you install the book applications as shown in figure 2-11.

Figure 2-14   A summary of the directories and files for the book applications

Perspective

The goal of this chapter has been to show you how to install, configure, and use Tomcat on your own PC. Now, if you can use Tomcat to run the web applications that are included on the book's CD, that goal has been fulfilled. In that case, you're ready to move on to the next chapter where you'll learn how to develop your own HTML documents.

Summary

- After you install Tomcat on your own PC, you need to copy the servlet.jar file from Tomcat's common\lib directory to the SDK's jre\lib\ext directory. You also need to set the JAVA_HOME environmental variable so it points to the SDK that's installed on your PC.

- If you want Tomcat to recognize changes that are made to the servlet classes that are used, you need to turn on *servlet reloading* by modifying the servlet.xml file. Then, you don't have to stop and restart Tomcat every time you change a class.

- Before you can run servlets and JSPs on your own system, you need to open a DOS prompt window and use the startup batch file to start Tomcat. When you're done with Tomcat, you use the shutdown batch file to turn Tomcat off.

- When Tomcat is running, you can use your web browser to enter a *Uniform Resource Locator* (*URL*) that accesses an HTML document, a JSP, or a servlet. If you enter a URL that points to a directory that doesn't contain an index.htm, index.html file, or index.jsp, Tomcat displays a directory listing.

- Two common problems that occur when you enter a URL into your browser are (1) that Tomcat isn't running so the browser can't connect with the web server, and (2) that the URL is incorrect so Tomcat can't find the page you want. In either case, an error message is displayed.

- If Tomcat's default *port* is used by another application on your system, you may need to change the default port by modifying the servlet.xml file.

- A Java web application consists of a hierarchy of directories and files in a standard layout that's defined by the J2EE specification. This layout includes a *document root directory*, a WEB-INF directory, and classes and lib directories that are subordinate to the WEB-INF directory.

- The *deployment descriptor* for a web application is a web.xml file in the WEB-INF directory that can be used to configure the servlets and other components that make up the application.

Terms

Tomcat home directory
servlet reloading
Uniform Resource Locator (URL)
protocol
host
port
path
filename
document root directory
document root
JAR file
package
deployment descriptor

Objectives

- Install and configure Tomcat so it runs on your own PC.

- Start Tomcat from a DOS prompt window, and shut it down from this window.

- Turn on servlet reloading so you don't have to stop and restart Tomcat every time you want to change and test a servlet.

- Use your browser to enter a URL that accesses an HTML document, JSP, or servlet.

- If a port conflict occurs, change the port that's used by Tomcat.

- Describe two common errors that occur after you enter a URL into a browser.

- In general terms, describe the directory structure of a web application that's defined by the J2EE specfication.

- In general terms, describe the deployment descriptor of a web application.

Before you do the exercises for this chapter

If you haven't already done so, you need to install all of the software that's on the book's CD. You should also install the web applications that are on the CD. In appendix A, you'll find the procedures that you need for installing all of the software and applications, except for Tomcat.

Exercise 2-1   Install and test Tomcat

If you've installed and tested Tomcat as you went through this chapter, you don't need to do this exercise.

1. Install and configure Tomcat as described in this chapter.

2. To make sure you've installed Tomcat correctly, start Tomcat and run some of the Tomcat examples as shown in figure 2-7.

3. Shutdown Tomcat.

Exercise 2-2   Run the book applications

Before you do this exercise, you need to install the book applications from this book's CD as described in appendix A.

1. Display the index page for the murach book applications, and run any of the applications for chapters 4 through 16. If you like, bookmark the index page for these applications.

2. Start the Music Store application by entering the URL for its index page, and experiment with this application to make sure that the MySQL database has been installed correctly.

3. Use the Windows Explorer to review the directories and files for the murach book applications and the Music Store application.

3

A crash course in HTML

In a typical web application, HyperText Markup Language is used to provide the user interface. Then, the user can navigate through the HTML pages to view data, and the user can enter data into HTML forms that pass the data to JavaServer Pages or servlets. That's why you need to have a basic set of HTML skills before you can code JSPs or servlets. And that's why this chapter presents a crash course in HTML.

If you already know how to code HTML, of course, you can skip this chapter. And if you want to learn more about HTML after you read this chapter, you can get a book that's dedicated entirely to HTML. Keep in mind, though, that this chapter presents all the HTML that you will need to know as you use this book.

An introduction to HTML **62**
Tools for working with HTML 62
An HTML document 64

How to code and view an HTML page **66**
How to code an HTML document 66
Where and how to save an HTML document 68
How to view an HTML page 70

More skills for coding HTML documents **72**
How to code links to other HTML pages 72
How to code tables 74
Attributes for working with table tags 76
How to include images in an HTML page 78
How to use a style sheet 80

How to code HTML forms **82**
How to code a form 82
How to code text boxes, password boxes, and hidden fields 84
How to code buttons 86
How to code check boxes and radio buttons 88
How to code combo boxes and list boxes 90
How to code text areas 92
How to set the tab order of controls 94

Perspective **96**

An introduction to HTML

This topic introduces you to HTML and to the editors and IDEs that you can use for coding HTML. Once you understand that, you can learn the specifics of HTML coding.

Tools for working with HTML

When you're coding HTML or JSPs, you can use a general text editor like Notepad or TextPad. In fact, TextPad can be set up so it uses colors to identify the various parts of the HTML syntax, which makes it quite efficient for HTML editing.

Another alternative, though, is to use an editor that's specifically designed for working with HTML pages and JSPs. One of the most popular of these editors is Macromedia's HomeSite, which is shown in figure 3-1. HomeSite not only uses color, boldfacing, and italics to identify various parts of the HTML syntax, but it also provides tools that can help you enter and edit HTML code. For example, this figure shows a pop-up box that can help you write specific types of code.

If you want to experiment with HomeSite, you'll find a trial copy on the CD that comes with this book. Then, if you decide that you want to continue using it, you can purchase it for a cost of about $85. If cost is an issue, though, you can do all of the HTML and JSP editing that this book requires by using TextPad, which is also available on the CD.

A third alternative for entering and editing HTML code and JSPs is to use an *Integrated Development Environment* (*IDE*) that's designed for developing web applications. Of these, Macromedia's Dreamweaver is the industry leader. It not only provides an editor for HTML and JSPs, but also visual tools for designing and maintaining web pages.

Because an IDE like Dreamweaver presents its own learning problems, we think it's best to start by using TextPad or HomeSite instead of an IDE. Once you master the skills in this book, though, you shouldn't have any trouble mastering an IDE like Dreamweaver. And if you've been using HomeSite, you'll find that it integrates well with Dreamweaver since they're both made by the same company.

Macromedia's HomeSite

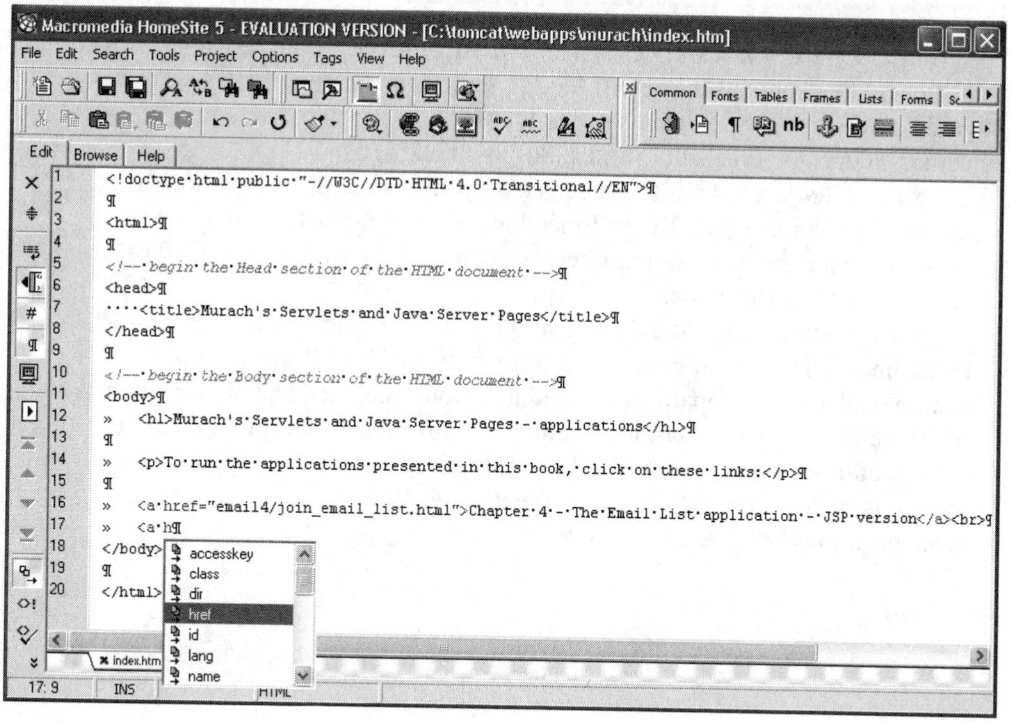

Description

- *HyperText Markup Language*, or *HTML*, is used to provide the user interface for web applications.

- To write and edit HTML code and JSPs, you can use a general text editor like TextPad, a text editor that's specifically designed for working with HTML, or an *Integrated Development Environment*, or *IDE*, that's designed for developing web applications.

- Macromedia's HomeSite is a text editor that's specifically designed for working with HTML and JSPs, and it is one of the most popular HTML editors on the market.

- Macromedia's Dreamweaver is the industry-leading IDE that lets you create and manage web sites and Internet applications. It provides visual layout tools and extensive editing support.

Figure 3-1   Tools for working with HTML

An HTML document

Figure 3-2 shows a simple *HTML page* in a browser along with the *HTML document* that contains the HTML code for the page. Within the HTML code, *HTML tags* define the elements of the HTML page. Each of these tags is coded within an opening bracket (<) and a closing bracket (>).

Since HTML tags aren't case sensitive, you can use upper or lowercase letters when you code your tags. Since lowercase is easier to read and type, most programmers use lowercase when coding HTML tags, and that's how the tags are coded in this book.

When coding an HTML document, you can use spaces, indentation, and blank lines to make your code easier to read. In this HTML document, for example, blank lines separate the Head and Body sections, and all tags within the Head and Body sections are indented. As a result, it's easy to tell where these sections begin and end. Similarly, the text after the heading in the body section is broken into two lines to make it easier to read. However, the web browser displays this text as a single line.

An HTML page viewed in a browser

The HTML document for the page

```html
<html>

<head>
    <title>Murach's Java Servlets and JSP</title>
</head>

<body>
    <h1>Murach's Java Servlets and JSP applications</h1>
    <p>To run the applications presented in this book,
        click on these links:</p>
</body>

</html>
```

Description

- An *HTML document* is used to define each *HTML page* that's displayed by a web browser.
- Within an HTML document, *HTML tags* define how the page will look when it is displayed. Each of these HTML tags is coded within a set of brackets (< >).
- Since HTML tags aren't case sensitive, you can use upper or lowercase letters for your tags.
- To make your code easier to read, you can use spaces, indentation, and blank lines.

Figure 3-2   An HTML document

How to code and view an HTML page

Now that you have a general idea of how HTML works, you're ready to learn more about coding, saving, and viewing an HTML page. To start, you'll learn about some of the most common HTML tags.

How to code an HTML document

Figure 3-3 shows how to code some of the most common HTML tags. Most of these tags require both an opening tag and a closing tag. Although the closing tags are similar to opening tags, they begin with a slash. For example, you can boldface text like this:

```
<b>This text will be boldfaced</b> but this text won't be.
```

On the other hand, some HTML tags don't require a closing tag. For example, you can insert a line break like this:

```
The text for line 1<br>
The text for line 2
```

To start the HTML document, the code in this figure uses a DocType tag that identifies the type of document that's being sent to the browser:

```
<!doctype html public "-//W3C//DTD HTML 4.0 Transitional//
EN">
```

This tag lets the browser know that this HTML document is an HTML 4.0 document that transitionally conforms to the W3C standard and is in the English language. As a Java programmer, you don't need to completely understand this tag, but you usually begin your web pages with this DocType tag or one that's similar to it. Some HTML editors will automatically insert this tag for you.

After the DocType tag, the opening HTML tag identifies the start of the HTML document, and the closing HTML tag identifies the end of the HTML document. Then, within the HTML tags, the Head and Body tags identify the Head and Body sections of the HTML document. Within the Head tags, the Title tag identifies the title that's displayed in the title bar of the browser. Within the Body tags, the H1 tag identifies a level-1 heading, the H2 tag identifies a level-2 heading, and the P tag identifies a paragraph. Since these tags are coded within the Body tags, they're displayed within the main browser window.

To document your HTML code, you can use *comments* in the same way that you use them in other languages. In this example, comments are used to identify the beginning of the Head and Body sections, but that's just for the purpose of illustration. You can also use comments to "comment out" portions of HTML code that you don't want rendered by the browser. Then, if you want to restore the code, you can just remove the comment's opening and closing tags.

The code for an HTML document that contains comments

```
<!doctype html public "-//W3C//DTD HTML 4.0 Transitional//EN">

<html>

<!-- begin the Head section of the HTML document -->
<head>
    <title>Murach's Java Servlets and JSP</title>
</head>

<!-- begin the Body section of the HTML document -->
<body>
    <h1>Murach's Java Servlets and JSP applications</h1>
        <p>Here are links to the applications presented in this book:</p>
</body>

</html>
```

Basic HTML tags

Tag	Description
`<!doctype ... >`	Identifies the type of HTML document. This tag is often inserted automatically by the HTML editor.
`<html> </html>`	Marks the beginning and end of an HTML document.
`<head> </head>`	Marks the beginning and end of the Head section of the HTML document.
`<title> </title>`	Marks the title that is displayed in the title bar of the browser.
`<body> </body>`	Marks the beginning and end of the Body section of the HTML document.
`<h1> </h1>`	Tells the browser to use the default format for a heading-1 paragraph.
`<h2> </h2>`	Tells the browser to use the default format for a heading-2 paragraph.
`<p> </p>`	Tells the browser to use the default format for a standard paragraph.
` `	Inserts a line break.
`<b> </b>`	Marks text as bold.
`<i> </i>`	Marks text as italic.
`<u> </u>`	Marks text as underlined.
`<!-- -->`	Defines a comment that is ignored by the browser.

Description

- The DocType tag lets the browser know what version of HTML is being used, what standards it conforms to, and what language is used.
- Within the Head tags, you code any tags that apply to the entire page such as the Title tag.
- Within the Body tags, you code the text and other components for the body of the HTML page. When working with text, you can use the H1, H2, and P tags to apply the default formatting that's assigned to heading-l, heading-2, and standard paragraphs. You can also use the B, I, and U tags to apply bold, italics, or underlining.
- *Comments* can be used anywhere within an HTML document to document portions of code or to tell the browser not to process portions of code.

Figure 3-3 How to code an HTML document

Where and how to save an HTML document

Figure 3-4 shows where and how to save HTML documents to make them available to a web application. To start, this figure shows the directories where you can store HTML files and shows how to name your HTML files. Then, this figure shows the Save As dialog box for a typical HTML editor.

To make HTML pages available to a web application, you must store them in a directory that's available to the web server. Although this directory varies from one server to another, you can use any subdirectory of the webapps directory when you're working with Tomcat 4.0. For instance, all of the applications that are presented in the first 16 chapters of this book are stored in Tomcat's webapps\murach directory. You can also use the webapps\ROOT directory that's created when you install Tomcat. And you can create your own subdirectories under the webapps or ROOT directory for storing your HTML files.

When you save an HTML file, you must make sure to include an extension of htm or html. In addition, you shouldn't use any spaces in the filename. By convention, most web programmers use underscore characters instead of spaces. However, you can also use a mixture of uppercase and lowercase letters. If you're using a text editor that isn't designed for working with HTML documents, you may need to enclose the filename of the HTML document in quotes. Otherwise, the text editor might not include the extension for the file.

The root directory for the applications in the first 16 chapters of this book

```
c:\tomcat\webapps\murach
```

Other directories for saving HTML documents in Tomcat 4.0

```
c:\tomcat\webapps\yourDocumentRoot
c:\tomcat\webapps\yourDocumentRoot\yourSubdirectory
c:\tomcat\webapps\ROOT
c:\tomcat\webapps\ROOT\yourSubdirectory
```

Typical names for HTML documents

```
index.htm
index.html
join_email_list.htm
join_email_list.html
```

A dialog box for saving an HTML document

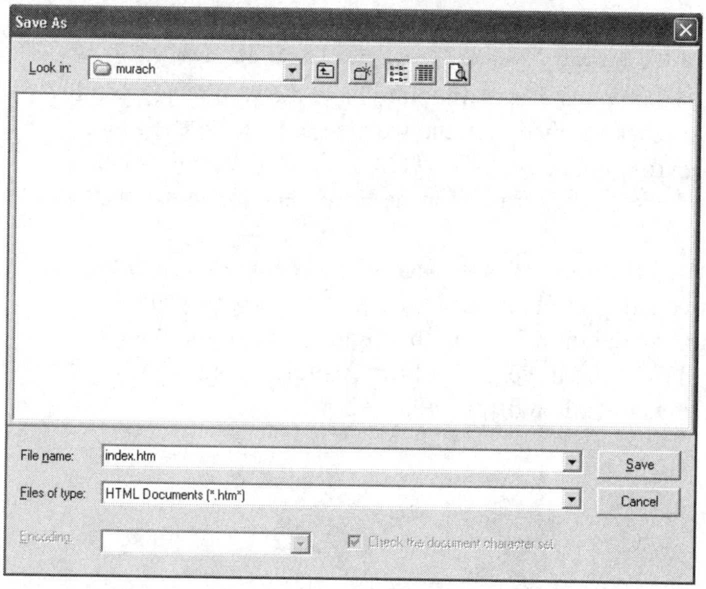

Description

- To make an HTML document available to a user, you must save it in a directory that's available to the web server. If you're starting to work on a new system, you need to find out what directories are available for your web pages.

- For Tomcat 4.0, you must save your HTML files in a subdirectory of Tomcat's webapps directory.

- All HTML files that are presented in the first 16 chapters of this book are stored in the webapps\murach directory or one of its subdirectories.

- When naming an HTML file, don't use spaces. Use underscores instead. In addition, you must be sure that the file is saved with an extension of htm or html.

- In the Save As dialog box, you can make sure that the filename is saved with the right extension by entering the filename and extension within quotation marks.

Figure 3-4   Where and how to save an HTML document

How to view an HTML page

Once you've coded an HTML document and saved it in a directory that's available to the web server, you can view the HTML page as shown in figure 3-5. To do that, you start your web browser and enter an HTTP URL as shown in this figure.

If, for example, you have saved an HTML file named index.htm in the webapps\murach directory, you can view that file by entering

```
http://localhost:8080/murach/index.htm
```

Or, since most web servers will automatically look for an index file when you enter a directory, you can get the same file by entering

```
http://localhost:8080/murach
```

Finally, if you want to view a web page named join_email_list.htm that's stored in the murach\email directory, you can enter the name of the file like this:

```
http://localhost:8080/murach/email/join_email_list.htm
```

While you're coding a web page, it's common to have the web page open in a browser. Then, when you make a change to the web page, you can easily view the change in the browser. To do that, use your HTML editor to save the change, switch to the browser, and click the Refresh (for the Explorer) or Reload button (for Netscape).

Incidentally, you can also view an HTML page without going through the web server by entering the path and file name in the Address box of your browser. This is illustrated by the third URL in this figure. And if you double-click on the name of an HTML file in your Windows Explorer, your web browser will open and the page will be displayed.

An HTML page viewed in a browser

How Tomcat maps directories to HTTP calls

Directory	URL
c:\tomcat\webapps\murach	http://localhost:8080/murach/
c:\tomcat \webapps\murach\email	http://localhost:8080/murach/email
c:\tomcat \webapps\root	http://localhost:8080/
c:\tomcat \webapps\root\email	http://localhost:8080/email

A URL that requests an HTML page from a local server

```
http://localhost:8080/murach/email/join_email_list.htm
```

A URL that requests an HTML page from an Internet server

```
http://www.murach.com/email/join_email_list.htm
```

A URL that requests an HTML page without going through a server

```
c:\tomcat\webapps\murach\email\join_email_list.htm
```

Description

- To use HTTP to view a local HTML page, start the Tomcat server and enter a URL that calls the page.
- To use HTTP to view a web page that's on the Internet, connect to the Internet and enter the URL for the page.
- If you modify the HTML for a page and save your changes, you can view the new results in the browser by clicking the Refresh button (for the Internet Explorer) or the Reload button (for Netscape).
- You can also view an HTML page without going through the web server by entering its path and filename or by double-clicking on it in the Windows Explorer. However, this won't work correctly for JSPs, which need to go through the web server.

Figure 3-5   How to view an HTML page

More skills for coding HTML documents

Now that you know how to code, save, and view a simple HTML document, you're ready to learn more of the skills for working with HTML documents. In particular, you're going to learn the HTML tags that are used in most commercial web pages. These, of course, are the tags that Java programmers need to know and understand.

How to code links to other HTML pages

Any web site or web application is a series of web pages that are connected by *links*. To code a link to another web page, you can use an Anchor, or A tag, as shown in figure 3-6. Within the opening tag, you code an *attribute* that contains a *value* that identifies the linked page. Between the opening and closing tags, you code the text that describes the link. When viewed in a browser, this text is usually underlined. Then, the user can click on the link to jump to the page that's specified by the link.

To code an attribute, you code the name of the attribute, the equals sign, and the value, with no intervening spaces. However, if you code two or more attributes within a single tag, you separate the attributes with spaces. Although it's generally considered a good coding practice to include quotation marks around the attribute's value, that's not required. As a result, you may come across HTML code that doesn't include the quotation marks.

The first group of examples in this figure shows how to use a *relative link*. Here, the first link specifies a web page named join_email_list.htm that's in the same directory as the current web page. Then, the second link specifies the join_email_list.htm page that's stored in the email subdirectory of the current directory. If necessary, you can code a link that navigates down several directories like this:

```
books/java/ch01/toc.htm
```

The second group of examples shows how to navigate up the directory hierarchy. To do that, you can start your link with a slash or two periods (..). The first two examples in this group use two periods to navigate up one or two directory levels. Since these examples don't include the name of a web page, they select the index page for that directory. The third and forth examples in this group show how to use a slash to navigate to the directory that's defined as the root directory by your web server.

The third group of examples shows how to use an *absolute link* to specify a web page. Here, the first link shows how to specify a web page named join_email_list.htm that's stored in the email subdirectory of the root HTML directory for the www.murach.com web site. The second link specifies the same web page, but it uses an IP address instead of a URL. Although you rarely need to use IP addresses, you do need to use them for sites that haven't yet been assigned their domain names.

Two Anchor tags viewed in a browser

The Email List application 1
The Email List application 2

Examples of Anchor tags

Anchor tags with relative URLs that are based on the current directory

```
<a href="join_email_list.htm">The Email List application 1</a><br>
<a href="email/join_email_list.htm">The Email List application 2</a><br>
```

Anchor tags with relative URLs that navigate up the directory structure

```
<a href="../">Go back one directory level</a>
<a href="../../">Go back two directory levels</a>
<a href="/">Go to the root level for HTML files</a>
<a href="/murach">Go to the murach subdirectory of the root level</a>
```

Anchor tags with absolute URLs

```
<a href="http://www.murach.com/email">An Internet address</a>
<a href="http://64.71.179.86/email">An IP address</a>
```

The Anchor tag

Tag	Description
`<a>  </a>`	Defines a link to another URL. When the user clicks on the text that's displayed by the tag, the browser requests the page that is identified by the Href attribute of the tag.

One attribute of the Anchor tag

Attribute	Description
`href`	Specifies the URL for the link.

How to code attributes for tags

- Within the starting tag, code a space and the attribute name. Then, if the attribute requires a value, code the equals sign followed by the value between quotation marks with no intervening spaces.

- If more than one attribute is required, separate the attributes with spaces.

Description

- A tag can have one or more *attributes*, and most attributes require values. Although it's considered a good coding practice to code values within quotation marks, the quotation marks aren't required.

- The Href attribute of the Anchor tag is used to specify the URL that identifies the HTML page that the browser should request when the user clicks on the text for this tag.

- When you code a *relative URL* in the Href attribute, you base it on the current directory, which is the one for the current HTML page. To go to the root directory for web pages, you can code a slash. To go up one level from the current directory, you can code two periods and a slash. And so on.

- When you code an *absolute URL*, you code the complete URL. To do that, you can code the name of the host or the IP address for the host.

Figure 3-6   How to code links to other HTML pages

How to code tables

If you do any serious work with HTML, you need to use one or more *tables* to present data in *rows* and *columns* as shown in figure 3-7. To start, you use the Table tag to identify the start and end of the table. Within the Table tag, you use the Table Row tag, or TR tag, to specify a new row, and you use the Table Data tag, or TD tag, to specify a new column. In this figure, for example, the table contains three rows and two columns.

The intersection of a row and column is known as a *cell*. Typically, each cell of a table stores text as shown in this figure. However, cells can store any type of data including links to other pages, images, controls, and even other tables. In fact, it's common for a web page to contain one or more tables nested within other tables. As a Java programmer, though, you will probably only have to work with one table at a time.

The HTML code for a table

```
<p>Here is the information that you entered:</p>

<table cellspacing="5" cellpadding="5" border="1">
  <tr>
    <td align="right">First name:</td>
    <td>John</td>
  </tr>
  <tr>
    <td align="right">Last name:</td>
    <td>Smith</td>
  </tr>
  <tr>
    <td align="right">Email address:</td>
    <td>jsmith@hotmail.com</td>
  </tr>
</table>
```

The table displayed in a browser

Here is the information that you entered:

First name:	John
Last name:	Smith
Email address:	jsmith@hotmail.com

The tags for working with tables

Tag	Description
`<table> </table>`	Marks the start and end of the table.
`<tr> </tr>`	Marks the start and end of each row.
`<td> </td>`	Marks the start and end of each cell within a row.

Description

- A *table* consists of *rows* and *columns*. The intersection of a row and column creates a *cell* that can hold data.
- Although this figure shows a single table that stores text within each cell, it's common to store other types of data within a cell such as images, links, or even another table.
- The attributes in figure 3-8 can be used with the Table, TR, and TD tags to control the formatting of the table.

Figure 3-7   How to code tables

Attributes for working with table tags

When coding the HTML for a table, you usually need to use some of the attributes that are summarized in figure 3-8. In the last figure, for example, you can see the use of the Border, CellSpacing, and CellPadding attributes of the Table tag. They make the table border visible and add some spacing and padding between the cells of the table. That example also uses the Align attribute of the TD tag to align the text in the first column with the right edge of that column.

When you're creating and modifying tables, you can set the Border attribute to 1 so you can see the cells within the table. This makes it easier to organize the rows and columns of the table and to set the attributes of the table. Then, when you've got the table the way you want it, you can set the Border attribute to 0 to hide the borders of the table.

Although this figure doesn't present all of the attributes for working with tables, it does present the most useful ones. If you experiment with them, you should be able to figure out how they work. In addition, a good HTML editor will provide pop-up lists of other attributes that you can use when you're working with tables.

When working with a table, you can use *pixels* to specify most height and width measurements. Pixels are the tiny dots on your computer's monitor that display the text and images that you see. Today, many computers display a screen that's 800 pixels wide and 600 pixels tall. However, some computers run at higher resolutions such as 1024 pixels wide by 728 pixels tall. When coding a table, then, it's a good practice to make the total width of your table less than the total number of pixels for your target resolution. That usually means coding tables where all cell spacing and width measurements add up to be less than 780 (800 pixels wide minus 20 pixels for the vertical scroll bar).

Attributes of the Table tag

Attribute	Description
border	Specifies the visual border of the table. To turn the border off, specify a value of 0. To specify the width of the border in pixels, specify a value of 1 or greater.
cellspacing	Specifies the number of pixels between cells.
cellpadding	Specifies the number of pixels between the contents of a cell and the edge of the cell.
width	Specifies the width of the table. To specify the width in pixels, use a number such as 300. To specify a percent of the browser's display space, use a number followed by the percent sign such as 60%.
height	Specifies the height of the table in pixels or as a percentage of the browser's display space. This works like the Width attribute.

Attributes of the TR tag

Attribute	Description
valign	Specifies the vertical alignment of the contents of the row. Acceptable values include Top, Bottom, and Middle.

Attributes of the TD tag

Attribute	Description
align	Specifies the horizontal alignment of the contents of the cell. Acceptable values include Left, Right, and Center.
colspan	Specifies the number of columns that the cell will span.
rowspan	Specifies the number of rows that the cell will span.
height	Specifies the height of the cell in pixels.
width	Specifies the width of the cell in pixels.
valign	Specifies the vertical alignment of the contents of the row. Acceptable values include Top, Bottom, and Middle and will override any settings in the TR tag.

Description

- Although there are other attributes for working with tables, these are the ones that are commonly used.

Figure 3-8   Attributes for working with table tags

How to include images in an HTML page

Although text and links are an important part of any web site, most web pages include one or more images. Figure 3-9 shows how to use the Image (or IMG) tag to display an image. Unlike most of the tags presented so far, the IMG tag doesn't have a closing tag. As a result, you just need to code the tag and its attributes.

The example in this figure shows how to code an IMG tag and its three required attributes. Here, you must code the Source (SRC) attribute to specify the image that you want to include. In this case, the SRC attribute specifies the filename of an image that's stored in the images directory. If you have any trouble specifying the file for the image, please refer to figure 3-6 because many of the skills that apply to the Href attribute of the Anchor tag also apply to the SRC attribute of the IMG tag.

After the SRC attribute, you can code the Width and Height attributes. The values for these attributes must specify the height and width of the image in pixels. If you use one of your HTML editor's tools to insert an image, all three of these attributes may be automatically specified for you. Otherwise, you may need to open the image in an image editor to determine the number of pixels for the width and height.

The last five attributes described in this figure aren't required, but they're commonly used. For example, the Alt attribute is commonly used to specify text that's displayed if an image can't be loaded. This text is usually displayed when a web browser takes a long time to load all of the images on a page, but it can also be displayed for text-only browsers. If you experiment with the attributes described in this list, you shouldn't have any trouble using them.

When you include images in a web page, you can use a *Graphic Interchange Format* file, or *GIF* file, or you can use a *Joint Photographic Experts Group* file, or *JPEG* file. Typically, a web designer will use imaging software such as Adobe's Photoshop to create and maintain these files for a web site and will save these files in a directory named images or graphics. In this book, for example, all images used by the applications for the first 16 chapters are stored in the murach\images directory. Although GIF files are stored with a GIF extension, JPEG files can be stored with either a JPEG or JPG extension.

HTML code that includes an image

```
<p>Here is the image for the Murach logo:</p>
<img src="../images/murachlogo.gif" width="150" height="65">
```

The HTML code displayed in a browser

Here is the image for the Murach logo:

The Image tag

Tag	Description
<img>	Specifies how to place a GIF or JPEG image within an HTML page.

Common attributes of the Image tag

Attribute	Description
src	Specifies the relative or absolute URL for the GIF or JPEG file.
height	Specifies the height of the image in pixels.
width	Specifies the width of the image in pixels.
alt	Specifies the text that's displayed when the image can't be displayed.
border	Specifies the width of the border in pixels with 0 specifying no border at all.
hspace	Specifies the horizontal space in pixels. This space is added to the left and right of the image.
vspace	Specifies the vertical space in pixels. This space is added to the top and bottom of the image.
align	Specifies the alignment of the image on the page. Acceptable values include Left, Right, Top, Bottom, and Middle.

Other examples

```
<img src="../../images/java.jpg" width="175" height="243">
<img src="http://www.murach.com/images/murachlogo.gif" width="150" height="65">
```

Description

* The two types of image formats that are supported by most web browsers are the *Graphic Interchange Format* (*GIF*) and the *Joint Photographic Experts Group* (*JPEG*). JPEG files, which have a JPEG or JPG extension, are typically used for photographs and scans, while GIF files are typically used for other types of images.

* GIF, JPG, and JPEG files are typically stored in a separate directory named images or graphics. All of the GIF, JPG, and JPEG files used by the applications for the first 16 chapters of this book are stored in the webapps\murach\images directory.

* If you use an HTML editor to insert the image tag into your page, the HTML editor usually sets the SRC, Height, and Width attributes automatically.

Figure 3-9   How to include images in an HTML page

How to use a style sheet

Although you can code formatting attributes such as fonts, colors, margins, and alignment within a web page, most commercial web sites store this information in a file known as a *style sheet*. That way, all of the web pages within a site will have a uniform look that can be quickly and easily modified if necessary. Figure 3-10 shows how you can code a style sheet and link it to your web pages.

To start, this figure shows the code for a style sheet that's stored in a file named murach.css in the webapps\murach\styles directory. Since this style sheet is stored in its own file and must be linked to web pages, it's known as an *external style sheet* or a *linked style sheet*. The styles in this style sheet set the font, color, indentation, and alignment for the P, A, H1, H2, and H3 tags. A style sheet like this is normally developed by the web designer.

Next, this figure shows how to link a web page to an external style sheet. To do that, you can code the Link tag and its attributes in the Head section of the HTML document. Here, the Rel attribute should always be set to "stylesheet", and the Href attribute works like it does for the Anchor tag in figure 3-6. Web programmers use this type of tag so the styles developed by the web designer are used in the web pages.

An external style sheet represents the highest level of a series of *cascading style sheets*. To override the styles in an external style sheet, you can code a style sheet within an opening and closing Style tag in the Head section of an HTML document. Similarly, you can override a Style tag coded in the Head section by coding a Style attribute within a tag. Most programmers, though, don't need to override or modify styles. Instead, they use the external style sheet developed by the web designer.

The code for a style sheet

```
p {font-family: Arial, sans-serif; font-size: 12px}
a:hover {text-decoration : underline; color : #CC0000}

h1 { font-family: Arial, sans-serif; font-size: 16px; color: #003366;
    vertical-align: top; margin-top: 10px; margin-bottom: 0px
  }
h2 { font-family: Arial, sans-serif; font-size: 16px; color: #003366}
h3 { font-family: Arial, sans-serif; font-size: 14px; color: #003366}
```

The code in the HTML document that links to a style sheet

```
<head>
    <title>Murach's Servlets and Java Server Pages</title>
    <link rel="stylesheet" href="../styles/murach.css">
</head>
```

An HTML page after the style sheet above has been applied to it

Murach's Java Servlets and JSP applications

To run the applications presented in this book, click on these links:

Chapter 4 - The Email List application - JSP version
Chapter 5 - The Email List application - servlet version
Chapter 6 - The Email List application - MVC version

The Link tag

Tag	Description
`<link>`	Specifies the external style sheet.

Attributes of the Link tag

Attribute	Description
`href`	Specifies the location of the style sheet.
`rel`	Specifies the type of link. To specify a style sheet, supply a value of "stylesheet".

Description

* A *style sheet* can be used to define the font *styles* that are applied to the text of an HTML page. To identify the location of the style sheet that should be used for a page, you use the Link tag within the Head tags of the page.

* This type of style sheet can be referred to as an *external style sheet*, or *linked style* sheet, and it is actually the top style sheet in a series of *cascading style sheets*. An external style sheet is typically stored in its own directory, and css is used as the extension for its file name.

* The style sheet for the first 16 chapters of this book is named murach.css, and it is stored in the webapps\murach\styles directory.

* As a Java web programmer, you shouldn't have to create style sheets of your own, but you should know how to use them if they are available to you.

Figure 3-10   How to use a style sheet

How to code HTML forms

This topic shows how to code an HTML *form* that contains one or more *controls* such as text boxes and buttons. In this topic, you'll learn how to code 11 types of controls to gather data. In the next chapter, you'll learn how to process the data that's gathered by these controls.

How to code a form

Figure 3-11 shows how to code a form that contains three controls: two text boxes and a button. To code a form, you begin by coding the opening and closing Form tags. Within the opening Form tag, you must code an Action attribute that specifies the servlet or JSP that will be called when the user clicks on the Submit button. In addition, you can code a Method attribute that specifies the HTTP method that will be used. Between the two Form tags, you code the controls for the form.

This example shows a form that contains two text boxes and a Submit button. When the user clicks on the Submit button, the data that's in the text boxes will be passed to the JSP named entry.jsp that's specified by the Action attribute of the form. Although a form can have many controls, it should always contain at least one control that executes the Action attribute of the form. Typically, this control is a Submit button like the one shown in this figure.

You can use the Input tag to code several types of controls. This figure shows how to use the Input tag to code a text box and a button, but you'll learn more about coding these controls in the next two figures.

When coding controls, you can use the Name attribute to specify a name that you can use in your Java code to access the parameter that's passed from the HTML form to a servlet or JSP. To access the data in the two text boxes in this figure, for example, you can use firstName to access the data that's been entered in the first text box, and you can use lastName to access the data in the second text box.

In contrast, you can use the Value attribute to specify a value for a control. This works differently depending on the control. If, for example, you're working with a button, the Value attribute specifies the text that's displayed on a button. But if you're working with a text box, the Value attribute specifies the default text that's displayed in the box.

The HTML code for a form

```
<p>Here's a form that contains two text boxes and a button:</p>

<form action="entry.jsp" method="post">
  <p>
  First name: <input type="text" name="firstName"><br>
  Last name: <input type="text" name="lastName">
  <input type="submit" value="Submit">
  </p>
</form>
```

The form displayed in a browser after the user enters data

Here's a form that contains two text boxes and a button:

First name: John

Last name: Smith   Submit

Tags for working with a simple form

Tag	Description
`<form> </form>`	Defines the start and end of the form.
`<input>`	Defines the input type. You'll learn more about this tag in the next two figures.

Attributes of the Form tag

Attribute	Description
`action`	The Action attribute specifies the URL of the servlet or JSP that will be called when the user clicks on the Submit button. You'll learn more about specifying this attribute in the next two figures.
`method`	The Method attribute specifies the HTTP method that the browser will use for the HTTP request. The default method is the Get method, but the Post method is also commonly used. You'll learn more about these methods in the next chapter.

Common control attributes

Attribute	Description
`name`	The name of the control. When writing Java code, you can use this attribute to refer to the control.
`value`	The default value of the control. This varies depending on the type of control. For a text box, this attribute sets the default text that's displayed in the box. For a button, this attribute sets the text that's displayed on the button.

Description

- A *form* contains one or more *controls* such as text boxes, buttons, check boxes, and list boxes.
- A form should always contain at least one control like a Submit button that activates the Action attribute of the form. Then, any data in the controls is passed to the servlet or JSP that is identified by the URL in the Action attribute.

Figure 3-11   How to code a form

How to code text boxes, password boxes, and hidden fields

Figure 3-12 shows how to use the Input tag to code three types of *text boxes*. You can use a *standard text box* to accept text input from a user. You can use a *password box* to let a user enter a password that is displayed as one asterisk for each character that's entered. And you can use a *hidden field* to store text that you don't want to display on the HTML page.

To create a text box, you set the Type attribute to Text, Password, or Hidden. Then, you code the Name attribute so you'll be able to access the text that's stored in the text box from your Java code.

If you want the text box to contain a default value, you can code the Value attribute. Although all three of the text boxes shown in this figure have Value attributes, you often don't need to code them for standard text boxes and password boxes. Then, the user can enter values for these text boxes. In contrast, since a user can't enter text into a hidden field, you commonly code a Value attribute for a hidden field.

When coding text boxes, you can use the Size attribute to control the width of the text box. To set this attribute, you should specify the approximate number of characters that you want to display. However, since the Size attribute is based upon the average width of the character for the font that's used, it isn't exact. As a result, to be sure that a text box is wide enough to hold all of the characters, you can add a few extra characters. If, for example, you want a text box to be able to display 40 characters, you can set the size attribute to 45.

You can also use the MaxLength attribute to specify the maximum number of characters that can be entered into a text box. This can be helpful if you create a database that can only store a fixed number of characters for certain fields. If, for example, the FirstName field in the database accepts a maximum of 20 characters, you can set the MaxLength attribute of its textbox to 20. That way, the user won't be able to enter more than 20 characters for this field.

The code for three types of text controls

```
Username: <input type="text" name="username" value="jsmith"><br>
Password: <input type="password" name="password" value="opensesame"><br>
          <input type="hidden" name="productCode" value="jr01"><br>
```

The text controls displayed in a browser

Username: jsmith
Password: ●●●●●●●●●●

Attributes of these text controls

Attribute	Description
type	Specifies the type of input control. Acceptable types for text boxes are Text, Password, and Hidden.
name	Specifies the name of the control. This is the name that is used to refer to the data in the control from a servlet or JSP.
value	Specifies the value of data in the control.
size	The width of the text control field in characters based on the average character width of the font.
maxlength	The maximum number of characters that can be entered into the text box.

Description

- The Type attribute identifies the type of *text box* to be used. A value of Text creates a *standard text box*. A value of Password creates a *password box* that displays asterisks instead of text. And a value of Hidden creates a *hidden field* that can store text but isn't shown by the browser.

- For a standard text box or a password box, you can use the Value attribute to provide a default value. For a hidden field, you always use the Value attribute to supply a value that can be used by a servlet or JSP.

- Since the Size attribute specifies an approximate number of characters, you may want to make a text box slightly larger than necessary to make sure that all characters will fit within the box.

Figure 3-12   How to code text boxes, password boxes, and hidden fields

How to code buttons

Figure 3-13 shows how to use the Input tag to code three types of *buttons*. A *submit button* executes the Action attribute that's specified in the Form tag. A *reset button* resets all controls on the current form to the default values that are set by their Value attributes. And a *JavaScript button* executes the JavaScript method that's specified by its OnClick attribute.

To create a button, you set the Type attribute of the Input tag to Submit, Reset, or Button. Then, you can code a Value attribute that contains the text that's displayed on the button. For submit and reset buttons, that's all you need to do.

For a JavaScript button, though, you also need to code an OnClick attribute that specifies the JavaScript method that should be called. In chapter 6, you'll learn how to code some simple JavaScript methods for data validation so don't be bothered if you don't know JavaScript right now. In this example, the JavaScript button calls a JavaScript method named validate that accepts the current form as an argument. To specify the current form, this code uses the *this* keyword and the *form* keyword.

When coding a web page, you often to need to have two or more buttons per page that link to different servlets or JSPs. However, each form can only contain one submit button. As a result, you often need to code more than one form per page. In some cases, that means that you code a form that only contains one button. For instance, the second example in this figure actually shows two forms where the first form contains only the Continue Shopping button and the second form contains only the Checkout button.

The code for three types of buttons

```
<input type="submit" value="Submit">
<input type="reset" value="Reset">
<input type="button" value="Validate" onClick="validate(this.form)">
```

The buttons displayed in a browser

Submit   Reset   Validate

The code for two submit buttons on the same page

```
<form action="/murach/cart/index.jsp" method="post">
  <input type="submit" value="Continue Shopping">
</form>
<form action="/murach/servlet/cart.CustomerServlet" method="post">
  <input type="submit" value="Checkout">
</form>
```

The buttons displayed in a browser

Continue Shopping

Checkout

Attributes of these buttons

Attribute	Description
type	Specifies the type of input control. Acceptable types are Submit, Reset, and Button.
onclick	Specifies the JavaScript method that the button will execute when the user clicks the button.

Description

- The Type attribute identifies the type of *button* to be used.
- A Type attribute of Submit creates a *submit button* that activates the Action attribute of the form when it's clicked.
- A Type attribute of Reset creates a *reset button* that resets all controls on the form to their default values when it's clicked.
- A Type attribute of Button creates a *JavaScript button*. When this type of button is clicked, the JavaScript method that's specified by the OnClick attribute of the button is executed.
- To pass the current form to a JavaScript method in the OnClick attribute, you can use the *this* keyword and the *form* keyword. You'll learn more about JavaScript in chapter 6.

Figure 3-13   How to code buttons

How to code check boxes and radio buttons

Figure 3-14 shows how to use the Input tag to code *check boxes* and *radio buttons*. Although check boxes work independently of other check boxes, radio buttons can be set up so the user can select only one radio button from a group of radio buttons. In this figure, for example, you can select only one of the three radio buttons. However, you can select or deselect any combination of check boxes.

To create a check box, you set the Type attribute of the Input tag to Checkbox. Then, you can set the Name attribute for the check box so you can access the value from your Java code. If you want the check box to be checked by default, you can also code the Checked attribute. Unlike the Type and Name attributes, you don't need to supply a value for the Checked attribute.

To create a radio button, you can set the Type attribute of the Input tag to Radio. Then, you can set the Name attribute just as you do for other controls. However, you can specify the same name for all of the radio buttons in a group. In this figure, for example, all three radio buttons are named contactVia. That way, the user will only be able to select one of these radio buttons at a time. When coding radio buttons, you typically supply a value for each radio button. Later, when you write your Java code, you can access the value that's coded for the selected radio button.

The code for four checkboxes and three radio buttons

```
<input type="checkbox" name="addEmail" checked>
Yes, add me to your mailing list.<br>
<br>
Contact me by:<br>
<input type="radio" name="contactVia" value="Email">Email
<input type="radio" name="contactVia" value="Postal Mail">Postal mail
<input type="radio" name="contactVia" value="Both" checked>Both<br>
<br>
I'm interested in these types of music:<br>
<input type="checkbox" name="rock">Rock<br>
<input type="checkbox" name="country">Country<br>
<input type="checkbox" name="bluegrass">Bluegrass<br>
```

The check boxes and radio buttons when displayed in a browser

Here's a form that contains 4 check boxes and 3 radio buttons:

☑ Yes, add me to your mailing list.

Contact me by:
○ Email ○ Postal mail ◉ Both

I'm interested in these types of music:
☐ Rock
☐ Country
☐ Bluegrass

Attributes of these buttons

Attribute	Description
type	Specifies the type of control. A value of Checkbox creates a check box while a value of Radio creates a radio button.
checked	Selects the control. When several radio buttons share the same name, only one radio button can be selected at a time.

Description

* You can use *check boxes* to allow the user to supply a true/false value.
* You can use *radio buttons* to allow a user to select one option from a group of options. To create a group of radio buttons, use the same name for all of the radio buttons.
* If you don't group radio buttons, more than one can be on at the same time.

Figure 3-14   How to code check boxes and radio buttons

How to code combo boxes and list boxes

Figure 3-15 shows how to code *combo boxes* and *list boxes*. You can use a combo box to allow the user to select one option from a drop-down list, and you can use a list box to allow the user to select one or more options. In this figure, for example, the combo box lets you select one country, and the list box lets you select more than one country.

To code a combo or list box, you must use the Select tag and two or more Option tags. To start, you code an opening and closing Select tag. Within the opening Select tag, you must code the Name attribute. Within the two Select tags, you can code two or more Option tags. These tags supply the options that are available for the box. Within each Option tag, you must code a Value attribute. After the Option tag, you must supply the text that will be displayed in the list. This text is often similar to the text of the Value attribute.

The Multiple attribute of the Select tag allows you to create a list box. If you don't code this attribute, the Select tag will produce a combo box that lets the user select one option. If you do code this attribute, the Select tag will produce a list box that lets the user select multiple options. In fact, the only difference between the combo box and list box in this figure is that the Multiple attribute is supplied for the list box.

If you want to select a default option for a combo or list box, you can code the Selected attribute within the Option tag. Since a combo box only allows one option to be selected, you should only code one Selected attribute per combo box. However, for a list box, you can code the Selected attribute for one or more options.

The code for a combo box

```
Select a country:<br>
<select name="country">
  <option value="USA" selected>United States
  <option value="Canada">Canada
  <option value="Mexico">Mexico
</select>
```

The combo box displayed in a browser

How to convert a combo box to a list box

```
<select name="country" multiple>
```

The combo box displayed as a list box

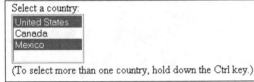

Attributes of the Select tag

Attribute	Description
multiple	Converts a combo box to a list box.

Attributes of the Option tag

Attribute	Description
selected	Selects the option.

Description

- A *combo box* provides a drop-down list that lets the user select a single option. A *list box* provides a list of options and lets the user select one or more of these options.
- To select adjacent options from a list box, the user can click the top option, hold down the Shift key, and click the bottom option.
- To select non-adjacent options from a list box, the user can click one option, hold down the Ctrl key, and click other options.

Figure 3-15   How to code combo boxes and list boxes

How to code text areas

Figure 3-16 shows how to code a *text area*. Although a text area is similar to a text box, a text area can display multiple lines of text. By default, a text area wraps each line of text to the next line and provides a vertical scroll bar that you can use to scroll up and down through the text.

To code a text area, you can begin by coding the opening and closing TextArea tags. Within the opening TextArea tag, you can code a Name attribute so you can access the control through Java. You can also code the Rows attribute to specify the number of visible rows, and you can code the Cols attribute to specify the width of the text area. Here, the Cols attribute works like the Width attribute of a text box.

Within the opening and closing TextArea tags, you can code any default text that you want to appear in the text area. By default, a text area automatically wraps text to the next line.

The code for a text area

```
Comments:<br>
<textarea name="comment" rows="5" cols="60"></textarea>
```

The text area displayed in a browser

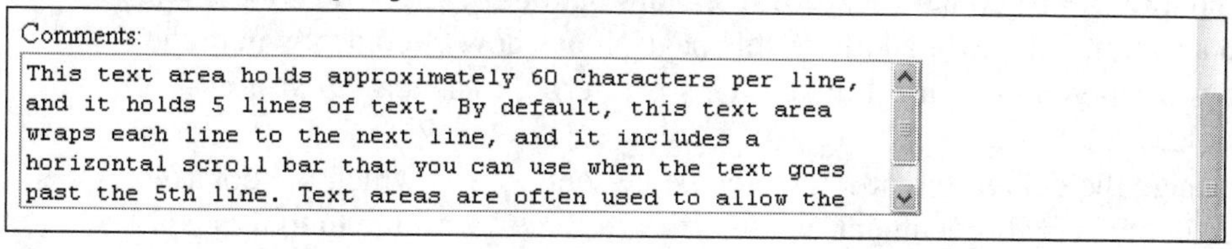

Comments:

```
This text area holds approximately 60 characters per line,
and it holds 5 lines of text. By default, this text area
wraps each line to the next line, and it includes a
horizontal scroll bar that you can use when the text goes
past the 5th line. Text areas are often used to allow the
```

Attributes of the TextArea tag

Attribute	Description
rows	Specifies the number of visible lines in the text area. If the number of lines in the text box exceeds this setting, the text area will display a vertical scroll bar.
cols	Specifies the width of the text area based on the average character width of the font that's being used.

Description

* A *text area* is similar to a text box, but it can display multiple lines of text.
* To specify a default value for a text area, you can code the text within the opening and closing TextArea tags.

Figure 3-16   How to code text areas

How to set the tab order of controls

Figure 3-17 shows an HTML page that takes many of the skills described in this chapter and puts them all together. This page uses an external style sheet, tables, and a form that contains text boxes, radio buttons, a check box, a combo box, and a submit button. In addition, this page shows how to control where the focus goes when you press the Tab key. This is referred to as the *tab order* of the controls.

To change the default tab order, which is the sequence in which the controls are coded in the HTML document, you use the TabIndex attribute to assign a number to each control. In this figure, for example, the TabIndex attribute has been set so the focus moves from the text boxes to the first radio button and then to the submit button. In other words, it skips the check box and the combo box. In this case, modifying the default tab order isn't that useful, but it can be when the default tab order doesn't work the way you want it to.

When you code the TabIndex attribute, you should know that it doesn't work on some older versions of Netscape. But that's usually okay because the tab order isn't critical to the operation of the form.

Since the HTML page presented here summarizes many of the skills presented in this chapter, you may want to view the complete code for this page. To do that, you can open the survey.htm file that's stored in Tomcat's webapps\murach directory. Then, you can read through its code and experiment with it. Once you understand how this code works, you're ready to begin coding HTML pages of your own.

An HTML page for a survey

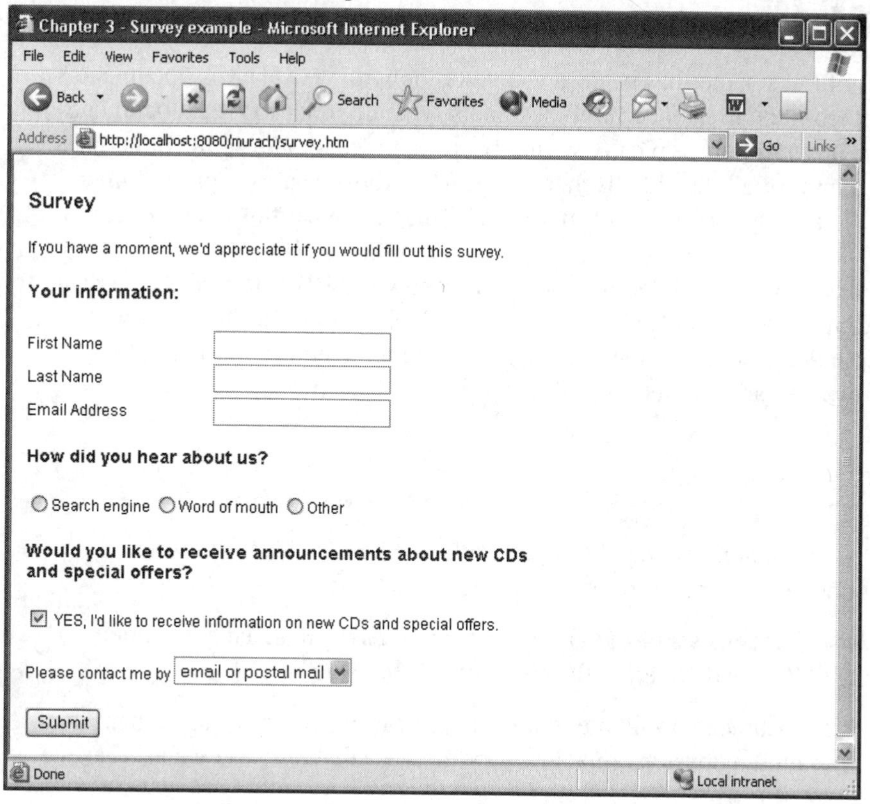

Code that controls the tab order of the survey page

```
<input type="text" name="firstName" size="20" tabindex="1">
<input type="text" name="lastName" size="20" tabindex="2">
<input type="text" name="emailAddress" size="20" tabindex="3">
<input type=radio name="heardFrom" value="Search Engine" tabindex="4">
<input type=submit value="Submit" tabindex="5">
```

Description

- The *tab order* determines the sequence in which the controls on a form will receive the focus when the Tab key is pressed. By default, the tab order is the same as the sequence in which the controls are coded in the HTML document.

- To modify the default tab order, you can use the TabIndex attribute of any visible control. Then, if you omit the TabIndex attribute for some controls, they will be added to the tab order after the controls that have TabIndex attributes.

- The TabIndex attribute only works for the first radio button in a group. And some older versions of Netscape ignore the TabIndex attribute.

- To view the complete code for this page, use a text or HTML editor to open the survey.htm file that's stored in Tomcat's webapps\murach directory.

Figure 3-17   How to set the tab order of controls

Perspective

The goal of this chapter has been to show you how to code HTML documents that get input from the user. Since web designers typically code HTML documents and Java web programmers typically write servlets and JSPs that use the data that's gathered, this may be all the HTML that you need to know as a Java programmer. Remember, though, that there's a lot more to HTML than what this chapter presents.

In the next chapter, you'll learn how to code and test JSPs that process the data that's sent from the forms on HTML documents. Once you master that, you will have a better understanding of how the controls need to be coded so their values can be used by JSPs and servlets.

Summary

- *HyperText Markup Language*, or *HTML*, is the language that a web browser converts into the user interface for a web application.

- An *HTML document* consists of the HTML for one *HTML page*. This document contains the *HTML tags* that define the elements of the page.

- To make HTML documents available to a web application, you must save them in files with htm or html extensions in a directory that's available to the web server.

- To view an HTML page, you enter a URL in the address box of your web browser. These URLs are directly related to the directories on the web server that stores the HTML files.

- To move from one web page to another, you can code *links* within the HTML. These can be *relative links* that are based on the current directory or *absolute links*.

- *Tables* that consist of *rows* and *columns* are used for the design of many web pages. The *cells* within the table can be used to store links, images, controls, and even other tables.

- An HTML page can include images in *Graphic Interchange Format* (*GIF*) or *Joint Photographic Experts Group* (*JPEG*) format.

- To insure consistent formatting, the formatting for the web pages of an application can be stored in an *external style sheet*, or just *style sheet*. Then, each web page can refer to that style sheet.

- An *HTML form* contains one or more controls like text boxes, check boxes, radio buttons, combo boxes, and list boxes. It should also contain a submit button that calls a JSP or servlet when the user clicks it. If necessary, one HTML document can contain two or more forms.

- The *tab order* of the controls on a form determines where the focus goes when the user presses the Tab key.

Terms

Hypertext Markup Language (HTML)	row	text box
Integrated Development Environment (IDE)	column	standard text box
	cell	password box
HTML page	pixel	hidden field
HTML document	Graphic Interchange Format (GIF)	button
HTML tag	Joint Photographic Experts Group (JPEG)	submit button
comment	style sheet	reset button
link	external style sheet	JavaScript button
attribute	linked style sheet	check box
value	cascading style sheet	radio button
relative link	form	combo box
absolute link	control	list box
table		text area
		tab order

Objectives

1. Code the HTML for an HTML document using any of the tags and attributes presented in this chapter.

2. Save your HTML documents in a directory that is appropriate for your web server.

3. Use your browser to view your own HTML pages or any other HTML pages on a local or Internet server.

4. Describe the use of the Head, Title, and Body tags that are used for HTML documents.

5. Describe the use of the Anchor (A), Table, and Image (IMG) tags.

6. Describe the use of check boxes, radio buttons, combo boxes, list boxes, and text areas.

7. Explain how the directories and HTML files on a web server directory are related to the URLs that refer to these files.

8. Explain how a submit button in an HTML form is used to pass control to a JSP or a servlet.

9. Explain how a standard text box is used to pass data to a JSP or servlet.

Exercise 3-1   Modify the survey page

This exercise steps you the process of modifying the survey page shown in figure 3-17. After each step, you can save and view the page to make sure your modifications are working correctly.

1. Use your editor to open the survey web page that's stored in the webapps\murach directory. Then, edit the survey page so it displays the image for the Murach logo at the top of the page.

2. Add another row to the table that provides for the date of birth.

3. Add an Advertising option button before the Other option button, and turn the Search engine button on as the default for the group.

4. Add a text area for comments before the Submit button.

Section 2

The essence of servlet and JSP programming

The best way to learn how to develop web applications in Java is to start developing them. That's why the chapters in this section take a hands-on approach to developing web applications. In chapter 4, you'll learn how to code JavaServer Pages (JSPs), which is one way to develop web applications. In chapter 5, you'll learn how to code servlets, which is another way to develop web applications. And in chapter 6, you'll learn how to structure your web applications so you combine the best features of JSPs and servlets.

With that as background, you'll be ready to learn the other web programming essentials. In chapter 7, you'll learn how to work with sessions and cookies so your application can keep track of its users. In chapter 8, you'll learn how to build better applications by using JavaBeans. And in chapter 9, you'll learn how to simplify the code in your JSPs by using custom tags. When you complete this section, you'll have the essential skills that you need for designing, coding, and testing web applications that use JSPs and servlets.

4

How to develop JavaServer Pages

In this chapter, you'll learn how to develop a web application that consists of HTML pages and JavaServer Pages (JSPs). As you will see, JSPs work fine as long as the amount of processing that's required for each page is limited. When you complete this chapter, you should be able to use JSPs to develop simple web applications of your own.

The Email List application **102**
The user interface for the application 102
The code for the HTML page that calls the JSP 104
The code for the JSP 106

How to create a JSP **108**
How to code scriptlets and expressions 108
How to use the methods of the request object 110
Where and how to save a JSP 112
How to request a JSP 114
When to use the Get and Post methods 116

How to use regular Java classes with JSPs **118**
The code for the User and UserIO classes 118
Where and how to save and compile regular Java classes 120
A JSP that uses the User and UserIO classes 122

How to use three more types of JSP tags **124**
How to import classes 124
How to code comments in a JSP 126
How to declare instance variables and methods 128
A JSP that imports classes and declares instance variables 130

How to work with JSP errors **132**
How to debug JSP errors 132
How to use a custom error page 134
When and how to view the servlet that's generated for a JSP ... 136

Perspective **138**

The Email List application

This topic introduces you to a simple web application that consists of one HTML page and one *JavaServer Page*, or *JSP*. Once you get the general idea of how this application works, you'll be ready to learn the specific skills that you need for developing JSPs.

The user interface for the application

Figure 4-1 shows the two pages that make up the user interface for the Email List application. The first page is an HTML page that asks the user to enter a first name, last name, and email address. Then, when the user clicks on the Submit button, the HTML page calls the JSP and passes the three user entries to that page.

When the JSP receives the three entries, it could process them by checking them for validity, writing them to a file or database, and so on. In this simple application, though, the JSP just passes the three entries back to the browser so it can display the second page of this application. From this page, the user can return to the first page by clicking the Back button in the web browser or by clicking the Return button that's displayed on this page.

As simple as this application is, you're going to learn a lot from it. In this chapter, you'll learn how enhance this application so it uses regular Java classes to save the user entries in a text file. Then, in later chapters, you'll learn how to modify this application to illustrate other essential skills that apply to servlet and JSP programming.

The HTML page

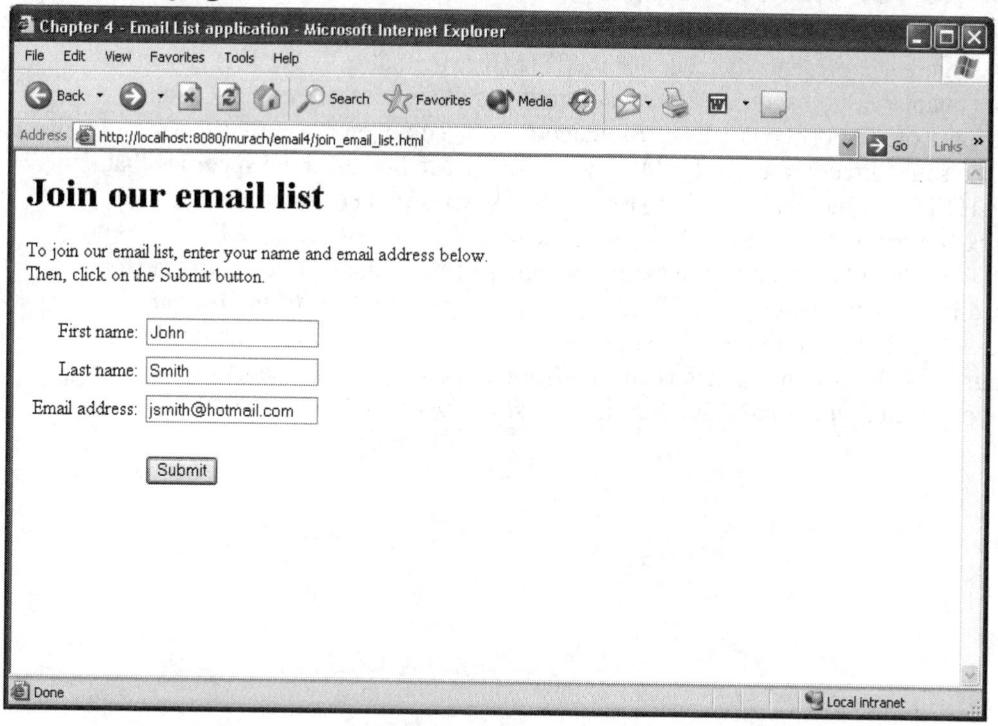

The JSP

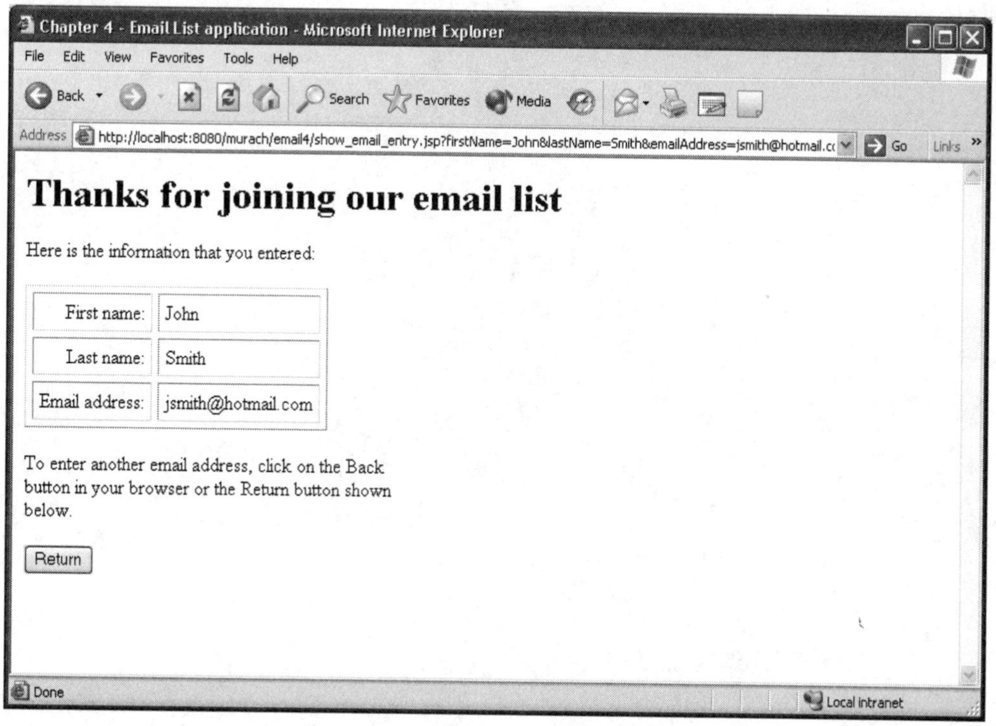

Figure 4-1   The user interface for the application

The code for the HTML page that calls the JSP

Figure 4-2 presents the code for the HTML page that calls the JSP. If you've read chapter 3, you shouldn't have any trouble following it. Here, the Action attribute of the Form tag calls a JSP named show_email_entry.jsp that's stored in the same directory as the HTML page, and the Method attribute specifies that the HTTP Get method should be used with this action. Then, when the user clicks on the Submit button, the browser will send a request for the JSP.

You should also notice the Name attributes of the three text boxes that are used in the table within this HTML page. These are the names of the *parameters* that are passed to the JSP when the user clicks on the Submit button. In figure 4-1, the parameter names are firstName, lastName, and emailAddress and the parameter values are John, Smith, and jsmith@hotmail.com.

The code for the HTML page

```
<!doctype html public "-//W3C//DTD HTML 4.0 Transitional//EN">
<html>

<head>
  <title>Chapter 4 - Email List application</title>
</head>

<body>
  <h1>Join our email list</h1>
  <p>To join our email list, enter your name and
     email address below. <br>
     Then, click on the Submit button.</p>

  <form action="show_email_entry.jsp" method="get">
  <table cellspacing="5" border="0">
    <tr>
      <td align="right">First name:</td>
      <td><input type="text" name="firstName"></td>
    </tr>
    <tr>
      <td align="right">Last name:</td>
      <td><input type="text" name="lastName"></td>
    </tr>
    <tr>
      <td align="right">Email address:</td>
      <td><input type="text" name="emailAddress"></td>
    </tr>
    <tr>
      <td></td>
      <td><br><input type="submit" value="Submit"></td>
    </tr>
  </table>
  </form>
</body>

</html>
```

Description

- The Action and Method attributes for the Form tag set up a request for a JSP that will be executed when the user clicks on the Submit button.

- The three text boxes represent *parameters* that will be passed to the JSP when the user clicks the Submit button.

- The parameter names are firstName, lastName, and emailAddress, and the parameter values are the strings that the user enters into the text boxes.

Figure 4-2   The code for the HTML page that calls the JSP

The code for the JSP

Figure 4-3 presents the code for the JSP. As you can see, much of the JSP code is HTML. In addition, though, Java code is embedded within the HTML code in the form of JSP *scriptlets* and *expressions*. Typically, a scriptlet is used to execute one or more Java statements while a JSP expression is used to display text. To identify scriptlets and expressions, JSPs use tags. To distinguish them from HTML tags, you can refer to them as *JSP tags*.

When you code a JSP, you can use the methods of the *request object* in your scriptlets or expressions. Since you don't have to explicitly create this object when you code JSPs, this object is sometimes referred to as the *implicit request object*. The scriptlet in this figure contains three statements that use the getParameter method of the request object. Each of these statements returns the value of the parameter that is passed to the JSP from the HTML page. Here, the argument for each getParameter method is the name of the textbox on the HTML page.

Once the scriptlet is executed, the values for the three parameters are available as variables to the rest of the page. Then, the three expressions can display these variables. Since these expressions are coded within the HTML tags for a table, the browser will display these expressions within a table.

After the table, the JSP contains some HTML that defines a form. This form contains only one control, a submit button named Return. When it is clicked, it takes the user back to the first page of the application. If you have any trouble visualizing how this button or the rest of the page will look when displayed by a browser, please refer back to figure 4-1.

As you read this book, remember that it assumes that you already know the basics of Java programming. If you have any trouble understanding the Java code in this chapter, you may need a refresher course on Java coding. To quickly review the basics of Java coding, we recommend that you use *Murach's Beginning Java 2* because it contains all the Java skills that you'll need for working with this book.

The code for the JSP

```
<!doctype html public "-//W3C//DTD HTML 4.0 Transitional//EN">
<html>
<head>
  <title>Chapter 4 - Email List application</title>
</head>
<body>

<%
  String firstName = request.getParameter("firstName");
  String lastName = request.getParameter("lastName");
  String emailAddress = request.getParameter("emailAddress");
%>
```
— JSP scriptlet
```
<h1>Thanks for joining our email list</h1>

<p>Here is the information that you entered:</p>

  <table cellspacing="5" cellpadding="5" border="1">
    <tr>
      <td align="right">First name:</td>
      <td><%= firstName %></td>
    </tr>
    <tr>
      <td align="right">Last name:</td>
      <td><%= lastName %></td>
    </tr>
    <tr>
      <td align="right">Email address:</td>
      <td><%= emailAddress %></td>
    </tr>
  </table>
```
— JSP expression
```
<p>To enter another email address, click on the Back <br>
button in your browser or the Return button shown <br>
below.</p>

<form action="join_email_list.html" method="post">
  <input type="submit" value="Return">
</form>

</body>
</html>
```

Description

- Although a JSP looks much like an HTML page, a JSP contains embedded Java code.
- To code a *scriptlet* that contains one or more Java statements, you use the <% and %> tags. To display any *expression* that can be converted to a string, you use the <%= and %> tags.
- When you code a JSP, you can use the *implicit request object*. This object is named request. You can use the getParameter method of the request object to get the values of the parameters that are passed to the JSP.

Figure 4-3   The code for the JSP

How to create a JSP

Now that you have a general idea of how JSPs are coded, you're ready to learn some specific skills for creating a JSP. To start, you need to know more about coding scriptlets and expressions.

How to code scriptlets and expressions

Figure 4-4 summarizes the information you need for coding scriptlets and expressions within a JSP. To code a scriptlet, for example, you code Java statements that end with semicolons within the JSP scriptlet tags. To code an expression, you code any Java expression that evaluates to a string. Since primitive data types like integers or doubles are automatically converted to strings, you can also use expressions that evaluate to these data types.

When you're coding a scriptlet or an expression, you can use any of the methods of the implicit request object. In this figure, only the getParameter method is used, but you'll learn about two more methods of the request object in the next figure.

In this figure, the first two examples show different ways that you can display the value of a parameter. The first example uses a scriptlet to return the value of the firstName parameter and store it in a String object. Then, this example uses an expression to display the value. In contrast, the second example uses an expression to display the value of the firstName parameter without creating the firstName object.

The last example in this figure shows how two scriptlets and an expression can be used to display an HTML line five times while a Java variable within the HTML line counts from 1 to 5. Here, the first JSP scriptlet contains the code that begins a while loop. Then, a line of HTML code uses a JSP expression to display the current value of the counter for the loop. And finally, the second scriptlet contains the code that ends the loop.

The syntax for a JSP scriptlet

```
<% Java statements %>
```

The syntax for a JSP expression

```
<%= any Java expression that can be converted to a string %>
```

The syntax for getting a parameter from the implicit request object

```
request.getParameter(parameterName);
```

Examples that use scriptlets and expressions

A scriptlet and expression that display the value of the firstName parameter

```
<%
    String firstName = request.getParameter("firstName");
%>
The first name is <%= firstName %>.
```

An expression that displays the value of the firstName parameter

```
The first name is <%= request.getParameter("firstName") %>.
```

Two scriptlets and an expression that display an HTML line 5 times

```
<%
    int numOfTimes = 1;
    while (numOfTimes <= 5){
%>
    <h1> This line is shown <%= numOfTimes %> of 5 times in a JSP.</h1>
<%
        numOfTimes++;
    }
%>
```

Description

- Within a scriptlet, you can code one or more complete Java statements. Because these statements are Java statements, you must end each one with a semicolon.

- Within a JSP expression, you can code any Java expression that evaluates to a string. This includes Java expressions that evaluate to any of the primitive types, and it includes any object that has a toString method. Because a JSP expression is an expression, not a statement, you don't end it with a semicolon.

Figure 4-4   How to code scriptlets and expressions

How to use the methods of the request object

In the last figure, you learned how to use the getParameter method to return the value that the user entered into a textbox. Now, figure 4-5 summarizes that method and illustrates it in a new context. This figure also summarizes and illustrates two more methods of the implicit request object.

In most cases, the getParameter method returns the value of the parameter. For a textbox, that's usually the value entered by the user. But for a group of radio buttons or a combo box, that's the value of the button or item selected by the user.

For checkboxes or independent radio buttons that have a Value attribute, the getParameter method returns that value if the checkbox or button is selected and a null value if it isn't. For checkboxes or independent radio buttons that don't have a Value attribute, though, the getParameter method returns an "on" value if the checkbox or button is selected and a null value if it isn't. This is illustrated by the first example in this figure.

To retrieve multiple values for one parameter name, you can use the getParameterValues method as illustrated by the second example. This method is useful for controls like list boxes that allow multiple selections. After you use the getParameterValues method to return an array of String objects, you can use a loop to get the values from the array.

To get the names of all the parameters sent with a request, you can use the getParameterNames method to return an Enumeration object that contains the names. Then, you can search through the Enumeration object to get the parameter names, and you can use the getParameter method to return the value for each parameter name. This is illustrated by the third example.

If you're not familiar with the Enumeration class, you can learn more about it through the API. For most purposes, though, you only need to know that an Enumeration object is a collection that can be searched element by element. To determine if more elements exist in the collection, you can use the hasMoreElements method, which returns a boolean value. And to get the next element in the collection, you can use the nextElement method.

Three methods of the request object

Method	Description
`getParameter(String param)`	Returns the value of the specified parameter as a string if it exists or null if it doesn't. Often, this is the value defined in the Value attribute of the control in the HTML page or JSP.
`getParameterValues(String param)`	Returns an array of String objects containing all of the values that the given request parameter has or null if the parameter doesn't have any values.
`getParameterNames()`	Returns an Enumeration object that contains the names of all the parameters contained in the request. If the request has no parameters, the method returns an empty Enumeration object.

A scriptlet that determines if a checkbox is checked

```
<%
    String rockCheckBox = request.getParameter("Rock");
    // returns the value or "on" if checked, null otherwise.
    if (rockCheckBox != null){
%>
        You checked Rock music!
<%  }
%>
```

A scriptlet that reads and displays multiple values from a list box

```
<%
    String[] selectedCountries = request.getParameterValues("country");
    // returns the values of items selected in list box.
    for (int i = 0; i < selectedCountries.length; i++){
%>
        <%= selectedCountries[i] %> <br>
<%
    }
%>
```

A scriptlet that reads and displays all request parameters and values

```
<%
    Enumeration parameterNames = request.getParameterNames();
    while (parameterNames.hasMoreElements()){
        String parameterName = (String) parameterNames.nextElement();
        String parameterValue = request.getParameter(parameterName);
%>
        <%= parameterName %> has value <%= parameterValue %>. <br>
<%
    }
%>
```

Description

- You can use the getParameter method to return the value of the selected radio button in a group or the selected item in a combo box. You can also use it to return the value of a selected check box or independent radio button, but that value is null if it isn't selected.

- If an independent radio button or a checkbox doesn't have a Value attribute, this method returns "on" if the control is selected or null if it isn't.

Figure 4-5   How to use the methods of the request object

Where and how to save a JSP

As figure 4-6 shows, you normally save the JSPs of an application in the same directory that you use for the HTML pages of the application. The difference is that the name for a JSP requires a jsp extension. So if you're using a text editor that's not designed for working with JSPs, you may have to place the filename in quotation marks to make sure the file is saved with the jsp extension.

Like HTML pages, JSPs must be saved in a directory that's available to the web server. For Tomcat 4.0, you can use any directory under the webapps directory. The root directory for the web applications that are presented in the first 16 chapters of this book is the webapps\murach directory, and the subdirectory for the Email List application that's presented in this chapter is email4. Note, however, that you can also use the webapps\ROOT directory that Tomcat sets up as the default root directory. Or, you can create your own subdirectories under the webapps directory.

Where the show_email_entry.jsp page is saved

```
c:\tomcat\webapps\murach\email4
```

Other places you can save your JSPs

```
c:\tomcat\webapps\yourDocumentRoot
c:\tomcat\webapps\yourDocumentRoot\yourSubdirectory
c:\tomcat\webapps\ROOT
c:\tomcat\webapps\ROOT\yourSubdirectory
```

A standard dialog box for saving a JSP

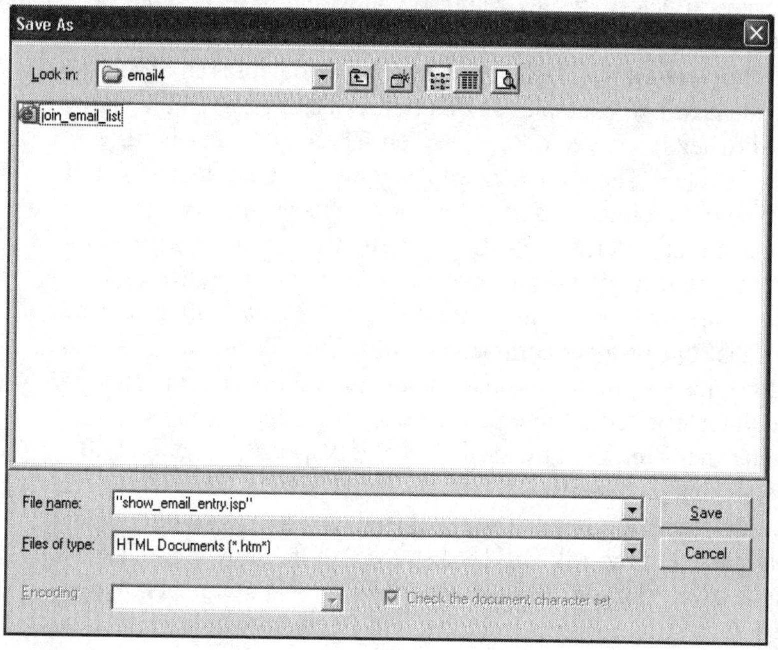

Description

- JSPs are normally saved in the same directory as the HTML pages. This directory should be a subdirectory of the web applications directory for your server. If you're running Tomcat on your PC, that directory is usually c:\tomcat\webapps or c:\jakarta-tomcat\webapps.

- For the first 16 chapters of this book, the document root directory for all applications is the murach directory. As a result, the HTML and JSP files for each application are stored in this directory or one of its subdirectories.

- If you're using Tomcat on your local system, you can also use webapps\ROOT as the root directory for your applications. The ROOT directory is automatically set up when you install Tomcat, and it is the default document root directory.

- To make sure that the filename for a JSP is saved with the jsp extension when you're using an HTML or text editor, you can enter the filename within quotes.

Figure 4-6   Where and how to save a JSP

How to request a JSP

After you create a JSP, you need to test it. One way to do that is to click on a link or a button on an HTML page that requests the JSP. Another way is to enter a URL into a web browser that requests the JSP. Figure 4-7 shows how to request a JSP either way.

To request a JSP from an HTML form, you use the Action attribute of the form to provide a path and filename that point to the JSP. This is illustrated by the first example in this figure. Here, the assumption is that the HTML page and the JSP are in the same directory. If they weren't, you would have to supply a relative or absolute path for the JSP file.

To request a JSP by entering its URL into a browser, you enter an absolute URL as shown by the next two examples in this figure. The first example shows the URL for the JSP when it's stored on a local web server in the email4 directory of the murach directory. The second example shows the URL for the JSP if the JSP was deployed on the Internet server for *www.murach.com*.

When you test a JSP by entering a URL, you will often want to pass parameters to it. To do that, you can add the parameters to the end of the URL as shown by the last examples in this figure. Here, the question mark after the jsp extension indicates that one or more parameters will follow. Then, you code the parameter name, the equals sign, and the parameter value for each parameter that is passed, and you separate multiple parameters with ampersands (&). If you omit a parameter that's required by the JSP, the getParameter method will return a null value for that parameter.

When you use a Get method to request a JSP from another page, any parameters that are passed to the JSP will be displayed in the browser's URL address. In this figure, for example, you can see the first two parameters that have been attached to the URL. However, in the next figure, you'll learn that the Post method works differently.

A URL that includes parameters

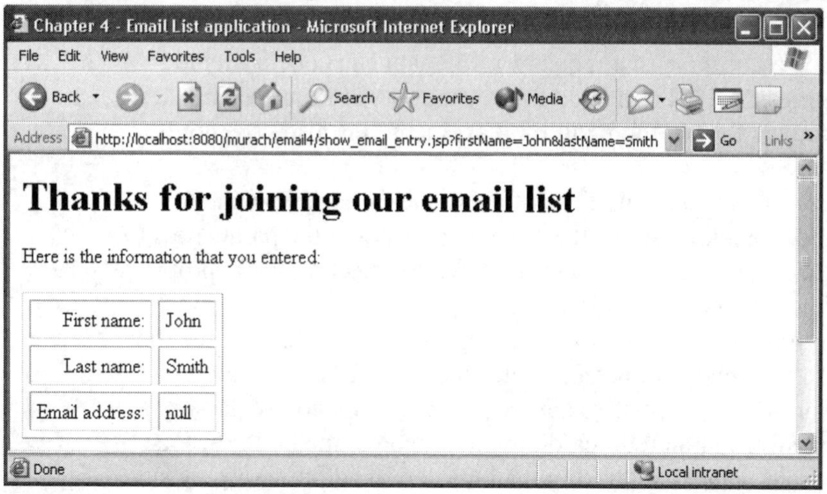

How Tomcat maps directories to HTTP calls

Tomcat directory	URL
c:\tomcat\webapps\murach	http://localhost:8080/murach/
c:\tomcat\webapps\murach\email4	http://localhost:8080/murach/email4
c:\tomcat\webapps\ROOT	http://localhost:8080/
c:\tomcat\webapps\ROOT\email4	http://localhost:8080/email4

A Form tag that requests a JSP

```
<form action="show_email_entry.jsp" method="get">
```

Two URLs that request a JSP

```
http://localhost:8080/murach/email4/show_email_entry.jsp
http://www.murach.com/email4/show_email_entry.jsp
```

How to include parameters

```
show_email_entry.jsp?firstName=John
show_email_entry.jsp?firstName=John&lastName=Smith
```

Description

- When you use the Get method to request a JSP from an HTML form, the parameters are automatically appended to the URL.

- When you code or enter a URL that requests a JSP, you can add a parameter list to it starting with a question mark and with no intervening spaces. Then, each parameter consists of its name, an equals sign, and its value. To code multiple parameters, use ampersands (&) to separate the parameters.

Figure 4-7   How to request a JSP

When to use the Get and Post methods

When you code a Form tag that requests a JSP, you can code a Method attribute that specifies the HTTP method that's used for the request. The Get method is the default HTTP method, but the Post method is also commonly used.

Figure 4-8 presents the pros and cons of using the Get and Post methods. With either method, you can still test the page by appending the parameters to the URL string. So the question really comes down to selecting the appropriate method for the finished web application.

There are two primary reasons for using the Post method. First, since the Post method doesn't append parameters to the end of the URL, it is more appropriate for working with sensitive data. If, for example, you're passing a parameter for a password or a credit card number, the Post method prevents these parameters from being displayed in the browser. In addition, it prevents the web browser from including these parameters in a bookmark for a page. Second, you need to use the Post method if your parameters contain more than 4 KB of data.

For all other uses, the Get method is preferred. It runs slightly faster than the Post method, and it lets the user bookmark the page along with the parameters that were sent to the page.

An HTML form tag that uses the Post method

```
<form action="show_email_entry.jsp" method="post">
```

A JSP that's requested through the Post method

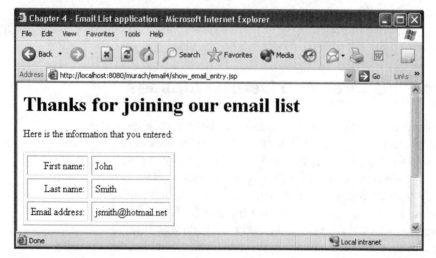

When to use the Get method

- If you want to transfer data as fast as possible.
- If the HTML form only needs to transfer 4 KB of data or less.
- If it's okay for the parameters to be displayed in the URL.
- If you want users to be able to include parameters when they bookmark a page.

When to use the Post method

- If you're transferring over 4 KB of data.
- If it's not okay for the parameters to be appended to the URL.

Description

- The visible difference between the Get and Post methods is the URL that's displayed in the browser. For Get requests from an HTML page, the parameters are appended to the URL. For Post requests, the parameters are still sent, but they're not displayed in the browser.
- You can test a JSP that uses either method by appending the parameters to the URL.

Figure 4-8   When to use the Get and Post methods

How to use regular Java classes with JSPs

In this topic, you'll learn how to use regular Java classes to do the processing that a JSP requires. In particular, you'll learn how to use two classes named User and UserIO to do the processing for the JSP of the Email List application.

The code for the User and UserIO classes

Figure 4-9 presents the code for a business class named User and an I/O class named UserIO. The package statement at the start of each class indicates where each class is stored. Here, the User class is stored in the business directory because it defines a business object while the UserIO class is stored in the data directory because it provides the data access for the application.

The User class defines a user of the application. This class contains three instance variables: firstName, lastName, and emailAddress. It includes a constructor that accepts three values for these instance variables. And it includes get and set methods for each instance variable.

In contrast, the UserIO class contains one static method named addRecord that writes the values stored in a User object to a text file. This method accepts two parameters: a User object and a string that provides the path for the file. If this file exists, the method will add the user data to the end of it. If the file doesn't exist, the method will create it and add the data at the beginning of the file.

If you've read the first six chapters of *Murach's Beginning Java 2*, you should understand the code for the User class. And if you've read chapters 16 and 17, you should understand the code in the UserIO class. The one exception is the use of the synchronized keyword in the addRecord method declaration. But this keyword just prevents two users from writing to the file at the same time, which could lead to an error.

The code for the User class

```
package business;

public class User{
    private String firstName;
    private String lastName;
    private String emailAddress;

    public User(){}

    public User(String first, String last, String email){
        firstName = first;
        lastName = last;
        emailAddress = email;
    }

    public void setFirstName(String f){
        firstName = f;
    }
    public String getFirstName(){ return firstName; }

    public void setLastName(String l){
        lastName = l;
    }
    public String getLastName(){ return lastName; }

    public void setEmailAddress(String e){
        emailAddress = e;
    }
    public String getEmailAddress(){ return emailAddress; }
}
```

The code for the UserIO class

```
package data;

import java.io.*;
import business.User;

public class UserIO{
    public synchronized static void addRecord(User user, String filename)
                                    throws IOException{
        PrintWriter out = new PrintWriter(
                        new FileWriter(filename, true));
        out.println(user.getEmailAddress()+ "|"
                    + user.getFirstName() + "|"
                    + user.getLastName());
        out.close();
    }
}
```

Note

- The synchronized keyword in the declaration for the addRecord method of the UserIO class prevents two users of the JSP from using that method at the same time.

Figure 4-9   The code for the User and UserIO classes

Where and how to save and compile regular Java classes

If you're using Tomcat 4.0, figure 4-10 shows where and how to save your compiled Java classes (the .class files) so Tomcat can access them. Usually, you'll save your source code (the .java files) in the same directory, but that's not required.

The two paths shown at the top of this figure show where the User and UserIO classes that come with this book are saved. After that, the figure presents the syntax for other paths that can be used to store Java classes. If you review these paths, you'll see that each one places the Java classes in a subdirectory of the WEB-INF\classes directory.

Since the User class contains a package statement that corresponds to the business directory, it must be located in the WEB-INF\classes\business directory. In contrast, if the package statement specified "murach.email", the compiled classes would have to be located in the WEB-INF\classes\murach\email directory.

Since TextPad is designed for working with Java, you can use it to compile regular Java classes. However, you may need to configure your system as described in appendix A before it will work properly. In particular, you may need to add the appropriate WEB-INF\classes directory to your classpath.

If you use the DOS prompt window to compile your classes, you can do that as shown in this figure. Here, a DOS prompt is used to compile the User class. To start, the cd command changes the current directory to the \WEB-INF\classes directory. Then, the javac command is used with "business\User.java" as the filename. This compiles the User class and stores it in the business package, which is what you want.

Where the User class is saved

```
c:\tomcat\webapps\murach\WEB-INF\classes\business
```

Where the UserIO class is saved

```
c:\tomcat\webapps\murach\WEB-INF\classes\data
```

Other places to save your Java classes

```
c:\tomcat\webapps\yourDocumentRoot\WEB-INF\classes
c:\tomcat\webapps\yourDocumentRoot\WEB-INF\classes\packageName
c:\tomcat\webapps\ROOT\WEB-INF\classes
c:\tomcat\webapps\ROOT\WEB-INF\classes\packageName
```

The DOS prompt window for compiling the User class

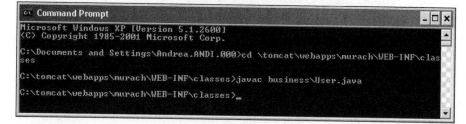

Description

- Although you can save the source code (the .java files) in any directory, you must save the class files (the .class files) in the WEB-INF\classes directory or one of its subdirectories. This can be subordinate to the ROOT directory or your own document root directory.

- To compile a class, you can use TextPad's Compile Java command, your IDE's compile command, or the javac command from the DOS prompt window.

- If you have trouble compiling a class, make sure your system is configured correctly as described in appendix A.

Figure 4-10   Where and how to save and compile regular Java classes

A JSP that uses the User and UserIO classes

Figure 4-11 shows the code for the JSP in the Email List application after it has been enhanced so it uses the User and UserIO classes to process the parameters that have been passed to it. In the first statement of the body, a special type of JSP tag is used to import the business and data packages that contain the User and UserIO classes. You'll learn how to code this type of tag in the next figure. For now, though, you should focus on the other shaded lines in this JSP.

In the scriptlet of the JSP, the getParameter method is used to get the values of the three parameters that are passed to it, and these values are stored in String objects. Then, the next statement uses these strings as arguments for the constructor of the User class. This creates a User object that contains the three values. Last, this scriptlet uses the addRecord method of the UserIO class to add the three values of the User object to a file named UserEmail.txt that's stored in the WEB-INF\etc directory. Since the WEB-INF\etc directory isn't web-accessible, this prevents users of the application from accessing this file.

After the scriptlet, the code in the JSP defines the layout of the page. Within the HTML table definitions, the JSP expressions use the get methods of the User object to display the first name, last name, and email address values. Although these JSP expressions could use the String objects instead, the code in this figure is intended to show how the get methods can be used.

The code for a JSP that uses the User and UserIO classes

```
<!doctype html public "-//W3C//DTD HTML 4.0 Transitional//EN">
<html>

<head>
  <title>Chapter 4 - Email List application</title>
</head>

<body>
<%@ page import="business.*, data.*" %>
<%
    String firstName = request.getParameter("firstName");
    String lastName = request.getParameter("lastName");
    String emailAddress = request.getParameter("emailAddress");

    User user = new User(firstName, lastName, emailAddress);
    UserIO.addRecord(user, "../webapps/murach/WEB-INF/etc/UserEmail.txt");
%>

<h1>Thanks for joining our email list</h1>

<p>Here is the information that you entered:</p>

  <table cellspacing="5" cellpadding="5" border="1">
    <tr>
      <td align="right">First name:</td>
      <td><%= user.getFirstName() %></td>
    </tr>
    <tr>
      <td align="right">Last name:</td>
      <td><%= user.getLastName() %></td>
    </tr>
    <tr>
      <td align="right">Email address:</td>
      <td><%= user.getEmailAddress() %></td>
    </tr>
  </table>

<p>To enter another email address, click on the Back <br>
button in your browser or the Return button shown <br>
below.</p>

<form action="join_email_list.html" method="post">
  <input type="submit" value="Return">
</form>

</body>
</html>
```

Description

- This JSP uses a scriptlet to create a User object and add it to a file, and it uses JSP expressions to display the values of the User object's instance variables.
- Since the User and UserIO classes are stored in the business and data packages, the JSP must import these packages as shown in figure 4-12.

Figure 4-11   A JSP that uses the User and UserIO classes

How to use three more types of JSP tags

So far, you've learned how to use the JSP tags for scriptlets and expressions. Now, you'll learn how to use three more types of JSP tags. All five types of JSP tags are summarized at the top of figure 4-12.

How to import classes

Figure 4-12 also shows how to use a *JSP directive* to import classes in a JSP. The type of directive that you use for doing that is called a *page directive*, and the shaded statement at the start of the JSP shows how to code one.

To code a page directive for importing classes, you code the starting tag and the word *page* followed by the Import attribute. Within the quotation marks after the equals sign for this attribute, you code the names of the Java classes that you want to import just as you do in a Java import statement. In the example in this figure, all the classes of the business and data packages are imported, plus the Date class in the java.util package.

Once the page directive imports the packages, the JSP can access the User and UserIO classes and the Date class. The scriptlet that follows creates a User object from the User class and uses the addRecord method of the UserIO class to write the data for the User object to a text file. The last line in this example uses the default constructor of the Date class as an expression in an HTML line. This works because the JSP will automatically convert the Date object that's created by the constructor into a string.

The JSP tags presented in this chapter

Tag	Name	Purpose
<% %>	JSP scriptlet	To insert a block of Java statements.
<%= %>	JSP expression	To display the string value of an expression.
<%@ %>	JSP directive	To set conditions that apply to the entire JSP.
<%-- --%>	JSP comment	To tell the JSP engine to ignore code.
<%! %>	JSP declaration	To declare instance variables and methods for a JSP.

JSP code that imports Java classes

```
<%@ page import="business.*, data.*, java.util.Date" %>

<%
    String firstName = request.getParameter("firstName");
    String lastName = request.getParameter("lastName");
    String emailAddress = request.getParameter("emailAddress");

    User user = new User(firstName, lastName, emailAddress);
    UserIO.addRecord(user, "../webapps/murach/WEB-INF/etc/UserEmail.txt");
%>

Today's date is <%= new Date() %>.
```

Description

* To define the conditions that the JSP engine should follow when converting a JSP into a servlet, you can use a *JSP directive*.

* To import classes in a JSP, you use the import attribute of the *page directive*. This makes the imported classes available to the entire page.

* You can also use the page directive to define other conditions like error handling and content type conditions. You'll learn more about this directive throughout this book.

Figure 4-12   How to import classes

How to code comments in a JSP

Figure 4-13 shows how to code *JSP comments*, and it shows how you can code Java comments and HTML comments in a JSP. As a result, you need to understand how the three types of comments are processed.

Like Java comments, any code within a JSP comment isn't compiled or executed. In contrast, any code within an HTML comment is compiled and executed, but the browser doesn't display it. This is illustrated by the HTML comment in this figure. Here, the HTML line within the comment isn't displayed by the browser, but the integer variable in the comment is incremented each time the page is accessed. To prevent this integer variable from being incremented, you have to use a JSP comment instead of an HTML comment.

A JSP comment

```
<%--
    Today's date is <%= new java.util.Date() %>.
--%>
```

Java comments in a JSP scriptlet

```
<%
    //These statements retrieve the request parameter values
    String firstName = request.getParameter("firstName");
    String lastName = request.getParameter("lastName");
    String emailAddress = request.getParameter("emailAddress");

    /*
    User user = new User(firstName, lastName, emailAddress);
    UserIO.addRecord(user, "../webapps/murach/WEB-INF/etc/UserEmail.txt");
    */
%>
```

An HTML comment in a JSP

```
<!--
    <i>This page has been accessed <%= ++i %> times.</i>
-->
The value of the variable i is <%= i %>.
```

Description

- When you code *JSP comments*, the comments aren't compiled or executed.
- When you code Java comments within a scriptlet, the comments aren't compiled or executed.
- When you code HTML comments, the comments are compiled and executed, but the browser doesn't display them.

Figure 4-13   How to code comments in a JSP

How to declare instance variables and methods

When a JSP is requested for the first time, one *instance* of the JSP is created and loaded into memory, and a *thread* is started that executes the Java code in the JSP. For each subsequent request for the JSP, another thread is started that can access the one instance of the JSP. When you code variables in scriptlets, each thread gets its own copy of each variable, which is usually what you want.

In some cases, though, you may want to declare instance variables and methods that can be shared between all of the threads that are accessing a JSP. To do that, you can code *JSP declarations* as shown in figure 4-14. Then, the instance variables and methods are initialized when the JSP is first requested. After that, each thread can access those instance variables and methods.

This is illustrated by the accessCount variable that's declared as an instance variable in this figure. This variable is incremented by one each time the JSP is requested. Once it's incremented, the current value is stored in a local variable. Later, when the variable is displayed, it represents the total number of times that the page has been accessed.

In this figure, the synchronized keyword prevents two threads from using the method or modifying the instance variable at the same time. This results in a *thread-safe* JSP. Without the synchronized keyword for the method, for example, two or more threads could write to the text file at the same time, which could lead to an I/O error if one thread tries to open the file before the previous thread closes it. Without the synchronized and this keywords for the block of code, two or more threads could update the accessCount variable at the same time. If, for example, user 4 updates the accessCount before it is stored in the localCount variable, the access count that's displayed for user 3 will be 4. Although that's highly unlikely and insignificant in this case, this illustrates the type of problem that can occur.

In most cases, though, it's okay for multiple threads to access a method or instance variable at the same time because no harm can come from it. That's why you only need to code a thread-safe JSP when multiple threads could cause inaccurate or faulty results. The potential for this often arises when an instance variable is modified by a thread or when a method accesses a data store. Then, you can decide whether you need to provide for this by coding a thread-safe JSP.

If you find your JSP becoming cluttered with declarations, you should consider restructuring your program. In some cases, you may want to use regular Java classes like the ones shown in this chapter. In other cases, you may want to use a servlet as described in the next chapter. Better yet, you may want to use a combination of servlets, JSPs, and other Java classes as described in chapter 6.

JSP code that declares an instance variable and a method

```
<%@ page import="business.*, data.*, java.util.Date, java.io.*" %>

<%! int accessCount = 0; %>
<%!
    public synchronized void addRecord(User user, String filename)
                              throws IOException{
        PrintWriter out = new PrintWriter(
                          new FileWriter(filename, true));
        out.println(user.getEmailAddress()+ "|"
                    + user.getFirstName() + "|"
                    + user.getLastName());
        out.close();
    }
%>
<%
    String firstName = request.getParameter("firstName");
    String lastName = request.getParameter("lastName");
    String emailAddress = request.getParameter("emailAddress");

    User user = new User(firstName, lastName, emailAddress);
    addRecord(user, "../webapps/murach/WEB-INF/etc/UserEmail.txt");

    int localCount = 0;
    synchronized (this) {
        accessCount++;
        localCount = accessCount;
    }
%>
    .
    .
    .
<p><i>This page has been accessed <%= localCount %> times.</i></p>
```

Description

- You can use *JSP declarations* to declare instance variables and methods for a JSP. Unlike the variables defined in scriptlets, one set of instance variables and methods are used by all the users of the JSP.

- To code a *thread-safe* JSP, you must synchronize access to instance variables and methods that should only be called by one thread at a time. Otherwise, two threads may conflict when they try to modify the same instance variable at the same time or when they try to execute the same method that accesses a data store at the same time.

- To synchronize access to a method, you can use the synchronized keyword in the method declaration. To synchronize access to a block of code, you can use the synchronized keyword and the this keyword before the block.

Figure 4-14   How to declare instance variables and methods

A JSP that imports classes and declares instance variables

To illustrate how these JSP tags work together, figure 4-15 presents an enhanced version of the Email List application. Here, the page that's displayed is the same as the page shown in figure 4-1 except that it displays two lines below the Return button. The first line displays the date and time that the user accessed the page. The second displays the number of times the page has been accessed since it was initialized.

In the code for the JSP, the page directive imports the required classes including the User and UserIO classes from the business and data packages. This directive is followed by two declarations. The first declares an instance variable for the number of users that access the JSP. The second declares an instance variable for the path of the text file that will store the user data. The scriptlet that follows is one that you've already seen so you should understand how it works.

Since you've already seen the HTML tags that display the data for this JSP, this figure doesn't show these tags. They are the same HTML tags that are shown in figure 4-11.

The first shaded line at the end of this JSP uses the constructor for the Date class to return the current date and time. Since this constructor is coded within an expression, each user of the JSP will get its own copy of the date and time. As a result, the HTML line will display a different time for each user. In contrast, as explained earlier, the second shaded line displays the value of an instance variable that is incremented by one for each thread.

A JSP that displays the date and an instance variable

The code for the JSP

```
<!doctype html public "-//W3C//DTD HTML 4.0 Transitional//EN">
<html>
<head>
  <title>Chapter 4 - Email List application</title>
</head>

<body>
<%@ page import= "business.User, data.UserIO, java.util.Date, java.io.*" %>
<%! int accessCount = 0; %>
<%! String file = "../webapps/murach/WEB-INF/etc/UserEmail.txt"; %>
<%  String firstName = request.getParameter("firstName");
    String lastName = request.getParameter("lastName");
    String emailAddress = request.getParameter("emailAddress");
    User user = new User(firstName, lastName, emailAddress);
    UserIO.addRecord(user, file);
    int localCount = 0;
    synchronized (this) {
        accessCount++;
        localCount = accessCount;
    }
%>

<!-- missing code that's the same as figure 4-11 -->

Today's date is <%= new Date() %>. <br>
<i>This page has been accessed <%= localCount %> times.</i>

</body>
</html>
```

Figure 4-15 A JSP that imports classes and declares instance variables

How to work with JSP errors

When you develop JSPs, you will inevitably encounter errors. That's why the last three figures in this chapter show you how to work with JSP errors.

How to debug JSP errors

Figure 4-16 presents the two most common JSP errors. HTTP Status 404 means that Tomcat received the HTTP request but couldn't find the requested resource. You've already seen this in chapter 2. To fix this type of problem, make sure that you've entered the correct path and filename for the request and that the requested file is in the right location.

In contrast, HTTP Status 500 means that the server received the request and found the resource but couldn't fill the request. This usually means that the JSP engine wasn't able to compile the JSP due to a coding error in the JSP. To fix this type of problem, you can review the other information provided by the error page. In the error page in this figure, for example, you can see that a semicolon is missing at the end of one of the statements in the JSP scriptlet.

To correct this type of error, you should fix the JSP so it will compile correctly. To do this, you can open the JSP, add the semicolon, save it, and refresh the screen. Then, the JSP engine will recognize that the JSP has been modified and it will automatically attempt to compile and load the JSP.

This figure also gives some tips for debugging JSP errors. The first three tips will help you solve most status 404 errors. The fourth one will help you find the cause of most status 500 errors. And when all else fails, you can look at the servlet that's generated from the JSP as explained in figure 4-18.

An error page for a common JSP error

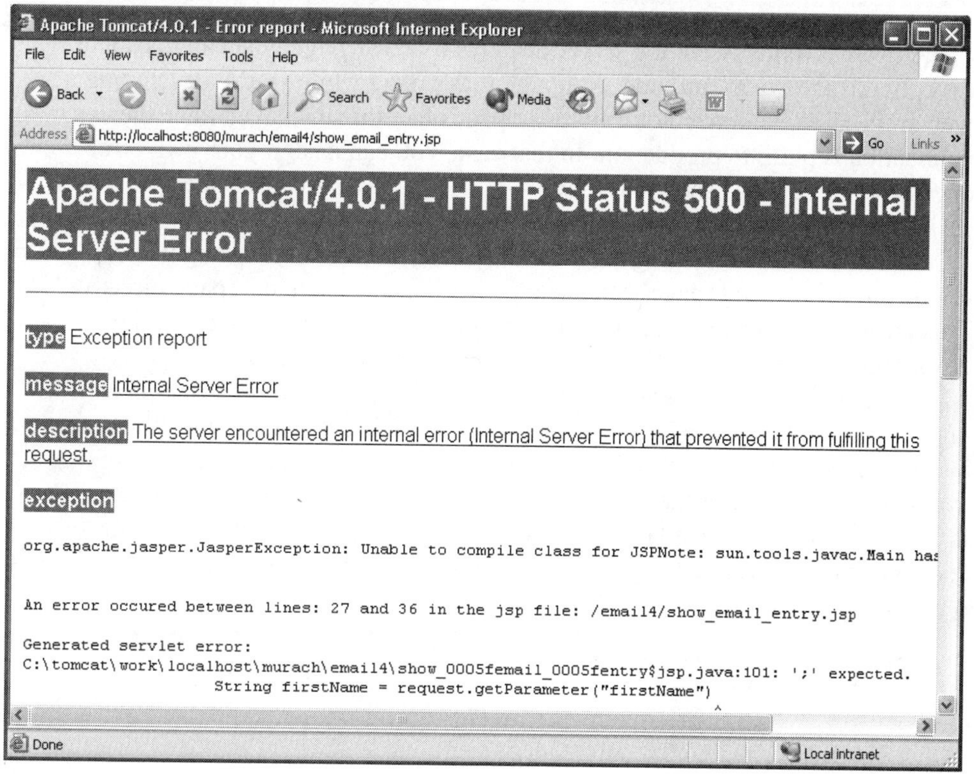

Common JSP errors

- HTTP Status 404 – File Not Found Error
- HTTP Status 500 – Internal Server Error

Tips for debugging JSP errors

- Make sure the Tomcat server is running.
- Make sure that the URL is valid and that it points to the right location for the requested page.
- Make sure all of the HTML, JSP, and Java class files are in the correct locations.
- Read the error page carefully to get all available information about the error.
- As a last resort, look at the servlet that's generated for the JSP as shown in figure 4-18.

Figure 4-16   How to debug JSP errors

How to use a custom error page

As you have just seen, the server displays its *error page* when an uncaught exception is thrown at run time. Although that's okay while you're developing a web application, you may not want error pages like that displayed once the application is put into production. In that case, you can design your own error pages and use them as shown in figure 4-17. That makes the user interface easier to understand.

To designate the error page that should be used when any uncaught exception is thrown by a JSP page, you use the errorPage attribute of a page directive. This attribute designates the JSP or HTML page that you want to use as the error page. This is illustrated by the first example in this figure.

Then, if you want the error page to have access to the *implicit exception object*, you set the isErrorPage attribute of its page directive to true as illustrated by the second example in this figure. This makes an object named exception available to the page. In the second example, you can see how this object is used in a JSP expression to display the exception type and description. (When you code an object name in an expression, its toString method is invoked.)

A custom error page in a browser

Two more attributes of a page directive

Attribute	Use
errorPage	To designate an error page for any uncaught exceptions that are thrown by the page.
isErrorPage	To identify a page as an error page so it has access to the implicit exception object.

A page directive that designates a custom error page

```
<%@ page errorPage="show_error_message.jsp" %>
```

A JSP that is designated as a custom error page

```
<!DOCTYPE HTML PUBLIC "-//W3C//DTD HTML 4.01 Transitional//EN">

<html>
<head>
    <title>Chapter 4 - Email List application</title>
</head>

<body>
    <%@ page isErrorPage="true" %>
    <h1>Error</h1>
    <p>There was a problem adding your email to our list.
       Please try back later.</p>
    <p><i><%= exception %></i></p>
</body>
</html>
```

Description

- You can use the errorPage attribute of a JSP page directive to designate an error page that is requested if an uncaught exception is thrown at runtime. That error page can be either a JSP or an HTML page.

- If you want the error page to have access to the JSP *implicit exception object*, the error page must be a JSP that includes a page directive with the isErrorPage attribute set to true. Since the implicit exception object is an object of the java.lang.Throwable class, you can call any methods in this class from the exception object.

Figure 4-17   How to use a custom error page

When and how to view the servlet that's generated for a JSP

As you work with JSPs, you should keep in mind that JSPs are translated into servlets and compiled before they are run. As a result, when a Status 500 error occurs, it's usually because the JSP engine can't compile the generated servlet, even though that problem is caused by bad code in the related JSP.

As you have seen in figure 4-16, you can usually find the cause of a Status 500 error by reading the error page and proceeding from there. As a last resort, though, it sometimes makes sense to view the servlet that has been generated from the JSP. For instance, figure 4-18 shows the servlet that's generated for the JSP in figure 4-15.

Before you take a closer look at that servlet, though, you need to understand how a servlet is generated, compiled, and instantiated. In particular, you need to keep these facts in mind. First, each JSP is translated into a servlet class. Second, the servlet class is compiled when the first user requests the JSP. Third, one instance of the servlet class is instantiated when the first user requests the JSP. Fourth, each user is treated as a thread by the servlet, and each thread gets its own copy of the local variables of the servlet methods. With this conceptual background, the generated servlet should make more sense.

At the start of this figure, you can see the path and filename for the servlet that's generated from the JSP in figure 4-15. Although all generated servlets are stored in the work\localhost directory for Tomcat 4.0, the rest of the path is dependent on the location of the actual JSP. If, for example, the JSP is saved in the email4 directory of the murach application directory, then the generated servlet is saved in the work\localhost\murach\email4 directory. The filename of this servlet is generated from the JSP filename.

If you find the servlet file and open it with a text editor, you will probably find the code overwhelming at first. But the partial code in this figure should give you an idea of what's going on. Somewhere near the start of the code, you'll find the instance variables of the JSP declarations declared as variables of the class.

After that, you'll find a JSP service method that contains all of the code from the JSP scriptlet. Because this method is called for each user, each user (or thread) will get a copy of the local variables used by this method. Then, after the code that's generated for the scriptlets, you'll find out.write statements that return HTML to the browser and out.print statements that return Java expressions to the browser.

After you read the next chapter, which shows you how to develop servlets, the code for this servlet should make more sense. But if you compare the code for the JSP in figure 4-15 with its servlet code, you should get a good idea of what's going on. Remember, though, that you usually don't need to view the generated servlets for debugging purposes.

The location of the servlet class for the JSP in figure 4-15

```
C:\tomcat\work\localhost\murach\email4\show_0005femail_0005fentry$jsp.java
```

Part of the servlet class that's generated from the JSP in figure 4-15

```java
public class show_0005femail_0005fentry$jsp extends HttpJspBase {

    int accessCount = 0;
    String file = "../webapps/murach/WEB-INF/etc/UserEmail.txt";
    ...
}

public void _jspService(HttpServletRequest request, HttpServletResponse
        response) throws java.io.IOException, ServletException {
    ...
    String firstName = request.getParameter("firstName");
    String lastName = request.getParameter("lastName");
    String emailAddress = request.getParameter("emailAddress");

    User user = new User(firstName, lastName, emailAddress);
    addRecord(user, file);
    int localCount = 0;
    synchronized (this) {
        accessCount++;
        localCount = accessCount;
    }
    ...
    out.write("... <td align=\"right\">First name:</td> ...");
    out.print( firstName );
    ...
    }
}
```

Instance variables from JSP declarations

Local data from a JSP scriptlet

A write statement for HTML tags

A print statement from a JSP expression

How a servlet is generated, compiled, and instantiated from a JSP

- When a JSP is first requested, the JSP engine translates the page into a servlet class and compiles the class. When it does, it places all JSP scriptlets into a service method. As a result, all variables defined by the scriptlets are local variables to the service method.

- After the servlet class is compiled, one instance of the class is instantiated and a new thread is created. Then, the service method is called.

- For each subsequent user that requests the JSP, a new thread is created from the instance of the servlet class and the service method is called. This method delivers a copy of the local variables for each thread, but all threads share the instance variables.

When and how to view the servlet that's generated for a JSP

- Although you need to know that your JSPs are translated into servlets before they are executed, you normally don't need to view them. For advanced debugging problems, though, it is sometimes useful to view the servlet for a JSP.

- If you're using Tomcat 4.0 or later, you can find the code for the Java servlet class in the subdirectory of the tomcat\work\localhost directory. Starting with that directory, you'll find a directory structure that corresponds to the one for your JSPs.

- If you're using another JSP engine, you should find the servlet class in a similar directory structure.

Figure 4-18   When and how to view the servlet that's generated for a JSP

Perspective

The goal of this chapter has been to provide you with the basics of coding, saving, and viewing JSPs. At this point, you should be able to code simple, but practical, JSPs of your own. In addition, you should understand how HTML pages communicate with JSPs, how JSPs communicate with regular Java classes, and how to fix some of the most common JSP errors.

In the next chapter, you'll learn how to use the same types of skills with servlets. In fact, the next chapter uses the same application that's presented in this chapter, but it uses a servlet instead of a JSP.

Summary

- A *JavaServer Page*, or *JSP*, consists of HTML code plus Java code that's embedded in *scriptlets* and *expressions*. Within the scriptlets and expressions, you can use the methods of the *implicit request object* to get the *parameters* that are passed to the JSP.

- The JSPs for an application are stored in the document root directory or one of its subdirectories. Then, you can view a JSP by entering a URL that corresponds to its directory location.

- When you use the Get method to pass parameters to a JSP, the parameters are displayed in the URL. When you use the Post method, they aren't. Although the Get method transfers data faster than the Post method, you can't use the Get method to transfer more than 4K of data.

- You can use business and data classes from within scriptlets and expressions just as you use them from Java classes. However, the business and data classes must be stored in the WEB-INF\classes directory or one of its subdirectories.

- You use a *JSP directive* known as a *page directive* to import classes for use in a JSP.

- When you use *JSP comments*, the comments aren't compiled or executed. In contrast, HTML comments are compiled and executed, but the browser doesn't display them.

- You use *JSP declarations* to declare instance variables and methods for a JSP. To code a *thread-safe* JSP, you must synchronize access to these instance variables and methods.

- You can use a page directive to designate an error page for an uncaught exception. You can code this directive so it has access to the JSP *implicit exception object* and you can use this object's methods.

- When a JSP is first requested, the JSP engine translates the page into a servlet and compiles it. Then, one instance of the class is instantiated. For each subsequent request, a new thread is created from this single instance of the servlet class. This means that each requestor gets its own copy of the local variables, but all requestors share the same instance variables.

Terms

JavaServer Page (JSP)	implicit request object	JSP declaration
parameter	JSP directive	thread-safe
scriptlet	page directive	error page
JSP expression	JSP comment	implicit exception
JSP tag	instance	object
request object	thread	

Objectives

- Code and test JavaServer Pages that require any of the features presented in this chapter including scriptlets, expressions, page directives, JSP comments, JSP declarations, and custom error pages.

- Describe the directory structure that should be used for JSPs, business, and data classes.

- List two differences between the Get and Post methods that can be used to pass parameters to a JSP.

- Describe the difference between JSP comments and HTML comments.

- Explain what is meant by a thread-safe JSP and describe what you have to do to develop one.

- Describe the process of running a JSP and its effect on local and instance variables.

Exercise 4-1   Create a custom error page

In this exercise, you'll create a custom error page for the Email List application.

1. Run the HTML document named join_email_list.html that's in the webapps\murach\email4 directory so it accesses and runs the JSP named show_email_entry.jsp.

2. Create a custom error page named show_error_page.jsp that displays the type of error, the current date, and the number of times the error page has been accessed. Save this JSP in the webapps\murach\email4 directory.

3. Edit the JSP file named show_email_entry.jsp that's in the email4 directory so it uses the show_error_page.jsp.

4. Test the custom error page. To do that, you can cause an exception by changing the properties of the file so it's read-only. In Windows, you can do this by right clicking the file icon in Explorer, selecting Properties, and selecting Read-only.

Exercise 4-2   Create a new JSP

In this exercise, you'll modify the HTML document for the Email List application, and you'll create a new JSP that responds to the HTML document.

1. Modify the HTML document named join_email_list.html that's in the email4 directory so it has this line of text after the Email address box: "I'm interested in these types of music." Then, follow this line with a list box that has options for Rock, Country, Bluegrass, and Folk music. This list box should be followed by the Submit button, and the Submit button should link to a new JSP named show_music_choices.jsp

2. Create a new JSP named show_music_choices.jsp that responds to the changed HTML document. This JSP should start with an H1 line that reads like this:

    Thanks for joining our email list, John Smith.

    And this line should be followed by text that looks like this:

    We'll use email to notify you whenever we have new releases for these types of music:

    Country
    Bluegrass

    In other words, you list the types of music that correspond to the items that are selected in the list box. And the entire web page consists of just the heading and text lines that I've just described.

3. Test the HTML document and the new JSP by running them. Note the parameter list that is passed to the JSP by the HTML document. Then, test the new JSP by using a URL that includes a parameter list.

5

How to develop servlets

In chapter 4, you learned how to develop a web application that consisted of an HTML page and a JavaServer Page. In this chapter, you'll learn how to create the same application using a servlet instead of a JSP. When you complete this chapter, you should be able to use servlets to develop simple web applications of your own.

The Email List application **142**
The user interface for the application 142
The code for the EmailServlet class 144
How to create a servlet **146**
How to code a servlet 146
How to save and compile a servlet 148
How to request a servlet 150
Other skills for working with servlets **152**
The methods of a servlet 152
How to code instance variables 154
How to code thread-safe servlets 156
How to debug servlets **158**
Common servlet problems 158
How to print debugging data to the console 160
How to write debugging data to a log file 162
Perspective **164**

The Email List application

In this topic, you'll see how the Email List application that was presented in the last chapter works when it uses a servlet instead of a JSP. Once you get the general idea of how this works, you'll be ready to learn the specific skills that you need for developing servlets.

The user interface for the application

Figure 5-1 shows the two pages that make up the user interface for the Email List application. These pages are the same as the pages that are shown in the last chapter except that the second page uses a servlet instead of a JSP.

Like the last chapter, the first page is an HTML page that asks the user to enter a first name, last name, and email address. However, when the user clicks on the Submit button for this application, the HTML page calls a servlet instead of a JSP and passes the three user entries to the servlet. This is shown by the URL that's displayed in the browser for the second page.

The HTML page

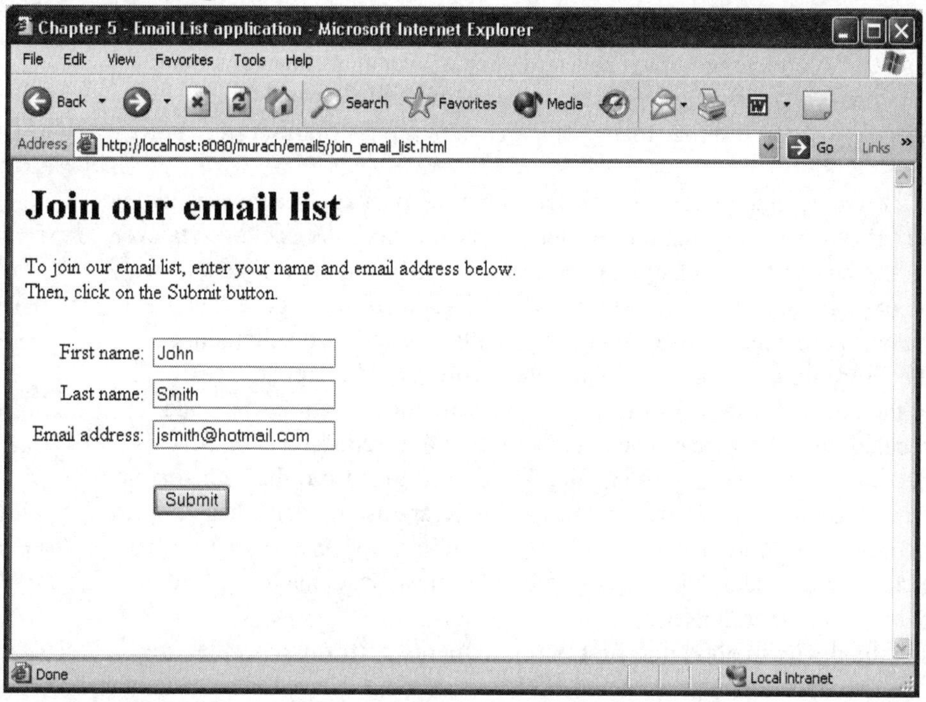

The servlet page

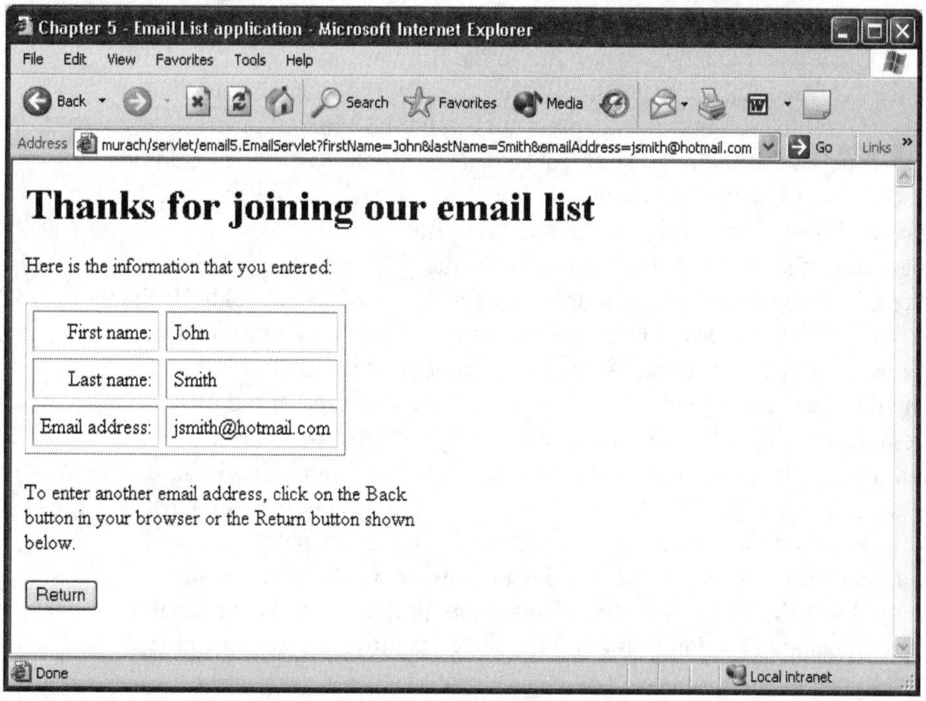

Figure 5-1   The user interface for the application

The code for the EmailServlet class

In chapter 1, you learned that a *servlet* is just a Java class that runs on a server. You also learned that a servlet for a web application extends the HttpServlet class. In figure 5-2, then, you can see that the EmailServlet class extends this class.

The first six statements for this servlet create the package for the servlet and import all the other classes that the servlet will need. First, the package statement puts the servlet in a package named email5. Then, the next three statements import some packages from the servlet API and from the core Java API. These packages are needed by all servlets. Finally, the last two statements import the User and UserIO classes from the business and data packages.

After the declaration for the class, the doGet method provides the code that's executed when a browser uses the Get method to request a servlet. This doGet method accepts two arguments that are passed to it from the web server: an HttpServletRequest object and an HttpServletResponse object. These objects are commonly referred to as the *request object* and the *response object*. In fact, the implicit request object that you learned about in the last chapter is actually an object of the HttpServletRequest class.

Within the doGet method, the first two statements perform tasks that are common to most servlets that return an HTML document. Here, the first statement sets the *content type* that will be returned to the browser. In this case, the content type is set so that the servlet returns an HTML document, but it's possible to return other content types. Then, the second statement returns a PrintWriter object that's used to return data to the browser later on.

After the first two statements of the doGet method, the shaded statements perform the same processing that was presented in the last chapter. First, the getParameter method of the request object returns the three parameters entered by the user. Then, a User object is created from these three parameters, and the UserIO class adds the User object to the specified file.

The last statement in the doGet method uses the println method of the PrintWriter object to return HTML to the browser. This is the same HTML that was used in the JSP in the last chapter. However, this HTML is more difficult to code and read now that it's coded as a string argument of the println method. That's why the next chapter will show how to remove this type of tedious coding from your servlets by combining the use of servlets with JSPs.

Within the println string, only the firstName, lastName, and emailAddress variables are displayed outside of quotation marks. Also, the quotation marks within the string, like the quotation marks around HTML attributes, are preceded by a backslash (\). Otherwise, the Java compiler would interpret those quotation marks as the end of the string. Since the quotation marks within the HTML statements aren't actually required, you can remove them to simplify the code, but the code is still clumsy.

The code for the EmailServlet class

```
package email5;

import javax.servlet.*;
import javax.servlet.http.*;
import java.io.*;
import business.*;
import data.*;

public class EmailServlet extends HttpServlet{

    public void doGet(HttpServletRequest request,
                      HttpServletResponse response)
                      throws IOException, ServletException{

        response.setContentType("text/html");
        PrintWriter out = response.getWriter();

        String firstName = request.getParameter("firstName");
        String lastName = request.getParameter("lastName");
        String emailAddress = request.getParameter("emailAddress");
        User user = new User(firstName, lastName, emailAddress);
        UserIO.addRecord(user, "../webapps/murach/WEB-INF/etc/UserEmail.txt");

        out.println(
          "<!doctype html public \"-//W3C//DTD HTML 4.0 Transitional//EN\">\n"
        + "<html>\n"
        + "<head>\n"
        + "   <title>Chapter 5 - Email List application</title>\n"
        + "</head>\n"
        + "<body>\n"
        + "<h1>Thanks for joining our email list</h1>\n"
        + "<p>Here is the information that you entered:</p>\n"
        + "   <table cellspacing=\"5\" cellpadding=\"5\" border=\"1\">\n"
        + "   <tr><td align=\"right\">First name:</td>\n"
        + "       <td>" + firstName + "</td>\n"
        + "   </tr>\n"
        + "   <tr><td align=\"right\">Last name:</td>\n"
        + "       <td>" + lastName + "</td>\n"
        + "   </tr>\n"
        + "   <tr><td align=\"right\">Email address:</td>\n"
        + "       <td>" + emailAddress + "</td>\n"
        + "   </tr>\n"
        + "   </table>\n"
        + "<p>To enter another email address, click on the Back <br>\n"
        + "button in your browser or the Return button shown <br>\n"
        + "below.</p>\n"
        + "<form action=\"/murach/email5/join_email_list.html\" "
        + "      method=\"post\">\n"
        + "   <input type=\"submit\" value=\"Return\">\n"
        + "</form>\n"
        + "</body>\n"
        + "</html>\n");
    }
}
```

Figure 5-2   The code for the EmailServlet class

How to create a servlet

Now that you have a general idea of how servlets are coded, you're ready to learn some specific skills for creating a servlet. To start, you need to know how to begin coding the class for a servlet.

How to code a servlet

Figure 5-3 shows the basic structure for a typical servlet that performs some processing and returns an HTML document to the browser. You can use this basic structure for all the servlets you write. For now, that's all you need to get started, but you'll learn another way to structure servlets in the next chapter.

Since most servlets are stored in a package, the first statement in this servlet specifies the package for the servlet. This package must correspond to the directory that the servlet is saved in. In the next figure, you'll learn more about how this works.

The next three statements are the import statements that are required by all servlets. The javax.servlet.http package is required because it contains the HttpServletRequest and HttpServletResponse classes. The javax.servlet class is required because it contains the ServletException class. And the java.io class is required because it contains the IOException class.

After the first four statements, the class declaration provides the name for the servlet and indicates that it extends the HttpServlet class. Although in theory a servlet can extend the GenericServlet class, all servlets for web applications extend the HttpServlet class.

The doGet and doPost methods in this figure accept the same arguments and throw the same exceptions. Within these methods, you can use the methods of the request object to get incoming data, and you can use the methods of the response object to set outgoing data. In this structure, since the doPost method calls the doGet method, an HTTP request that uses the Post method will actually execute the doGet method of the servlet. This is a common programming practice that allows a servlet to use the same code to handle both the Get and Post methods of an HTTP request.

In the doGet method, the first statement calls the setContentType method of the response object. This sets the content type for the HTTP response that's returned to the browser to "text/html," which specifies that the servlet returns text or HTML. In chapter 15, you'll learn how to return other types of data.

The second statement in the doGet method obtains a PrintWriter object named out from the response object. This object can be used to return character data to the client. Once you have this object, you can use one println statement or a series of print and println statements to return HTML or other text to the browser. However, as you learned in the last figure, you must code a backslash before any quotation marks that don't start or end a string. Otherwise, the servlet won't compile properly.

The basic structure of a servlet class

```
package packageName;

import javax.servlet.*;
import javax.servlet.http.*;
import java.io.*;

public class ServletName extends HttpServlet{

    public void doGet(HttpServletRequest request,
                    HttpServletResponse response)
                    throws IOException, ServletException{

        response.setContentType("text/html");
        PrintWriter out = response.getWriter();

        //business processing

        out.println("response as HTML");
    }

    public void doPost(HttpServletRequest request,
                    HttpServletResponse response)
                    throws IOException, ServletException {
        doGet(request, response);
    }

}
```

Description

- All web-based servlets extend the HttpServlet class. To extend this class, the servlet must import the javax.servlet, javax.servlet.http, and java.io packages.
- The doGet method overrides the doGet method of the HttpServlet class and processes all HTTP requests that use the Get method, and the doPost method overrides the doPost method of the HttpServlet class and processes all HTTP requests that use the Post method.
- The doGet and doPost methods use two objects that are passed to it by the web server: (1) the HttpServletRequest object, or the *request object*, and (2) the HttpServletResponse object, or the *response object*.
- The setContentType method of the response object sets the *content type* of the response that's returned to the browser. Then, the getWriter method of the response object returns a PrintWriter object that can be used to send HTML to the browser.
- Before you can create a PrintWriter object, you must set the content type. This allows the getWriter method to return a PrintWriter object that uses the proper content type.

Figure 5-3   How to code a servlet

How to save and compile a servlet

In chapter 4, you learned how to save and compile regular Java classes in Tomcat. Now, figure 5-4 shows you how to save and compile servlet classes.

Since the EmailServlet class contains a package statement that specifies a package named email5, it must be placed in the email5 subdirectory of the WEB-INF\classes directory that is subordinate to the document root directory. For the book applications, this root directory is webapps\murach.

This figure also presents four other directory paths that you can use to store your servlet classes. All of these paths store the servlet classes in the WEB-INF\classes directory that's subordinate to the document root directory. That can be your own document root directory or the default document root directory (ROOT) that's provided by Tomcat 4.0. Then, if you use packages, you continue the directory structure with one directory for each package level. If, for example, you use a class named EmailServlet in a package named business.email, the directory path for the servlet must be WEB-INF\classes\business\email.

If you're using TextPad to save and compile your servlets, you will need to set your classpath so it includes the directory that contains your class files as described in appendix A. Then, TextPad's Compile Java command will work properly.

Otherwise, you can use a DOS prompt to compile your packaged classes. To do that, you use the cd command to change the current directory to the WEB-INF\classes directory for your application. Then, you use the javac command to compile the class. When you do that, you can enter the javac command, followed by a space, followed by the package name, followed by a backslash (\), followed by the name of the Java class.

Where the EmailServlet class is saved

    c:\tomcat\webapps\murach\WEB-INF\classes\email5

Other places to save your servlet classes

    c:\tomcat\webapps\yourDocumentRoot\WEB-INF\classes\packageName
    c:\tomcat\webapps\yourDocumentRoot\WEB-INF\classes\
    c:\tomcat\webapps\ROOT\WEB-INF\classes\
    c:\tomcat\webapps\ROOT\WEB-INF\classes\packageName

The TextPad dialog box for saving Java files

The DOS prompt window for compiling the EmailServlet class

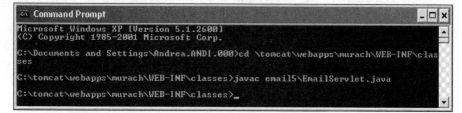

Description

- Although you can save the source code (.java file) for a servlet in any directory, you must save the compiled class (.class file) in the \WEB-INF\classes subdirectory of the document root directory or in a subdirectory that corresponds to the Java package that the class is in.

- For simplicity, you can store your servlet source files in the same directory as the corresponding class files, but the source files for a production application are likely to be stored in other directories.

- To compile your servlets, you can use TextPad's Compile Java command, your IDE's compile command, or the javac command from a DOS prompt window.

Figure 5-4   How to save and compile a servlet

How to request a servlet

Now that you can code, save, and compile a servlet, you're ready to test the servlet by viewing it in a web browser. To do that, the web server and the servlet engine must be running. Then, you can request the servlet as shown in figure 5-5.

To test a servlet, you can enter a URL directly in a web browser. However, once you're done testing a servlet, you'll usually want to code a web page that requests the servlet. You can do that by coding a Form tag or an Anchor tag that specifies a URL that requests the servlet.

To request a servlet by entering the URL into a browser, you enter an absolute URL like the two examples in this figure. If you've read the last two chapters, you shouldn't have much trouble understanding how this works. The main difference is that you must enter "servlet" after the document root directory to indicate that you want to run a servlet. Then, you enter the package name for the servlet, followed by a period (or dot), followed by the name of the servlet.

The first example shows the URL for a servlet that's stored on a local web server in the email5 directory of the murach directory. The second example shows the URL for the servlet after it's deployed on the Internet server for *www.murach.com*.

When you test a servlet, you will often want to pass parameters to it. To do that, you can add the parameters to the end of the URL. Here, the question mark after the servlet name indicates that one or more parameters will follow. Then, you can code the parameter name, the equals sign, and the parameter value for each parameter that is passed, and you can separate multiple parameters with ampersands (&).

If you omit a parameter that's required by the servlet, the getParameter method will return a null value for that parameter. In this figure, for example, only the first parameter value is added to the end of the URL. As a result, two of the values displayed by the servlet are null values.

To request a servlet from an HTML form, you use the Action attribute of the form to provide a path and filename that points to the servlet. This is illustrated by the last two examples in this figure. Here, the assumption is that the HTML page is in a subdirectory of the document root directory. As a result, the path specified in the Action attribute begins with two periods to navigate back one level to the root directory. Then, the word "servlet" specifies that you want to call a servlet. Last, the package and class names point to the class for the servlet.

When you use an HTML form to request a servlet, you can use the Method attribute to specify whether you want to use the Get method or the Post method. If you use a Get method to request a servlet from another page, any parameters that are passed to the servlet will be displayed in the browser at the end of the URL. But if you use the Post method to request a servlet, the parameters won't be displayed at the end of the URL.

How to request the EmailServlet class

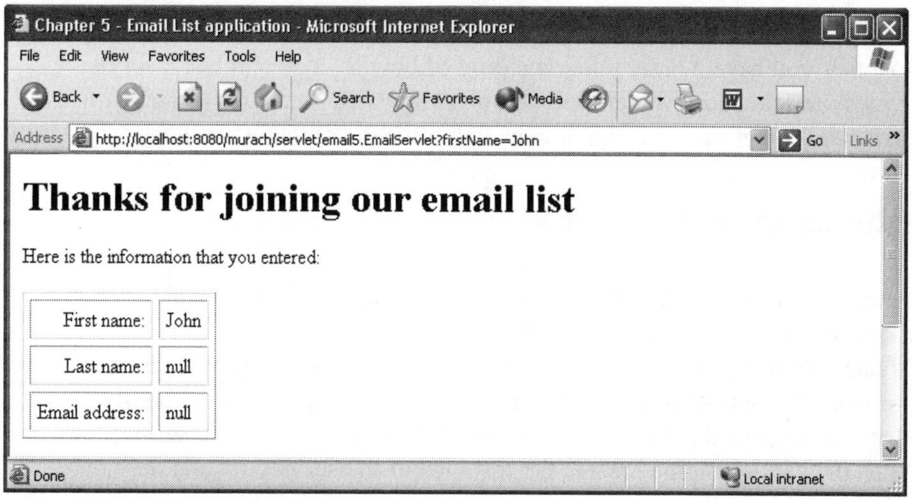

The syntax for requesting a servlet

```
http://host:port/documentRoot/servlet/packageName.ServletName
```

Two URLs that request a servlet

```
http://localhost:8080/murach/servlet/email5.EmailServlet
http://www.murach.com/servlet/email5.EmailServlet
```

How to add parameters to a URL

```
EmailServlet?firstName=John&lastName=Smith
EmailServlet?firstName=John&lastName=Smith&emailAddress=jsmith@hotmail.com
```

Two Form tags that request a servlet

```
<form action="../servlet/email5.EmailServlet" method="get">
<form action="../servlet/email5.EmailServlet" method="post">
```

Description

- To request a servlet without using an HTML form, enter a URL that requests the servlet in the browser. If necessary, add parameters to the end of the URL.

- When you code or enter a URL that requests a servlet, you can add a parameter list to it starting with a question mark and with no intervening spaces. Then, each parameter consists of its name, an equals sign, and its value. To code multiple parameters, use ampersands (&) to separate them.

- If an HTML form that uses the Get method requests a servlet, the URL and its parameters will be displayed by the browser. If an HTML form that uses the Post method requests a servlet, the URL will be displayed in the browser, but the parameters won't be.

Figure 5-5   How to request a servlet

Other skills for working with servlets

Now that you have a basic understanding of how to code and test a servlet, you're ready to learn some other skills for working with servlets. To start, you can learn about other methods that are available when you code servlets.

The methods of a servlet

Figure 5-6 presents some common methods of the HttpServlet class. When you code these methods, you need to understand that the servlet engine only creates one instance of a servlet. This usually occurs when the servlet engine starts or when the servlet is first requested. Then, each request for the servlet starts (or "spawns") a thread that can access that one instance of the servlet.

When the servlet engine creates the instance of the servlet, it calls the init method. Since this method is only called once, you can override it in your servlet to supply any necessary initialization code. In the next figure, you'll see an example of this.

After the servlet engine has created the one instance of the servlet, each request for that servlet spawns a thread that calls the service method of the servlet. This method checks the method that's specified in the HTTP request and calls the appropriate doGet or doPost method.

When you code servlets, you shouldn't override the service method. Instead, you should override the appropriate doGet or doPost methods. To handle a request that uses the Get method, for example, you can override the doGet method. If, on the other hand, you want to handle a request that uses the Post method, you can override the doPost method. To handle both types of requests, you can override both of them and have one call the other as shown in figure 5-3.

If a servlet has been idle for some time or if the servlet engine is shut down, the servlet engine unloads the instances of the servlets that it has created. Before unloading a servlet, though, it calls the destroy method of the servlet. If you want to provide some cleanup code, such as writing a variable to a file or closing a database connection, you can override this method. However, the destroy method may not be called if the server crashes. As a result, you shouldn't rely on it to execute any code that's critical to your application.

Five common methods of a servlet

```
public void init() throws ServletException{}

public void service(HttpServletRequest request,
                    HttpServletResponse response)
                throws IOException, ServletException{}

public void doGet(HttpServletRequest request,
                    HttpServletResponse response)
                throws IOException, ServletException{}

public void doPost(HttpServletRequest request,
                    HttpServletResponse response)
                throws IOException, ServletException{}

public void destroy(){}
```

How the server handles a request for a servlet

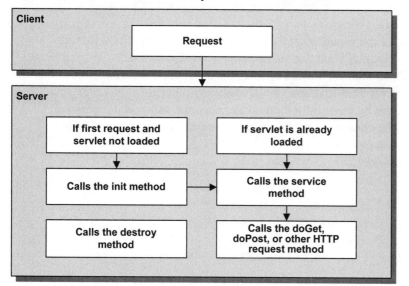

The life cycle of a servlet

- A server loads and initializes the servlet by calling the init method.
- The servlet handles each browser request by calling the service method. This method then calls another method to handle the specific HTTP request type.
- The server removes the servlet by calling the destroy method. This occurs either when the servlet has been idle for some time or when the server is shutdown.

Description

- All the methods shown above are located in the abstract HttpServlet class. This means you can override these methods in your own servlets. However, you shouldn't need to override the service method. Rather, you should override a method like doGet or doPost to handle a specific HTTP request.

Figure 5-6   The methods of a servlet

How to code instance variables

Figure 5-7 shows how to code *instance variables* in a servlet. Since multiple threads access a single instance of a servlet, the instance variables of a servlet are used by all the threads. For that reason, you may need to synchronize the access to some instance variables if there's a chance that use by two or more threads at the same time could corrupt the data.

The code in this figure shows how to add an instance variable named accessCount to the EmailServlet. To initialize a variable like this, you can code its declaration in the init method. This will ensure that the variable is initialized when the instance of the servlet is first created.

If you shut down the server and restart it, though, the servlet will be destroyed and a new instance of the servlet will be created. As a result, any instance variables will be initialized again. If that's not what you want, you can write the value of the instance variable to a file so the data isn't lost when the servlet is destroyed.

In this example, the synchronized and this keywords prevent two threads from running the block of code that updates the accessCount instance variable at the same time. Then, after the thread updates the accessCount variable, its value is stored in a local variable so it can't be accessed by other threads. Later, this local variable is used by the println method to return the value to the browser. This is similar to the code that you saw in the scriptlet for the JSP in the last chapter.

Code that adds an instance variable to the EmailServlet class

```
public class EmailServlet extends HttpServlet{

    private int accessCount;

    public void init() throws ServletException{
        accessCount = 0;
    }

    public void doGet(HttpServletRequest request,
                      HttpServletResponse response)
                  throws IOException, ServletException{

        // missing code

        int localCount = 0;
        synchronized(this){
            accessCount++;
            localCount = accessCount;
        }

        // missing code

        out.println(
        // missing code
        + "<i>This page has been accessed " + localCount + " times.</i>"
        // missing code
        );
    }
}
```

Description

- An *instance variable* of a servlet belongs to the one instance of the servlet and is shared by any threads that request the servlet.
- You can initialize an instance variable in the init method.
- If you don't want two or more threads to modify an instance variable at the same time, you must synchronize the access to the instance variables.
- To synchronize access to a block of code, you can use the synchronized keyword and the this keyword.

Figure 5-7   How to code instance variables

How to code thread-safe servlets

A *thread-safe* servlet, like a thread-safe JSP, is one that works correctly even if more than one servlet thread is running at the same time. To code a thread-safe servlet, you not only have to synchronize the use of any instance variables that could be corrupted, but also any methods that could cause problems if they were used by two or more threads at the same time.

In figure 5-8, you can see how to limit the use of code to a single thread at three different levels. First, you can synchronize a block of code by using the synchronized and this keywords. Second, you can synchronize an entire method. Third, you can use the SingleThreadModel interface to limit the use of an entire servlet to a single thread. That way, you don't have to synchronize any of the code within the servlet.

As you code thread-safe servlets, you must remember that one thread has to wait while another thread is using a synchronized block of code, a synchronized method, or a single-thread servlet. Since that can affect the performance of a web application, your general goal should be to synchronize as little code as possible. As a result, synchronizing a block of code within a method is best for performance, synchronizing a method is next best, and coding single-thread servlets should usually be avoided.

But those decisions also depend on other factors like how long it takes to run a servlet or a method and how many users are likely to access a servlet at any given time. If the pages on your web site get accessed thousands of times each day, performance is obviously an issue. But if your web site gets only a few dozen visitors a day, performance may not be an issue at all.

A block of synchronized code

```
synchronized(this){
    accessCount++;
    if (accessCount == 1000){
        LogUtil.logToFile("We reached 1000 users on "
                            + new java.util.Date());
    }
}
```

A synchronized method

```
public static synchronized int addRecord(Connection connection, User user)
                                    throws SQLException{
    String query =
            "INSERT INTO User " +
            "(EmailAddress, FirstName, LastName) " +
            "VALUES ('" + SQLUtil.encode(user.getEmailAddress()) + "', " +
                    "'" + SQLUtil.encode(user.getFirstName()) + "', " +
                    "'" + SQLUtil.encode(user.getLastName()) + "')";
    Statement statement = connection.createStatement();
    int status = statement.executeUpdate(query);
    statement.close();
    return status;
}
```

A servlet that prevents multiple thread access

```
public class EmailServlet extends HttpServlet implements SingleThreadModel{…
}
```

Description

- A *thread-safe* servlet is one that works correctly when more than one thread is running at the same time.
- To synchronize access to a method or a block of code, you can use the synchronized keyword. Then, only one thread at a time can access the code in the block or the method.
- To prevent multiple threads from accessing the code in a servlet, you can implement the SingleThreadModel interface. This is a tagging interface that prevents two threads from accessing the servlet's service method at the same time.

Note

- A tagging interface is one that has no methods.

Figure 5-8   How to code thread-safe servlets

How to debug servlets

When you develop servlets, you will encounter errors. That's why this topic gives you some ideas on how to debug servlets when you're using a text editor to develop your servlets. If you're using an IDE, though, it may provide advanced debugging tools that let you step through code and monitor variables so you won't the need to use the techniques that follow.

Common servlet problems

Figure 5-9 lists four common problems that can occur when you're working with servlets. Then, it lists some possible solutions for each of these problems.

If your servlet won't compile, the error message that's displayed by the compiler should give you an idea of why the servlet won't compile. If the compiler can't find a class that's in one of the Java APIs, for example, you may need to install the API. If the compiler can't locate your custom classes, you may need to modify your classpath. And if the compiler has a problem locating a package, your package statement for the class might not correspond with the directory that contains the class.

If the servlet compiles but won't run, it may be because the servlet engine isn't running. To solve this problem, of course, you can start the servlet engine. However, if the servlet engine is already running, you should double-check the URL to make sure that it's pointing to the correct host, path, and package for the servlet. A common mistake, for example, is to forget to include the package name when specifying a URL for a servlet.

If you make changes to a servlet and the changes aren't apparent when you test it, it may be because the servlet engine hasn't reloaded the modified class. Then, if you're using Tomcat in a stand-alone development environment, you can either make sure that servlet reloading is turned on as explained in chapter 2. Or, you can shutdown Tomcat and restart it so the changed servlet will be reloaded the next time that it's requested.

If the HTML response page doesn't look right when it's rendered by the browser, the servlet is probably sending bad HTML to the browser. To fix this problem, you can use the Source command (for Internet Explorer) or the Page Source command (for Netscape) to view the HTML that has been returned to the browser. Then, you can identify the problem and modify the servlet to fix it.

Common servlet problems

Problem	Possible solutions
The servlet won't compile	Make sure the compiler has access to the JAR files for all necessary APIs.
	Make sure the classpath is pointing to the directory that contains your user-defined packages.
	Make sure the class is in the correct directory with the correct package statement.
The servlet won't run	Make sure the web server is running.
	Make sure you're using the correct URL.
The changes aren't showing up	Make sure servlet reloading is on, or shutdown and startup the server so it reloads the class that you modified.
The HTML page doesn't look right	Select the Source or Page Source command from your browser's View menu to view the HTML code. Then, you can read through the HTML code to identify the problem, and you can fix the problem in the servlet.

Note

- Appendix A shows how to install the Java APIs and how to set the classpath.

Figure 5-9   Common servlet problems

How to print debugging data to the console

If you're using Tomcat in a stand-alone development environment, you can print debugging messages to the console for the servlet engine as shown in figure 5-10. To do that, you can use the println method of the System.out and System.err objects. You can use these messages to help track the methods that are executed or the changes to variables.

If you aren't using Tomcat in a stand-alone environment, you might not be able to view the debugging messages in the console. In some cases, though, you may be able to make them appear in the console by starting the servlet engine from a command line. In other cases, the println statements may automatically be written to a text file that you can view. Otherwise, you'll need to print this data to a log file as described in the next figure.

When you use println statements to check the value of a variable, you'll often want to include the name of the class and the name of the variable. That way, your messages will be easier to understand. This also makes it easier to find and remove the println statements once the error is debugged.

How Tomcat displays println statements

Code that prints debugging data to the console

```
public void doGet(HttpServletRequest request,
                  HttpServletResponse response)
                  throws IOException, ServletException{
    // code
    String emailAddress = request.getParameter("emailAddress");
    System.out.println("EmailServlet emailAddress: " + emailAddress);
    // code
}
```

Description

- When you're testing an application on your local system, you may be able to use the println method of the System.out or System.err objects to display debugging messages on the console for the servlet engine.
- When you use debugging messages to display variable values, it's a good practice to include the class name and variable name so the messages are easy to interpret.

Figure 5-10   How to print debugging data to the console

How to write debugging data to a log file

If you can't print debugging data to the console, you can print debugging data to a *log file* as shown in figure 5-11. Although each servlet engine uses log files a little differently, you should be able to use these log methods with any servlet engine. However, you may need to check the documentation for your servlet engine to see how it works with log files.

To write data to a log file, you can use the two log methods of the HttpServlet class. If you just want to write a message to a log file, you can use the first log method. But if you want to write a message to the log file along with the stack trace for an exception, you can use the second log method. A *stack trace* is a series of messages that presents the chain of method calls that precede the current method.

The code in this figure uses the first log method to display the value for the emailAddress variable of the EmailServlet class. Then, it uses the second log method to print a message and a stack trace for an IOException. The data that's printed by these two log methods is shown in the TextPad window.

Tomcat 4.0 stores all log files in its logs directory. Within this directory, Tomcat stores several types of log files with one file of each type for each date. In the TextPad window, you can see the contents of the localhost_log.2002-10-15.txt file. This log file contains the value of the emailAddress variable as well as the stack trace for an IOException.

Often, the servlet engine automatically writes other information in the same log file that the log methods of the HttpServlet class use. In that case, you can write your debugging information to a separate text file to make it easier to view your debugging messages. To do that, you can create your own class that writes error messages to a file.

To illustrate, the CD that comes with this book includes a LogUtil class in the util package that contains log methods that work like the log methods shown in this figure. However, you can easily modify this class to specify a name and location for the log file. Then, you can use the log methods in this class to write your debugging information to the file.

Two methods of the HttpServlet class used to log errors

Method	Description
log(String message**)**	Writes the specified message to the server's error log.
log(String message, Throwable t**)**	Writes the specified message and stack trace for the exception to the server's error log.

Servlet code that prints data to a server specific log file

```
String emailAddress = request.getParameter("emailAddress");
log("EmailServlet emailAddress: " + emailAddress);
User user = new User(firstName, lastName, emailAddress);
try{
    UserIO.addRecord(user, file);
}
catch(IOException ioe){
    log("EmailServlet IOException in UserIO", ioe);
}
```

The location of log files in Tomcat 4.0

```
\tomcat\logs
```

A typical log file

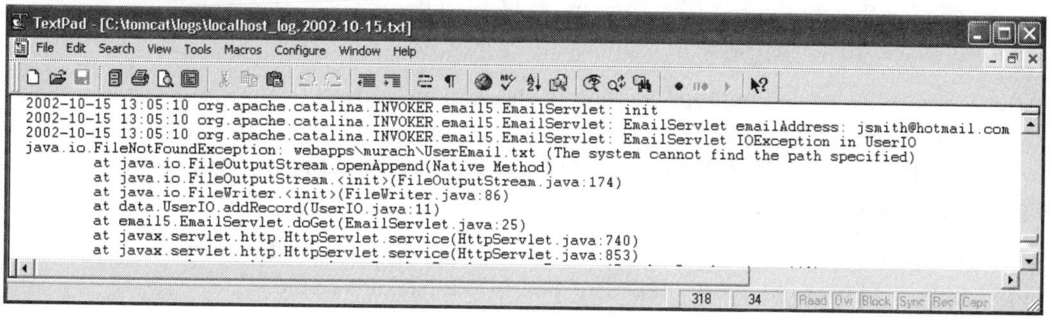

Description

- You can use the log methods of the HttpServlet class to write debugging information to a *log file*. Tomcat 4.0 stores its log files in a directory named logs.

- The name and location of the log files for a servlet engine may vary depending on the servlet engine. To find the name and location of your log files, check the documentation for your servlet engine.

- A *stack trace* is the chain of method calls for any statement that calls a method.

Figure 5-11   How to write debugging data to a log file

Perspective

The goal of this chapter has been to teach you the basics of coding, saving, and testing servlets. So at this point, you should be able to develop simple, but practical, servlets of your own. In addition, you should have a basic understanding of how servlets are executed.

Note, however, that you usually don't use servlets to send the HTML code back to the browser as shown in this chapter. Instead, you structure your web applications so servlets do the processing that's required and JSPs send the HTML code back to the browser. In that way, you combine the best features of servlets with the best features of JSPs, and that's what you'll learn how to do in the next chapter.

Summary

- A *servlet* is a Java class that runs on a server, and a servlet for a web application extends the HttpServlet class.

- When you write servlets, you override the doGet and doPost methods to provide the processing that's required. These methods receive the *request object* and the *response object* that are passed to them by the server.

- After you use the setContentType method of the response object to set the *content type* of the response that's returned to the browser, you use the getWriter method to create a PrintWriter object. Then, you can use the println and print methods of that object to send HTML back to the browser.

- The class files for servlets must be stored in the WEB-INF\classes directory of an application or in a subdirectory that corresponds to a package name.

- To request a servlet from a URL, you include the word "servlet" after the document root directory in the path. This is followed by the package name, a dot, and the servlet name.

- You can override the init method of a servlet to initialize its instance variables. These variables are then available to all of the threads that are spawned for the one instance of the servlet.

- When you code a *thread-safe* servlet, you prevent two or more users from accessing the same block of code at the same time.

- To print debugging data to the server console, you can use the println method of the System.out or System.err object. An alternative is to use the log methods of the HttpServlet class to write debugging data to a *log file*.

Terms

servlet
request object
response object
content type
instance variable
thread-safe
log file
stack trace

Objectives

- Code and test servlets that require any of the features presented in this chapter.
- Provide debugging data for a servlet by writing messages to either the console or a log file.
- Describe the directory structure that must be used for servlet classes.
- Describe the difference between the URL for a JSP and the URL for a servlet.
- Describe the use of the init, doGet, and doPost methods in a servlet.
- Describe the execution of a servlet, and explain its effect on local and instance variables.
- Explain what is meant by a thread-safe servlet and describe what you have to do to develop one.

Exercise 5-1   Modify the EmailServlet class

1. Enter a URL in your browser that requests the EmailServlet class that's located in the murach/WEB-INF/classes/email5 directory and sends two parameters to it.
2. Run the HTML document named join_email_list.html in the email5 directory so it accesses and runs the EmailServlet class.
3. Add the accessCount instance variable to the EmailServlet class as described in figure 5-7. Then, run the servlet from the HTML document. This will test whether servlet reloading has been turned on as described in chapter 2. If it isn't on, you will have to stop and restart Tomcat before the changes to the servlet show up. (You may have to refresh your browser for the changes to take effect.)
4. Modify the HTML document so it uses the Post method instead of the Get method, and modify the servlet so it works properly.
5. Print a debugging message to the console that shows the value of the accessCount variable. Then, run the servlet two or more times to see how this message appears in the console.
6. Repeat step 5, but use a log file this time.

Exercise 5-2   Create a new servlet

In this exercise, you'll modify the HTML document for the Email List application, and you'll create a new servlet that responds to the HTML document. This is comparable to what you did for exercise 4-2, but the details are repeated here.

1. Modify the HTML document named join_email_list.html that's in the email5 directory so it has this line of text after the Email address box: "I'm interested in these types of music." Then, follow this line with a list box that has options for Rock, Country, Bluegrass, and Folk music. This list box should be followed by the Submit button, and the Submit button should link to a new servlet named MusicChoicesServlet.

2. Create a new servlet named MusicChoicesServlet that responds to the changed HTML document. This servlet should respond with an H1 line that looks like this:

    `Thanks for joining our email list, John Smith.`

    And this line should be followed by text that looks like this:

    `We'll use email to notify you whenever we have new releases for`
    `these types of music:`

    `Country`
    `Bluegrass`

    In other words, you list the types of music that correspond to the items that are selected in the list box. And the entire web page consists of just the heading and text lines that I've just described.

3. Test the HTML document and the new servlet by running them. Note the parameter list that is passed to the servlet by the HTML document. Then, test the new servlet by using a URL that includes a parameter list.

6

How to structure a web application

In chapter 4, you learned how to use a JSP to create a simple web application. Then, in chapter 5, you learned how to use a servlet to create the same application. Now, in this chapter, you will learn how to use servlets and JSPs to structure an application so it takes advantage of the best features of servlets and JSPs. You'll also learn some other skills for structuring the code in an application so it's easier to code and maintain.

The Email List application **168**
The code for the servlet 168
The code for the JSP 170
How to structure servlets and JSPs **172**
An introduction to the Model 1 architecture 172
An introduction to the Model-View-Controller pattern 174
How to forward and redirect requests and responses 176
How to validate data on the client **178**
An HTML page that uses JavaScript to validate data 178
A dialog box that displays a validation message 180
How to validate data on the server **182**
A servlet that validates data 182
A JSP that displays a data validation message 184
How to include code from a file in a JSP **186**
A JSP that includes code from other files 186
How to include a file in a JSP 188
How to work with the web.xml file **190**
An introduction to the web.xml file 190
How to set initialization parameters 192
How to get initialization parameters 194
How to implement servlet mapping 196
How to implement custom error handling 198
Perspective **200**

The Email List application

In this topic, you'll learn to modify the Email List application that was presented in the last chapter so it uses a servlet and a JSP. In this application, the servlet will handle all of the processing for the application, and the JSP will handle the presentation. Once you see how this works for this simple application, you'll be ready to learn how to use this technique for more complex applications.

The code for the servlet

Figure 6-1 presents the code for the EmailServlet class that does the processing for the Email List application. Unlike the EmailServlet class presented in chapter 5, this one doesn't use println statements to send HTML back to the browser. Instead, it forwards the request and response objects to the JSP shown in the next figure so the JSP can do that.

In figure 6-5, you'll learn the coding details for forwarding these objects. For now, all you need to know is that the highlighted code in this figure forwards the request and response objects to the JSP named show_email_entry.jsp. To forward these objects to another JSP, though, you just change the URL.

The EmailServlet class

```
package email6;

import java.io.*;
import javax.servlet.*;
import javax.servlet.http.*;
import business.User;
import data.UserIO;

public class EmailServlet extends HttpServlet{

    public void doGet(HttpServletRequest request,
                      HttpServletResponse response)
                      throws IOException, ServletException{

        String firstName = request.getParameter("firstName");
        String lastName = request.getParameter("lastName");
        String emailAddress = request.getParameter("emailAddress");

        User user = new User(firstName, lastName, emailAddress);
        UserIO.addRecord(user,
                    "../webapps/murach/WEB-INF/etc/UserEmail.txt");

        RequestDispatcher dispatcher =
            getServletContext().getRequestDispatcher(
               "/email6/show_email_entry.jsp");
        dispatcher.forward(request, response);
    }

    public void doPost(HttpServletRequest request,
                      HttpServletResponse response)
                      throws ServletException, IOException {
        doGet(request, response);
    }
}
```

Description

- Instead of sending HTML code to a browser, this servlet forwards the request and response objects to the JSP shown in the next figure.

Figure 6-1   The code for the servlet

The code for the JSP

Figure 6-2 presents the JSP code for the show_email_entry.jsp file. Since this JSP works like the JSP in chapter 4, you shouldn't have any trouble understanding it. You should realize, though, that this JSP is accessing the request object that has been passed to it from the servlet, not the original HTML page. In addition, since the servlet has already used the User and UserIO classes to write the user's data to a file, this JSP doesn't need to do that. Instead, it only needs to handle the presentation for the application by displaying the user's data.

For a simple application like this one, the benefits of using servlets for processing and JSPs for presentation may not be obvious. As your applications become more complex, though, you'll realize how this structuring method results in servlets and JSPs that are easier to code and maintain.

The JSP code for show_email_entry.jsp

```
<!doctype html public "-//W3C//DTD HTML 4.0 Transitional//EN">
<html>
<head>
  <title>Chapter 6 - Email List application</title>
</head>

<body>

<%
  String firstName = request.getParameter("firstName");
  String lastName = request.getParameter("lastName");
  String emailAddress = request.getParameter("emailAddress");
%>

<h1>Thanks for joining our email list</h1>

<p>Here is the information that you entered:</p>

  <table cellspacing="5" cellpadding="5" border="1">
    <tr>
      <td align="right">First name:</td>
      <td><%= firstName %></td>
    </tr>
    <tr>
      <td align="right">Last name:</td>
      <td><%= lastName %></td>
    </tr>
    <tr>
      <td align="right">Email address:</td>
      <td><%= emailAddress %></td>
    </tr>
  </table>

<p>To enter another email address, click on the Back <br>
button in your browser or the Return button shown <br>
below.</p>

<form action="/murach/email6/join_email_list.html" method="post">
  <input type="submit" value="Return">
</form>
</body>
</html>
```

Description

- The EmailServlet class in the last figure forwards the request and response objects to this JSP.
- Since the EmailServlet class has already done all of the processing for the requested page, this JSP only needs to handle the presentation for the page.

Figure 6-2   The code for the JSP

How to structure servlets and JSPs

Now that you have a general idea of how to structure a simple application, you're ready to learn about the two structuring patterns that are commonly used for web applications.

An introduction to the Model 1 architecture

In chapter 4, you learned how to create a simple application that consisted of an HTML page and a JSP. This approach used the *Model 1 architecture* that's shown in figure 6-3. With this architecture, a JSP is responsible for handling both the request and response of the application.

To do that, the JSP interacts with business classes that are coded as *JavaBeans*. These classes represent the data of the business objects in the application and provide the methods that do the business processing. In the chapter 4 application, the User class is coded as a JavaBean, and you'll learn more about JavaBeans in chapter 8.

To save the data of the business classes, the application maps the data to a database or files that can be called the *data store* for the application. This is also known as *persistent data storage* because it exists after the application ends. Usually, data classes like the UserIO class in chapter 4 are used to store the data of the business objects in the data stores. So far in this book, the UserIO class has stored the data for each User object in a file, but you'll learn how to use a database or an XML file as a data store later in this book.

In general, the Model 1 architecture works well when the processing requirements are limited. But once your JSPs become cluttered with scriptlets, you should consider the approach you saw in figures 6-1 and 6-2. That approach can be called the Model 2 architecture, and you'll learn more about it in the next figure.

The Model 1 architecture

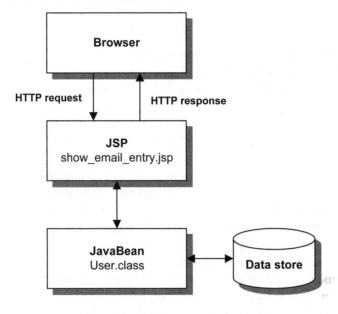

Description

- The *Model 1 architecture* is commonly used for web applications with limited processing requirements. With this architecture, JSPs handle both the requests and the responses.

- The business classes in the Model 1 architecture are coded as *JavaBeans*, which you'll learn about in chapter 8. These classes represent the data of the application and also do the business processing of the application.

- The *data store* can be a database or one or more disk files. It holds the business data that is represented by the JavaBeans. This is often referred to as *persistent data storage* because it exists after the application ends.

- The application that you studied in chapter 4 uses the Model 1 architecture, and the User class for that application is actually a JavaBean.

- Usually, the methods of data classes like the UserIO class are used to access and store the data of the data store. That isn't done directly by the JavaBeans.

Figure 6-3   An introduction to the Model 1 architecture

An introduction to the Model-View-Controller pattern

A *pattern* is a standard approach that is used by programmers to solve common programming problems. One of these patterns is the *Model-View-Controller pattern*, or *MVC pattern*, that's introduced in figure 6-4. As its name implies, the MVC pattern has three layers: the model, the view, and the controller. This pattern is also known as the *Model 2 architecture*, and it works better than the Model 1 architecture whenever the processing requirements are substantial.

In the MVC pattern, the *model* defines the business layer of the application. This layer is usually implemented by JavaBeans, which you'll learn more about in chapter 8. For now, you can think of the User class as the model for the Email List application, and it is a JavaBean. This type of class defines the data for the business objects and provides the methods that do the business processing.

The *view* defines the presentation layer of the application. Since it's cumbersome to use a servlet to send HTML to a browser, an MVC application uses HTML documents or JSPs to present the view to the browser.

The *controller* manages the flow of the application, and this work is done by servlets. In particular, a servlet usually does the processing for a request using JavaBeans whenever necessary, and then forwards it to one of several possible JSPs for presentation based on the logic of that processing.

Here again, most applications need to map the data in the model to a data store. But the JavaBeans usually don't provide the methods for storing their own data. Instead, data classes like the UserIO class provide those methods. That's designed to separate the business logic from the I/O operations.

When you use the MVC pattern, you should try to keep the model, view, and controller as independent of each other as possible. That makes it easier to modify an application later on. If, for example, you decide to modify an application so it presents the view in a different way, you should be able to modify the view layer without making any changes to the controller or model layers. In practice, it's difficult to separate these layers completely, but in theory complete independence is the goal.

Note, however, that you don't have to use the MVC pattern to implement every page in a web application. For those pages that have substantial processing requirements, this pattern will make it easier to code, test, and maintain the pages. But for web pages with simple processing requirements, it's usually easier to use the Model 1 architecture. In particular, if all your models are JavaBeans, you can use special JSP tags to work directly with the data in the JavaBeans as described in chapter 8.

The Model-View-Controller pattern

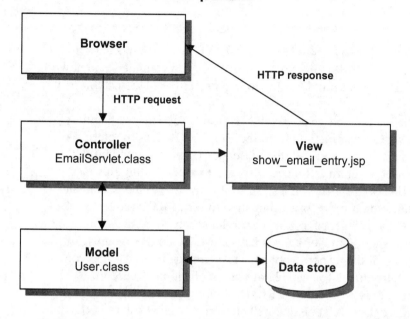

Description

- The *Model-View-Controller pattern*, or *MVC pattern*, is commonly used to structure web applications that have significant processing requirements. That makes them easier to code and maintain. This pattern is also known as the *Model 2 architecture*.

- The *model* in the MVS pattern consists of JavaBeans. The *view* consists of HTML documents and JSPs. And the *controller* consists of servlets.

- Usually, the methods of data classes like the UserIO class are used to access and store the data of the data store. That isn't done directly by the JavaBeans.

- When you use the MVC pattern, you try to construct each layer so it's as independent as possible. Then, if you need to make changes to one layer, any changes to the other layers are minimized.

Figure 6-4   An introduction to the Model-View-Controller pattern

How to forward and redirect requests and responses

Figure 6-5 shows how to *forward* the request and response objects from a servlet to an HTML page, a JSP, or another servlet. Once you understand how to write this type of code, you should be able to implement the MVC pattern in your applications.

To forward the request and response objects from a servlet, you begin by calling the getServletContext method from the HttpServlet class to return a ServletContext object. Then, you call the getRequestDispatcher method of the ServletContext object to return a RequestDispatcher object. Within this method, you must code a URL that starts with a slash so it is relative to the document root directory. Then, you use the forward method to forward the request and response objects to the HTML page, JSP, or servlet specified by the URL.

This figure also shows how to *redirect* a response. To do that, you use the sendRedirect method of the response object. This is typically used when you want to transfer control to a URL outside of your application. To use this method, you often supply an absolute URL. However, you can also supply a relative URL because the servlet engine will convert it to an absolute URL. If you begin the pathname with a slash, the servlet engine interprets the path as relative to the servlet engine root directory.

When you call the sendRedirect method, the server sends an absolute URL to the browser. Then, the browser sends a request for that URL. Since the processing occurs on the client side rather than the server side, this isn't as efficient as forwarding a request object. In addition, the sendRedirect method doesn't transfer the request and response objects. As a result, you should only use the sendRedirect method when you want to redirect to a URL that's running on another server.

How to forward the request and response objects

Syntax

```
RequestDispatcher objectName =
    getServletContext().getRequestDispatcher(
        "/url");
objectName.forward(request, response);
```

Examples

```
RequestDispatcher dispatcher =
    getServletContext().getRequestDispatcher(
        "/email6/get_missing_fields.jsp");
dispatcher.forward(request, response);

RequestDispatcher dispatcher =
    getServletContext().getRequestDispatcher(
        "/email6/join_email_list.html");
dispatcher.forward(request, response);

RequestDispatcher dispatcher =
    getServletContext().getRequestDispatcher(
        "/servlet/email6.ValidateUserServlet");
dispatcher.forward(request, response);
```

How to redirect a response from a servlet

Syntax

```
response.sendRedirect("url");
```

Examples

```
response.sendRedirect("http://www.murach.com/index.htm");
response.sendRedirect("/murach/email6/show_email_entry.jsp");
```

Description

- The forward method of the RequestDispatcher object is typically used to transfer control to a resource on the same server. Then, all processing takes place on the server, and the specified resource has access to the request and response objects.

- To get a RequestDispatcher object, you use the getRequestDispatcher method of the ServletContext interface. To get the ServletContext object, you use the getServletContext method of the HttpServlet class.

- The sendRedirect method of the response object is typically used to transfer control to a resource on another server. When you use this method, the specified resource doesn't have access to the request and response objects and the processing is split between the server and the browser.

Figure 6-5   How to forward and redirect requests and responses

How to validate data on the client

When a user enters data into an application, the application often needs to check the data to make sure that the data is valid. This is referred to as *data validation*. Then, if the user enters data that isn't valid, the application can display an error message and give the user another chance to enter the data.

When coding a web application, you can use *JavaScript* to validate data on the client. Although there are other ways to validate data on the client, using JavaScript is one of the most popular ways.

An HTML page that uses JavaScript to validate data

Figure 6-6 shows how to use JavaScript to do some simple data validation. Since all modern web browsers can execute JavaScript, this data validation runs entirely on the client. As a result, it's more efficient than sending a request to the server that includes invalid data only to receive a response that indicates that the data isn't valid.

Although the syntax of JavaScript is similar to the syntax of Java, JavaScript is a different language. So to learn how to use JavaScript, you need to get a book on that subject. For now, all I'm trying to show you is how JavaScript and client-side data validation can be used in a Java web application because that affects the structure of an application.

The JavaScript in this figure just checks to make sure the user has entered values into all three text boxes of a form. Here, the opening and closing Script tags identify the JavaScript code to the browser. Within these tags, JavaScript uses a *function* that accepts the HTML form as an argument. This JavaScript function is similar to a Java method.

Within this function, if statements check to make sure that a value has been entered into each text box. If a value hasn't been entered in a text box, the alert method causes the browser to display a dialog box like the one in the next figure. Then, the focus method moves the focus to that text box. Otherwise, the submit method submits the form.

The HTML in this figure uses a JavaScript button rather than a standard Submit button. Here, the onClick attribute of the JavaScript button calls the validate function that's coded within the Script tags. This code uses the this and form keywords to specify the current form as the argument for the function.

Although most modern browsers support JavaScript, some older browsers don't. To prevent these older browsers from displaying the text that's inside the Script tags, you can place an HTML comment around the scripting statements as shown in this figure. This won't affect the execution of the JavaScript in browsers that support it, but it will prevent the code from being displayed as text in browsers that don't support it.

JavaScript that validates a form

```
<script language="JavaScript">
  <!-- hide this script from older browsers
    function validate(form) {
        if (form.firstName.value=="") {
            alert("Please fill in your first name");
            form.firstName.focus();
        }
        else if (form.lastName.value=="") {
            alert("Please fill in your last name");
            form.lastName.focus();
        }
        else if (form.emailAddress.value=="") {
            alert("Please fill in your email address");
            form.emailAddress.focus();
        }
        else {
            form.submit();
        }
    }
  // end hiding -->
</script>

<body>

<h1>Join our email list</h1>
<p>To join our email list, enter your name and
email address below. <br>
Then, click on the Submit button.</p>

<form action="../servlet/email6.EmailServlet" method="get">
<table cellspacing="5" border="0">
  <tr><td align="right">First name:</td>
    <td><input type="text" name="firstName"></td>
  </tr>
  <tr><td align="right">Last name:</td>
    <td><input type="text" name="lastName"></td>
  </tr>
  <tr><td align="right">Email address:</td>
    <td><input type="text" name="emailAddress"></td>
  </tr>
  <tr><td></td>
    <td><input type="button" value="Submit"
        onClick="validate(this.form)"></td>
  </tr>
</table>
</form>

</body>
```

Description

- To validate data on the client side, you can add *JavaScript* to an HTML page or a JSP. This improves the performance of an application by preventing unnecessary requests and responses from being passed between the server and browser.

- Although JavaScript uses a syntax that's similar to Java, it is a different language.

Figure 6-6   An HTML page that uses JavaScript to validate data

A dialog box that displays a validation message

Figure 6-7 shows the type of dialog box that's displayed when you use JavaScript. In this case, this dialog box is issued when the user doesn't enter any text in the text box for the email address. When the user clicks the OK button in the dialog box, the focus will move to that text box. Then, the user can enter an email address and submit the form again.

When you validate data, you may not want to display validation messages in a dialog box like this one. In that case, you can validate data on the server as shown in the next two figures. Although this allows you to customize your data validation messages, which can make your application more user-friendly, it isn't as efficient as validating data on the client side.

The dialog box that's displayed when an entry isn't made

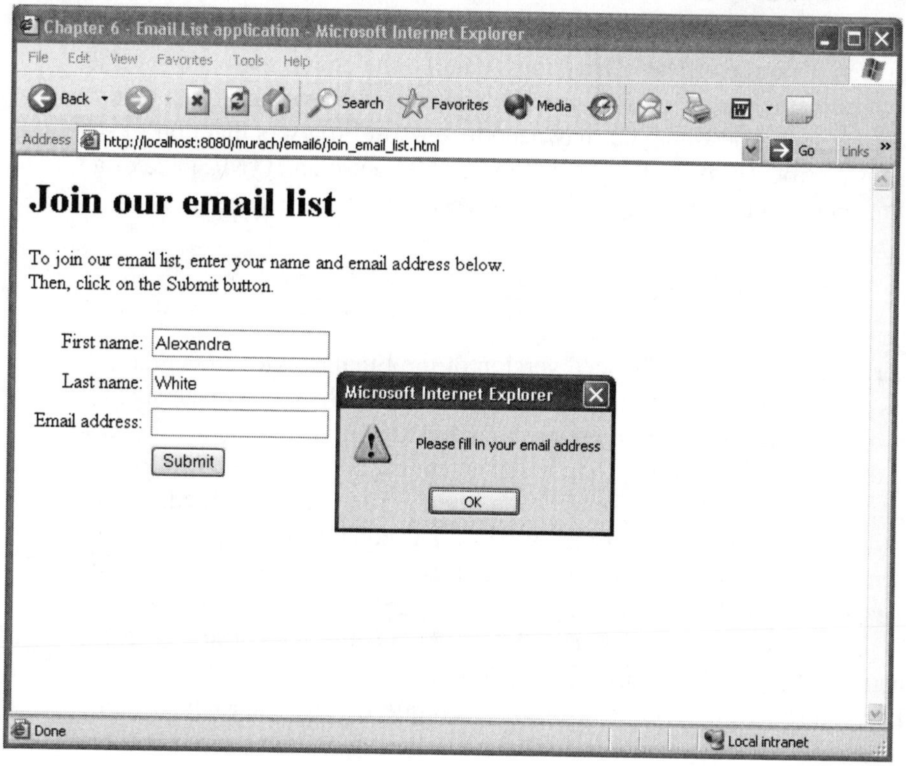

Description

- When you use JavaScript to display validation messages, they appear in standard dialog boxes.

- If you want to display error messages in an HTML page or JSP, you can use servlets to validate data on the server side.

Figure 6-7 A dialog box that displays a data validation message

How to validate data on the server

Although it's more efficient to validate data on the client, there are several reasons to validate data on the server. First, you may need to check data that's stored on the server. Second, you may need to support browsers that don't support JavaScript. Third, you may want to be able to use an HTML page or a JSP to customize your data validation messages.

A servlet that validates data

Figure 6-8 presents an enhanced version of the EmailServlet class that validates data on the server. Here, the highlighted code checks to make sure that the user enters values for all three request parameters. If any of the parameters is equal to an empty string, this code transfers control to the JSP shown in the next figure. As a result, the rest of the code in the servlet isn't executed.

On the other hand, if none of the parameters is equal to an empty string, the servlet creates a User object from the parameters and uses the UserIO class to write the data in this object to a file. Then, it forwards the request to a JSP that displays the data to the user. This should give you a better idea of how a servlet can function as a controller in the MVC pattern.

When you're writing code that forwards a request, you need to make sure that your servlet doesn't attempt to forward a request more than once per thread. If you write code that attempts to do this, the server will display an error when you try to request the servlet. In that case, you can use one or more if statements to restructure your code.

Since this servlet works with strings, you don't need to write any code to convert data. But let's say you want to make sure that the user enters an integer. To do that, the servlet code can attempt to parse the string to an integer within a try/catch statement. Then, if the parsing fails and an exception is thrown, the servlet can supply code in the catch statement that forwards the request to an appropriate JSP.

A servlet method that validates data

```
public void doGet(HttpServletRequest request,
                  HttpServletResponse response)
                  throws IOException, ServletException{

    String firstName = request.getParameter("firstName");
    String lastName = request.getParameter("lastName");
    String emailAddress = request.getParameter("emailAddress");

    // if any required fields are missing,
    // display a JSP to get the missing fields
    if ((firstName.length()==0) || (lastName.length()==0) ||
        (emailAddress.length()==0)){
        RequestDispatcher dispatcher =
            getServletContext().getRequestDispatcher(
                "/email6/get_missing_fields.jsp");
        dispatcher.forward(request, response);
    }

    // otherwise, write the data to a file and display the entry
    User user = new User(firstName, lastName, emailAddress);
    UserIO.addRecord(user,
        "../webapps/murach/WEB-INF/etc/UserEmail.txt");
    RequestDispatcher dispatcher =
        getServletContext().getRequestDispatcher(
        "/email6/show_email_entry.jsp");
    dispatcher.forward(request, response);
}
```

Description

- If the code in this servlet determines that any parameter values that have been passed to the servlet are invalid, the servlet forwards the request and response objects to a JSP like the one shown in the next figure. Then, the code in the rest of the servlet isn't executed.

- If the code in this servlet determines that all parameter values are valid, it writes the data to a file and forwards the request and response objects to a JSP that displays the data.

- If you try to write code that forwards the request and response objects to more than one resource, the servlet won't compile.

Figure 6-8   A servlet that validates data

A JSP that displays a data validation message

Figure 6-9 shows the JSP that the request and response objects are forwarded to if a user doesn't enter a value for each of the three text boxes. This JSP displays a validation message that asks the user to fill out all three text boxes, and it displays any values that the user has already entered within the text boxes. That way, the user doesn't have to re-enter any values that have already been entered.

When the user clicks the Submit button, this page sends the values in the text boxes back to the EmailServlet class. Then, if a value is still missing, the EmailServlet class forwards the request to this JSP again. In other words, this request and response cycle continues until the user enters valid data or ends the application. This of course is quite inefficient when compared with client-side data validation.

The JSP that's displayed when an entry isn't made

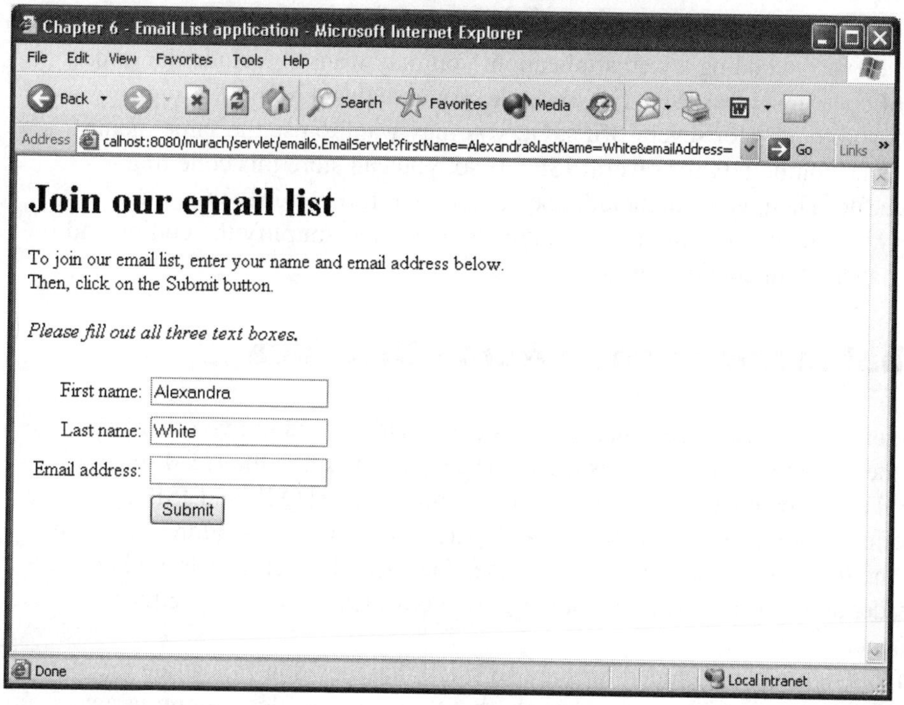

Some code for the JSP

```
<%
   String firstName = request.getParameter("firstName");
   String lastName = request.getParameter("lastName");
   String emailAddress = request.getParameter("emailAddress");
%>

<h1>Join our email list</h1>
<p>To join our email list, enter your name and
email address below. <br>
Then, click on the Submit button.</p>
<p><i>Please fill out all three fields.</i></p>

<form action="../servlet/email6.EmailServlet" method="get">
<table cellspacing="5" border="0">
  <tr>
    <td align="right">First name:</td>
    <td><input type="text" name="firstName" value="<%= firstName %>"></td>
  </tr>
  <tr>
    <td align="right">Last name:</td>
    <td><input type="text" name="lastName" value="<%= lastName %>"></td>
  </tr>
  <tr>
    <td align="right">Email address:</td>
    <td><input type="text" name="emailAddress"
        value="<%= emailAddress %>"></td>
  </tr>
```

Figure 6-9   A JSP that displays a data validation message

How to include code from a file in a JSP

When you're coding a web application, you may want to include the same block of code in several JSPs. For example, you may want to use the same headers and footers for several JSPs. Or, you may want to use the same menus or the same combo box for several JSPs. If so, you can store this code in a separate file. Then, you can include the code in that file in a JSP. When used properly, this technique can reduce redundant code and simplify the coding and maintenance of an application.

A JSP that includes code from other files

Figure 6-10 shows a JSP that includes code that's stored in two other files. Here, the header.htm file contains the HTML tags that define the Head section of the HTML document. The footer.jsp file contains the HTML and JSP tags that define a footer for a document that displays the user's email address and the date. And the show_email_entry.jsp file uses the shaded statements to include the header and footer files. In the next figure, you'll learn how to code these statements.

In this figure, the included files are so small that they don't illustrate the value of this technique. Imagine, though, that the included files contain larger blocks of code and that they are appropriate for many different JSPs. Then, this coding technique can reduce the total amount of code in the application and make the application easier to maintain. If, for example, you want to change the header for all the JSPs that include the header file, you just have to change one file.

A JSP that uses two include files

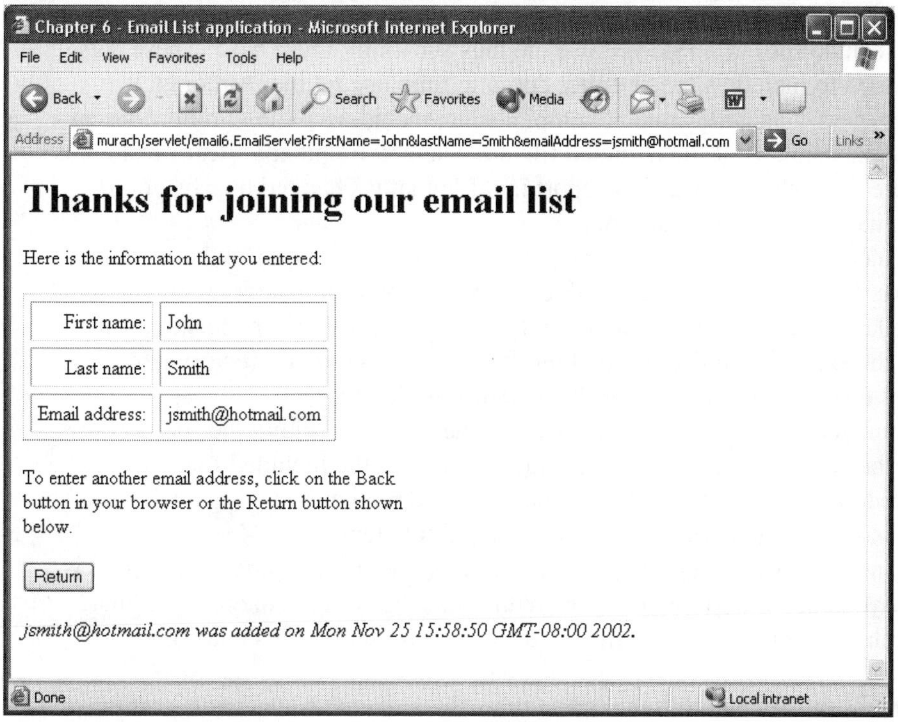

The code for the header.htm file

```
<head>
  <title>Chapter 6 - Email List application</title>
</head>
```

The code for the footer.jsp file

```
<%@ page import="java.util.Date" %>
<p><i><%= emailAddress %> was added on <%= new Date() %>.</p>
```

The code for the show_email_entry.jsp file

```
<!doctype html public "-//W3C//DTD HTML 4.0 Transitional//EN">
<html>

<jsp:include page="/includes/header.htm" flush="true" />

<body>
    // missing code that displays the body of the page
    <%@ include file="/includes/footer.jsp" %>
</body>

</html>
```

Figure 6-10   A JSP that includes code from other files

How to include a file in a JSP

To include files in a JSP, you use the tags shown in figure 6-11. These tags can be used to include a file at either compile-time or runtime. Although it's more efficient to include a file at compile-time, including a file at runtime works better if the contents of the included file are changed frequently. If, for example, you store the code for a weather report in a file that is changed hourly, you'll want to include the file at runtime.

To include a file at compile-time, or *translation time*, you use the *include directive*. To do that, you code a JSP directive tag. Within this tag, you type the include keyword followed by the file attribute and the relative pathname of the file. In the examples in this figure, both files are located in a directory named includes that's subordinate to the document root directory.

When you include a file at translation time, the code within the file becomes part of the generated servlet. As a result, a change to the included file isn't displayed in the JSP until the JSP is modified and recompiled. That's why you should include a file at runtime if it is changed frequently.

To include a file at runtime, or *request time*, you use the *include action*. To do that, you code the jsp:include tag. Within this tag, you set the page attribute to the relative pathname of the include file, and you set the flush attribute to true.

When you include a file at request time, the included file never becomes part of the generated servlet. As a result, a change to the included file is displayed in the JSP the next time the page is requested. That's why this method works better for files that are changed frequently.

How to include a file in a JSP at translation time

Syntax

```
<%@ include file="fileLocationAndName" %>
```

Examples

```
<%@ include file="/includes/header.htm" %>
<%@ include file="/includes/footer.jsp" %>
```

How to include a file in a JSP at request time

Syntax

```
<jsp:include page="fileLocationAndName" flush="true" />
```

Examples

```
<jsp:include page="/includes/header.htm" flush="true" />
<jsp:include page="/includes/footer2.jsp" flush="true" />
```

Description

- To include a file in a JSP at compile-time, or *translation time*, you use the *include directive*.

- When you use the include directive, the code in the included file becomes part of the generated servlet. As a result, any changes to the included file don't appear in the JSP until the JSP is retranslated and recompiled.

- To include a file in a JSP at runtime, or *request time*, you use the *include action*.

- When you use the include action, the included code is not part of the generated servlet, and any changes to the included file appear in the JSP the next time it is requested.

- When you include a file at translation time, the included file has access to all variables and methods defined in the JSP, including the request object. When you include a file at request time, the included file doesn't have access to these variables.

Figure 6-11   How to include a file in a JSP

How to work with the web.xml file

In chapter 2, you learned that every application has one web.xml file that contains information about how the application is configured. Now, you'll learn how to modify that web.xml file to control the operation of an application.

This topic assumes that you're using Tomcat 4.0. So if you're using a different servlet engine, you may need to modify the code presented in this topic so it works with your servlet engine. In general, though, the concepts presented here should still apply.

An introduction to the web.xml file

Figure 6-12 shows the web.xml file that works with the application presented in this chapter. Since this file is stored in the webapps\murach\WEB-INF directory, it also works with all other applications subordinate to the murach directory.

This web.xml file begins with two tags that define the type of XML document that's being used. For now, you don't need to understand this code. However, you should include them at the beginning of each web.xml file. To do that, you can copy them from another web.xml file.

After this code, the web.xml file contains *XML tags* that define *elements*. For example, the opening and closing web-app tags define the web-app element. Since all other elements are coded within this element, the web-app element is known as the *root element*. Any element coded within this element or a lower-level element is known as a *child element*.

To modify a web.xml file, you can use a text editor to add, modify, or remove the file's XML elements. If you want to leave the code in the file but you don't want the servlet engine to use the code, you can use *comments* to comment out a portion of the web.xml file. These comments work the same way HTML comments do. Once you're done modifying the file, you must restart Tomcat so that the changes take effect.

When you modify the web.xml file, you should take care to code the XML elements in the order shown in this figure. Otherwise, when you start Tomcat, it won't be able to read the web.xml file. As a result, it will display an error message that indicates that the elements aren't in the correct order. To solve this problem, you can edit the web.xml file and restart Tomcat to read the file again.

A web.xml file

```xml
<?xml version="1.0" encoding="ISO-8859-1"?>
<!DOCTYPE web-app
    PUBLIC "-//Sun Microsystems, Inc.//DTD Web Application 2.2//EN"
    "http://java.sun.com/j2ee/dtds/web-app_2_2.dtd">

<web-app>
  <context-param>
    <param-name>dbName</param-name>
    <param-value>murach</param-value>
  </context-param>

  <servlet>
    <servlet-name>email6.EmailServlet</servlet-name>
    <servlet-class>email6.EmailServlet</servlet-class>
    <init-param>
      <param-name>filename</param-name>
      <param-value>../webapps/murach/WEB-INF/etc/UserEmail.txt</param-value>
    </init-param>
  </servlet>

  <servlet-mapping>
    <servlet-name>email6.EmailServlet</servlet-name>
    <url-pattern>/email6/email.jsp</url-pattern>
  </servlet-mapping>

  <!-- To implement error handling, remove the following comment -->
  <!--
  <error-page>
    <exception-type>java.lang.Throwable</exception-type>
    <location>/email6/error.htm</location>
  </error-page>

  <error-page>
    <error-code>404</error-code>
    <location>/email6/show_error_page.jsp</location>
  </error-page>
  -->
</web-app>
```

Description

- The web.xml file is stored in the WEB-INF directory for an application. When the servlet engine starts, it reads the web.xml file.

- You use *XML tags* to define *elements*. An element can have several *child elements*. Since all elements must be coded within the web-app element, it is the *root element*.

- You can use *comments* to document the XML tags and to comment out certain portions of the web.xml file. The tags for XML comments are the same as the tags for HTML comments.

- If the elements in the web.xml aren't in the correct order, Tomcat will display an error message when it reads the web.xml file.

- After you modify the web.xml file, you must restart Tomcat so the changes take effect.

Figure 6-12   An introduction to the the web.xml file

How to set initialization parameters

If you want to store some *initialization parameters* for an application in a central location, you can add them to the web.xml file as shown in figure 6-13. Then, your servlets can read these parameters as shown in the next figure.

To define a *context initialization parameter* that will be available to all servlets in the entire web application, you code a context-param element. In this figure, the context-param element has two child elements: the param-name element and the param-value element. To define multiple context parameters, you can code additional context-param elements after the first one.

To define a *servlet initialization parameter* that will be available to a specific servlet, you can code an init-param element within a servlet element. Within the servlet element, you must start by coding the servlet-name and servlet-class elements to specify the servlet. In this example, the value of the servlet-name element is the same as the value of the servlet-class element. However, you can use any name that you like for the servlet-name element. Then, throughout the rest of the web.xml file, you use that name to refer to that servlet.

After you define the servlet-name and servlet-class elements, you use the init-param element to define the initialization parameter. Within this element, you must code the param-name and param-value elements to define the name and value of the parameter. To define multiple initialization parameters for a servlet, you can code additional init-param elements after the first one.

XML tags that set initialization parameters in a web.xml file

```
<web-app>

    <context-param>
        <param-name>dbName</param-name>
        <param-value>murach</param-value>
    </context-param>

    <servlet>
        <servlet-name>email6.EmailServlet</servlet-name>
        <servlet-class>email6.EmailServlet</servlet-class>
        <init-param>
            <param-name>filename</param-name>
            <param-value>../webapps/murach/UserEmail.txt</param-value>
        </init-param>
    </servlet>

</web-app>
```

XML elements for working with initialization parameters

Element	Description
`<web-app>`	The root element of web.xml. All other elements must be coded within this element.
`<context-param>`	Defines a parameter that's available to all servlets within an application.
`<servlet>`	Identifies a specific servlet within the application.
`<servlet-name>`	Defines the name for the servlet that's used in the rest of the web.xml file.
`<servlet-class>`	Identifies the servlet by specifying the servlet's package and class name.
`<init-param>`	Defines a name/value pair for an initialization parameter for a servlet.
`<param-name>`	Defines the name of a parameter.
`<param-value>`	Defines the value of a parameter.

Description

- To create an *initialization parameter* that will be available to all servlets (called a *context initialization parameter*), you code the param-name and param-value elements within the context-param element.

- To create an initialization parameter that will be available to a specific servlet (called a *servlet initialization parameter*), you code the param-name and param-value elements within the init-param element. But first, you must identify the servlet by coding the servlet, servlet-name, and servlet-class elements.

Figure 6-13   How to set initialization parameters

How to get initialization parameters

Figure 6-14 shows you how to read initialization parameters like the ones set by the web.xml file in the last figure. To do that, you begin by overriding the init method of the servlet. Within this method, you can read the parameters and set the instance variables. That way, the parameters will be available to the rest of the servlet.

To retrieve an initialization parameter that's available to the current servlet, you call the getInitParameter method from the ServletConfig object. When you call this method, you must specify the name of the parameter. If the parameter exists, the getInitParameter method returns the value of the parameter as a string. Otherwise, this method returns a null value. As a result, your code should be able to handle a null value.

To retrieve an initialization parameter that's available to all servlets, you can use the getInitParameter method from the ServletContext object. To retrieve the ServletContext object, you can call the getServletContext method from the ServletConfig object. Other than that, the getInitParameter method works the same whether you call it from the ServletConfig object or the ServletContext object.

Code that gets servlet initialization parameters

```
public class EmailServlet extends HttpServlet{
    private String file;

    public void init() throws ServletException{
        ServletConfig config = getServletConfig();
        file = config.getInitParameter("filename");
    }
```

Code that gets context initialization parameters

```
public class EmailServlet extends HttpServlet{
    private String dbName;

    public void init() throws ServletException{
        ServletConfig config = getServletConfig();
        ServletContext context = config.getServletContext();
        dbName = context.getInitParameter("dbName");
    }
```

Description

- To get an initialization parameter for a specific servlet, you use the getInitParameter method of the ServletConfig object. To get a ServletConfig object, you call the getServletConfig method of the HttpServlet class.

- To get an initialization parameter that's available to all servlets, you use the getInitParameter method of the ServletContext object. To get a ServletContext object, you call the getServletContext method of the ServletConfig object.

- If the parameter specified in the getInitParameter method exists, this method returns the value for the parameter as a string. Otherwise, it returns a null value.

Figure 6-14   How to get initialization parameters

How to implement servlet mapping

Figure 6-15 shows how to implement *servlet mapping* to redirect requests for a URL to a servlet. This prevents the URL for the servlet from being displayed in the user's browser, and it allows you to use shorter URLs in your code. If, for example, the URLs for some servlets are long and unwieldy, you can map shorter URLs to these servlets.

The example in this figure shows how to map a request for /email6/ email.jsp to /servlet/email6.EmailServlet. Since all requests for this JSP will be mapped to that servlet, you want to make sure that the JSP doesn't actually exist. Otherwise, the JSP will never be run. You should know that to test this JSP directly in the browser, though, you need to append parameter names and values to the URL.

To implement servlet mapping in the web.xml file, you must code a servlet element that identifies the name and class of the servlet. Then, you must code a servlet-mapping element that identifies the name of the servlet and the URL pattern. If the URL pattern specifies a directory, a request for that directory will be mapped to the specified servlet. Otherwise, the servlet engine will map the filename specified by the URL to the specified servlet.

You can use servlet mapping to map all requests for any file in a directory to one servlet that controls the flow of the application. Then, you can use that servlet to do the logic that forwards the request to the appropriate HTML document or JSP.

XML tags that add servlet mapping to the web.xml file

```
<servlet>
  <servlet-name>email6.EmailServlet</servlet-name>
  <servlet-class>email6.EmailServlet</servlet-class>
</servlet>

<servlet-mapping>
  <servlet-name>email6.EmailServlet</servlet-name>
  <url-pattern>/email6/email.jsp</url-pattern>
</servlet-mapping>
```

How servlet mapping works

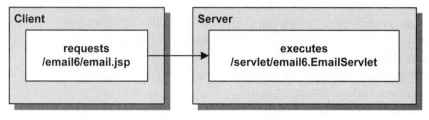

The opening Form tag that requests the servlet

```
<form action="/murach/email6/email.jsp" method="post">
```

The URL displayed in the browser

```
http://localhost:8080/murach/email6/email.jsp
```

XML elements for working with servlet mapping

Element	Description
`<servlet-mapping>`	Enables the ability to map URLs to servlets.
`<servlet-name>`	Specifies the name of the servlet. This must correspond with the servlet-name element that's specified within the servlet element.
`<url-pattern>`	Specifies the URL or URLs that are to be redirected to the servlet specified within the servlet-mapping element. To avoid conflicts, you should specify a directory or filename that doesn't actually exist.

Some URL patterns

Pattern	Description
`email6`	Specifies any file in the email6 directory.
`email6/show`	Specifies a file in the email6 directory named show that has no extension.

Description

- You can use *servlet mapping* to map any URL pattern to a servlet.
- In the web.xml file, you must code the servlet-mapping element after the servlet element. Then, you can code one servlet-mapping element for each URL pattern you want to map.

Figure 6-15   How to implement servlet mapping

How to implement custom error handling

In chapter 4, you learned how to create a custom error page for a single JSP. Now, figure 6-16 shows you how to use the web.xml file to specify custom error pages that apply to the entire application.

When you're developing an application, you probably won't want to implement custom error pages. That way, when an error occurs, Tomcat will display an error page that you can use to debug the error. Before you deploy an application, though, you may want to implement custom error pages that present errors in a way that's consistent with the rest of your application.

To specify a custom error page that's displayed when an uncaught exception is thrown, you begin by coding an error-page element. Within this element, you code two child elements: the exception-type element and the location element. The exception-type element specifies the type of exception by identifying the package name and the class name for the exception. The location element specifies the location of the custom error page.

In the first example in this figure, the exception-type element specifies the java.lang package and the Throwable class. Since all exceptions inherit this class, this causes a custom error page to be displayed for all uncaught exceptions. However, if you want to display different error pages for different types of exceptions, you can code multiple error-page elements. For example, you can display one error page for exceptions of the NullPointerException type and another error page for exceptions of the ServletException type.

To specify the path for the location element, you can begin the path with a slash followed by a path that's relative to the application root. In this first example, the custom error page is a static HTML page that's stored in the error.htm file that's in the email6 subdirectory of the application's root directory.

Another way to implement custom error handling is to provide error pages for specific types of errors that are represented by *HTTP status codes*. To do that, you code error-code elements instead of exception-type elements, but otherwise this works the same. For instance, the second example in this figure shows how to specify a custom error page for the 404 status code.

The 404 status code indicates that the server wasn't able to find a file at the requested URL. To test an error page for this error, then, you request a URL that doesn't exist. As you gain more experience with web programming, you'll become familiar with other HTTP status codes. And some of the more common ones are summarized in chapter 15.

When you code a custom error page, you can use an HTML document or a JSP. If you use a JSP, you can use the request object to customize the page. However, your error pages won't be able to access the exception object that's described in chapter 4.

XML tags that provide error-handling for specific exception types

```
<error-page>
  <exception-type>java.lang.Throwable</exception-type>
  <location>/email6/error.htm</location>
</error-page>
```

XML tags that provide error-handling for specific error codes

```
<error-page>
  <error-code>404</error-code>
  <location>/email6/error_404.jsp</location>
</error-page>
```

XML elements for working with error handling

Element	Description
`<error-page>`	Specifies an HTML page or JSP that's displayed when the application encounters an uncaught exception or a certain type of HTTP status code.
`<exception-type>`	Uses the fully qualified class name to specify a Java exception.
`<error-code>`	Specifies the number of a valid HTTP status code.
`<location>`	Specifies the location of the HTML page or JSP that's displayed.

Description

- In the web.xml file, you can use the error-page element to specify the error pages that should be displayed when the application encounters (1) uncaught exceptions or (2) specific HTTP status codes.

- In the web.xml file, you must place all error-page elements after all servlet and servlet-mapping elements.

- For more information about HTTP status codes, see chapter 15.

Figure 6-16   How to implement custom error handling

Perspective

The primary goal of this chapter has been to show you how to use the Model-View-Controller pattern, or Model 2 architecture, to structure a web application. In addition, this chapter has presented other skills that should help you structure your code so it's easier to develop and maintain. In the next few chapters, you'll learn some additional servlet and JSP skills that expand upon the principles presented in this chapter.

Summary

- The *Model 1 architecture* is commonly used for web applications with limited processing requirements. In this architecture, JSPs are used to handle both requests and responses, and *JavaBeans* are the business classes that represent the business data and do the business processing.

- The *Model-View-Controller (MVC) pattern,* or *Model 2 architecture*, is commonly used for web applications with significant processing requirements. In this pattern, servlets are the *controllers*, JSPs deliver the *views*, and JavaBeans are the business classes that *model* the business objects.

- The data for the business objects in a web application are stored in *data stores* like files and databases, which can be referred to as *persistent data storage*. The I/O operations for these stores are usually done by the methods in data classes.

- When using the MVC pattern, a servlet uses the RequestDispatcher object to forward the request and response objects to the JSP that's going to present the view.

- You can use JavaScript for *data validation* on the client. Or, you can use a servlet for data validation on the server.

- You can include files in a JSP at *translation time* or *request time*.

- The web.xml file consists of *XML tags* that define XML *elements*. The *root element* for this file is the web-app element. When one element is coded within another element, it can be called a *child element*.

- You can use the web.xml file to provide *initialization parameters* that apply to the entire web application or to specific servlets. Then, you can get the values of these parameters in the init method of a servlet.

- You can use the web.xml file to provide *servlet mapping* that maps the URL for a directory or filename to a specific servlet.

- You can use the web.xml file to provide custom error pages for specific exception types or for errors represented by specific *HTTP status codes*.

Terms

Model 1 architecture
pattern
Model-View-Controller pattern
MVC pattern
model
view
controller
Model 2 architecture
persistent data storage
data store
forward
redirect
data validation
JavaScript

function
translation time
include directive
request time
include action
XML tag
element
root element
child element
comment
initialization parameter
servlet initialization parameter
context initialization parameter
servlet mapping
HTTP status code

Objectives

- Use the MVC pattern to develop your web applications so servlets control the processing and JSPs do the presentation.

- Provide for server-side data validation in your applications.

- Include files in your JSPs at translation time or request time.

- Use the web.xml file to set initialization parameters and use your servlets to get the parameters.

- Use the web.xml file to provide servlet mapping and custom error handling.

- Describe the Model 1 architecture and the applications for which it is appropriate.

- Describe the Model-View-Controller pattern, and explain how it can help you develop web applications that are easier to develop and maintain.

- Describe the way the controller, view, model, and data store are used within an application that follows the MVC pattern.

- Distinguish between the use of JavaScript and servlets for data validation.

- Describe the use of include files.

- Describe the use of the web.xml file.

Exercise 6-1   Use include and web.xml files

1. Run the HTML document named join_email_list.html in the email6 directory so it runs the EmailServlet class, which runs show_email_entry.jsp if the data is valid or get_missing_fields.jsp if it isn't.

2. Modify the show_email_entry.jsp so it uses the two include files shown in figure 6-10. These files are located in the includes directory. First, include them at translation time, and then at request time.

3. Use a servlet initialization parameter to supply the location and name of the text file that's passed to the UserIO class. Make sure that your servlet code handles a null value if this parameter can't be read properly.

4. Implement servlet mapping so a URL for email6/email.jsp will be mapped to the EmailServlet class. To test this, modify the join_email_list.html page so it requests this URL rather than the EmailServlet class.

Exercise 6-2   Modify the Email List application

In this exercise, you'll modify the HTML document and the servlet for the Email List application that you worked with in exercise 6-1. You will also create a new JSP that provides for another type of error message.

1. Modify the HTML document named join_email_list.html that's in the email6 directory so it has this line of text after the Email address box: "I'm interested in these types of music." Then, follow this line with a list box that has options for Rock, Country, Bluegrass, and Folk music, but don't provide a selected value. When you're done, this document should still link to the EmailServlet class in the email6 directory.

2. Add more data validation to the EmailServlet class so it not only checks to make sure that the three text boxes have entries, but also that at least one of the music options has been selected in the list box. Then, if one or more text boxes don't have entries, the servlet should still call the JSP named get_missing_fields.jsp (don't bother to change that JSP). And if all the data is valid, the servlet should still call the JSP named show_email_entry.jsp (don't bother to change that one either). But if the text boxes are okay and no music option has been selected, the servlet should call a new JSP that's named no_music_option.jsp. This JSP should have this message above the list box: "Please select at least one music option." Be sure not to add a record to the data store until all data is validated.

3. Test the HTML document, the servlet, and the JSPs by running the application.

7

How to work with sessions and cookies

In all but the simplest of web applications, you need to keep track of the user as the user moves through the web application. Fortunately, the servlet API makes it relatively easy to do this. In this chapter, you'll learn how to use the servlet API to keep track of sessions, and you'll learn how to use the servlet API to work with cookies.

An introduction to session tracking **204**
Why session tracking is difficult with HTTP 204
How session tracking works in Java 204
An application that needs session tracking 206
How to work with sessions **208**
How to set and get session attributes 208
More methods of the session object 210
How to enable or disable cookies 212
How to use URL encoding to track sessions without cookies 214
How to work with cookies **216**
An introduction to cookies 216
How to create and use cookies 218
How to view and delete cookies 220
Four methods for working with cookies 222
A utility class for working with cookies 224
How to work with URL rewriting and hidden fields **226**
How to use URL rewriting to pass parameters 226
How to use hidden fields to pass parameters 228
The Download application **230**
The user interface 230
The file structure 230
The code for the JSPs and servlets 230
Perspective **240**

An introduction to session tracking

Keeping track of users as they move around a web site is known as *session tracking*. So to start, you'll learn how the servlet API tracks sessions, and you'll be introduced to a web application that needs session tracking.

Why session tracking is difficult with HTTP

Figure 7-1 shows why session tracking is more difficult for web applications that use HTTP than it is for other types of applications. To start, a browser on a client requests a page from a web server. After the web server returns the page, it drops the connection. Then, if the browser makes additional requests the web server has no way to associate the browser with its previous requests. Since HTTP doesn't maintain *state*, it is known as a *stateless protocol*. (In contrast, FTP maintains state between requests so it is known as a *stateful protocol*.)

How session tracking works in Java

Figure 7-1 also shows how the servlet API keeps track of sessions. To start, a browser on a client requests a JSP or servlet from the web server, which passes the request to the servlet engine. Then, the servlet engine checks if the request includes an ID for the Java session. If it doesn't, the servlet engine creates a unique ID for the session plus a *session object* that can be used to store the data for the session. From that point on, the web server uses the session ID to relate each browser request to the session object, even though the server still drops the HTTP connection after returning each page.

By default, the servlet API uses a *cookie* to store the session ID within the client's browser. This is an extension of the HTTP protocol. Then, when the next request is made, this cookie is added to the request. However, if cookies have been disabled within a browser, this type of session tracking won't work.

To get around this problem, the servlet API provides a way to rewrite the URL so it includes the session ID. This is known as *URL encoding*, and it works even if cookies have been disabled within a browser. However, you have to provide for this encoding in your servlets and JSPs as shown in figure 7-6. In contrast, cookies are automatically used for session tracking so you don't have to provide any code for them.

Why session tracking is difficult with HTTP

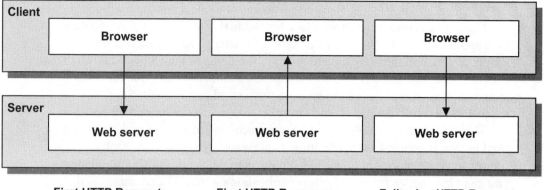

First HTTP Request:
The browser requests a
page.

First HTTP Response:
The server returns the
requested page and drops
the connection.

Following HTTP Requests:
The browser requests a
page. The web server has no
way to associate the browser
with its previous request.

How Java keeps track of sessions

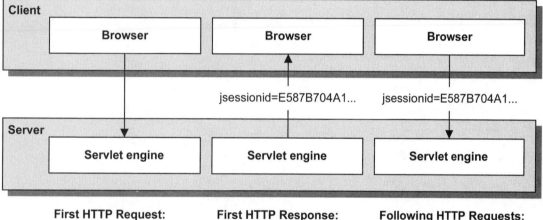

First HTTP Request:
The browser requests a
JSP or servlet. The servlet
engine creates a session
object and assigns
an ID for the session.

First HTTP Response:
The server returns the
requested page and the
ID for the session.

Following HTTP Requests:
The browser requests a JSP
or servlet. The servlet engine
uses the session ID to
associate the browser
with its session object.

Description

- HTTP is a *stateless protocol*. Once a browser makes a request, it drops the connection to the server. So to maintain *state*, a web application must use *session tracking*.
- By default, the servlet API uses a *cookie* to store a session ID in each browser. Then, the browser passes the cookie to the server with each request.
- To provide session tracking when cookies are disabled in the browser, you can use *URL encoding* to store the session ID in the URL for each page of an application.
- To store the data for each session, the server creates a *session object*.

Figure 7-1   An introduction to session tracking

An application that needs session tracking

Figure 7-2 shows the user interface for the first two pages of a Shopping Cart application. Here, the first page allows the user to add an item to the shopping cart, and the second page displays the items in the cart and allows the user to update the quantity or remove an item. Without session tracking, this application wouldn't be able to associate the second request with the first request. As a result, the cart would never be able to display more than one item.

Throughout this chapter, you'll be introduced to snippets of code that are used in this Shopping Cart application. If necessary, you can refer back to these figures to view the user interface. To see the complete code for this application, you can view the source code for this application on the CD that comes with this book. The JSP code is stored in the murach\cart7 directory, and the servlet code is stored in the murach\WEB-INF\classes\cart7 directory.

The Index page

Chapter 7 - The Shopping Cart application - Microsoft Internet Explorer

File   Edit   View   Favorites   Tools   Help

Back ▼ ▼ Search Favorites Media

Address http://localhost:8080/murach/cart7/index.jsp   Go   Links »

CD list

Description	Price	
86 (the band) - True Life Songs and Pictures	$14.95	Add To Cart
Paddlefoot - The first CD	$12.95	Add To Cart
Paddlefoot - The second CD	$14.95	Add To Cart
Joe Rut - Genuine Wood Grained Finish	$14.95	Add To Cart

Local intranet

The Cart page

Chapter 7 - The Shopping Cart application - Microsoft Internet Explorer

File   Edit   View   Favorites   Tools   Help

Back ▼ ▼ Search Favorites Media

Address http://localhost:8080/murach/servlet/cart7.CartServlet?productCode=pf01   Go   Links »

Your shopping cart

Qty	Description	Price	Amount	
1 Update	86 (the band) - True Life Songs and Pictures	$14.95	$14.95	Remove Item
1 Update	Paddlefoot - The first CD	$12.95	$12.95	Remove Item
To change the quantity, enter the new book quantity and click on the Update button.				

Continue Shopping

Checkout

Done   Local intranet

Description

- To view the code for this version of the Shopping Cart application, you can view the JSP code that's in the murach\cart7 directory and the servlet code that's in the murach\WEB-INF\classes\cart7 directory.

Figure 7-2   An application that needs session tracking

How to work with sessions

This topic shows how to use the servlet API to track sessions. To start, it shows how to track sessions when cookies are enabled in the user's browser. Then, it shows how to track sessions even if cookies have been disabled in the user's browser.

How to set and get session attributes

Figure 7-3 shows how to get a session object and how to get and set the attributes of that object. Since the session object is a built-in JSP object, you only need to get a session object when you're working with servlets. To do that, you can call the getSession method of the request object as shown in the first example. Then, if the session object doesn't exist, this method creates a new one. Usually, though, it just accesses the one that already exists.

From the session object, you can call the setAttribute method to set any Java object as an attribute of the current session. To do that, you specify a name for the attribute and the name of the object that you want to store. For instance, the second and third examples show how to store a String object and a Cart object. Here, the Cart object is a business object that is used to store all of the items for a Shopping Cart application.

Similarly, you can use the getAttribute method to return any attribute that you've set. To do that, you specify the name of the attribute. Since this method returns an object of the Object class, though, you need to cast each object to the appropriate class as shown by the fourth and fifth examples. In addition to these get and set methods, you can use the removeAttribute method to delete any attribute from a session object.

If you work with an older web application, you may find that it uses the putValue, getValue, and removeValue methods instead of the setAttribute, getAttribute, and removeAttribute methods. That's because the Attribute methods are newer methods that were introduced in version 2.2 of the servlet API. The Value methods have been deprecated in the later releases, which means they should no longer be used. As a result, all new web applications should use the Attribute methods.

Common methods for working with sessions

A method of the request object

```
public HttpSession getSession()
```

Three methods of the session object

```
public void setAttribute(String name, Object value)
public Object getAttribute(String name)
public void removeAttribute(String name)
```

Java code for working with session objects

Code that gets a session object

```
HttpSession session = request.getSession();
```

Code that sets an attribute to a String object

```
session.setAttribute("productCode", productCode);
```

Code that sets an attribute to a user-defined object

```
Cart cart = new Cart(productCode);
session.setAttribute("cart", cart);
```

Code that gets a String object

```
String productCode = (String) session.getAttribute("productCode");
```

Code that gets a user-defined object

```
Cart cart = (Cart) session.getAttribute("cart");
if (cart == null)
    cart = new Cart();
```

Code that removes an object

```
session.removeAttribute("productCode");
```

Description

- Since the session object is a built-in JSP object, you don't need to create the session object when working with JSPs. It is created when a browser makes the first request to a site. It is destroyed when the session ends.

- A session ends when a specified amount of time elapses without another request or when the user exits the browser.

- The getSession method of the HttpRequest object provides access to the built-in session object. This method only creates a session object if one doesn't already exist.

- The setAttribute, getAttribute, and removeAttribute methods were introduced in version 2.2 of the servlet API. With older versions of the servlet API, you can use the putValue, getValue, and removeValue methods to accomplish the same tasks, but these methods are now deprecated.

Figure 7-3   How to set and get session attributes

More methods of the session object

Most of the time, you'll use the methods presented in the last figure to work with the session object. However, figure 7-4 presents some other methods of the session object that you may want to use.

You can use the getAttributeNames method of the session object to return the names of all attributes stored in the session object. To do that, you use the getAttributeNames method to return an Enumeration object. Then, you can use the hasMoreElements and nextElement methods of the Enumeration object to loop through the names as shown in the code example. This can be useful for debugging.

You can use the getId method to return the ID that the servlet engine is using for the current session. This ID is a long string that uniquely identifies each Java session. Here again, this can be useful for debugging.

You can use the isNew method to check if the client is new or if the client chooses to not join the session. This method returns a true value if the client is accessing the site for the first time in a new session or if cookies have been disabled on the browser.

You can use the last two methods to control when a session is invalidated. When this happens, all objects that have been stored in the session object are released from the session object. By default, the session will be invalidated if a user is inactive for half an hour, but you can use the setMaxInactiveInterval method to change this default. If, for example, you supply an argument of –1, the session object won't be invalidated until the user exits the browser. If necessary, though, you can call the invalidate method whenever you want to invalidate the session. If you call a method from the session object after it has been invalidated, that method will throw an IllegalStateException.

More methods of the session object

public Enumeration getAttributeNames()

This method returns a java.util.Enumeration object that contains the names of all attributes in the HttpSession object. It replaces the deprecated getValueNames method that returns an array of String values.

public String getId()

This method returns the unique Java session identifier that the servlet engine generates for each session.

public boolean isNew()

This method returns a true value if the client does not yet know about the session or if the client chooses not to join the session. This can happen if the session relies upon cookies and the browser doesn't accept cookies.

public void setMaxInactiveInterval(int seconds)

By default, the session object sets the maximum inactive interval to 1800 seconds (30 minutes). As a result, if the user is inactive for 30 minutes, the session will be invalidated. To increase or decrease this interval, supply a positive integer value. To create a session that won't end until the user closes the browser, supply a negative integer such as –1.

public void invalidate()

This method invalidates the session and unbinds any objects that are bound to it.

Examples

A method that gets all the names of the attributes for a session

```
Enumeration names = session.getAttributeNames();
while (names.hasMoreElements()){
    System.out.println((String) names.nextElement());
}
```

A method that gets the ID for a session

```
String jSessionId = session.getId();
```

A method that sets the inactive interval for a session

```
session.setMaxInactiveInterval(60*60*24);   // one day
session.setMaxInactiveInterval(-1);         // until the browser is closed
```

A method that invalidates the session and unbinds any objects

```
session.invalidate();
```

Description

- If the session object has been explicitly or implicitly invalidated, all methods of the session object will throw an IllegalStateException.

- For more information about these and other methods of the session object, you can look up the HttpSession interface in the javax.servlet.http package in the documentation for the Servlet and JavaServer Pages API.

Figure 7-4   More methods of the session object

How to enable or disable cookies

There are two types of cookies. A *per-session cookie* is stored on the browser until the user closes the browser, and a *persistent cookie* can be stored on the user's hard disk for up to 3 years. Since the session tracking code in the previous two figures relies on per-session cookies, it won't work unless per-session cookies are enabled in the user's browser.

That's why figure 7-5 shows how to enable or disable cookies in a browser. To test sessions that rely on cookies, you'll need to enable cookies in your browser. Conversely, to test code that's intended to work even if cookies have been disabled, you'll need to disable cookies in your browser.

If you're using the Internet Explorer 6.0, the recommended privacy setting is Medium. This default setting enables per-session and persistent cookies. To disable both per-session cookies and persistent cookies, you can select a privacy setting that blocks all cookies as shown in this figure. However, you can use the Advanced button to override the default settings so that your browser accepts per-session cookies but disables persistent cookies.

For earlier versions of Internet Explorer, you control cookies through the Security tab. Here, the recommended security level is the Medium security level. The default settings for this level enable per-session and persistent cookies. In contrast, the defaults for the High security level disable both per-session cookies and persistent cookies. However, you can use the Custom tab to modify the defaults for the High security level so this level allows per-session cookies.

An Internet Explorer dialog box with disabled cookies

How to enable cookies for the Internet Explorer 6.0

1. Pull down the Tools menu and select the Internet Options command.
2. Select the Privacy tab.
3. Use the slider control to set the security level to accept cookies.

How to enable cookies for the Internet Explorer 5.5 and earlier

1. Pull down the Tools menu and select the Internet Options command.
2. Select the Security tab.
3. Use the slider control to set the security level to Medium, Medium-Low, or Low.

How to enable cookies for Netscape

1. Pull down the Edit menu and select the Preference command.
2. Click on the Advanced option.
3. Choose one of the options that accept cookies.

Description

*   If you're using Internet Explorer 6.0, click on the Advanced button to enable or disable *persistent cookies* that are permanently stored on the user's computer or *per-session cookies* that are deleted when the user closes the browser. For earlier versions of Internet Explorer, you can do this by selecting the Custom Level button in the Security tab.

Figure 7-5   How to enable or disable cookies

How to use URL encoding to track sessions without cookies

Although cookies are enabled by default on most web browsers, some people choose to disable cookies in their browsers. When you're programming a web application, you have to take this into account. If the web application isn't a critical part of the web site, it may be acceptable to display a message that explains that this part of the site won't work properly if cookies have been disabled. Otherwise, you can make the application work even when cookies have been disabled by using *URL encoding* to track sessions as shown in figure 7-6.

To use URL encoding, you must convert all of the HTML pages in the application to JSPs. Then, you can use the encodeURL method of the response object to encode all the URLs for the JSPs that are used in the application. Once you do that, the session ID is added to a URL whenever the URL is requested from a browser with disabled cookies. In the Address box of the browser in this figure, for example, you can see that an ID has been added to the end of the URL, but before the parameters.

When you use URL rewriting, you must be sure to encode all URLs in the application. If you forget one, the application will lose track of the session as soon as the web server returns a response object that contains a URL that isn't encoded. However, if a servlet forwards a request to a JSP in an MVC pattern, you don't need to encode the URL because it isn't sent to the browser.

To test an application that uses URL encoding, you need to disable cookies in your browser as shown in the previous figure. Then, the URL for each page in the application should include the ID for the Java session. However, if you enable cookies in your browser, the URLs of the application won't display the ID for the Java session. This shows that the encodeURL method only rewrites the URLs of the application when necessary.

The syntax for the encodeURL method of the response object

```
public String encodeURL(String url)
```

How to encode a URL

In a JSP that calls a servlet

```
<%
    String encodedURL = response.encodeURL("../servlet/cart7.CartServlet");
%>
<form action="<%=encodedURL%>" method="post">
```

In a JSP that uses a single tag and a second parameter

```
<a href="
    <%=response.encodeURL("../servlet/cart7.CartServlet?productCode=jr01")%>
">Add to Cart</a>
```

A URL after it has been encoded

Description

- If the user has disabled per-session cookies, you can use *URL encoding* to keep track of the ID for the session. To do that, you must convert any relevant HTML pages to JSPs, and you must encode all relevant URLs.
- When you encode a URL, the session ID is passed to the browser in the URL.

Figure 7-6   How to use URL encoding to track sessions without cookies

How to work with cookies

In the last topic, you learned that the servlet API uses per-session cookies. Now, you'll learn more about working with cookies including how to create a persistent cookie that can be stored on the user's computer for up to three years.

An introduction to cookies

Figure 7-7 introduces you to some basic facts about cookies. To start, it shows some examples of cookies. These examples show that a cookie is nothing more than a name/value pair. For example, the name of the first cookie is jsessionid, and its value is

```
D1F15245171203E8670487F020544490
```

This is a typical value for the cookie that's generated by the servlet API to keep track of sessions. However, you can create your own cookies to store any type of string data.

Once you create a cookie, you include it in the server's response to the browser. Then, the browser will store the cookie on the client machine, and it will send it back to the server with all subsequent requests. Remember, though, that some browsers have disabled cookies so you can't always count on using them.

Once you have stored a cookie on a browser's PC, you can use it to make your web application work better for the user. For instance, you can use cookies to verify that users have registered before so they don't have to register again. You can use them to customize pages that display information that's specific to the users. And you can use them to focus advertising that is likely to appeal to the users.

Examples of cookies

```
jsessionid=D1F15245171203E8670487F020544490
user_id=87
email=jsmith@hotmail.com
userName=jsmith
passwordCookie=opensesame
```

How cookies work

- A cookie is a name/value pair that is stored in a browser.

- On the server, a web application creates a cookie and sends it to the browser. On the client, the browser saves the cookie and sends it back to the server every time it accesses a page from that server.

- Cookies can be set to persist within the user's browser for up to 3 years.

- Some users disable cookies in their browsers. As a result, you can't always count on all users having their cookies enabled.

- Browsers generally accept only 20 cookies from each site and 300 cookies total. In addition, they can limit each cookie to 4 kilobytes.

- A cookie can be associated with one or more subdomain names.

Typical uses for cookies

- **To allow users to skip login and registration forms** that gather data like user name, password, address, or credit card data.

- **To customize pages** that display information like weather reports, sports scores, and stock quotations.

- **To focus advertising** like banner ads that target the user's interests.

Description

- A per-session cookie that holds the session ID is automatically created for each session. That cookie is used to relate the browser to the session object.

- You can also create and send other cookies to a user's browser. You can use these cookies to access user-specific data that's stored in a file or database.

Figure 7-7   An introduction to cookies

How to create and use cookies

To create and use cookies, you use the constructors and methods shown in figure 7-8. After you use the constructor of the Cookie class to create a cookie, you can use the methods of this class to set parameters for the cookie and to get its name and value. Then, you can use the addCookie method of the response object to add a cookie to a browser's PC. And you can use the getCookies method of the request object to get an array of all the cookies on the browser's PC. These methods are illustrated by the two examples.

The first example uses four statements to create a cookie and add it to the response object. The first statement creates the Cookie object. The second statement calls the setMaxAge method to set the life of the cookie on the browser's PC to two years (60 seconds times 60 minutes times 24 hours times 365 days times 2 years). The third statement sets the path for the cookie so it's available to the entire web application. And the fourth statement adds the cookie to the response object so it will be returned to the browser and added to the browser's PC.

The second example retrieves a cookie from the request object that's been sent from a browser. Here, the first statement returns an array of Cookie objects from the request object. Then, the following statements loop through the array to return the cookie that's named userIdCookie. To do that, these statements use the getName and getValue methods of the Cookie object.

Constructors and methods

The constructor of the Cookie class

```
public Cookie(String cookieName, String cookieValue)
```

The methods of the Cookie class

```
public void setMaxAge(int lifeInSeconds)
public void setPath(String path)
public String getName()
public String getValue()
```

A method of the response object

```
public void addCookie(Cookie cookieName)
```

A method of the request object

```
public Cookie[] getCookies()
```

Examples

Code that creates and sets a cookie

```
Cookie userIdCookie = new Cookie("userIdCookie", userId);
userIdCookie.setMaxAge(60*60*24*365*2); //set the age to 2 years
userIdCookie.setPath("/"); // allow access by the entire application
response.addCookie(userIdCookie);
```

Code that gets the cookie

```
Cookie[] cookies = request.getCookies();
String cookieName = "userIdCookie";
String cookieValue = "";
for (int i=0; i<cookies.length; i++) {
    Cookie cookie = cookies[i];
    if (cookieName.equals(cookie.getName()))
        cookieValue = cookie.getValue();
}
```

Description

- To create a persistent cookie, you must use the setMaxAge method to a positive number. If, for example, you set the age of the cookie to 60*60*24*365, the cookie will persist for 1 year (60 seconds times 60 minutes times 24 hours times 365 days).

- To create a per-session cookie, set the maximum age to −1. Then, the cookie will be deleted when the user exits the browser.

- To allow the entire application to access the cookie, you must use its setPath method to set its path to "/".

Figure 7-8   How to create and use cookies

How to view and delete cookies

When you're testing or debugging an application, you may want to view all of the cookies for a browser to make sure the right ones are being stored. Similarly, you may want to delete all the cookies from the browser so you can add new cookies to it. In figure 7-9, you can learn how to do both of these tasks.

To display all the cookies for a browser, you can write a JSP that uses the getCookies method of the request object to get an array of cookies. Then, you can code a loop that gets each name in the array and displays it. This is illustrated by the first example.

To delete all the cookies for a browser, you can get the array of cookies again. Then, you can code a loop that uses the setMaxAge method to set the age of each cookie to zero. This is illustrated by the second example.

A JSP that shows all cookies for the current server

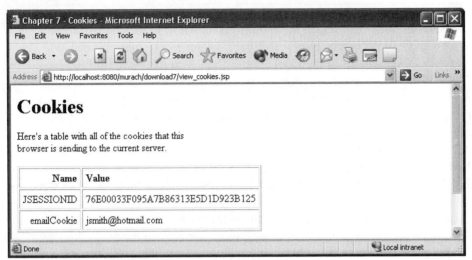

Code that displays all cookies

```
<%
  Cookie[] cookies = request.getCookies();
  for (int i=0; i<cookies.length; i++) {
      Cookie cookie = cookies[i];
%>
  <tr>
    <td align="right"><%= cookie.getName() %></td>
    <td><%= cookie.getValue() %></td>
  </tr>
<%
  }
%>
```

Code that deletes all persistent cookies

```
<%
  Cookie[] cookies = request.getCookies();
  for (int i=0; i<cookies.length; i++) {
      Cookie cookie = cookies[i];
      cookie.setMaxAge(0); //delete the cookie
      cookie.setPath("/"); //allow the entire application to access it
      response.addCookie(cookie);
  }
%>
```

Description

- To delete a persistent cookie from a browser, set the age of a cookie to 0.
- To view the complete code for JSPs that display and delete cookies, you can open the JSP files named view_cookies.jsp and delete_cookies.jsp that are stored in the murach\download7 directory on the CD that comes with this book.

Figure 7-9   How to view and delete cookies

Four methods for working with cookies

Most of the time, you'll use the techniques shown in in the last two figures to work with Cookie objects. However, figure 7-10 presents more information about four of the methods of the Cookie object that you may find useful.

As you've already seen, you can use the setPath method to set the path for a cookie. By default, when a browser returns a cookie, it returns it to the directory that originally sent the cookie to the browser and to all subdirectories of that directory. But that's often not what you want. If, for example, a servlet sends a cookie to the browser, then all servlets will be able to access the cookie, but JSPs won't be able to access that cookie. As a result, it's common to use the setPath method to set the path for the cookie to a slash (/) so that the entire web application can access the cookie.

You can use the setDomain method to set the domain for the cookie. By default, when a browser returns a cookie, it returns it only to the exact domain name that originally sent the cookie to the browser. Since that's usually what you want, you usually don't need to use this method. But if you have a web site that uses server subdomains, you can use this method to return the cookie to all of the subdomains. To illustrate, assume that you have a website named *www.murach.com* that has two subdomains *www.java.murach.com* and *www.cobol.murach.com*. Then, if you set the domain to

```
.murach.com
```

all three of these websites can access the cookie. In other words, when the browser sends the cookie to one subdomain, it's possible for the other subdomains to retrieve the cookie.

You can use the setSecure method to create a secure cookie. By default, a browser will return a cookie across a regular HTTP connection or across a secure, encrypted connection. But if you're sending sensitive data such as a password or a credit card number, you can use this method to specify that the cookie should only be sent across a secure connection.

You can use the setVersion method to set the version of the cookie protocol that you want to use. By default, a cookie uses version 0 of the cookie protocol. Since this protocol has been around the longest and is the most widely supported, that's usually what you want. But if there's a compelling reason to use version 1 of the cookie protocol, you can use this protocol by specifying an integer value of 1 for this method.

Four methods of the Cookie class

public void setPath(String path**)**

By default, when you send a cookie to a browser, the browser will return the cookie to all servlets and JSPs within the directory that sent the cookie and all subdirectories of that directory. To make a cookie available to the entire application, you can set the path to a slash (/). To make a cookie available to a directory and its subdirectories, you can specify a path like /cart. Then, the browser will return the cookie to the cart directory and all subdirectories. However, the directory that originally sent the cookie must be within this directory or one of its subdirectories.

public void setDomain(String domainPattern**)**

By default, the browser only returns a cookie to the host that sent the cookie. To return a cookie to other hosts within the same domain, you can set a domain pattern like .ads.com. Then, the browser will return the cookie to any subdomain of www.ads.com like www.travel.ads.com or www.camera.ads.com.

public void setSecure(boolean flag**)**

By default, the browser sends a cookie over a regular connection or an encrypted connection. To protect cookies that store sensitive data such as passwords or credit card number, you can supply a true value for this method. Then, the cookie will only be sent over a secure connection.

public void setVersion(int version**)**

By default, Java creates cookies that use version 0 of the cookie protocol that was developed by Netscape. Since this is the cookie protocol that has been around the longest, it is the most widely supported. However, you can specify an int value of 1 for this method to use the new version of the cookie protocol, which is version 1.

Description

- All of these set methods have corresponding get methods.
- For more information about these methods and other methods for working with cookies, use your web browser to look up the Cookie class in the javax.servlet.http package that's in the documentation for the Servlet and JavaServer Pages API.

Figure 7-10   Four methods for working with cookies

A utility class for working with cookies

As you've already seen, you must loop through an array of cookies whenever you want to get the value for one cookie. Since this can be tedious, it's common to place the code that loops through the array of cookies in a utility class like the one shown in figure 7-11. Then, you can easily retrieve the value of a cookie by calling the utility class.

The CookieUtil class shown in this figure contains one static method named getCookieValue. This method accepts an array of cookies and the name of the cookie that you want to get. Then, it loops through the array of cookies and returns the value that matches the name of the cookie. If it doesn't find the name of the cookie in the array, this method returns an empty string.

Since you might want to access this class from more than one servlet or JSP, you should store this class in a central location. For instance, this class is stored in the util package for the murach applications. In that case, though, you need to import the package that contains the utilities. Once you do that, you can use Java statements like the two at the bottom of this figure to get the value of any cookie.

A utility class that gets the value of a cookie

```
package util;

import javax.servlet.*;
import javax.servlet.http.*;

public class CookieUtil {

    public static String getCookieValue(Cookie[] cookies,
        String cookieName) {

        String cookieValue = "";
        Cookie cookie;
        for (int i=0; i<cookies.length; i++) {
            cookie = cookies[i];
            if (cookieName.equals(cookie.getName())){
                cookieValue = cookie.getValue();
            }
        }
        return cookieValue;
    }

}
```

Code that uses the CookieUtil class to get the value of a cookie

```
Cookie[] cookies = request.getCookies();
String emailAddress = CookieUtil.getCookieValue(cookies, "emailCookie");
```

Description

- To make it easier to get the value of a cookie, you can create a utility class that contains a method that accepts an array of Cookie objects and the name of the cookie and then returns the value of the cookie.

Figure 7-11   A utility class for working with cookies

How to work with URL rewriting and hidden fields

In the early days of web programming, programmers used URL rewriting and hidden fields to track sessions. Today, you can use the servlet API to track sessions. However, you can still use URL rewriting and hidden fields to pass parameters between the browser and the server.

In particular, URL rewriting and hidden fields are handy if you need to pass data for a single request. Rather than storing that type of data in the session object, which takes up memory, you can use URL rewriting and hidden fields to pass data from page to page.

How to use URL rewriting to pass parameters

Figure 7-12 shows how to use *URL rewriting* to pass parameters from the browser to the server. This should already be familiar to you because that's how parameters are passed from HTML documents to a JSP or servlet when the Get method is used.

For instance, the first example shows how to code a URL that adds a product to a cart. Here, the URL calls the CartServlet and passes a parameter named productCode with a value of 8601 to the servlet. Since URL rewriting always uses the Get method of the HTTP protocol, this will cause the productCode parameter to be displayed in the browser as shown in this figure.

The second example shows that you can use URL rewriting to pass a parameter to a JSP and that you can use URL rewriting within a Form tag. Then, the last example shows that you can use a JSP expression to pass a value to a URL. Here, the product code is an expression that's evaluated at runtime.

Although URL rewriting works even if cookies have been disabled, it has the four limitations that are summarized in this figure. One way to get around some of these limitations is to use hidden fields as shown in the next figure. But as you will see, hidden fields aren't secure either.

The syntax for URL rewriting

```
url?parameterName1=parameterValue1&parameterName2=parameterValue2&...
```

An example of URL rewriting that adds a product code to a URL

```
<a href="../servlet/cart7.CartServlet?productCode=8601">Add to cart</a>
```

The link displayed in a browser

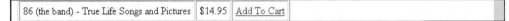

| 86 (the band) - True Life Songs and Pictures | $14.95 | Add To Cart |

The URL that's displayed when you click on the link

More examples

URL rewriting that calls a JSP from a Form tag

```
<form action="../cart7/cart.jsp?productCode=jr01">
```

URL rewriting that uses a JSP expression for the product code

```
<a href="../servlet/cart7.CartServlet?productCode=<%= productCode %>" >
   Add to cart</a>
```

Four limitations of URL rewriting

- Most browsers limit the number of characters that can be passed by a URL to 2,000 characters.
- Since URL rewriting only works with the HTTP Get method, all variables are visible in the browser's URL field.
- If a user creates a bookmark for a page that uses URL rewriting, the parameters for the page are included in the bookmark, which usually isn't what you want.
- You can't include white spaces and it's difficult to include special characters such as the ? and & characters in parameter values.

Description

- You can use *URL rewriting* to pass parameters to a servlet or JSP. To do that, you add the parameters to the end of the URL.
- Whenever necessary, you can code variables that provide the values of the parameters in the URL.

Figure 7-12   How to use URL rewriting to pass parameters

How to use hidden fields to pass parameters

In chapter 3, you learned how to code *hidden fields* within an HTML form. Now, figure 7-13 shows how to use hidden fields to pass a parameter from a browser to the server. In particular, it shows how to pass a parameter named productCode to a servlet named CartServlet.

Although the first example in this figure accomplishes the same task as the URL rewriting example in the previous figure, there are a couple advantages to hidden fields. First, a hidden field can contain white spaces and other special characters that are difficult to work with when using URL rewriting. Second, since a hidden field is part of a form, it can be passed to the server with the Post method. As a result, the parameter isn't shown in the URL.

The second example in this figure shows that you can use a JSP expression to assign a value to a hidden field. Here, the form contains a hidden field that contains the product code, a text box for the quantity, and an Update button. However, the value for the hidden field isn't hard-coded. Instead, a JSP expression retrieves the value for the hidden field. That way, when the user clicks on the Update button, the servlet can tell which product the user wants to update.

The code for a form that uses hidden text fields

```
<form action="../servlet/cart7.CartServlet" method="post">
  <input type="submit" value="Add To Cart">
  <input type="hidden" name="productCode" value="8601">
</form>
```

The form displayed in a browser

86 (the band) - True Life Songs and Pictures	$14.95	Add To Cart

The URL that's displayed when you click on the button

The code for a form that sets a hidden field with a JSP expression

```
<form action="/murach/servlet/cart7.servlet.CartServlet" method="post">
  <input type="hidden" name="productCode"
         value="<%=lineItem.getProductCode()%>" >
  <input type=text size=2 name="quantity"
         value="<%=lineItem.getQuantity()%>" >
  <input type="submit" name="updateButton" value="Update">
</form>
```

Description

- When you use *hidden fields*, you can use the HTTP Post method so the parameters aren't displayed in the browser.
- Because hidden fields are displayed in the source code for the page that's returned to the browser, anyone can view the parameters by selecting the Source command from the View menu of the browser. As a result, hidden fields aren't appropriate for secure data like passwords and credit card numbers.

Figure 7-13   How to use hidden fields to pass parameters

The Download application

At this point, you should have the basic skills for working with sessions, cookies, URL rewriting, and hidden fields. But it's hard to understand how to use these skills without seeing them in a complete application. That's why figure 7-14 presents an application that lets registered users download sound files from a web site. Although studying this application will take some page flipping because it's seven parts long, you can learn a lot from it.

The user interface

The user interface for the Download application consists of three pages. The Index page lets a user select a CD. Then, if the user hasn't already registered with the site, the Register page registers the user by gathering the user's first name, last name, and email address. Once the user is registered, the Downloads page lets the user select a song and format to download. If, for example, the user clicks on the MP3 link to the right of a song, that song is downloaded and played. Then, the user can return to the Index page by clicking on the Return to the Index page link.

The file structure

In part 2 of this figure, you can see the files that make up the Download application. To start, you can see that this application uses six JSP files: one for the Index page, one for the Register page, and one for the Download page for each of the four albums. Here, the Download pages follow a rigid naming convention. All of these pages begin with a four-character product code that identifies the CD, followed by an underscore character, followed by "download.jsp".

The sound files that are used by the CD follow a similar naming convention. These files are all stored in a subdirectory of the murach\sound directory where the subdirectory uses the four-character product code for the CD. Then, the RealAudio files have an extension of "rm", and the MP3 files have an extension of "mp3". When a modern browser goes to the URL for one of these files, it downloads and plays it.

The code for the JSPs and servlets

The code for the Index page in part 3 of this figure should be easy to follow. Note, however, that it provides URLs that pass the product code for the selected CD to the DownloadServlet. Since this JSP uses the encodeURL method of the response object to encode all four URLs, these URLs should be able to track the session even if cookies are disabled in the browser. Remember, though, that all of the URLs for the other JSPs have to be encoded too or session tracking will fail.

The Index page

The Register page

The Downloads page

Figure 7-14   The Download application (part 1 of 7)

The file structure for the jsp files

```
murach/download7/index.jsp
                 register.jsp
                 8601_download.jsp
                 pf01_download.jsp
                 pf02_download.jsp
                 jr01_download.jsp
```

The file structure for the servlets

```
murach/WEB-INF/classes/download7/DownloadServlet
                                  RegisterServlet
```

The file structure for the sound files

```
murach/sound/8601/*.rm
                  *.mp3
murach/sound/pf01/*.rm
                  *.mp3
murach/sound/pf02/*.rm
                  *.mp3
murach/sound/jr01/*.rm
                  *.mp3
```

Description

- The Download application is implemented by the six JSPs, two servlets, and two sound files for each downloadable song.

- The directory locations of these JSPs, servlets, and sound files is consistent with the structure of all web applications.

Figure 7-14   The Download application (part 2 of 7)

The code for the Index JSP

```
<!doctype html public "-//W3C//DTD HTML 4.0 Transitional//EN">
<html>

<head>
  <title>Chapter 7 - The Download application</title>
</head>

<body>

<h1>List of downloads</h1>

<p>Select the CD that you want to download from.</p>

<p>
<a href="<%= response.encodeURL(
        "../servlet/download7.DownloadServlet?productCode=8601") %>
        ">86 (the band) - True Life Songs and Pictures</a><br>

<a href="<%= response.encodeURL(
        "../servlet/download7.DownloadServlet?productCode=pf01")%>
        ">Paddlefoot - The first CD</a><br>

<a href="<%= response.encodeURL(
        "../servlet/download7.DownloadServlet?productCode=pf02")%>
        ">Paddlefoot - The second CD</a><br>

<a href="<%= response.encodeURL(
        "../servlet/download7.DownloadServlet?productCode=jr01")%>
        ">Joe Rut - Genuine Wood Grained Finish</a><br>

</body>

</html>
```

Description

- The index page provides URLs that pass the product code for the CD to the DownloadServlet.

- All of the URLs are encoded so they can be used to track the session if the browser has disabled cookies.

Figure 7-14   The Download application (part 3 of 7)

The code for the DownloadServlet gets the product code from the request object that was passed from the Index page. Then, it creates a session object by using the getSession method of the request object, and it sets the product code as an attribute of the session object. From this point on, this product code can be retrieved from the session object.

After that, the code creates a new User object and tries to get the data for this object from the User attribute of the session object. Then, if the session object contains a User object, which means that the user has called this servlet at least once before in this session, the new User object will get the data from the session object. Otherwise, the new User object will be set to null, which means that the user is calling this servlet for the first time.

The nested if statements that follow provide for three possibilities. First, if the User object is null and a cookie named emailCookie isn't available from previous sessions, the code forwards the request and response objects to the Register JSP. Second, if the User object is null but the cookie exists, which means the user has registered before, the code (1) uses the getUser method of the UserIO class to get the data for the User object from a file; (2) attaches the User object to the session object; and (3) forwards the request and response objects to the appropriate Download JSP. Third, if the User object exists, which means that either the emailCookie was available or the user has already registered in this session, the code forwards the request and response objects to the appropriate Download JSP.

If you study this code, you should be able to follow it. It may help to understand, though, that the RegisterServlet creates a User object from the user entries and adds this object to the session object. It also creates an emailCookie and adds it to the response object. Then, if your browser has cookies enabled, you won't have to register the next time you use this application. Otherwise, you will have to register each time you use this application. In part 6 of this figure, you can see the code for the RegisterServlet.

The code for DownloadServlet

```
package download7;
import java.io.*;
import javax.servlet.*;
import javax.servlet.http.*;
import business.User;
import data.UserIO;
import util.*;

public class DownloadServlet extends HttpServlet{

    public void doGet(HttpServletRequest request,
                      HttpServletResponse response)
                      throws IOException, ServletException {

        String productCode = request.getParameter("productCode");
        HttpSession session = request.getSession();
        session.setAttribute("productCode", productCode);
        User user = (User) session.getAttribute("user");

        // if the User object doesn't exist, check for the email cookie
        if (user == null){
            Cookie[] cookies = request.getCookies();
            String emailAddress =
                CookieUtil.getCookieValue(cookies, "emailCookie");

            // if the email cookie doesn't exist, go to the registration page
            if (emailAddress == null || emailAddress.equals("")){
                RequestDispatcher dispatcher =
                    getServletContext().getRequestDispatcher(
                        "/download7/register.jsp");
                dispatcher.forward(request, response);
            }

            // if the email cookie does exist, create the User object
            // from the email cookie and skip the registration page
            else{
                user = UserIO.getUser(emailAddress,
                    "../webapps/murach/web-inf/etc/UserEmail.txt");
                session.setAttribute("user", user);
                RequestDispatcher dispatcher =
                    getServletContext().getRequestDispatcher(
                        "/download7/" + productCode + "_download.jsp");
                dispatcher.forward(request, response);
            }
        }

        // if the User object exists, skip the registration page
        else{
            RequestDispatcher dispatcher =
                getServletContext().getRequestDispatcher(
                    "/download7/" + productCode + "_download.jsp");
            dispatcher.forward(request, response);
        }
    }
}
```

Figure 7-14   The Download application (part 4 of 7)

Since the code for the Register page works similarly to the Email List application of the previous chapters, it should be easy to follow. The only difference is that the Register page uses the encodeURL method of the response object to encode the URL in the Form tag, which is essential for browsers with disabled cookies.

What's more interesting is the code for the RegisterServlet in part 6 of this figure. It starts by retrieving the parameters that the user entered on the Register page. Then, this servlet creates a User object from these parameters and uses the UserIO class to write the User object to a file that's stored in the murach\WEB-INF\etc directory. After writing the file, this servlet stores the User object in the session object and creates a persistent cookie that stores the user's email address for two years. Last, this servlet uses the productCode variable to forward the request and response objects to the appropriate Download page.

The code for the Download page begins by retrieving the product code from the session object. Then, it uses the product code to locate the sound files for the CD. Depending on how the user's system is configured, clicking on a link may display the Download dialog box, or it may cause the sound file to download and automatically begin playing.

To understand how this application works without cookies, notice that the encodeURL method of the response object has been used to encode every URL that's returned to the client. That insures that session tracking will take place so the User object that's attached to the session object will be available until the session ends. Since all of the servlets forward the response object to a JSP, though, you don't have to encode the URLs in the servlets.

The code for the Register JSP

```
<!doctype html public "-//W3C//DTD HTML 4.0 Transitional//EN">
<html>

<head>
  <title>Chapter 7 - The Download application</title>
</head>

<body>

<h1>Download registration</h1>

<p>To register for our downloads, enter your name and email <br>
   address below. Then, click on the Submit button.</p>

<form action="<%= response.encodeURL("../servlet/download7.RegisterServlet")%>"
      method="post">

  <table cellspacing="5" border="0">
    <tr>
      <td align="right">First name:</td>
      <td><input type="text" name="firstName"></td>
    </tr>
    <tr>
      <td align="right">Last name:</td>
      <td><input type="text" name="lastName"></td>
    </tr>
    <tr>
      <td align="right">Email address:</td>
      <td><input type="text" name="emailAddress"></td>
    </tr>
    <tr>
      <td></td>
      <td><input type="submit" value="Submit"></td>
    </tr>
  </table>

</form>
</body>

</html>
```

Description

* This JSP is similar to the ones for the Email List application. The primary difference is that the URL is encoded so it provides for session tracking if the browser has cookies disabled.

Figure 7-14   The Download application (part 5 of 7)

The code for RegisterServlet

```
package download7;

import java.io.*;
import javax.servlet.*;
import javax.servlet.http.*;
import util.*;
import business.User;
import data.UserIO;

public class RegisterServlet extends HttpServlet{

    public void doPost(HttpServletRequest request,
                       HttpServletResponse response)
                       throws IOException, ServletException {

        String firstName = request.getParameter("firstName");
        String lastName = request.getParameter("lastName");
        String emailAddress = request.getParameter("emailAddress");

        User user = new User();
        user.setFirstName(firstName);
        user.setLastName(lastName);
        user.setEmailAddress(emailAddress);
        UserIO.addRecord(user,
            "../webapps/murach/web-inf/etc/UserEmail.txt");

        HttpSession session = request.getSession();
        session.setAttribute("user", user);
        String productCode = (String) session.getAttribute("productCode");

        Cookie emailCookie = new Cookie("emailCookie", emailAddress);
        emailCookie.setMaxAge(60*60*24*365*2); //set its age to 2 years
        emailCookie.setPath("/"); //allow the entire application to access it
        response.addCookie(emailCookie);

        RequestDispatcher dispatcher =
            getServletContext().getRequestDispatcher(
                "/download7/" + productCode + "_download.jsp");
        dispatcher.forward(request, response);

    }
}
```

Description

- This servlet gets the parameters from the Register JSP and uses them to create a User object. Then, it stores the data for the user object in a disk file.

- After this servlet creates a session object, it gets the value of the product code from the object. Later, it uses this code in the URL for the downloadable file.

- After preparing the session object, this servlet creates a cookie that contains the email address of the user and adds it to the response object so it will be added to the user's PC if cookies are enabled. Then, you won't have to register the next time you access this application.

Figure 7-14   The Download application (part 6 of 7)

The code for the 8601_Download JSP

```
<html>

<head>
  <title>Chapter 7 - The Download application</title>
</head>

<body>

<%
  String productCode = (String) session.getAttribute("productCode");
%>

<h1>Downloads</h1>

<table cellpadding="5" border="1">
  <tr><td colspan="3"><b>86 (the band) - True Life Songs and Pictures</b></td></tr>
  <tr><td width="200"><b>Song title</b></td>
      <td colspan="2"><b>Audio Format</b></td>
  </tr>
  <tr><td>How To Get There</td>
      <td><a href="../sound/<%= productCode%>/how_to.mp3">MP3</a></td>
      <td><a href="../sound/<%= productCode%>/how_to.rm">Real Audio</a></td>
  </tr>
  <tr><td>You Are a Star</td>
      <td><a href="../sound/<%= productCode%>/star.mp3">MP3</a></td>
      <td><a href="../sound/<%= productCode%>/star.rm">Real Audio</a></td>
  </tr>
  <tr><td>Don't Make No Difference</td>
      <td><a href="../sound/<%= productCode%>/no_difference.mp3">MP3</a></td>
      <td><a href="../sound/<%= productCode%>/no_difference.rm">Real Audio</a>
  </td>
</tr>
</table>

<p><a href="<%= response.encodeURL("../download7/index.jsp")%>">
    Return to the Index page</a>.</p>

</body>

</html>
```

Description

- This is one of the four JSPs for downloading songs from CDs. The others are similar.
- When a browser receives the URL for a sound file, it downloads and plays it. That's one of the capabilities of a modern browser.
- This JSP gets the product code from the session object and uses it in the URLs for the sound files. This isn't necessary, though, because the URLs could be hard-coded.
- Another way to handle the downloads is to write one JSP that works for all of the CDs. To implement that, you can store the data for the downloadable songs in one file for each CD. Then, the download JSP can get the product code from the session object, read the related file, and load its data into the table.

Figure 7-14   The Download application (part 7 of 7)

Perspective

The goal of this chapter has been to show you how to use the servlet API to track sessions and work with cookies. If you understand the code in the Download application that's presented at the end of this chapter, this chapter has achieved its goal. As a result, you should now be able to develop web applications that require session tracking.

In the next chapter, you'll learn how to work with a special type of Java class known as a JavaBean. You can use JavaBeans to implement the business classes in a web application. In a typical application, it's common to store a JavaBean in the session object so the next chapter will build on what you've learned here.

Summary

- Because HTTP is a *stateless protocol*, web applications must provide for *session tracking*. That way, an application is able to relate each browser request to a specific browser and to the data for that browser session.

- To provide for session tracking, Java creates one *session object* for each browser session. Then, you can add attributes like variables and objects to this session object, and you can retrieve the values of these attributes in any of the servlets and JSPs that are run during the session.

- One way to implement session tracking is to use *cookies*. Then, the session ID is stored in a cookie on the user's browser and that ID can be related to the session object. This type of session tracking is done automatically by the servlet API, but it doesn't work unless the browser enables cookies.

- The other way to implement session tracking is to use *URL encoding*. With this technique, you have to encode each URL in the JSPs with an ID that identifies the browser for the session, but this works even when the browser doesn't enable cookies.

- *Persistent cookies* are stored on the user's PC, while *per-session cookies* are deleted when the session ends.

- To create cookies, you use methods of the Cookie class. Then, to add a cookie to the response object so it gets stored on the user's browser or PC, you use the addCookie method of the response object. And to get the cookies from a browser's PC, you use the getCookies method of the request object.

- Because the getCookies method gets an array of all cookies on a browser's PC, it's common to create and use a static method that gets a specific cookie.

- To pass parameters to a servlet or a JSP, you can use *URL rewriting* or *hidden fields*. When you use hidden fields, you can use the Post method so the parameters aren't shown in the URL, and you can include white space and special characters in your parameter values.

Terms

session tracking   session object   persistent cookie
state   cookie   URL rewriting
stateless protocol   URL encoding   hidden field
stateful protocol   per-session cookie

Objectives

- Develop web applications that (1) provide for session tracking by using both cookies and URL encoding, and (2) provide for parameter passing by using URL rewriting or hidden fields.

- Test your web applications with cookies enabled and with cookies disabled.

- Write a utility class that includes a static method for getting a specific cookie from a user's browser.

- Describe the way HTTP works without session tracking.

- Describe the way cookies are used for session tracking.

- Describe the way URL encoding works for session tracking.

- Distinguish between persistent cookies and per-session cookies.

- Distinguish between the use of URL rewriting and the use of hidden fields as ways to implement parameter passing.

Exercise 7-1   Use URL encoding and hidden fields

1. Modify the Shopping Cart application shown in figure 7-2 so it works even when cookies have been disabled. To do that, use URL encoding as shown in figure 7-6.

2. Modify the Cart page for the Shopping Cart application so it uses hidden fields and the Post method instead of URL rewriting.

Exercise 7-2   Add and retrieve a cookie

1. Run the Download application shown in figure 7-14 and test it to make sure it works correctly with and without cookies. To do that, you may need to use the View All Cookies link to view all cookies and the Delete All Persistent Cookies link to delete all cookies.

2. Modify this application by creating a cookie that stores the first name of the user and adds it to the user's PC after the user registers for the first time. To do this, create the cookie in the RegisterServlet class.

3. Open the Index page for the Download application and add a line of text to the top of the page that says "Welcome back, *first name*" if the user has the first name cookie. To do this, you can use a JSP scriptlet to retrieve the cookie.

Exercise 7-3   Create and use a session attribute

1. Create a String object in the DownloadServlet class of the Download application named productDescription that holds the name of the artist and title for the current product. To get this string, you can use the readRecord method in the ProductIO class that's located in the business package to return a Product object. Then, you can use the getDescription method to return the artist name and title as follows:

    ```
    Product product = ProductIO.readRecord(productCode,
                    "../webapps/murach/WEB-INF/etc/products.txt");
    String productDescription = product.getDescription();
    ```

2. Store this String object as a session attribute.

3. For each product's download.jsp page, retrieve the String object from the session object and use it to display the artist and title in the JSP.

4. Instead of using the String object to display the artist and title in each JSP, store the Product object in the session object in the DownloadServlet class and use it to display the artist and title in the JSP.

Exercise 7-4   Work with a vector in a session

1. Create a Vector object in the DownloadServlet class that contains a list of downloadable songs for the "8601" product code. To do this, you can use the getDownloads method in the DownloadIO class that's located in the data package as follows:

    ```
    Vector songList8601 = DownloadIO.getDownloads(
                    "../webapps/murach/WEB-INF/etc/8601downloads.txt");
    ```

2. Store this Vector object in the session object.

3. Open the 8601_download.jsp page and use the Vector object created in the DownloadServlet class to display the name of each song in the JSP.

8

How to create and use JavaBeans

In chapters 4 through 6, you learned how to use the User class to create User objects that contain the data for a user of a web application. In this chapter, you'll learn that this class follows all the rules for a JavaBean, which means that you can use special JSP tags to work with the class. This can minimize the amount of Java code that's used in your JSPs and make it easier for non-programmers to create the JSPs that work with business classes.

An introduction to JavaBeans **244**
How to code a JavaBean 244
A JSP that uses a JavaBean 246
How to code JSP tags for JavaBeans **248**
How to code the useBean tag 248
How to code the getProperty and setProperty tags 250
How to set the properties of a bean from request parameters ... 252
How to set non-string data types in a bean 254
How to use interface and abstract class types with beans 256
The Email List application with beans **258**
The application when the MVC pattern is used 258
The application when the Model 1 architecture is used 262
Perspective **264**

An introduction to JavaBeans

Once you code a class that defines a *JavaBean*, or *bean*, you can use special JSP tags to work with it. In this topic, you'll learn how to define a JavaBean, and you'll be introduced to three types of JSP tags that you can use to create a bean and work with its properties.

How to code a JavaBean

Figure 8-1 shows the code for the User class along with the three rules that must be applied if you want a class like this to be a JavaBean. Since the User class follows all three of these rules, it is a JavaBean.

First, a JavaBean must contain a constructor that doesn't accept any arguments. In this example, this constructor doesn't execute any statements. However, this constructor could contain initialization statements.

Second, a JavaBean can't declare any public instance variables. In this example, all of the instance variables are declared as private. However, it's also possible to declare instance variables as protected.

Third, a JavaBean must contain get and set methods for all of the *properties* that need to be accessed by JSPs. In this example, the methods provide access to all of the instance variables of the class, which represent the properties, so this class qualifies as a bean. Of course, you can also code get and set methods that provide access to other properties in a bean.

To provide access to a boolean value, you code is and set methods instead of get and set methods. For example, you could code methods named isEmailUpdates and setEmailUpdates to provide access to a boolean property named emailUpdates that indicates whether the user wants to receive new product news via email.

When you code the get, set, and is methods, you must follow the capitalization conventions used in this figure. In other words, each method name must start with a lowercase letter and each property name must start with an uppercase letter.

When coding a web application, it's common to use JavaBeans to define the business objects of an application. These beans can be called *invisible JavaBeans* because they don't define visible components. The focus of this book is on this type of JavaBean.

You should realize, though, that JavaBeans are capable of doing much more than defining business objects. For instance, JavaBeans can be used to define buttons and other user interface controls. In fact, the JavaBean API describes a JavaBean as a self-contained, reusable software component that can be visually manipulated. Then, these beans can be used to build the visual interface of an application.

You should also realize that there's another type of JavaBean called an *Enterprise JavaBean*, or *EJB*. Although EJBs are similar in some ways to invisible JavaBeans, an EJB requires an additional server that's not required by JavaBeans. In chapter 17, you can learn more about EJBs.

The code for the User bean class

```
package business;

public class User{

    // three private instance variables (properties)
    private String firstName;
    private String lastName;
    private String emailAddress;

    // a zero-argument constructor
    public User(){}

    public User(String first, String last, String email){
        firstName = first;
        lastName = last;
        emailAddress = email;
    }

    // get and set methods for all three properties
    public void setFirstName(String f){
        firstName = f;
    }
    public String getFirstName(){ return firstName; }

    public void setLastName(String l){
        lastName = l;
    }
    public String getLastName(){ return lastName; }

    public void setEmailAddress(String e){
        emailAddress = e;
    }
    public String getEmailAddress(){ return emailAddress; }
}
```

How to create a JavaBean

* Include a zero-argument constructor.
* Don't code any public instance variables.
* Provide get, set, and is methods for all of the properties that need to be accessed by JSPs.

Description

* A *JavaBean*, or *bean*, is a Java class that follows the three rules above. When you develop web applications, beans are commonly used for the business objects.
* A JavaBean that doesn't define a visual component like a control can be referred to as an *invisible JavaBean*, so the JavaBeans for business objects are invisible.
* The *properties* of a bean are its instance variables. To provide access to the non-boolean properties of a bean, you code get and set methods. To provide access to the boolean properties, you code is and set methods.
* JavaBeans are not the same as *Enterprise JavaBeans*, or *EJBs* (see chapter 17).

Figure 8-1   How to code a JavaBean

A JSP that uses a JavaBean

The main benefit that you get from coding your business classes so they qualify as JavaBeans is that you can then use special JSP tags for working with the beans. This is illustrated by the JSP in figure 8-2. Here, the useBean tag accesses the User bean. Then, if a User object with the same name already exists within the session object, this tag accesses that User object. Otherwise, this tag creates the object by calling the zero-argument constructor of the User class. Because the object is created from a bean class, it can be called a *bean*.

After the bean has been created, the setProperty tag sets the properties of the User bean from the parameters of the request object. Then, the three getProperty tags display the values of the properties that have been set in the bean. Later in this chapter, you'll learn more about how this works. For now, you just need to understand that you can use the setProperty and getProperty tags to set and get the properties of a bean.

This figure also shows a JSP that does the same task by using scriptlets and expressions. Since this code is an unwieldy mix of Java code and HTML, it shows how using JavaBeans and JSP tags can make your JSPs easier to code and maintain. In fact, the JSP that uses the JSP tags doesn't require any Java code at all. This makes it easier for non-programmers to code JSPs.

A JSP that uses JSP tags to access the User bean

```
<jsp:useBean id="user" scope="session" class="business.User"/>
<jsp:setProperty name="user" property="*" />

<table cellspacing="5" cellpadding="5" border="1">
    <tr>
      <td align="right">First name:</td>
      <td><jsp:getProperty name="user" property="firstName"/></td>
    </tr>
    <tr>
      <td align="right">Last name:</td>
      <td><jsp:getProperty name="user" property="lastName"/></td>
    </tr>
    <tr>
      <td align="right">Email address:</td>
      <td><jsp:getProperty name="user" property="emailAddress"/></td>
    </tr>
  </table>
```

The same JSP without using JSP tags to access the User bean

```
<%@ page import="business.*" %>
<%
    User user = (User) session.getAttribute("user");
    if (user == null){
        user = new User();
    }
    user.setFirstName(request.getParameter("firstName"));
    user.setLastName(request.getParameter("lastName"));
    user.setEmailAddress(request.getParameter("emailAddress"));
    session.setAttribute("user", user);
%>

  <table cellspacing="5" cellpadding="5" border="1">
    <tr>
      <td align="right">First name:</td>
      <td><%= user.getFirstName() %></td>
    </tr>
    <tr>
      <td align="right">Last name:</td>
      <td><%= user.getLastName()%></td>
    </tr>
    <tr>
      <td align="right">Email address:</td>
      <td><%= user.getEmailAddress()%></td>
    </tr>
  </table>
```

Description

- JSP tags for using JavaBeans make it easier for non-programmers to use beans because they don't require the use of Java code.

Figure 8-2   A JSP that uses a JavaBean

How to code JSP tags for JavaBeans

In the last figure, you were introduced to the three JSP tags that you can use to work with Java beans. Now, you'll learn the details for coding those tags.

How to code the useBean tag

Figure 8-3 shows how to code the useBean tag to access a bean. Although this tag looks and works much like an HTML tag, all of the JSP tags for working with JavaBeans use XML syntax. As a result, when you code these tags, you must use lowercase and uppercase characters as shown in this figure; you must code a front slash to mark the end of the opening tag or the start of a closing tag; and you must code single or double quotation marks around all attributes of a tag.

To code a simple useBean tag, you code the name of the tag followed by the attributes of the tag. In this example, the ID attribute specifies the name that's used to access the bean, the Class attribute specifies the package and class of the bean, and the Scope attribute specifies the *scope* of the bean.

When you code the Scope attribute, you can specify one of four values: page, request, application, and session. The value of the Scope attribute specifies the object that stores the bean and that determines how long the bean will be available to the rest of the application. For instance, the first example sets the Scope attribute to session, which means that the bean is bound to the session object. As a result, any JSP or servlet that has access to the session object will have access to this bean. If you don't specify the Scope attribute, the scope will be set to "page" by default, which means that the bean will only be available to the current JSP.

If a bean that matches the attributes specified in the useBean tag exists, this tag creates a reference to that object. Otherwise, the useBean tag creates a new object by calling the zero-argument constructor of the specified class. If you study the first example and its equivalent scriptlet, you should get a better idea of how the useBean tag works.

If you want to initialize a bean the first time it's created, you can use an opening and closing useBean tag. To do that, you code the front slash at the beginning of the closing tag instead of coding it at the end of the opening tag. Then, you can code initialization statements within the opening and closing tags. In this figure, the initialization statements set all of the properties of the User bean to string values. However, these statements will only be executed if a bean that matches the specified attributes isn't found.

The useBean tag

Syntax

```
<jsp:useBean id="beanName" class="package.Class" scope="scopeValue" />
```

Example

```
<jsp:useBean id="user" class="business.User" scope="session" />
```

Equivalent scriptlet

```
<%@ page import="business.*" %>
<%
    User user = (User) session.getAttribute("user");
    if (user == null){
        user = new User();
        session.setAttribute("user", user);
    }
%>
```

How to include initialization statements for a bean

```
<jsp:useBean id="user" class="business.User" scope="session" >
    <!-- Note: these statements run only if a new bean is created -->
    <jsp:setProperty name="user" property="firstName" value="John" />
    <jsp:setProperty name="user" property="lastName" value="Smith" />
    <jsp:setProperty name="user" property="emailAddress"
                     value="jsmith@hotmail.com" />
</jsp:useBean>
```

Scope values

Value	Description
page	The bean is stored in the implicit pageContext object for the JSP and is only available to the current page. This is the default setting.
request	The bean is stored in the HttpServletRequest object and is available to all JSPs and servlets that have access to the current request object.
session	The bean is stored in the HttpSession object and is available to all JSPs and servlets that have access to this object. For more information about session objects, see chapter 7.
application	The bean is stored in the ServletContext object and is available to all JSPs and servlets that have access to this object.

Description

- The useBean tag is used to access a bean and, if necessary, create a bean from the JavaBean class.

- The *scope* of a bean refers to the object that stores the bean. This controls how long the bean is available to the rest of the application.

- The JSP tags for working with beans use XML syntax. As a result, these tags are case-sensitive, a front slash indicates the end of the opening tag or the start of a closing tag, and all attributes must be enclosed by single or double quotes.

Figure 8-3   How to code the useBean tag

How to code the getProperty and setProperty tags

Once you code a useBean tag to access or create a bean, you can use the getProperty tag to get the values stored in the bean, and you can use the setProperty tag to set the values stored in the bean. Figure 8-4 shows how.

To get the value of a property that's stored in a bean, you code a getProperty tag. Here, the Name attribute specifies the name of the bean, so it should match the ID attribute of the useBean tag. If, for example, you set the Name attribute to "user," this attribute accesses the User bean specified by the useBean tag in the last figure. Then, the Property attribute specifies the name of the property that you want to access. For example, a value of "firstName" accesses the firstName property of the User bean.

To set a property of a bean, you code a setProperty tag. In this tag, you code the Name attribute and the Property attribute to specify the name of the bean and the property that you want to set. Then, you code the Value attribute to specify the value that you want the property set to as shown in this figure or the Param attribute as shown in the next figure.

If you need to code one of the special characters shown in this figure as part of a Value attribute, you can use the escape sequences shown here. If, for example, you're using single quotes to identify your attributes, you can use an escape sequence like the one in the first escape sequence example to set the lastName property of the User bean to O'Neil. However, you can often avoid using escape sequences by switching the type of quotation mark that you use to identify an attribute. This is illustrated by the second escape sequence example.

When you work with the getProperty tag, you should be aware that it won't get the value of a property if the value is null or an empty string. Similarly, you can't use the setProperty tag to set the value of a property to null or an empty string. If you need to do that, though, you can do it in the constructor of the bean or in a servlet that accesses the bean.

The getProperty tag

Syntax

```
<jsp:getProperty name="beanName" property="propertyName" />
```

Example

```
<jsp:getProperty name="user" property="firstName" />
```

Equivalent JSP expression

```
<%= user.getFirstName() %>
```

The setProperty tag with a Value attribute

Syntax

```
<jsp:setProperty name="beanName" property="propertyName" value="value" />
```

Example

```
<jsp:setProperty name="user" property="firstName" value="John" />
```

Equivalent scriptlet

```
<% user.setFirstName("John"); %>
```

Escape sequences within attributes

Character	Escape sequence
'	\'
"	\"
\	\\
<%	<\%
%>	%\>

How to use an escape sequence

```
<jsp:setProperty name='user' property='lastName' value='O\'Neil' />
```

How to avoid an escape sequence

```
<jsp:setProperty name="user" property="lastName" value="O'Neil" />
```

Description

- The Name attribute for the getProperty and setProperty tags must match the ID attribute in the useBean tag.

- To code special characters within an attribute, you can use escape sequences. However, if you enclose an attribute in double quotes, you don't need to use escape sequences for single quotes. Conversely, if you enclose an attribute in single quotes, you don't need to use the escape sequence for double quotes.

- The getProperty tag can't be used to get a null value or an empty string, and the setProperty tag can't be used to set a property to a null value or an empty string. However, you can use the constructor of a bean or the code in a servlet to set a property to a null value or an empty string.

Figure 8-4   How to code the getProperty and setProperty tags

How to set the properties of a bean from request parameters

Figure 8-5 shows you how to use the setProperty tag to set the properties of a bean from the parameters of a request object. To do that, you use the Param attribute instead of the Value attribute. Or, if the name of the property matches the name of the parameter, you can omit the Param attribute.

If the names of the property and the parameter are different, you need to code the Param attribute to specify the name of the parameter that you want to get from the request object. This is illustrated by the first example. Here, the name of the property is "firstName" and the name of the parameter is "userFirstName," so the value of that parameter will be stored in the property.

If the names of the property and the parameter are the same, you don't need to code the Param attribute as shown in the second example. Here, the name of both the property and the parameter is "firstName," so the corresponding parameter value will be stored in the firstName property.

If the names of several properties and parameters are the same, you can take this one step further as shown by the third example. Here, an asterisk is coded for the Property attribute. Then, all of the properties in the bean with matching parameter names in the request object will be set to the values of those parameters. Since the parameter names should match the corresponding property names if you use consistent naming conventions, this is a common JSP coding technique.

The syntax of the setProperty tag with a Param attribute

```
<jsp:setProperty name="name" property="varName" param="paramName" />
```

Example 1: Setting a property that has a different name than the parameter

```
<jsp:setProperty name="user" property="firstName" param="userFirstName" />
```

Equivalent scriptlet

```
<% user.setFirstName(request.getParameter("userFirstName")); %>
```

Example 2: Setting a property that has the same name as the parameter

```
<jsp:setProperty name="user" property="firstName" />
```

Equivalent scriptlet

```
<% user.setFirstName(request.getParameter("firstName")); %>
```

Example 3: Setting all properties to the parameters with the same names

```
<jsp:setProperty name="user" property="*" />
```

Equivalent scriptlet

```
<%
    user.setFirstName(request.getParameter("firstName"));
    user.setLastName(request.getParameter("lastName"));
    user.setEmailAddress(request.getParameter("emailAddress"));
%>
```

Description

- You can use the Param attribute of the setProperty tag to set the property of a bean to the value of a parameter of the request object.
- If the parameter name is the same as the property name, you can omit the Param attribute.
- If the names of the bean properties are the same as the names of the parameters in the request object, you can set the bean properties by specifying an asterisk in the property attribute.

Figure 8-5   How to set the properties of a bean from request parameters

How to set non-string data types in a bean

So far, all of the examples in this chapter use the setProperty tag to set properties to strings. But what happens if you use the setProperty tag to set properties with primitive data types or their wrapper classes? The good news is that the setProperty method automatically does these conversions for you as shown in figure 8-6. As a result, you set properties with these data types the same way that you set properties with string values.

To convert the data types, the JSP engine uses the valueOf method of the wrapper class and, if necessary, converts the object to the corresponding primitive data type. For instance, the first example assumes that the price property of the Product bean uses a double value. Here, the setProperty tag sets the value of the price property to a value of "15.50". Since the setPrice method in the Product bean class accepts a double data type, the JSP engine uses the static valueOf method of the Double class to return a Double object. Then, it calls the doubleValue method from that object to return a double data type. This sets the price property of the Product bean to the double value of 15.50.

The second example shows that these automatic conversions work even when working with the parameters of the request object, which are always returned as strings. When the JSP engine reads the setProperty tag in this example, it performs the same conversion as in the first example.

The servlet code in this figure shows that the JSP engine has automatically converted the string to the appropriate data type. Here, the getPrice method of the Product object returns a double type. This code also shows how to access a bean that has application scope. To do that, you begin by calling the getServletContext method to return a ServletContext object. Then, you can call the getAttribute method of the ServletContext object to return the Product bean.

How the JSP engine automatically converts data types

Type	Conversion calls
double	**Double.valueOf**(valueOrParamString)**.doubleValue()**
Double	**Double.valueOf**(valueOrParamString)
int	**Integer.valueOf**(valueOrParamString)**.intValue()**
Integer	**Integer.valueOf**(valueOrParamString)
float	**Float.valueOf**(valueOrParamString)**.floatValue()**
Float	**Float.valueOf**(valueOrParamString)
long	**Long.valueOf**(valueOrParamString)**.longValue()**
Long	**Long.valueOf**(valueOrParamString)
short	**Short.valueOf**(valueOrParamString)**.shortValue()**
Short	**Short.valueOf**(valueOrParamString)
byte	**Byte.valueOf**(valueOrParamString)**.byteValue()**
Byte	**Byte.valueOf**(valueOrParamString)
boolean	**Boolean.valueOf**(valueOrParamString)**.booleanValue()**
Boolean	**Boolean.valueOf**(valueOrParamString)
char	**Character.valueOf**(valueOrParamString)**.charValue()**
Character	**Character.valueOf**(valueOrParamString)

How to use the setProperty method to set a non-string value

Example 1

```
<jsp:useBean id="product" class="business.Product" scope="application" />
<jsp:setProperty name="product" property="price" value="15.50"/>
```

Example 2

```
<jsp:useBean id="product" class="business.Product" scope="application" />
<jsp:setProperty name="product" property="price" param="productPrice" />
```

Servlet code that accesses a Product bean that has application scope

```
ServletContext servletContext = getServletContext();
Product product = (Product) servletContext.getAttribute("product");
double price = product.getPrice();
```

Description

- The setProperty method automatically converts all of the primitive data types and their wrapper classes to the data types of the properties.

Figure 8-6   How to set non-string data types in a bean

How to use interface and abstract class types with beans

Most of the time, you won't need to use an interface or abstract class type to refer to a bean. As a result, you may want to skip this complex topic until you face that requirement. If you do need to do that, though, you can code a Type attribute in the useBean tag as shown in figure 8-7.

In the examples in this figure, the JavaBean classes named Order and CatalogRequest implement the Addressable interface, and this interface contains set and get methods for instance variables named city and state. As a result, every class that implements this interface must implement the setCity, getCity, setState, and getState methods.

To start, this figure shows how to code a useBean tag to create an Order bean that can be referred to by the Addressable interface. Usually, though, you do that in a servlet. That's why this figure also shows servlet code that creates either an Order or a CatalogRequest bean that can be referred to by the Addressable interface.

Since the Order and CatalogRequest beans implement the Addressable interface, you can use the JSP tags to work with the properties that are defined in the interface. If you use JSP tags to access an existing bean, you don't need to include the Class attribute. But if the bean doesn't exist and the Class attribute isn't coded, the bean will be set to a null value. For that reason, you should code the Class attribute when you aren't sure that the bean exists.

How to create a bean of an interface or abstract class type

Syntax for creating a specific type of bean

```
<jsp:useBean id="beanName" class="package.Class"
             type="package.InterfaceOrAbstractClass" scope="scopeValue" />
```

Example

```
<jsp:useBean id="addr" class="business.Order" type="business.Addressable"
    scope="session" />
```

Equivalent scriptlet

```
<%@ page import="business.*" %>
<%
    Addressable addr = new Order();
    session.setAttribute("addr", addr);
%>
```

Servlet code that creates two Addressable beans in the session

```
Addressable addr = null;
if (source.equals("OrderForm"))
    addr = new Order();
else if (source.equals("Request"))
    addr = new CatalogRequest();
session.setAttribute("addr", addr);
```

How to access beans by interface or abstract class type

Syntax for accessing an interface type

```
<jsp:useBean id="beanName" type="package.InterfaceOrAbstractClass"
             scope="scopeValue" />
```

Example

```
<jsp:useBean id="addr" type="business.Addressable" scope="session" />
<jsp:getProperty name="addr" property="city" />
<jsp:getProperty name="addr" property="state" />
```

Equivalent scriptlet

```
<%@ page import="business.*" %>
<%
    Addressable addr = (Addressable) session.getAttribute("addr");
%>
<%= addr.getCity() %>
<%= addr.getState() %>
```

Description

- If you want to refer to a bean by an interface or abstract class type, you can code a Type attribute that specifies the interface or abstract class. For this to work, the bean class must implement the interface or extend the abstract class.

Figure 8-7   How to use interface and abstract class types with beans

The Email List application with beans

When you develop a web application with JavaBeans and JSP tags, you can use either the MVC pattern or the Model 1 architecture to structure the application. To illustrate, this chapter finishes by showing you the Email List application first when the MVC pattern is used and then when Model 1 architecture is used.

The application when the MVC pattern is used

Figure 8-8 presents a simple version of the Email List application that uses the MVC pattern. It consists of a first JSP that starts the application, a servlet that controls the application when the first JSP calls it, and a second JSP that presents the results of the servlet.

The JSP in part 1 of this figure starts the application. It uses the useBean tag to access the User bean and bind it to the current session. Then, it uses three getProperty tags to display the values of the properties that are stored in the User bean. The first time this JSP is requested in a session, though, the bean will contain null values for its properties so no values will be displayed in the table for this page.

Why then use a JSP instead of an HTML page to start this application? Because the bean will have properties once the user enters data and clicks the Submit button. Then, if the user returns to this JSP, it will display those values. If, for example, the user clicks the Back button to return to this page, those values will be displayed. For some applications, this is useful.

When the user clicks the Submit button on the first JSP, the Form tag requests the EmailServlet class. If you look ahead to part 2 of this figure, you can see that this servlet retrieves the parameters stored in the request object, creates a new User bean, sets the values for the User bean, and writes the User bean to a file. Next, this servlet retrieves the session object and binds the User bean to it, which replaces the bean created by the first JSP with the new bean. Then, the servlet forwards the request and response objects to the second JSP.

If you look ahead to part 3 of this figure, you can see that the second JSP begins by using the useBean tag to load the User bean that was stored in the session object by the servlet. Then, this page uses three getProperty tags to display the values that are stored in the bean. This shows that the JSP for the view doesn't require any Java code at all.

The code for join_email_list.jsp

```
<!doctype html public "-//W3C//DTD HTML 4.0 Transitional//EN">
<html>

<head>
  <title>Chapter 8 - Email List application</title>
</head>

<body>

<h1>Join our email list</h1>
<p>To join our email list, enter your name and
   email address below. <br>
   Then, click on the Submit button.</p>

<jsp:useBean id="user" scope="session" class="business.User"/>

<form action="../servlet/email8.EmailServlet" method="get">
  <table cellspacing="5" border="0">
    <tr>
      <td align="right">First name:</td>
      <td><input type="text" name="firstName"
          value="<jsp:getProperty name="user" property="firstName"/>">
      </td>
    </tr>
    <tr>
      <td align="right">Last name:</td>
      <td><input type="text" name="lastName"
          value="<jsp:getProperty name="user" property="lastName"/>">
      </td>
    </tr>
    <tr>
      <td align="right">Email address:</td>
      <td><input type="text" name="emailAddress"
          value="<jsp:getProperty name="user" property="emailAddress"/>">
      </td>
    </tr>
    <tr>
      <td></td>
      <td><input type="submit" value="Submit"></td>
    </tr>
  </table>
</form>

</body>

</html>
```

Description

- This MVC application starts with this JSP instead of an HTML document. The first time this JSP is requested, it creates a new User bean for the session. These properties aren't set to any values until the servlet sets the properties to the parameter values entered by the user.
- If this JSP is requested later in the session by clicking on the Back button, the property values that have been set by the servlet are displayed by the browser.

Figure 8-8   The Email List application in the MVC pattern with beans (part 1 of 3)

The code for the EmailServlet class

```java
package email8;

import java.io.*;
import javax.servlet.*;
import javax.servlet.http.*;
import business.User;
import data.UserIO;

public class EmailServlet extends HttpServlet{

    public void doGet(HttpServletRequest request,
                      HttpServletResponse response)
                throws IOException, ServletException{

        String firstName = request.getParameter("firstName");
        String lastName = request.getParameter("lastName");
        String emailAddress = request.getParameter("emailAddress");

        User user = new User();
        user.setFirstName(firstName);
        user.setLastName(lastName);
        user.setEmailAddress(emailAddress);

        UserIO.addRecord(user,
            "../webapps/murach/WEB-INF/etc/UserEmail.txt");

        HttpSession session = request.getSession();
        session.setAttribute("user", user);

        RequestDispatcher dispatcher =
                    getServletContext().getRequestDispatcher(
                        "/email8/show_email_entry.jsp");
        dispatcher.forward(request, response);

    }

    public void doPost(HttpServletRequest request,
                       HttpServletResponse response)
                throws ServletException, IOException {
        doGet(request, response);
    }

}
```

Description

- The EmailServlet class creates a new User bean and sets its three properties to the parameters that were retrieved from the request object.

- After the servlet writes the data for the bean to a file, it uses the getSession method of the request object to get the session object. Then, it sets the user attribute of this object to the new user bean, which replaces the bean that was created by the first JSP.

Figure 8-8   The Email List application in the MVC pattern with beans (part 2 of 3)

The code for show_email_entry.jsp

```
<!doctype html public "-//W3C//DTD HTML 4.0 Transitional//EN">
<html>

<head>
  <title>Chapter 8 - Email List application</title>
</head>

<body>

<h1>Thanks for joining our email list</h1>
<p>Here is the information that you entered:</p>

<jsp:useBean id="user" scope="session" class="business.User"/>

  <table cellspacing="5" cellpadding="5" border="1">
    <tr>
      <td align="right">First name:</td>
      <td><jsp:getProperty name="user" property="firstName"/></td>
    </tr>
    <tr>
      <td align="right">Last name:</td>
      <td><jsp:getProperty name="user" property="lastName"/></td>
    </tr>
    <tr>
      <td align="right">Email address:</td>
      <td><jsp:getProperty name="user" property="emailAddress"/></td>
    </tr>
  </table>

<p>To enter another email address, click on the Back <br>
  button in your browser or the Return button shown <br>
  below.</p>

<form action="../email8/join_email_list.jsp" method="post">
  <input type="submit" value="Return">
</form>

</body>

</html>
```

Description

- This is the JSP that's called by the servlet for the view layer of the application. It uses the properties of the bean to return the user entries to the browser.

Figure 8-8   The Email List application in the MVC pattern with beans (part 3 of 3)

The application when the Model 1 architecture is used

When the processing for an application is simple, the Model 1 architecture often works better than the MVC pattern (or Model 2 architecture). In fact, JavaBeans and JSP tags are designed to help make the Model 1 architecture easier to implement.

When you use this architecture, as you should remember from chapter 6, you don't use a servlet as the controller. Instead, a JSP handles both the processing and the presentation for the application. For the Email List application, then, the first JSP will call the second JSP instead of the servlet. That's the only change that needs to be made to the first JSP in figure 8-8.

In figure 8-9, you can see the second JSP for the Email List application when Model 1 architecture is used. Here, the first two JSP tags access the User bean that was created by the first JSP and set the properties of the bean to the parameter values of the request object. This shows that one JSP can access a bean created by another JSP without using a servlet as a controller.

Then, the JSP uses a scriptlet to write the data of the bean to a file. This shows that you often have to use some Java code in a JSP when you use the Model 1 architecture. Unfortunately, that makes it difficult for non-programmers to code JSPs, which usually means that the designers and programmers have to work together to create JSPs, even simple ones like this.

The code for show_email_entry.jsp when Model 1 architecture is used

```
<!doctype html public "-//W3C//DTD HTML 4.0 Transitional//EN">
<html>

<head>
  <title>Chapter 8 - Email List application</title>
</head>

<body>
<%@ page import="data.*" %>
<jsp:useBean id="user" scope="session" class="business.User"/>
<jsp:setProperty name="user" property="*" />

<%
    UserIO.addRecord(user, "../webapps/murach/WEB-INF/etc/UserEmail.txt");
%>

<h1>Thanks for joining our email list</h1>
<p>Here is the information that you entered:</p>


  <table cellspacing="5" cellpadding="5" border="1">
    <tr>
      <td align="right">First name:</td>
      <td><jsp:getProperty name="user" property="firstName"/></td>
    </tr>
    <tr>
      <td align="right">Last name:</td>
      <td><jsp:getProperty name="user" property="lastName"/></td>
    </tr>
    <tr>
      <td align="right">Email address:</td>
      <td><jsp:getProperty name="user" property="emailAddress"/></td>
    </tr>
  </table>

<p>To enter another email address, click on the Back <br>
   button in your browser or the Return button shown <br>
   below.</p>

<form action="/murach/email8/join_email_list.jsp" method="post">
  <input type="submit" value="Return">
</form>
</body>

</html>
```

Description

- When the Model 1 architecture is used for this application, the first JSP in figure 8-8 works the same but it calls this JSP when the Submit button is clicked. Then, this JSP does both the processing and the presentation for the application.

- Although JSP tags can be used to set the properties for the user bean, one scriptlet is required to store the data for the bean in a file.

Figure 8-9   The second JSP when Model 1 architecture is used

Perspective

The goal of this chapter has been to show you how to code JavaBeans and how to code the JSP tags that work with JavaBeans. Now, if you understand the Email List applications in figures 8-8 and 8-9, this chapter has achieved its goal. And that should make it easier for you to code the JSPs for your web applications.

In the next chapter, you'll learn how to create custom JSP tags. These tags are similar to the JSP tags for working with JavaBeans, but you can customize them to display different types of data. And that should make it easier still for you to code the JSPs for your web applications.

Summary

- A *JavaBean*, or *bean*, is a Java class that (1) has a zero-argument constructor, (2) doesn't include any public instance variables, and (3) provides get, set, and is methods for all of its *properties*, which are represented by the instance variables.

- When you use JavaBeans in your web applications, you can use JSP tags to create a bean object and get and set its properties. These tags help reduce the amount of Java code in a JSP and thus make it easier for non-programmers to code JSPs.

- The useBean tag lets you access or create a bean object. Then, the getProperty and setProperty tags let you get and set the properties of the object.

- The setProperty tag automatically converts the primitive data types and their wrapper classes to the data types of the properties.

- You can use JavaBeans and JSP tags with both the Model 1 architecture and the MVC pattern. The choice depends on the processing requirements of the application.

Terms

JavaBean
bean
property
invisible JavaBean
scope

Objectives

- Create business classes that are JavaBeans.

- Use the JSP tags presented in this chapter to work with JavaBeans.

- List the three rules for defining a JavaBean.

- Describe the use of these JSP tags: useBean, getProperty, and setProperty.

- Describe the benefit that you get from using JSP tags with JavaBeans.

- Describe the rationale for deciding when to use the Model 1 architecture and when to use the MVC pattern with JavaBeans and JSP tags.

Exercise 8-1   Modify the Email List application

In this exercise, you'll add a JavaBean to the Email List application that's presented throughout this chapter. For this exercise, all JSPs are located in the email8 directory and the servlet is located in the email8 package.

1. Run the Email List application for this chapter by requesting the join_email_list.jsp page. Once you submit your request, click on the Return button to return back to the original page. Notice that the text fields are empty.

2. Open the join_email_list.jsp page and add a User JavaBean to this page so that it displays user data when the page is requested more than once in a session. When you click the Return button in this version, the text fields will contain the current user's data.

3. Modify the Email List application so that it uses the Model 1 approach as shown in figure 8-9. When you're done, the application will consist of two JSPs and no servlets.

Exercise 8-2   Use a bean in the Download application

In this exercise, you'll enhance the Download application that you worked with in the last chapter so that the JSPs use a JavaBean to access product information. For this exercise, all JSPs are located in the download8 directory and the servlets are located in the download8 package.

1. Open the Product class that's located in the business package. Make sure that this class follows the rules for a JavaBean class.

2. Open the DownloadServlet class and add code that retrieves a Product object for the current product as described in exercise 7-3. Then, store this object in the session object.

3. Open the download.jsp page for each product and use a Product JavaBean for the Product object you created in the DownloadServlet class to access the product code and description.

9

How to work with custom JSP tags

In chapter 8, you learned how to code built-in JSP tags that work with JavaBeans. Now, you'll learn how to create custom JSP tags that can perform a wide range of custom tasks. Since it's difficult to understand how custom JSP tags work without seeing examples, this chapter starts with a simple example and works toward more complex examples.

How to code a custom tag that doesn't have a body **268**
The JSP 268
The TLD tags 270
The tag handler class 272

How to code a custom tag that has a body **274**
The JSP 274
The TLD tags 276
The tag handler class 276

How to code a custom tag that has attributes **278**
The JSP 278
The TLD tags 280
The tag handler class 282

How to code a custom tag that reiterates its body **284**
The JSP 284
The TLD tags 286
The tag handler class 286

How to work with scripting variables **290**
An introduction to scripting variables 290
The TEI class 292

Classes, methods, and fields for working with custom tags **294**
Methods and fields of the TagSupport class 294
Methods and fields of the PageContext class 296
Methods and fields of the BodyTagSupport class 298
Methods and fields of the BodyContent class 300

Perspective **302**

How to code a custom tag that doesn't have a body

This chapter begins by showing how to code the three components of a custom JSP tag that doesn't have a body. This is the simplest type of tag.

The JSP

Figure 9-1 shows how to code a *custom JSP tag*, or just *custom tag*, that inserts the current date into a JSP. Before you can use a custom tag in a JSP, though, you must code a *taglib directive* in the JSP. Within this directive, the URI attribute must specify the location of the Tag Library Descriptor (or TLD), which you'll learn more about in the next figure. Then, the Prefix attribute specifies a prefix that you can use for the custom tags that are defined by the TLD.

Once you code the taglib directive, you can use any of the custom tags in the TLD. To do that, you code an opening bracket (<), the prefix that's specified in the taglib directive, a colon, the name of the tag, and a slash followed by a closing bracket (/>). Although you can code the same tag by coding an opening and closing tag with nothing between them, you don't need to do that.

In this case, you could accomplish this same task by using a JSP scriptlet and expression, but using a custom tag has several advantages. First, using a custom tag requires less code in the JSP. Second, using a custom tag often doesn't require any Java code. Third, a custom tag can be used in more than one JSP. Fourth, Java programmers can create the custom tags and web designers can use them, which makes it easier for Java programmers and web designers to work together. Fifth, using custom tags provides another way for the Java programmer to organize the code of a web application. As you will see, these benefits also hold true for more complex custom tags.

The syntax for the taglib directive

```
<%@ taglib uri="TLDlocation" prefix="prefix" %>
```

The syntax for a tag that doesn't include a body

```
<prefix:tagName />
```

JSP code that uses a custom tag to display the date

```
<%@ taglib uri="../WEB-INF/tlds/murach.tld" prefix="mma" %>
<mma:today />
```

The page that displays the date

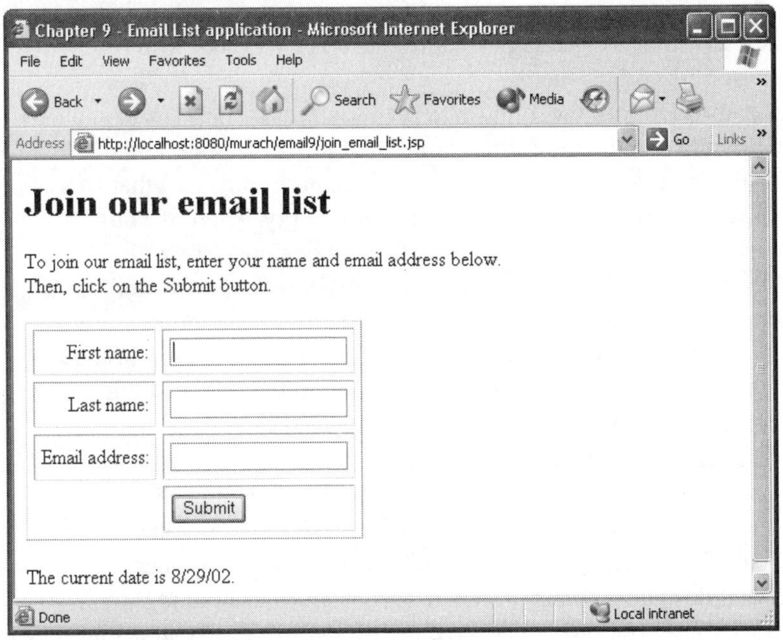

Description

- Before you can code a *custom tag* in a JSP, you must code a *taglib directive*. This directive must specify the location of the Tag Library Descriptor, or TLD, and it must specify a prefix that can be used for the custom tags that are defined by this TLD.

- To code a tag that doesn't have a body, you typically use a single tag. However, you can also code opening and closing tags with nothing between them like this:

```
<mma:today></mma:today>
```

Figure 9-1   A JSP that uses a tag that doesn't have a body

The TLD tags

Before you can use a custom tag in a JSP, you must create a *Tag Library Descriptor* file, or *TLD*, that describes the tag. To illustrate, figure 9-2 shows a TLD that contains two custom tags. As you progress through this chapter, you'll learn how to add other types of tags to this TLD. Although you can code as many TLDs as you like for an application, it's typical to code a single TLD that contains all of the custom tags for an application.

Since TLDs are XML documents, you must start a TLD with the standard XML header information. Since you don't need to understand this header information, you can just copy the header from an old TLD to the start of a new one. After the header information, the rest of the tags are XML tags that define the elements of the TLD. Since these tags are similar to HTML tags, you shouldn't have any trouble coding them.

After the header information, the TagLib element defines the *tag library*. Within this element, you code the tag library version, the JSP version, and a short name for the library. If you're not working with an authoring tool that requires a short name value, you can leave this element empty. Then, if you want to include a brief description of the tag library, you can code the Info element, which is optional. For Tomcat 4.0, both the tag library version and short name are required, but this may vary depending on the JSP engine.

After these elements, you code one Tag element for each custom tag in the tag library. When you create a Tag element, you're required to code a Name element that defines the name of the tag as well as a TagClass element that defines the class that carries out the actions of the tag. This class is often referred to as the *tag handler class*, which you'll learn more about in the next figure. Then, if you want to include a description of the custom tag, you can code an Info element. This description can be written so it will help other programmers and web designers decide whether they want to use the tag.

When you create a TLD file, you must save the file with a TLD extension. You must also save it in the WEB-INF directory or one of its subdirectories. In the applications that come with this book, for example, the TLD is saved in the WEB-INF\tlds directory.

A Tag Library Descriptor file that contains two tags

```
<?xml version="1.0" encoding="ISO-8859-1" ?>
<!DOCTYPE taglib
    PUBLIC "-//Sun Microsystems, Inc.//DTD JSP Tag Library 1.1//EN"
    "http://java.sun.com/j2ee/dtds/web-jsptaglibrary_1_1.dtd">

<taglib>
  <tlibversion>1.0</tlibversion>
  <jspversion>1.2</jspversion>
  <shortname></shortname>
  <info>The Tag Library Descriptor for the murach applications</info>

  <tag>
    <name>today</name>
    <tagclass>tags.SimpleDateTag</tagclass>
    <info>Returns the current date</info>
  </tag>

  <tag>
    <name>time</name>
    <tagclass>tags.CurrentTimeTag</tagclass>
  </tag>

</taglib>
```

Where the murach.tld file is saved

```
webapps/murach/WEB-INF/tlds/murach.tld
```

Description

- The *Tag Library Descriptor*, or *TLD*, is an XML document that describes a *tag library* that contains custom tags that can be used in an application. Although an application typically uses a single TLD to define all of its custom tags, there's no limit to the number of TLDs an application can have.

- The file for a TLD must be saved in the WEB-INF directory or one of its subdirectories, and it must be saved with an extension of TLD.

- If your application doesn't have an existing TLD, you can create one by copying the one that's on this book's CD. Then, you can add your custom Tag elements to this file.

- Within a Tag element, you must use the Name element to specify the name of the custom tag and the TagClass element to specify the *tag handler class* for the tag. The tag handler class is the Java class that does the actions of the tag as shown in the next figure.

- Within a Tag element, you can use the Info element to specify descriptive information about the tag, but this element is optional.

- The elements that are required by a TLD may vary depending on the JSP engine. As a result, if a TLD like the one in this figure doesn't work for you, you may need to consult the documentation for your JSP engine.

- Since Tomcat loads the TLD at startup, you must restart Tomcat whenever you modify this file. Otherwise, your changes won't take effect.

Figure 9-2   The TLD for two tags that don't have bodies

The tag handler class

Figure 9-3 presents the tag handler class for the Today tag shown in figure 9-1. This class displays the current date in this format, "The current date is MM/DD/YY".

To define a tag handler class for a custom tag, you must implement the Tag interface. Since you probably don't want to define every method in the Tag interface, though, it's easier to extend the TagSupport class instead. This class is a convenience class that implements the Tag interface. As a result, when you extend this class, you only need to define the methods that you want to use.

To define the actions of a custom tag, you can override the doStartTag method of the TagSupport class. This method is called when the custom tag is read. In the example in this figure, the first four statements in this method use the Calendar, Date, and DateFormat classes to get and format the current date. Then, a try/catch statement uses the built-in pageContext object to return a JspWriter object that's used to return the formatted date to the JSP. Last, the doStartTag method returns the SKIP_BODY constant that's defined in the TagSupport class. Whenever a tag doesn't have a body, you return the SKIP_BODY constant after you use the JspWriter to write the tag's data to the JSP.

When you code tag handler classes, you can save them in the same location as your other Java classes. However, it's common to store tag handler classes in a separate package. That's why all of the tag handler classes shown in this chapter are saved in the tags package.

At this point, you should have a pretty good idea of how custom tags work. When the JSP engine encounters a custom tag, it uses the tag prefix to relate the tag to the taglib directive, which points to the TLD for the tag. Then, the JSP engine uses the TLD to find the tag handler class that implements the custom tag. Once that's done, the JSP engine can translate the JSP into a servlet that calls the tag handler class.

A tag handler class for a tag that doesn't include a body

```
package tags;

import javax.servlet.jsp.*;
import javax.servlet.jsp.tagext.*;
import java.io.*;
import java.util.*;
import java.text.DateFormat;

public class SimpleDateTag extends TagSupport{

    public int doStartTag() throws JspException{

        Calendar calDate = new GregorianCalendar();
        Date now = calDate.getTime();
        DateFormat shortDate = DateFormat.getDateInstance(DateFormat.SHORT);
        String today = shortDate.format(now);

        try {
            JspWriter out = pageContext.getOut();
            out.print("The current date is " + today + ".");
        }
        catch (IOException ioe){
            System.out.println("SimpleDateTag IOException: " + ioe);
        }
        return SKIP_BODY;
    }
}
```

Where the SimpleDateTag class is saved

```
..\murach\WEB-INF\classes\tags
```

Description

- The *tag handler class* is the Java class that defines the actions of the tag. A tag handler class must implement the Tag interface.

- For a tag that doesn't have a body, you can implement the Tag interface by extending the TagSupport class of the javax.servlet.jsp.tagext package. Then, you can override the doStartTag method.

- To display text on the JSP, you use the print method of the JspWriter object that's stored in the javax.servlet.jsp package. Since this print method throws an IOException, you must use a try/catch statement to handle the exception.

- To get a JspWriter object, you use the getOut method of the pageContext object that's defined in the TagSupport class.

- For a tag that doesn't have a body, the doStartTag method must return the SKIP_BODY constant.

- Although you can store tag handler classes wherever you store your other Java classes, it's common to create a separate package for the tag handler classes of a tag library.

Figure 9-3   A tag handler class for a tag that doesn't have a body

How to code a custom tag that has a body

Now that you know how to create a custom tag that doesn't have a body, you're ready to learn how to create a custom tag that has a body.

The JSP

Figure 9-4 shows you how to use a custom tag with a body in a JSP. As with all custom tags, you must code a taglib directive before you can use the custom tag. Then, you code an opening tag, followed by the body of the tag, followed by the closing tag.

Although the custom tag shown in this figure doesn't appear to do anything, it determines when the body of the tag is displayed. As you will see, the tag handler class for this tag displays the body of the tag on Monday through Friday, but skips it on Saturday and Sunday. In this example, the body is displayed because it is a weekday.

The syntax of a tag that has a body

```
<prefix:tagName>
    body
</prefix:tagName>
```

JSP code that uses a custom tag with a body

```
<%@ taglib uri="../WEB-INF/tlds/murach.tld" prefix="mma" %>

<mma:weekday>
    <p>Live support available at 1-800-555-2222.</p>
</mma:weekday>
```

The page that displays the body only on Monday through Friday

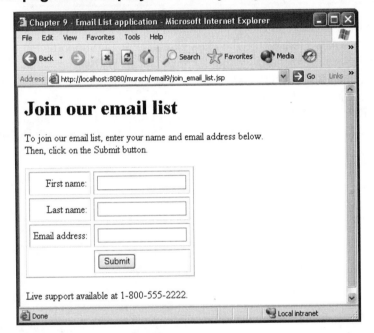

Description

- A tag that has a body must have an opening tag, a body, and a closing tag.
- The body of the tag can contain any HTML or JSP elements.
- The tag handler class for a custom tag can control whether the body of the tag is displayed in the JSP.

Figure 9-4   A JSP that uses a tag that has a body

The TLD tags

Figure 9-5 shows how to code the Tag element for a tag that contains a body. In general, this tag follows the same rules as a tag that doesn't have a body. As a result, you can just add the tag shown in this figure to a TLD like the one shown in figure 9-2. However, to inform the JSP engine that the tag has a body, you must code a BodyContent element that specifies a value of "JSP". In contrast, when you code a tag that doesn't have a body, you can omit the BodyContent element or you can specify a value of "empty".

The tag handler class

This figure also shows a tag handler class that displays the body of the tag when certain conditions are met. Here again, the class extends the TagSupport class and overrides the doStartTag method. Within the doStartTag method, though, this class returns the SKIP_BODY field if the day of the week is Saturday or Sunday. But if it isn't, this method returns the EVAL_BODY_INCLUDE field so the body is evaluated and displayed.

The Tag element in the TLD file

```
<tag>
  <name>weekday</name>
  <tagclass>tags.BodyWeekdayTag</tag-class>
  <bodycontent>JSP</bodycontent>
</tag>
```

A tag handler class that conditionally displays the body of the tag

```
package tags;

import javax.servlet.jsp.*;
import javax.servlet.jsp.tagext.*;
import java.io.*;
import java.util.*;

public class BodyWeekdayTag extends TagSupport{

    public int doStartTag() throws JspException{
        Calendar today = new GregorianCalendar();
        int day = today.get(Calendar.DAY_OF_WEEK);
        if ( (day==Calendar.SATURDAY) || (day==Calendar.SUNDAY) ){
            return SKIP_BODY;
        }
        else
            return EVAL_BODY_INCLUDE;
    }
}
```

Description

- When you add a tag that has a body to a TLD, you must specify a value of "JSP" for the BodyContent element. When you add a tag that doesn't have a body to a TLD, you can omit the BodyContent element or you can specify a value of "empty".

- To create a tag handler class for a tag that has a body, you can extend the TagSupport class and override the doStartTag method.

- To display the body of the tag in the JSP, the tag handler class should return the EVAL_BODY_INCLUDE constant. Otherwise, the tag handler class should return the SKIP_BODY constant.

Figure 9-5   The TLD and the tag handler class for a tag that has a body

How to code a custom tag that has attributes

In this topic, you'll learn how to add attributes to a custom tag. Although the example in this topic shows how to add attributes to a tag that doesn't have a body, you can also use attributes with a tag that has a body.

The JSP

Figure 9-6 shows a JSP that uses a custom tag to display an asterisk next to any text box that doesn't contain text. Here, a custom tag named checkfield is coded after each of the three text boxes. Within each tag, an attribute named field is set to an expression that's determined at runtime. This shows how you can use a runtime expression as the value of an attribute.

Then, the tag handler class uses that field to determine whether it contains an empty string. If it does, the tag handler displays an asterisk to the right of the text box for that field. If it doesn't, the tag handler doesn't do anything. In effect, then, the tag handler provides a type of data validation.

By default, the asterisk that's displayed will be red, but you can use the optional Color attribute to change that color. This is illustrated by the first use of the Checkfield tag, and this should work for all of the standard HTML colors like black, blue, red, green, and yellow. This shows how you can use a string as the value of an attribute.

A page that displays an asterisk next to an empty field

JSP code that uses a custom tag that has attributes

```
<%@ taglib uri="../WEB-INF/tlds/murach.tld" prefix="mma" %>
<%
    String firstName = request.getParameter("firstName");
    String lastName = request.getParameter("lastName");
    String emailAddress = request.getParameter("emailAddress");
%>
<form action="../servlet/email9.EmailServlet" method="get">
<table cellspacing="5" border="0">
  <tr><td align="right">First name:</td>
      <td><input type="text" name="firstName" value="<%= firstName %>">
          <mma:checkfield color="blue" field="<%= firstName %>"/></td>
  </tr>
  <tr><td align="right">Last name:</td>
      <td><input type="text" name="lastName" value="<%= lastName %>">
          <mma:checkfield field="<%= lastName %>"/></td>
  </tr>
  <tr><td align="right">Email address:</td>
      <td><input type="text" name="emailAddress" value="<%= emailAddress %>">
          <mma:checkfield field="<%= emailAddress %>"/></td>
  </tr>
```

Description

- The custom tags in this figure use attributes to send parameters from the JSP to the tag handler class.

- To code an attribute in a custom tag, you code the attribute after the name of the tag just as you would do with any other XML attribute.

Figure 9-6   A JSP that uses a tag that has attributes

The TLD tags

To use attributes in a custom tag, you must add information about the attributes to the TLD. For example, to define a Checkfield tag that has a Color attribute and a Field attribute, you can add the Tag element shown in figure 9-7 to the TLD.

To define an attribute, you code an Attribute element within the Tag element. Within the Attribute element, you can code the four elements shown in this figure. To start, you must code a Name element to specify the name of the attribute. Then, you can code the Required element to specify whether the attribute is required. In this figure, the Color element is optional while the Field attribute it required.

If an attribute is set to an expression that's determined at runtime, you must also set the RTExprValue element to true or yes. This informs the JSP engine that the value of the attribute won't be determined until the page is requested.

By default, an attribute that's determined by a runtime expression is returned as a string, but you can use the Type element to automatically convert a string attribute to a primitive data type or to an object of a wrapper class of a primitive data type. For instance, the last example in this figure shows the definition for the Count attribute of a tag that automatically converts an expression to an int value. Otherwise, you can use the tag handler class to convert the data type.

The syntax for the attribute element in a Tag element

```
<attribute>
  <name>attributeName</name>
  <required>true|false|yes|no</required>
  <rtexprvalue>true|false|yes|no</rtexprvalue>
  <type>data_type</type>
</attribute>
```

The Tag element with two attributes

```
<tag>
  <name>checkfield</name>
  <tagclass>tags.AttributeRequiredTag</tagclass>
  <bodycontent>empty</bodycontent>
  <attribute>
      <name>color</name>
      <required>false</required>
  </attribute>
  <attribute>
      <name>field</name>
      <required>true</required>
      <rtexprvalue>true</rtexprvalue>
  </attribute>
</tag>
```

An attribute element that uses the integer data type

```
<attribute>
  <name>count</name>
  <required>true</required>
  <rtexprvalue>true</rtexprvalue>
  <type>int</type>
</attribute>
```

The attribute child elements

Element	Description
`<name>`	The name of the attribute.
`<required>`	A true/false value that specifies whether this attribute is required. If it isn't required, the tag handler class should provide a default value.
`<rtexprvalue>`	A true/false value that specifies whether the value of the attribute is determined from a runtime expression. If so, the type element can be any data type. Otherwise, the type element will be a string.
`<type>`	The data type of the attribute value. You only need to code this element when the value of the attribute is determined from a runtime expression and the data type isn't a string.

Description

- The Tag element for a tag can include the definitions for one or more attributes.
- For each attribute, you should include at least the Name and Required elements.

Figure 9-7   The TLD for a tag that has attributes

The tag handler class

Figure 9-8 shows how to code a tag handler class that works with attributes. To start, the class must define each attribute as a private instance variable and provide a set method for each attribute.

When you code the set method, you must follow the standard Java naming conventions. For example, if you have an attribute named field, you must code a set method named setField. Similarly, if you have an attribute named height, you must have a set method named setHeight.

When this tag handler class is executed, it begins by declaring the instance variables named field and color. Then, it calls the setField method to set the field instance variable. Since this attribute is required, this method will always be called. This sets the value of the field instance variable equal to the value of the Field attribute in the custom JSP tag.

If a Color attribute has been coded in the custom JSP tag, this class will also call the setColor method to set the color attribute. Otherwise, the color variable will be equal to a null value.

Once the instance variables have been set, the doStartTag method is called. Within this method, the first statement checks the value of the color variable. If this variable is equal to a null value, it sets the variable to a string that specifies that the color should be red. Then, this method checks the value of the field variable. If the field is an empty string, the tag sends an asterisk to the JSP. Otherwise, the tag doesn't do anything.

A tag handler class that uses two attributes

```
package tags;

import javax.servlet.jsp.*;
import javax.servlet.jsp.tagext.*;
import java.io.*;

public class AttributeRequiredTag extends TagSupport{

    private String field;
    private String color;

    public void setField(String f){
        field = f;
    }

    public void setColor(String c){
        color = c;
    }

    public int doStartTag() throws JspException{
        if (color == null)
            color = "red";
        try{
            JspWriter out = pageContext.getOut();
            if ((field.length()==0)){
                out.print("<font color=" + color + ">*</font>");
            }
            return SKIP_BODY;
        }
        catch(IOException ioe){
            System.out.println("AttributeRequiredTag class: " + ioe);
            return SKIP_BODY;
        }
    }
}
```

How to code a tag handler that uses attributes

- Declare a private instance variable for each attribute.
- Define a set method for each attribute with the standard naming conventions.

Description

- This tag handler class will cause the custom JSP tag to display an asterisk if the Field attribute is an empty string.
- If the custom tag includes the Color attribute, the asterisk that's displayed is that color. Otherwise, the asterisk is red.

Figure 9-8   The tag handler class for a tag that has attributes

How to code a custom tag that reiterates its body

In this topic, you'll learn how to code a tag handler class that can repeat the body of a tag multiple times.

The JSP

Figure 9-9 presents a JSP that uses a custom tag to display all products contained in a Vector object. First, a JSP scriptlet uses the ProductIO class to return a vector that contains all Product objects and sets that vector as a session attribute. That way, the tag handler class will be able to access this vector. Then, a custom JSP tag displays one row of a table for each object in the vector.

To achieve this, the body of the custom JSP tag contains some HTML tags and some JSP expressions. These JSP expressions return the description, price, and product code of a product by calling the getAttribute method of the pageContext object. Although this body is coded only once, you'll soon see how the tag handler repeats it once for each object in the vector.

Although this example uses a JSP scriptlet to return the vector of Product objects, you could also store this code in a servlet. That way, you would be able to keep Java code out of your JSP. Although an alternative is to store this code in the tag handler class, it's better to create the vector in a servlet because that's consistent with the logic of the MVC pattern.

A page that displays all products in a text file

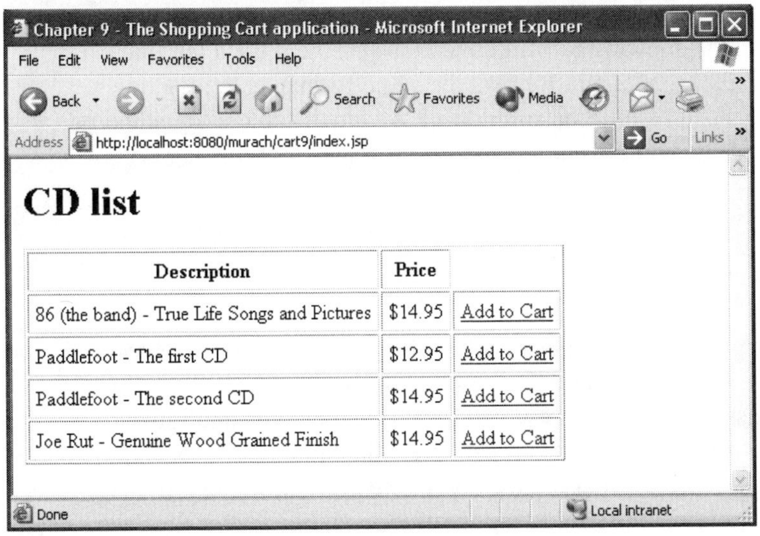

JSP code that uses a reiterating tag

```
<%@ page import="data.ProductIO, java.util.Vector" %>
<% Vector products = ProductIO.readRecords(
                    "../webapps/murach/WEB-INF/etc/products.txt");
   session.setAttribute("products", products);
%>

<%@ taglib uri="../WEB-INF/tlds/murach.tld" prefix="mma" %>
<mma:products>
  <tr valign="top">
    <td><p><%= pageContext.getAttribute("description") %></td>
    <td><p><%= pageContext.getAttribute("price") %></td>
    <td><a href= "../servlet/cart9.CartServlet?productCode=
            <%= pageContext.getAttribute("code") %>">Add to Cart</a></td>
  </tr>
</mma:products>
```

Description

- To pass data to the tag handler class, you can store that data as a session attribute.
- To get an attribute that has been set in the tag handler class, you can call the getAttribute method of the pageContext object.

Figure 9-9   A JSP that uses a tag that reiterates its body

The TLD tags

Figure 9-10 starts by showing how to code a Tag element for a tag that reiterates its body. This Tag element follows the same format as the tag described in figure 9-5. As a result, you shouldn't have any trouble understanding how it works. In short, the BodyContent element indicates that this tag does include a body.

The tag handler class

This figure also presents a tag handler class that reads a vector of objects and displays the data for those objects in the body of the custom JSP tag. In other words, this class loops through a vector of Product objects and returns the body of the tag with different attributes for each Product object.

To code a tag handler class that interacts with the body of the tag, the tag handler class must implement the BodyTag interface rather than the Tag interface. To do that, the tag handler class usually extends the BodyTagSupport class. Then, since this convenience class implements all methods of the BodyTag interface, you only need to override the methods that you want to use. Similarly, since the BodyTagSupport class extends the TagSupport class, all methods and fields that you've used so far will be available to any tag handler class that extends the BodyTagSupport class.

The tag handler class in this figure contains three instance variables. The first instance variable is a Vector object that stores the Product objects. The second instance variable is a counter that's used to loop through this vector. And the third instance variable is the Product object that's used to display data in the tag.

To determine if the tag body should be skipped or evaluated, the doStartTag method retrieves the vector of Product objects from the session and checks if it's empty. To do that, this method calls the findAttribute method of the pageContext object. This method will return any attribute stored in the page, request, session, or application scope.

If the vector of products is empty, the doStartTag method returns the SKIP_BODY constant. As a result, the body of the tag isn't displayed, and the rest of the class is skipped. Otherwise, the doStartTag method returns the EVAL_BODY_BUFFERED constant that's defined in the BodyTagSupport class. As a result, the tag handler class evaluates the body of the tag by calling the doInitBody and doAfterBody methods.

The doInitBody method initializes the body by preparing the first row of the tag. To do that, this method returns the first Product object in the vector. Then, it uses the setAttribute method of the pageContext object to set the three attributes of the Product. Last, it updates the counter variable so it points to the second Product object in the vector.

The Tag element for the TLD

```
<tag>
  <name>products</name>
  <tagclass>tags.ProductsTag</tagclass>
  <bodycontent>JSP</bodycontent>
</tag>
```

A tag handler class that reiterates the body of the tag

```java
package tags;

import javax.servlet.jsp.*;
import javax.servlet.jsp.tagext.*;
import java.io.*;
import java.util.*;
import java.text.NumberFormat;
import business.Product;
import data.ProductIO;

public class ProductsTag extends BodyTagSupport{

    private Vector products;
    private int count;
    private Product product;

    private static NumberFormat currency = NumberFormat.getCurrencyInstance();

// Get vector and skip the body if the vector is empty.

    public int doStartTag(){
        products = (Vector)(pageContext.findAttribute("products"));
        if (products.size() <= 0){
            return SKIP_BODY;
        }
        else{
            return EVAL_BODY_BUFFERED;
        }
    }

// Evaluate the body and add the data for the first vector element
// to the bodyContent object.

    public void doInitBody(){
        count = 0;
        product = (Product) products.get(count);
        pageContext.setAttribute("code", product.getCode());
        pageContext.setAttribute("description", product.getDescription());
        double price = product.getPrice();
        String priceAsString = currency.format(price);
        pageContext.setAttribute("price", priceAsString);
        count++;
    }
```

Figure 9-10   The TLD and the tag handler class for a reiterating tag (part 1 of 2)

After the doInitBody method finishes executing, the body is stored in the bodyContent object that's provided by the BodyTagSupport class. However, the body hasn't yet been displayed. To display the body, you must write the body to the JSP as shown in the doAfterBody method.

The doAfterBody method starts by checking if another element exists in the vector of products. If so, this method retrieves the Product object, and sets the pageContext attributes to the values for that product. Then, it returns the EVAL_BODY_AGAIN constant. This adds the body to the existing bodyContent object, and it calls the doAfterBody method to evaluate the body again. However, the body still hasn't been displayed.

Eventually, the doAfterBody method finishes looping through all of the products in the vector. Then, it displays the body. To do that, this method calls the getEnclosingWriter method of the bodyContent object to obtain a JspWriter object. Then, it calls the writeOut method of the bodyContent object and provides the JspWriter object as an argument. This writes the body to the JSP. Last, this method returns the SKIP_BODY constant to indicate that the tag has finished.

Since the writeOut method throws an IOException, you need to catch this exception. That's why all of the code for the doAfterBody method is enclosed in a try/catch statement.

The tag handler class that reiterates the tag body (continued)

```
    // Evaluate the body again and add the data
    // for the other vector elements to the bodyContent object.
    // Then, write the data of the bodyContent object to the JSP.

    public int doAfterBody() throws JspException{
        try{
            if (count < products.size()){
                product = (Product) products.get(count);
                pageContext.setAttribute("code", product.getCode());
                pageContext.setAttribute("description",
                    product.getDescription());
                double price = product.getPrice();
                String priceAsString = currency.format(price);
                pageContext.setAttribute("price", priceAsString);
                count++;
                return EVAL_BODY_AGAIN;
            }
            else{
                JspWriter out = bodyContent.getEnclosingWriter();
                bodyContent.writeOut(out);
                return SKIP_BODY;
            }
        }
        catch(IOException ioe){
            System.err.println("IOException doAfterBody: " + ioe);
            return SKIP_BODY;
        }
    }
}
```

Description

- To access a tag that has a body, the tag handler class must implement the BodyTag interface. The easiest way to do this is to extend the BodyTagSupport class. Since the BodyTagSupport class extends the TagSupport class, this provides access to all of the methods and fields of the TagSupport class.

- If the doStartTag method returns the EVAL_BODY_BUFFERED constant, the body of the tag will be evaluated by calling the doInitBody method and the doAfterBody method.

- The doInitBody method sets the initial values for the first row of the body.

- If the doAfterBody method returns the EVAL_BODY_AGAIN constant, the doAfterBody method will be called again.

- You can use the setAttribute method of the PageContext object to set any attributes that you need to access from the JSP tag.

- You can use the getEnclosingWriter and writeOut methods of the bodyContent object to write the body to the JSP.

Figure 9-10   The TLD and the tag handler class for a reiterating tag (part 2 of 2)

How to work with scripting variables

The example in the previous topic uses the pageContext object to display variables that were set as attributes in the tag handler class. Now, you'll learn how to create *scripting variables* that can make it easier to display these variables.

An introduction to scripting variables

Figure 9-11 shows how scripting variables can be used to access variables that have been stored as attributes of the pageContext object. Here, the first example shows a custom JSP tag that doesn't use scripting variables. As a result, this custom JSP tag must use the getAttribute method of the pageContext object to get the three variables that have been stored in the pageContext object by the tag handler class.

In contrast, the second example uses scripting variables. As a result, you only need to code the name of a scripting variable in an expression when you want to get the related attribute from the pageContext object.

To make this work, you have to do three tasks. First, the tag handler class must add the scripting variables to the pageContext object as shown in the third example in this figure. Second, you must code a TEI class that defines the scripting variables as shown in the next figure. And third, you must add a teiclass element to the Tag element in the TLD as shown in the last example in this figure.

A custom JSP tag without scripting variables

```
<mma:products>
    <tr>
        <td><%= pageContext.getAttribute("code") %></td>
        <td><%= pageContext.getAttribute("description") %></td>
        <td><%= pageContext.getAttribute("price") %></td>
    </tr>
</mma:products>
```

A custom JSP tag with scripting variables

```
<mma:products>
    <tr>
        <td><%= code %></td>
        <td><%= description %></td>
        <td><%= price %></td>
    </tr>
</mma:products>
```

The code in the tag handler class that adds the scripting variables to the pageContext object

```
pageContext.setAttribute("code", product.getCode());
pageContext.setAttribute("description", product.getDescription());
double price = product.getPrice();
String priceAsString = currency.format(price);
pageContext.setAttribute("price", priceAsString);
```

The Tag element in the TLD

```
<tag>
    <name>products</name>
    <tagclass>tags.ProductsTag</tagclass>
    <teiclass>tags.ProductsTEI</teiclass>
    <bodycontent>JSP</bodycontent>
</tag>
```

How to create a scripting variable

- The tag handler class must add the scripting variables to the pageContext object.
- The TEI class must define the scripting variables as shown in the next figure.
- The Tag element in the TLD must specify both the tag handler class and the TEI class for the custom tag.

Description

- To make attributes easier to access, you can use *scripting variables*. Then, you can code just the name of a scripting variable in an expression when you want to get the value of an attribute from the pageContext object.

Figure 9-11   An introduction to scripting variables

The TEI class

A *TEI class*, or *tag extra information class*, defines the scripting variables for a tag handler. To code a TEI class, you extend the TagExtraInfo class and override its getVariableInfo method. When you override that method, you must return an array of VariableInfo objects. These objects define the scripting variables.

For each scripting variable, you create a VariableInfo object using the constructor shown in this figure. When you code this constructor, you must provide a string that specifies the name of the variable and you must specify the data type of the variable. For the data type, you can specify a String object, a primitive data type, or a wrapper class for a primitive data type.

After coding the data type, you must code a boolean value that specifies whether the variable is a new scripting variable. If the variable has not been coded anywhere else, which is usually the case, you code a true value. Otherwise, you code a false value.

Last, you must define the scope of the scripting variable. Most of the time, you'll want to use the NESTED field. That way, the scripting variables will be available between the opening and closing tags.

The constructor of the VariableInfo class

```
VariableInfo(String varName, String dataType, boolean declare, int scope)
```

A TEI class that creates three scripting variables

```java
package tags;

import javax.servlet.jsp.tagext.*;

public class ProductsTEI extends TagExtraInfo{
    public VariableInfo[] getVariableInfo(TagData data){
        return new VariableInfo[]{
            new VariableInfo("code", "String", true, VariableInfo.NESTED),
            new VariableInfo("description", "String", true,
                            VariableInfo.NESTED),
            new VariableInfo("price", "String", true, VariableInfo.NESTED)
        };
    }
}
```

The VariableInfo constants that define the scope of a scripting variable

Constant	Scope
AT_BEGIN	From the start of the tag to the end of the JSP.
AT_END	From the end of the tag to the end of the JSP.
NESTED	From the start of the tag to the end of the tag.

Description

* To define scripting variables for a tag handler class, you create a *tag extra information class*, or *TEI class*. You can store this class in the same location as the tag handler classes.

* To code a TEI class, you extend the TagExtraInfo class in the javax.servlet.jsp.tagext package. Then, you override the getVariableInfo method to return an array of VariableInfo objects that define the scripting variables.

* For each scripting variable, you create a VariableInfo object that provides this data: the name and data type of the variable, a true/false value that tells whether the variable needs to be declared, and the scope of the variable.

* For the data type of a scripting variable, you can specify a String object, any primitive data type, or any wrapper class for a primitive type.

* To specify whether the scripting variable needs to be declared, you can usually specify a true value to indicate that the variable is new and should be declared.

* To declare the scope of a scripting variable, you can usually use the NESTED constant of the VariableInfo class to narrow the scope of the variable.

Figure 9-12   The TEI class for three scripting variables

Classes, methods, and fields for working with custom tags

This topic summarizes the most common classes, methods, and fields for working with custom tags. Since this chapter has already presented examples that use these classes, this topic should help you review the skills that you've already learned. In addition, it should give you some ideas for how to use other capabilities of custom tags.

Methods and fields of the TagSupport class

Figure 9-13 presents the common methods of the TagSupport class and shows the fields that these methods can return. When a tag is processed, the doStartTag method is called first, followed by the doEndTag method, followed by the release method. When you extend this class, you only need to override the methods that you want to code.

For many types of tags, you need to override the doStartTag method. If a tag doesn't have a body, you can return the SKIP_BODY field after the statements that process the tag. Then, the body of the tag won't be evaluated. However, if a tag does have a body, you can return the EVAL_BODY_INCLUDE field. Then, the body of the tag will be evaluated.

After the doStartTag method finishes executing, the doEndTag method is called. By default, this method returns the EVAL_PAGE field, which causes the rest of the JSP to be evaluated. Since that's usually what you want, you usually don't need to override this method. However, if you don't want to continue evaluating the JSP below the custom tag, you can override this method and return the SKIP_PAGE field. Then, any part of the JSP below the custom tag won't be displayed.

After the doEndTag method finishes executing, the release method is called. You can use this method to clean up any system resources that are in use. For example, you can use this method to close streams or database connections that you have used in the tag handler class.

Common methods and fields of the TagSupport class

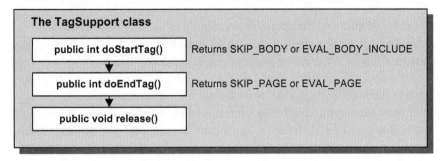

The TagSupport class

public int doStartTag()	Returns SKIP_BODY or EVAL_BODY_INCLUDE
public int doEndTag()	Returns SKIP_PAGE or EVAL_PAGE
public void release()	

Description

- The doStartTag method is the first method that's called for a custom tag. Typically, this method contains the statements that perform the processing for the tag.

- If a tag doesn't have a body, the doStartTag method should return the SKIP_BODY field. That way, the body of the tag won't be displayed.

- If a tag has a body, the doStartTag method should return the EVAL_BODY_INCLUDE field. That way, the body of the tag will be displayed.

- If you need to execute any statements at the end of the tag, you can override the doEndTag method.

- To display the rest of the JSP after the custom tag, the doEndTag method should return the EVAL_PAGE field.

- To not display the rest of the JSP after the custom tag, the doEndTag method should return the SKIP_PAGE field.

- If you need to execute any statements that release any system resources that the tag is using, you can code a release method.

Figure 9-13   Methods and fields of the TagSupport class

Methods and fields of the PageContext class

Figure 9-14 shows some of the methods and fields of the PageContext class. Since an instance of this class named pageContext is built-in for all JSPs and tag handler classes, it allows JSPs and tag handler classes to communicate by getting and setting objects and attributes.

To get objects from the calling JSP, you can use the first three methods shown in this figure. Since you've already seen how a tag handler class can use the getOut method to get the JspWriter object for the calling JSP, you shouldn't have much trouble understanding how the getRequest and getResponse methods can return the request and response objects for the calling JSP.

To set and get attributes, you can call any of the set and get methods of the pageContext class. If you don't explicitly specify a scope when setting an attribute, the attribute will only be available within page scope. However, you can use the fields of the PageContext class to specify the scope. Then, you can use these fields to specify the scope when you attempt to get the attribute, or you can use the findAttribute method to search through all four scopes from smallest to largest.

The pageContext object defined in the TagSupport class

`protected PageContext pageContext`

Common methods of the PageContext class

getOut()

Returns the JspWriter object from the JSP.

getRequest()

Returns the request object from the JSP.

getResponse()

Returns the response object from the JSP.

setAttribute(String name, Object value**)**

Sets the named attribute with page scope to the value.

setAttribute(String name, Object value, int scope**)**

Sets the named attribute with the specified scope to the value. To set the scope, you can use the fields shown below.

getAttribute(String name**)**

Searches the page scope for an attribute with the specified name. If this method finds the attribute, it returns an object of the Object type. Otherwise, it returns a null value.

getAttribute(String name, int scope**)**

Searches the specified scope for an attribute with the specified name. If this method finds the attribute, it returns an object of the Object type. Otherwise, it returns a null value. To set the scope, you can use the fields shown below.

findAttribute(String name**)**

Searches the page, request, session, and application scopes in that sequence for the specified attribute. If this method finds the specified attribute, it returns an object of the Object type. Otherwise, it returns a null value.

The fields of the PageContext class for setting scope

```
PAGE_SCOPE
REQUEST_SCOPE
SESSION_SCOPE
APPLICATION_SCOPE
```

Description

* You can use the pageContext object to set and get JSP objects and attributes.
* For more information about the PageContext class, you can look in the javax.servlet.jsp package in the servlet API.

Figure 9-14   Methods and fields of the PageContext class

Methods and fields of the BodyTagSupport class

Figure 9-15 shows some of the methods and fields of the BodyTagSupport class. Since this class extends the TagSupport class, you can access the pageContext object and its methods directly from the BodyTagSupport class. In addition, the doEndTag and release methods work much as they do in the TagSupport class.

By default, the doStartTag method of the BodyTagSupport class returns the EVAL_BODY_BUFFERED field. This field indicates that the tag has a body and it causes the doInitBody and doAfterBody methods to be called. As a result, you only need to override this method if you want to add code that writes data to the JSP before the body is evaluated, or if you want to skip the body under certain conditions. To skip the body, the doStartTag method can return the SKIP_BODY field. In that case, the doEndTag and release methods will be called.

If the doStartTag method returns EVAL_BODY_BUFFERED, the doInitBody method is called. Then, you can override this method to initialize any values before the body is evaluated for the first time. After the doInitBody method is executed, the body is evaluated. In other words, the body is read and placed in the built-in bodyContent object, which stores the body. In the next figure, you'll learn more about working with the bodyContent object.

After the doInitBody method finishes executing, the doAfterBody method is called. You can override this method to code statements that need to be executed each time the body is evaluated. If you want to evaluate the body again and add it to the bodyContent object, you return the EVAL_BODY_AGAIN field. Then, when you finish evaluating the body, you return the SKIP_BODY field. But first, you'll probably want to use the bodyContent object to write the body that's stored in the bodyContent object to the JSP.

Once the doAfterBody method returns the SKIP_BODY field, the doEndTag and release methods are called. Since the default values for these methods are usually adequate, you usually don't need to override these methods.

Common methods and fields of the BodyTagSupport class

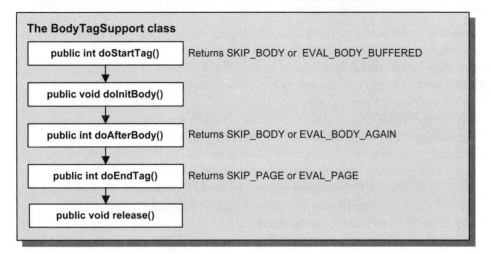

Description

- The BodyTagSupport class extends the TagSupport class. As a result, the methods and fields that are available in the TagSupport class are also available to the BodyTagSupport class.

- If you want to perform some initial processing for a tag, you can override the doStartTag method of the BodyTagSupport class.

- If the doStartTag method returns the EVAL_BODY_BUFFERED field, the doInitBody and doAfterBody methods will be called to display the body of the tag.

- The doInitBody method should contain all of the initialization statements that are needed for the first evaluation of the body.

- The doAfterBody method should contain all of the statements that are needed for additional evaluations of the body.

- If the doAfterBody method returns the EVAL_BODY_AGAIN field, the body will be added to the bodyContent object and the doAfterBody method will be called again.

- If the doAfterBody method returns the SKIP_BODY field, the processing for the tag will be finished and the body will be skipped.

Figure 9-15   Methods and fields of the BodyTagSupport class

Methods and fields of the BodyContent class

Figure 9-16 shows some methods and fields of the BodyContent class. When you extend the BodyTagSupport class, an instance of this class named bodyContent is automatically available to your tag handler class and it automatically stores the body of the tag. When the tag handler class is through evaluating the body of the tag, you can use the getEnclosingWriter and writeOut methods of the BodyContent class to write the body to the JSP.

Sometimes, you may need to use other methods of the BodyContent class. For example, you may need to use the getString method to return the text of the body as a String object. Or, you may need to use the clearBody method to clear the contents of the bodyContent object after the body is evaluated. To learn more about these and other methods of the BodyContent class, you can look them up in the documentation for the servlet API.

The bodyContent object defined in the BodyTagSupport class

```
protected BodyContent bodyContent
```

Common methods of the BodyContent class

clearBody()

Clears the body.

getEnclosingWriter()

Returns the JspWriter object for the body.

getString()

Returns the body as a String object.

writeOut(Writer out)

Writes the body to the specified out stream.

Description

- The bodyContent object stores the body of the tag before it is written to the JSP.

- To display the body in the JSP, you can use the getEnclosingWriter and writeOut methods of the BodyContent class.

- For more information about the BodyContent class, you can look in the javax.servlet.jsp.tagext package in the servlet API.

Figure 9-16   Methods and fields of the BodyContent class

Perspective

The goal of this chapter has been to show you how to create and use custom JSP tags. These tags make it easier for web designers to develop the JSPs for an application because they reduce the amount of Java code that's required. These tags can also help the Java programmer organize the code of an application and create code that can be used by more than one JSP.

Summary

- To create a *custom tag* that can be used in a JSP, you must create an XML file called the *Tag Library Descriptor*, or *TLD*. This TLD defines the *tag library* that defines the custom tags for an application.

- To implement a custom tag that's defined in the TLD, you code a *tag handler class*. This is a class that implements the Tag interface, usually by extending the TagSupport class.

- Before you can use a custom tag in a JSP, you must code a *taglib directive* that specifies the location of the TLD and a prefix. Then, to use a custom tag, you code the prefix followed by the name of the custom tag.

- You can use custom tags with a body, without a body, with attributes, and with a repeating body.

- *Scripting variables* can be used to get the attributes of the pageContext object. To provide for these variables, you need to code a *tag extra information (TEI) class* that is related to a tag handler class by the TLD.

- As you code the tag handler classes, you can use the methods and fields of the TagSupport, PageContext, BodyTagSupport, and BodyContent classes of the servlet API.

- When you create custom tags, you make it easier for web designers to code the JSPs of an application by reducing the amount of code that's required and by reducing the need for Java code. You also promote the reuse of code, which can improve productivity.

Terms

custom JSP tag
custom tag
taglib directive
Tag Library Descriptor (TLD)
tag library

tag handler class
scripting variable
TEI class
tag extra information class

Objectives

- Create a Tag Library Descriptor for custom tags, and write the tag handler classes that implement these tags. In your tag handler classes, you should be able to provide for tags with bodies, without bodies, with attributes, and with repeating bodies.

- Create scripting variables that can be used in your JSPs.

- Use custom JSP tags and scripting variables in the JSPs for your applications.

- Explain how a custom JSP tag gets associated with a tag handler class.

- Describe the benefits that you get from using custom tags.

Exercise 9-1   Create and use a custom tag

In this exercise, you'll create a custom tag and add it the Index page of the Cart application that you saw in chapter 7.

1. Create a custom tag that works like the tag shown in figures 9-1 through 9-3, but it should be used like this:

```
<mma:todayBody>
    <p>The current date is <%= pageContext.getAttribute("today") %>.</p>
</mma:todayBody>
```

   To do this, you should create the tag handler class and save it in the tags package, and then add the Tag element to the TLD located in the WEB-INF/tlds directory.

2. Open the Index page that's located in the cart9 directory and use the todayBody tag in this JSP. Request this page to make sure it works as you expect. (Be sure to restart Tomcat so that it can read your updated TLD file.)

3. Add an optional attribute named "format" to this tag that can be used to change the format of the date to the short, medium, or long formats described in the java.text.DateFormat class. If the JSP doesn't provide an attribute value, then use the short format by default. To do this, first edit the tag handler class so that it implements this attribute. Then, update the TLD. After that, modify the tag in the JSP.

Exercise 9-2 Work with scripting variables

1. Modify the Index page of the Cart application so it uses scripting variables as shown in figure 9-11.

2. Modify the custom tag that you created in the previous exercise so it uses a scripting variable to display the date. To do this, first create the TEI class. Then, edit the TLD. After that, modify the tag in the Index page so that it uses the scripting variable.

Exercise 9-3 Create and use a reiterating tag

In this exercise, you'll create a custom tag that reiterates through a vector of User objects. Then, you'll create a JSP that uses this tag to display the first name, last name, and email address of all users in the UserEmail.txt file that you've been working with throughout the book. For this exercise to run, the UserEmail.txt file must be correctly formatted. If you receive runtime errors, you should open the file and remove any invalid entries.

1. Create a tag handler class like the one in figure 9-10, but it should now work with User objects rather than Product objects. Then, create a Tag element for a Users custom tag in the TLD.

2. Create a JSP named users.jsp that uses the Users custom tag you created in step 1 to display a table of all users saved in the UserEmail.txt file. To do this, you may want to refer to figure 9-9. To retrieve a Vector object of all users in this file, you can use the readRecords method in the UserIO class that's located in the data package as follows:

```
Vector users = UserIO.readRecords(
                "../webapps/murach/WEB-INF/etc/userEmail.txt");
```

When you're done, save the JSP in the email9 directory. When it's rendered, it should look like this:

3. Add three scripting variables for the Users tag so the JSP doesn't have to use the pageContext object to access the first name, last name, and email address.

Section 3

The essential database skills

For most web applications, you need to save the data on the web server or a database server. Although you can often save the data for simple applications in text files like the ones used so far in this book, you often need to use a database for web applications. That's why the two chapters in this section present the essential database skills that you need for developing web applications.

In chapter 10, you'll learn how to use MySQL databases because MySQL is one of the most popular database management systems for Java web applications. Then, in chapter 11, you'll learn how to write servlets that connect to MySQL databases and work with the data that's stored in those databases. Because this works the same for all database management systems, these chapters present the essential skills that you need for working with any database.

10

How to use MySQL to work with a database

Although there are several databases that work well with web applications, this chapter shows how to work with MySQL because it's one of the most popular databases for Java web applications. It's also free for the purposes of this book. That's why we used it for the database that is used by the applications in this book. In this chapter, you'll learn how to create a MySQL database and how to use SQL statements to work with the data in that database.

Before you start this chapter, you should know that it assumes that you already have some database knowledge or experience. It assumes, for example, that you know that a relational database is made up of tables that consist of columns and rows, that the tables are related by keys, and that you use SQL statements to access and update the data in a database. Although this chapter does review some of these terms, its focus is on the specific skills that you need for using MySQL.

An introduction to MySQL **308**
What MySQL provides 308
What MySQL doesn't provide 308
Two ways to interact with MySQL 310
How to start and stop the MySQL database server 312

How to work with the mysql program **314**
How to start and stop the mysql program 314
How to create, select, and delete a database 316
How to create and delete a table 318
How to insert or load data into a table 320
How to configure the mysql program 322

The SQL statements for data manipulation **324**
How to select data from a single table 324
How to select data from multiple tables 326
How to insert, update, and delete data 328

Perspective **330**

An introduction to MySQL

Figure 10-1 presents an introduction to *MySQL*, which is an open-source database that you can download for free from the MySQL web site (*www.mysql.com*). It is also available as part of a hosting package from many ISPs.

What MySQL provides

Figure 10-1 begins by listing some of the reasons that MySQL enjoys such popularity among web developers. To start, it's inexpensive and easy to use when compared with products like Oracle or Microsoft SQL Server. It runs fast when compared to those products, especially when you consider the costs. And it runs on most modern operating systems, while Microsoft SQL Server runs only on Windows.

Even though it's free for most uses, MySQL provides most of the features that you would expect from a modern *relational database management system,* or *RDBMS*. In particular, it provides support for *Structured Query Language*, or *SQL*, which is the industry standard. It provides support for multiple clients. And it provides for connectivity and security.

In terms of web applications, that means you can write Java applications that use SQL statements to access and update the data in a MySQL database. You can connect a Java web application to a MySQL database that's running on an intranet or the Internet. And you can secure your data by restricting access to it.

What MySQL doesn't provide

This figure also lists three features that are commonly provided by commercial products, but that aren't provided by MySQL. If you're new to database programming, you probably don't know what referential integrity, subqueries, and transaction processing are, so you can skip the rest of this subtopic. But if you know what they are, you may be interested to know that these missing features aren't necessarily serious omissions.

For instance, although MySQL doesn't provide for declarative referential integrity, doing so degrades the performance of an RDBMS. Besides that, MySQL does support triggers, which you can use to enforce referential integrity. In addition, you can code your applications so they provide for referential integrity and your RDBMS doesn't have to. Similarly, although MySQL doesn't support subqueries, you can usually rewrite your SQL statements so you don't have to use subqueries. Or, you can use a combination of Java code and SQL to do the subquery and the query. Finally, although MySQL doesn't support transactions, you don't need that feature for many web applications. However, if transactional processing is critical to your applications, you can duplicate much of the functionality by making use of the MySQL log.

MySQL is...

- **Inexpensive.** MySQL is free for most uses and relatively inexpensive for other uses.
- **Fast.** By many accounts, MySQL is one of the fastest relational databases that's currently available.
- **Easy to use.** Compared to other database systems, MySQL is easy to install and use.
- **Portable.** MySQL runs on most modern operating systems including Windows, Unix, Solaris, and OS/2.

MySQL provides...

- **Support for SQL.** Like any modern database product, MySQL supports SQL, which is the standard language for working with data that's stored in relational databases.
- **Support for multiple clients.** MySQL supports access from multiple clients from a variety of interfaces and programming languages including Java, Perl, PHP, Python, and C.
- **Connectivity.** MySQL can provide access to data via an intranet or the Internet.
- **Security.** MySQL can protect access to your data so only authorized users can view the data.

MySQL doesn't provide...

- **Referential integrity.** Unlike Oracle or Microsoft SQL Server, standard MySQL tables don't support declarative referential integrity (DRI). However, referential integrity can be maintained by using SQL triggers or by the applications that maintain the data in the database.
- **Subqueries.** Although MySQL doesn't support SQL subqueries, the same results can often be achieved by writing a SQL statement in a different way or by using a combination of Java code and SQL code.
- **Transaction processing.** Unlike Oracle or Microsoft SQL Server, MySQL doesn't support transaction processing, which can prevent corruption of the database in the event of a system failure. For most web applications, however, this lack of support isn't necessary or can be duplicated by other means.

Figure 10-1   An introduction to MySQL

Two ways to interact with MySQL

Figure 10-2 shows two ways that you can interact with MySQL. When you install MySQL, it includes a command-line tool like the one at the top of this figure. Although this shows the DOS Prompt window for the Windows operating system, MySQL's command-line tool works similarly on all operating systems. In this example, the user has started the command-line tool, logged into a database named Murach, and displayed three rows from the User table in that database. You'll learn more about working with this tool in a moment.

If, on the other hand, you're accessing MySQL through an Internet service provider, you might have access to a web-based tool like the second one in this figure. This tool lets you work with a database by interacting with a series of web pages. In the next chapter, you'll learn how to create a web-based tool of your own that lets you enter SQL statements into a web page and display the results on a web page.

A command-line interface

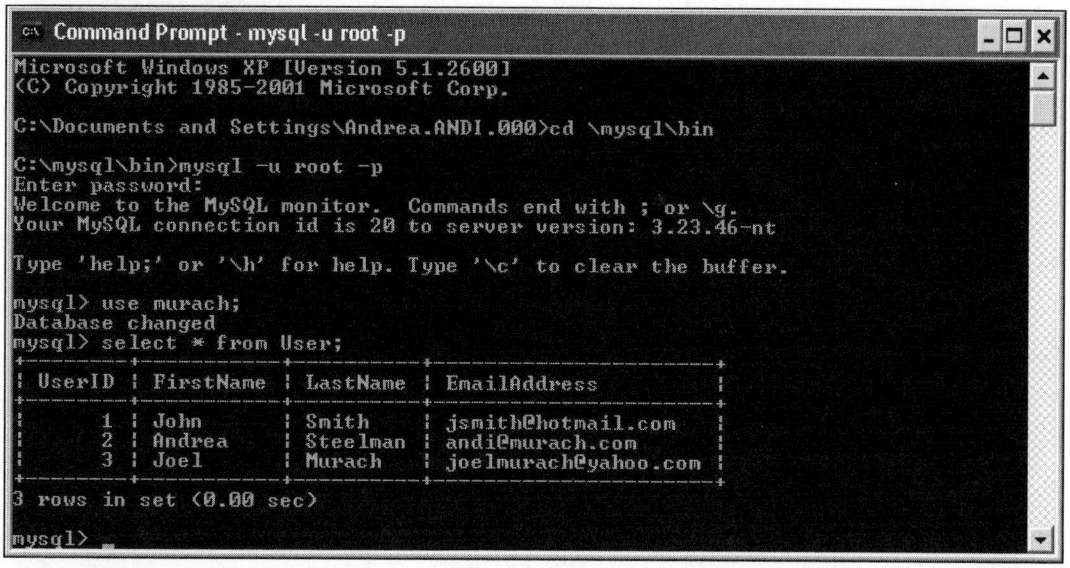

```
Command Prompt - mysql -u root -p                                    [_][□][x]
Microsoft Windows XP [Version 5.1.2600]
(C) Copyright 1985-2001 Microsoft Corp.

C:\Documents and Settings\Andrea.ANDI.000>cd \mysql\bin

C:\mysql\bin>mysql -u root -p
Enter password:
Welcome to the MySQL monitor.  Commands end with ; or \g.
Your MySQL connection id is 20 to server version: 3.23.46-nt

Type 'help;' or '\h' for help. Type '\c' to clear the buffer.

mysql> use murach;
Database changed
mysql> select * from User;
+--------+-----------+-----------+------------------------+
| UserID | FirstName | LastName  | EmailAddress           |
+--------+-----------+-----------+------------------------+
|      1 | John      | Smith     | jsmith@hotmail.com     |
|      2 | Andrea    | Steelman  | andi@murach.com        |
|      3 | Joel      | Murach    | joelmurach@yahoo.com   |
+--------+-----------+-----------+------------------------+
3 rows in set (0.00 sec)

mysql>
```

An HTML interface

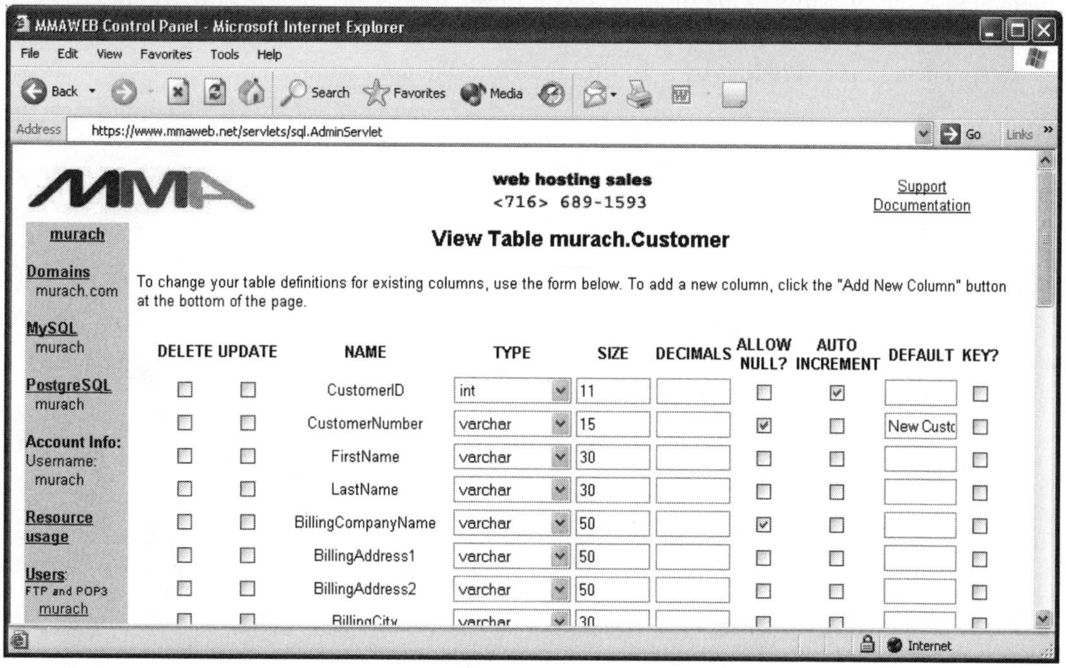

Figure 10-2   Two ways to interact with MySQL

How to start and stop the MySQL database server

Appendix A shows how to install MySQL, which is a simple procedure that you can do in a few minutes. As a result, this chapter assumes that you've already installed it or that you're using a client on a network that has MySQL running. As part of the installation, a *database server* is installed that provides for the management of your MySQL databases.

When you install MySQL on most Windows systems, the MySQL database server starts every time you start your computer. On some systems, this displays the MySQL icon in the tray. This icon looks like a stoplight, and the light is green when this server is running. On other systems, the server is running but the icon isn't displayed in the tray.

To display the MySQL icon, you can run the winmysqladmin.exe file that's in MySQL's bin directory. Then, you can stop the database server by selecting the "Stop this Service" or the "ShutDown this Server" command from the icon as shown in figure 10-3. If you select the "Stop this Service" command, the light on the icon will become red, and you can restart the server by selecting the "Start this Service" command from the icon.

MySQL also provides a GUI that lets you view some information about its database server. Most of the time, you won't need to use this GUI. But if you're curious, you can view it by selecting the Show Me command from the MySQL icon. Then, you can hide it by selecting the Hide Me command.

The icon for the MySQL server

MySQL icon

How to start the MySQL server and display the MySQL icon

* On most systems, the MySQL server starts every time you start your computer.
* If the MySQL server doesn't start when you start your computer, you can start the MySQL server by running the winmysqladmin.exe file in MySQL's bin directory.
* On some systems, the MySQL icon is displayed in the tray as shown above. On other systems, you must run the winmysqladmin.exe file to display the icon.

How to stop the MySQL server

* To stop the server, you can click on the MySQL icon. Then, you can select the "Win 9x" and "ShutDown this Server" commands, or you can select the "Win NT" and "Stop this Service" commands.

Description

* To install MySQL, you can follow the procedure in appendix A.
* When MySQL is installed, it includes a *database server* that provides for the management of your MySQL databases.
* Whenever necessary, you can stop and start MySQL by using the procedures above.

Figure 10-3   How to start and stop the MySQL database server

How to work with the mysql program

To make it easy to work with its databases, MySQL provides a command-line client program called the *mysql program*. After you use this program to connect to the database server, you can use it to work with the databases that are available from that server. So that's what you'll learn next.

How to start and stop the mysql program

Figure 10-4 shows how to start and stop the mysql program. To start it, you open a command prompt window like the DOS Prompt window and change to the mysql\bin directory. Then, you execute the mysql command by supplying all the appropriate parameters.

If the MySQL server is located on the same computer as the mysql client program and you haven't secured the database yet, you can log in with a username of "root" and no password. If the MySQL server is located on a remote computer, you may be able to access the database through a web-based interface. Otherwise, you'll need to specify the host name of the computer and a valid username. Then, MySQL will ask you for a valid password as shown by the example in this figure.

Although it can sometimes take some experimentation to find a connection string that works, you only need to figure it out once. Then, you can use that connection string for future sessions. To make that easier, though, you can save the parameters in a configuration file so you don't have to enter them every time you start the mysql program. You'll learn how to do that in figure 10-8.

Once you enter a successful connection string, the program will display a welcome message like the one shown in this figure, and it will display a mysql command prompt that looks like this:

```
mysql>
```

From this prompt, you can enter any MySQL command or SQL statement. To exit from the mysql program, for example, you can enter an Exit or Quit command like this one:

```
mysql>quit
```

The mysql program

How to start the mysql program

The syntax

```
mysql -h hostname -u username -p
```

Examples

```
c:\mysql\bin>mysql -h murach.com -u jmurach -p
c:\mysql\bin>mysql -u jmurach -p
c:\mysql\bin>mysql
```

How to exit the mysql program

The syntax

```
exit | quit
```

Examples

```
mysql>exit
```

Description

- MySQL provides a command-line client program called the *mysql program*. This program lets you enter MySQL commands and SQL statements that work with MySQL databases.

- To start the mysql program, open a command prompt window like the DOS Prompt window, change to the mysql\bin directory, and enter a mysql command that includes the username and the host name if it isn't the computer that you're logged in on. If it's required, MySQL will prompt you for a valid password.

- When you install MySQL, the database isn't secure so it allows anyone on the local machine to log into the database server with a username of 'root' and no password. If, however, the database has been secured or if you're accessing a database that's running on a remote server, you must obtain a valid username and password from the database administrator.

- To stop the mysql program, enter "exit" or "quit" at the command prompt.

Figure 10-4   How to start and stop the mysql program

How to create, select, and delete a database

Once the mysql program is connected to a database server, you can use it to run *MySQL commands* and *SQL statements* that work with the databases that are available from that server. As you read the rest of this chapter, you'll see examples of each. When you enter them at the prompt for the mysql program, though, that distinction is unimportant because they work the same way.

When you enter a command or statement, you must end it with a semicolon. Otherwise, the mysql prompt will display a second line when you press the Enter key like this:

```
mysql> show databases
    ->
```

This shows that the mysql program is waiting for you to finish your command or statement. As you will see, this makes it easy for you to enter commands or statements that require more than one line. To finish a command or statement and have it executed, you just type a semicolon and press the Enter key.

Figure 10-5 shows how use two MySQL commands and two SQL statements. To make it easy to distinguish them, the text in this chapter capitalizes just the first letters in the names of commands and all of the letters in the names of SQL statements. Thus, you use the Show Databases command to list the names of all the databases that are managed by the database server, and you use the CREATE DATABASE statement to create a database. When you enter commands or statements at the prompt for the mysql program, though, you can use all lowercase letters because it's easier to type them that way.

To create a database, you use the CREATE DATABASE statement as illustrated by the first example in this figure. Here, this statement creates a database named "murach", and the message after the command indicates that this has been done successfully. Note, however, that this database hasn't been defined yet and it doesn't contain any data. You'll learn how to define it and add data to it in the next two figures.

To list the names of the databases stored on a server, you use the Show Databases command as illustrated by the second example. Here, the "murach" database is the one created by the first example, the "mysql" database is an internal database that's used by the MySQL server, and the "test" database is a test database that comes with MySQL.

To select the database that you want to work with, you use the Use command as illustrated by the third example. This selects the "murach" database, and the message after this command says "Database changed" to indicate that the statement was successful. After you select a database, the commands and statements that you enter will work with that database.

To delete a database from the server, you use the DROP DATABASE statement as illustrated by the fourth example. Here, the "murach" database is deleted. When you successfully delete a database, the mysql program displays a message that says "Query OK" along with the number of rows that were deleted from the tables in the database.

How to create a database

```
mysql> create database murach;
Query OK, 1 row affected (0.06 sec)
```

How to list the names of all databases managed by the server

```
mysql> show databases;
+------------+
| Database   |
+------------+
| murach     |
| mysql      |
| test       |
+------------+
3 rows in set (0.00 sec)
```

How to select a database for use

```
mysql> use murach;
Database changed
```

How to delete a database

```
mysql> drop database murach;
Query OK, 3 rows affected (0.00 sec)
```

Description

*   You can use the mysql program to work with any of the MySQL databases that are managed by the database server. To do that, you can use MySQL commands and SQL statements.

*   You can use the CREATE DATABASE statement to create a database and the DROP DATABASE statement to delete a database. These are *SQL statements*, and the text uses all capital letters to refer to these statements.

*   You can use the Use command to select the database that you want to work with and the Show Databases command to list the names of all the databases for a server. These are *MySQL commands*, and the text capitalizes just the first letter to refer to these commands.

*   When you use the mysql program, the commands and statements aren't case-sensitive. As a result, must programmers enter them in lowercase letters because they're easier to type that way.

Figure 10-5   How to create, select, and delete a database

How to create and delete a table

As you probably know, a *relational database* consists of one or more *tables* that consist of *rows* and *columns*. These tables are related by the *keys* in the rows. The *primary key* is a column that provides a unique value that identifies each row in a table. A *foreign key* is a column that is used to relate each row in one table with one or more rows in another table, usually by the primary keys in those rows.

So after you create a database as shown in the last figure, you need to create its tables as shown in figure 10-6. To do that, you use the CREATE TABLE statement. This statement is used to name each table and to define its columns.

In the example in this figure, you can see that a table named User is created that consists of four columns (UserID, FirstName, LastName, and EmailAddress), and the primary key is the UserID field. Here, the UserID column is the integer data type, it can't contain a null value, and it uses MySQL's auto-increment feature to automatically generate a unique integer for each new row by incrementing the number for the last row. In contrast, the other three columns have the VarChar (variable character) data type and can hold a maximum of 50 characters.

Because entering a lengthy statement like this at the prompt is error prone, statements like this are often entered into separate text files known as *SQL scripts*. In fact, a SQL script can contain more than one statement so a single script can create a database and create all the tables for it. To run a SQL script, you enter the mysql command. This command must include a complete connection string, the name of the database, and the path for the SQL script as shown by the second example in this figure.

Once you've created the tables for a database, you can use the Show Tables command to list them. You can also use the DROP TABLE statement to delete one of them. That's useful when you want to modify the definitions for the columns in a table. An efficient way to do that is to drop the table you want to change, modify the script for the table, and rerun the script to recreate the table.

Please note, however, that the purpose of this figure is *not* to teach you how to create the tables for a database because that's more than can be done in a servlets book. Instead, the purposes of this figure are (1) to introduce you to the commands and statements for creating, listing, and deleting the tables in a database and (2) to show you how to use SQL scripts. As a result, you should now understand the SQL scripts that are used by the procedures in appendix A to create the databases that are used by the applications in this book.

These scripts are stored in a directory named MySQL_scripts. If you open them and study them, you should get a better feel for how the tables in a database are defined. In particular, you'll see definitions for other data types, primary keys, foreign keys, and so on. That in turn will make it easier for you to understand what's happening when you write SQL statements that retrieve and update the data in these databases.

How to create a table using the mysql program

```
mysql> create table User (
    -> UserID int not null auto_increment,
    -> FirstName varchar(50),
    -> LastName varchar(50),
    -> EmailAddress varchar(50),
    -> primary key(UserID)
    -> );
Query OK, 0 rows affected (0.05 sec)
```

How to create a table using a SQL script

A mysql command that runs a script

```
C:\mysql\bin>mysql -u jmurach -p murach < c:\murach\scripts\UserCreate.sql
Enter password: ******
```

The SQL script that's stored in a file named UserCreate.sql

```
CREATE TABLE User (
    UserID INT NOT NULL AUTO_INCREMENT,
    FirstName VARCHAR(50),
    LastName VARCHAR(50),
    EmailAddress VARCHAR(50),
    PRIMARY KEY(UserID)
)
```

How to list all of the tables in a database

```
mysql> show tables;
+------------------+
| Tables_in_murach |
+------------------+
| download         |
| user             |
+------------------+
2 rows in set (0.00 sec)
```

How to delete a table

```
mysql> drop table User;
Query OK, 0 rows affected (0.00 sec)
```

Description

- A *relational database* consists of one or more *tables* that consist of *rows* (*records*) and *columns* (*fields*). These tables are related by *keys*. The *primary key* in a table is the one that uniquely identifies each of the rows in the table. A *foreign key* is used to relate the rows in one table to the rows in another table.

- When you create a table, you define each of its columns and you identify its primary key. To define a column, you must supply the name and the data type, and you can also indicate whether a column accepts default values, whether it's automatically generated for new rows, and so on.

- A file that stores one or more SQL statements is a *SQL script*. To run a script, you use the mysql command.

- On Unix systems, the table and column names are case-sensitive.

Figure 10-6   How to create and delete a table

How to insert or load data into a table

Once you've created a table, you need to fill the table with some data. Figure 10-7 shows two ways to do that. First, you can use the INSERT statement to insert one or more rows into a table. Second, you can use the Load command to transfer the data that's stored in a tab-delimited text file into a table. Typically, the INSERT statement is used within the code for a web application to insert one row into a table while the Load command is used to load large amounts of data into a table.

This figure starts by showing two ways to execute an INSERT statement that inserts two rows into the User table that you learned how to create in the last figure. First, you can enter the statement directly into the mysql program. Second, you can store the statement in an SQL script and execute the script.

To begin an INSERT statement, you code the INSERT INTO keywords. Then, you code the table name followed by a set of parentheses. Within the parentheses, you code a list of the column names for the table. Although the SQL keywords aren't case-sensitive, the table and column names are case-sensitive on Unix systems. As a result, it's a good programming practice to code these names using the correct case.

After the list of column names, you code the VALUES keyword followed by a set of parentheses. Within these parentheses, you can code the values that should be inserted into each row. If you want to code more than one row of values, you can separate each row with a comma so the statement in this example inserts three rows. Note, however, that you don't need to include values for columns that use MySQL's auto increment feature or are defined with default values. In this case, since the value for the UserID column is automatically generated, you don't need to include it.

When you use the Load command to load the data from a tab-delimited text file into a table, the file must provide for all of the columns that are defined for the table. This is illustrated by the example in this figure, which has four fields for each record of the User table. Then, the Load command that follows is used to load the data from this file into the User table on the local computer.

To load data from your system into a table on a remote web server, though, you may need to use a Load command like the second one in this figure. Because this varies depending on how the remote server is configured, you may need to ask your Internet service provider how Load commands should be coded.

How to use the INSERT statement

With the mysql program

```
mysql> insert into User
    -> (FirstName, LastName, EmailAddress)
    -> values
    -> ('John', 'Smith', 'jsmith@hotmail.com'),
    -> ('Andrea', 'Steelman', 'andi@murach.com'),
    -> ('Joel', 'Murach', 'joelmurach@yahoo.com');
Query OK, 3 rows affected (0.06 sec)
```

In a SQL script stored in a file named UserInsert.sql

```
INSERT INTO User
  (FirstName, LastName, EmailAddress)
VALUES
  ('John', 'Smith', 'jsmith@hotmail.com'),
  ('Andrea', 'Steelman', 'andi@murach.com'),
  ('Joel', 'Murach', 'joelmurach@yahoo.com')
```

A Mysql command that runs the SQL script

```
C:\mysql\bin>mysql -u jmurach -p murach < c:\murach\scripts\UserInsert.sql
Enter password: ******
```

How to use the Load command

A tab-delimited text file that's stored in Users.txt

```
1    John      Smith       jsmith@hotmail.com
2    Andrea    Steelman    andi@murach.com
3    Joel      Murach      joelmurach@yahoo.com
```

A Load command that loads the data into a local table

```
mysql> load data local infile "c:/murach/scripts/Users.txt" into table User;
Query OK, 3 rows affected (0.00 sec)
Records: 3  Deleted: 0  Skipped: 0  Warnings: 0
```

A Load command that loads the data into a table on a remote Unix server

```
load data infile "/usr/local/etc/httpd/sites/murach.com/htdocs/Users.txt"
into table User
```

Description

- The INSERT statement lets you insert one or more rows into one table of a database. When you code it, you need to include data for all columns that aren't defined with default values or aren't automatically generated.

- The Load command lets you load a tab-delimited text file into a table. In this case, the text file must have the same number of columns as the table.

- On a Unix system, table and column names are case-sensitive.

- If you're loading data into a table on a remote web server, you need to find out how the Load command should be coded.

Figure 10-7   How to insert or load data into a table

How to configure the mysql program

Figure 10-8 shows how to store the parameters for the command that you use to start the mysql program. That way, you don't have to enter your connection parameters each time you start the program. To do that, you need to create a text file named my.cnf that contains your connection parameters. Then, you need to save this file in your home directory (which is c:\ on most Windows systems).

Because the my.cnf file is just a text file, you can use TextPad or any other text editor to create and modify it. This file must start with the [client] line. Then, it can specify one connection parameter per line. For example, the first two lines in this figure shows how to specify the user (-u) and password (-p) parameters. Then, this line shows how to specify the host (-h) parameter if you're connecting to your own PC. If you need to connect to a remote host, you can code provide a URL like *www.murach.com* for this parameter.

Once you've created and saved the my.cnf file, you can start the mysql program as shown by the three examples in this figure. The first example connects to the database server. The second example connects to the database server and selects the murach database. And the third example connects to the database server, selects the murach database, and runs the UserCreate script.

A c:\my.cnf configuration file for a Windows system

```
[client]
user=jsmith
password=sesame
host=localhost
```

The syntax for starting the mysql program using the my.cnf file

```
mysql databasename < sqlscriptpath
```

Three ways to start the mysql program using the my.cnf file

Start the mysql program only

```
c:\mysql\bin>mysql
```

Start the mysql program and select the murach database

```
c:\mysql\bin>mysql murach
```

Start the mysql program, select the murach database, and run a script

```
c:\mysql\bin>mysql murach < c:\murach\scripts\UserCreate.sql
```

Description

- If you create a configuration file for MySQL, you don't have to enter the user, password, and host parameters each time you start the mysql program.

- On a Windows system, the my.cnf file should be in the c:\ directory.

- To learn how to set up a configuration options file for other types of systems, check the MySQL website (*www.mysql.com*).

Figure 10-8   How to configure the mysql program

The SQL statements for data manipulation

With the exception of the INSERT statement, the SQL statements that you've seen thus far have been part of SQL's *Data Definition Language*, or *DDL*. These statements let you create databases, create tables, drop tables, and so on, but they don't work with the data in the tables.

In contrast, the statements that you'll learn about next make up SQL's *Data Manipulation Language*, or *DML*. These statements work with the data in a database, and they include the SELECT, INSERT, UPDATE, and DELETE statements. As a result, these are the statements that you will use in your Java applications.

How to select data from a single table

The SELECT statement is the most commonly used SQL statement. It can be used to retrieve data from one or more tables in a database. When you run a SELECT statement, it is commonly referred to as a *query* (although the execution of any SQL statement can also be referred to as a query). The result of this query is always a table known as a *result set*, or a *result table*.

In figure 10-9, the first example shows how to use this statement to retrieve all rows and columns from the User table. Here, the SELECT clause uses the asterisk wildcard to indicate that all of the columns in the table should be retrieved. Then, the FROM clause identifies the User table. In the result table, you can see the three rows and four columns that are returned by this query.

The second example shows how to use this statement to retrieve two columns and two rows from the User table. Here, the SELECT clause identifies the two columns, and the FROM clause identifies the table. Then, the WHERE clause limits the number of rows that are retrieved by specifying that the statement should only retrieve rows where the value in the UserID field is less than 3. Last, the ORDER BY clause indicates that the retrieved rows should be sorted in ascending order (from A to Z) by the LastName field.

The result set is a logical table that's created temporarily within the database. Then, the *current row pointer*, or *cursor*, keeps track of the current row. You can use this pointer from your web applications.

As you might guess, queries can have a significant effect on the performance of a database application. In general, the more columns and rows that a query returns, the more traffic the network has to bear. As a result, when you design queries, you should try to keep the number of columns and rows to a minimum.

The syntax for a SELECT statement that gets all columns

```
SELECT *
FROM table-1
[WHERE selection-criteria]
[ORDER BY field-1 [ASC|DESC] [, field-2 [ASC|DESC] ...]]
```

Example

```
SELECT * FROM User
```

Result set

```
+---------+-----------+-----------+----------------------+
| UserID  | FirstName | LastName  | EmailAddress         |
+---------+-----------+-----------+----------------------+
|       1 | John      | Smith     | jsmith@hotmail.com   |
|       2 | Andrea    | Steelman  | andi@murach.com      |
|       3 | Joel      | Murach    | joelmurach@yahoo.com |
+---------+-----------+-----------+----------------------+
```

The syntax for a SELECT statement that gets selected columns

```
SELECT field-1 [, field-2] ...
FROM table-1
[WHERE selection-criteria]
[ORDER BY field-1 [ASC|DESC] [, field-2 [ASC|DESC] ...]]
```

Example

```
SELECT FirstName, LastName
FROM User
WHERE UserID < 3
ORDER BY LastName ASC
```

Result set

```
+-----------+----------+
| FirstName | LastName |
+-----------+----------+
| John      | Smith    |
| Andrea    | Steelman |
+-----------+----------+
```

Description

- A SELECT statement is a SQL DML statement that returns a *result set* (or *result table*) that consists of the specified rows and columns.
- To specify the columns, you use the SELECT clause.
- To specify rows, you use the WHERE clause.
- To specify the table that the data should be retrieved from, you use the FROM clause.
- To specify how the result set should be sorted, you use the ORDER BY clause.

Figure 10-9   How to select data from a single table

How to select data from multiple tables

Figure 10-10 shows how to use the SELECT statement to retrieve data from two tables. This is commonly known as a *join*. The result of any join is a single result table.

An *inner join* is the most common type of join. When you use one, the data from the rows in the two tables are included in the result set only if their related columns match. In the example, the SELECT statement joins the data from the rows in the User and Download tables only if the value of the UserID field in the User table is equal to the UserID field in the Download table. In other words, if there isn't any data in the Download table for a user, that user won't be added to the result set.

Another type of join is an *outer join*. With this type of join, all of the records in one of the tables are included in the result set whether or not there are matching records in the other table. In a *left outer join*, all of the records in the first table (the one on the left) are included in the result set. In a *right outer join*, all of the records in the second table are included. To illustrate, assume that the SELECT statement in this figure had used a left outer join. In that case, all of the records in the User table would have been included in the result set...even if no matching record was found in the Download table.

To code a join, you use the JOIN clause to specify the second table and the ON clause to specify the fields to be used for the join. If a field in one table has the same name as a field in the other table, you code the table name, a dot, and the field name to specify the field that you want to use. You can see this in the ON clause of the example in this figure.

Although this figure only shows how to join data from two tables, you can extend this syntax to join data from additional tables. If, for example, you want to create a result set that includes data from three tables named User, Download, and Product tables, you could code the FROM clause of the SELECT statement like this:

```
FROM User
    INNER JOIN Download
        ON User.UserID = Download.UserID
    INNER JOIN Product
        ON Download.ProductCode = Product.ProductCode
```

Then, you could include any of the fields from the three tables in the field list of the SELECT statement.

The syntax for a SELECT statement that joins two tables

```
SELECT field-1 [, field-2] ...
FROM table-1
    {INNER | LEFT OUTER | RIGHT OUTER} JOIN table-2
    ON table-1.field-1 {=|<|>|<=|>=|<>} table-2.field-2
[WHERE selection-criteria]
[ORDER BY field-1 [ASC|DESC] [, field-2 [ASC|DESC] ...]]
```

A statement that gets data from related User and Download tables

```
SELECT EmailAddress, DownloadFilename, DownloadDate
FROM User
    INNER JOIN Download
    ON User.UserID = Download.UserID
WHERE DownloadDate > '2002-08-01'
ORDER BY EmailAddress ASC
```

Result set

```
+----------------------+-------------------+----------------------+
| EmailAddress         | DownloadFilename  | DownloadDate         |
+----------------------+-------------------+----------------------+
| andi@murach.com      | filter.rm         | 2002-08-02 18:31:46  |
| andi@murach.com      | so_long.rm        | 2002-08-02 18:31:46  |
| andi@murach.com      | corvair.rm        | 2002-08-02 18:31:46  |
| joelmurach@yahoo.com | filter.mp3        | 2002-08-02 18:31:46  |
+----------------------+-------------------+----------------------+
4 rows in set (0.05 sec)
```

Description

- To return a result set that contains data from two tables, you *join* the tables. To do that, you can use a JOIN clause. Most of the time, you'll want to code an *inner join* so that rows are only included when the key of a row in the first table matches the key of a row in the second table.

- In a *left outer join*, the data for all of the rows in the first table (the one on the left) are included in the table, but only the data for matching rows in the second table are included. In a *right outer join*, the reverse is true.

Figure 10-10   How to select data from multiple tables

How to insert, update, and delete data

Figure 10-11 shows how to use the INSERT, UPDATE, and DELETE statements to add, update, or delete one or more records in a database. Because these statements modify the data in a database, they are sometimes referred to as *action queries*.

The syntax and examples for the INSERT statement show how to use this statement to add one record to a database. To do that, the statement supplies the names of the fields that are going to receive values in the new record, followed by the values for those fields. Here, the first example inserts one row into the Download table. The second example also inserts one row into the Download table, but it uses the NOW function provided by MySQL to automatically insert the current date and time into the DownloadDate field.

Similarly, the syntax and examples for the UPDATE statement show how to update records. In the first example, the UPDATE statement updates the FirstName field in the record where the EmailAddress is equal to jsmith@hotmail.com. In the second example, the ProductPrice field is updated to 36.95 in all of the records where the ProductPrice is equal to 36.50.

Last, the syntax and examples for the DELETE statement show how to delete records. Here, the first example deletes the record from the User table where the EmailAddress equals jsmith@hotmail.com. Since each record contains a unique value in the EmailAddress field, this only deletes a single record. However, in the second example, two records in the Download table have a DownloadDate field that's less than August 1, 2002. As a result, this statement deletes both of these download records.

When you issue an INSERT, UPDATE, or DELETE statement from a Java application, you usually work with one record at a time. You'll see this illustrated by the Email List application in the next chapter. Action queries that affect more than one record are often issued by database administrators.

The syntax for the INSERT statement

```
INSERT INTO table-name [(field-list)]
    VALUES (value-list)
```

A statement that adds one row to the Download table

```
INSERT INTO Download (UserID, DownloadDate, DownloadFilename, ProductCode)
    VALUES (1, '2002-12-01', 'jr01-01.mp3', 'jr01')
```

A statement that uses the MySQL Now function to get the current date

```
INSERT INTO Download (UserID, DownloadDate, DownloadFilename, ProductCode)
    VALUES (1, NOW(), 'jr01-01.mp3', 'jr01')
```

The syntax for the UPDATE statement

```
UPDATE table-name
    SET expression-1 [, expression-2] ...
    WHERE selection-criteria
```

A statement that updates the FirstName column in one row

```
UPDATE User
    SET FirstName = 'Jack',
    WHERE EmailAddress = 'jsmith@hotmail.com'
```

A statement that updates the ProductPrice column in selected rows

```
UPDATE Products
    SET ProductPrice = 36.95
    WHERE ProductPrice = 36.50
```

The syntax for the DELETE statement

```
DELETE FROM table-name
    WHERE selection-criteria
```

A statement that deletes one row from the User table

```
DELETE FROM User WHERE EmailAddress = 'jsmith@hotmail.com'
```

A statement that deletes selected rows from the Downloads table

```
DELETE FROM Download WHERE DownloadDate < '2002-08-02'
```

Description

- Since the INSERT, UPDATE, and DELETE statements modify the data that's stored in a database, they're sometimes referred to as *action queries*. These statements don't return a result set. Instead, they return the number of rows that were affected by the query.

Figure 10-11   How to insert, update, and delete data

Perspective

The first goal of this chapter has been to present the basic skills that you need for using MySQL. The second goal has been to introduce you to SELECT, IN-SERT, UPDATE, and DELETE statements. If this chapter has succeeded, you should now be able to use the mysql program to run commands, scripts, and SQL statements.

In the next chapter, you'll learn how to use a servlet to connect to a MySQL database. You'll also learn how to use the SELECT, INSERT, UPDATE, and DELETE statements in your servlets so they can retrieve and modify the data in a database. That will show you how a database is used in the context of a web application.

Keep in mind, though, that this chapter has presented just a small subset of SQL skills. In particular, it has presented the least you need to know about SQL statements for understanding the Java code that is presented in the next chapter. For a complete mastery of SQL, you'll need to get a SQL book like *Murach's SQL for SQL Server*.

Summary

- *MySQL* is a *relational database management system*, or *RDBMS*, that can manage one or more *databases.* To retrieve and modify the data in one of its databases, MySQL provides support for *Structured Query Language*, or *SQL*, which is the standard language for working with databases.

- Whenever you use MySQL, its *database server* must be running. Usually, this server starts automatically whenever you start your system.

- To work with a MySQL *database*, you can use a client tool called the *mysql program*. It provides a command-line interface that lets you enter and run *MySQL commands* and *SQL statements*.

- A *SQL script* is a file that stores SQL statements. To run a script from the mysql program, you use the Mysql command.

- The SQL statements that you use for creating and deleting databases and tables are part of the *Data Definition Language*, or *DDL*.

- The SQL statements that you use for retrieving and modifying the data in a database make up the *Data Manipulation Language*, or *DML*. These are the SELECT, INSERT, UPDATE, and DELETE statements.

- The SELECT statement is used to get data from one or more tables and put it in a *result set*, or *result table*. This is commonly referred to as a *query*.

- The INSERT, UPDATE, and DELETE statements are used to add one or more rows to a table, update the data in one or more rows, and delete one or more rows. These statements don't return a result set, and they're sometimes referred to as *action queries*.

Terms

MySQL
Relational Database Management
    System (RDBMS)
Structured Query Language (SQL)
database server
mysql program
relational database
table
row
record
column
field
key
primary key
foreign key

SQL script
Data Definition Language (DDL)
Data Manipulation Language
  (DML)
query
result set
result table
current row pointer
cursor
join
inner join
outer join
left outer join
right outer join
action query

Objectives

- Use the mysql program to run commands, scripts, and DDL statements.
- Code simple SELECT, INSERT, UPDATE, and DELETE statements, and use the mysql program to run them.
- Distinguish between SQL's Data Definition Language and Data Manipulation Language.
- Describe the capabilities of a SELECT statement.
- Describe the capabilities of INSERT, UPDATE, and DELETE statements.
- Describe the use of a SQL script.

Before you do the exercises for this chapter

If you haven't already done so, you need to install MySQL. You also need to run the scripts that create the databases that are used by the applications in this book. The procedures for doing both are in appendix A.

Exercise 10-1   Use the mysql program

1. Start MySQL, start the mysql program, and run the Show Databases command to see which databases are installed on your system.
2. Select the murach database. Then, run the first SELECT statement in figure 10-9 to see the data stored in the User table.

3. Run the first UPDATE statement in figure 10-11 to see how that works. Then, run the first SELECT statement in figure 10-9 again to see how the data has been changed.

4. Exit from the mysql program.

Exercise 10-2 Run your own DML statements

1. Use TextPad or another text editor to open the scripts that come with this book. You'll find them in the MySQL_scripts directory on the CD. Here, you'll also find a MurachMaster script that contains all scripts for the murach database. Study the CREATE TABLE statements to see how the User and Download tables are constructed.

2. Start the mysql program, select the murach database, and run your own SELECT statements to retrieve data from the Download table in the database.

3. Write a SELECT statement that uses an inner join to return a result set that contains the first name, last name, and downloaded file names of a user whose email address is jsmith@hotmail.com.

Exercise 10-3 Create a database with tables and data

1. Use the mysql program to create a database named store.

2. Use the mysql program to create a table named Product in the store database that contains an auto-incremented ProductID field and the data located in the products.txt file that's stored in c:\webapps\murach\WEB-INF\etc. To create the ProductPrice field in this table, you can use the following line in the CREATE TABLE statement:

```
ProductPrice DECIMAL(7,2) NOT NULL DEFAULT '0.00',
```

3. Use a SELECT statement to view the data in the Product table.

4. Drop the Product table and the store database so they don't exist anymore.

5. Create a SQL script named StoreMaster.sql in a text editor that creates the Store database and creates the Product table. For an example that combines multiple scripts, you can view the MurachMaster script located in the MySQL_scripts folder.

6. Execute the StoreMaster.sql script at the mysql\bin prompt.

7. Use the mysql program to make sure the Product table was created as expected.

8. Change the price of all products with a price less than $13.00 to $13.25. Then, run a query to see whether the price change worked correctly.

11

How to use Java to work with a database

The basic skills for using Java to work with a database are the same for web applications as they are for other types of applications. So if you've used Java to work with a database before, you're probably already familiar with some of the skills presented in this chapter. In addition, though, you're going to see database programming in the context of web applications. And you're going to learn how to use a connection pool for a web application, which can improve the performance of the application.

How to work with JDBC **334**
How to obtain and install a database driver 334
How to connect to a database 336
How to return a result set and move the cursor through it 338
How to retrieve data from a result set 340
How to insert, update, and delete data 342
How to work with prepared statements 344

The SQL Gateway application **346**
The user interface 346
The code for the JSP 348
The code for the servlet 350
The code for the utility class 354

How to work with connection pooling **356**
How connection pooling works 356
How to install a connection pool 358
How to customize a connection pool 358
How to use a connection pool 360

The Email List application **362**
The user interface 362
The code for the JSP 362
The code for the servlet 364
The code for the UserDB class 366

Perspective **370**

How to work with JDBC

To write Java code that works with a database, you can use *JDBC*, which is sometimes referred to as *Java Database Connectivity*. The core JDBC API is stored in the java.sql package, which comes as part of the Java 2, Standard Edition. In this topic, you'll learn how to use JDBC to connect to a database, and you'll learn how to retrieve and modify the data that's stored in a database.

How to obtain and install a database driver

Before you can connect to a database, you must obtain and install a *database driver* so figure 11-1 lists the four types of JDBC database drivers that you can use. Then, it shows how to obtain and install a database driver that's appropriate for a web application. Since type-1 and type-2 database drivers require installation on the client side, they won't work for a web-based application. As a result, you'll need to use a type-3 or type-4 driver to connect to the database.

If you want to connect to a MySQL database, you can use the type-4 driver that's included on the CD that comes with this book. This is a popular open-source driver that's available for free. You can download drivers for other types of databases from the Java web site. The documentation for these drivers typically shows how to install and configure the driver.

To install the database driver, you put the jar file that contains the database driver into the correct directory within your servlet engine. For Tomcat 4.0, you put the jar file in the common\lib directory of Tomcat. If you're using another servlet engine, you can check the documentation for that servlet engine to learn where to place the jar file that contains the database driver. If that doesn't work, you can try copying the jar file to the WEB-INF\lib directory of your application or unpacking the jar file and copying the directories and class for the database driver to the WEB-INF\classes directory.

The four types of JDBC database drivers

Type 1   A *JDBC-ODBC bridge driver* converts JDBC calls into ODBC calls that access the DBMS protocol. This data access method requires that the ODBC drivers be installed on the client machines.

Type 2   A *native protocol partly Java driver* converts JDBC calls into calls in the native DBMS protocol. Since this conversion takes place on the client, some binary code must be installed on the client machine.

Type 3   A *net protocol all Java driver* converts JDBC calls into a net protocol that's independent of any native DBMS protocol. Then, middleware software running on a server converts the net protocol to the native DBMS protocol. Since this conversion takes place on the server side, no installation is required on the client machine.

Type 4   A *native protocol all Java driver* converts JDBC calls into a native DBMS protocol. Since this conversion takes place on the server side, no installation is required on the client machine.

Where to obtain database drivers

* For a MySQL database, you can use the driver that's included in the MySQL_Driver directory on the CD that comes with this book. It's an open-source, type-4 driver that's available for free.

* For other databases, you can usually download a database driver that's appropriate for the database that you're using from the Internet. To get information about the drivers that are currently available, check the Java web site at *www.java.sun.com/products/jdbc* and click on the List of Drivers Available link. For web applications, you'll want to download a type-3 or type-4 driver.

How to install a database driver

* For Tomcat 4.0, you can install a database driver by placing the jar file that contains the driver in the common/lib directory for Tomcat.

* For other servlet engines, the procedure for installing a database driver may differ. As a result, you may need to check the documentation for your servlet engine.

Figure 11-1   How to obtain and install a database driver

How to connect to a database

Before you can get or modify the data in a database, you must connect to it so figure 11-2 shows the syntax and code needed to do that. First, this figure shows the syntax that's used to specify the URL for the database. Then, this figure shows examples that connect to a database.

The first example shows how to use the type-4 MySQL driver that's included on the CD that comes with this book to connect to the murach database. To start, you use the forName method of the Class class to load the driver. The argument for this method provides the driver name, and you can get this name from the documentation for the driver.

Then, you use the getConnection method of the DriverManager class to return a Connection object. To use that method, you must supply a URL for the database, a username, and a password. The URL for all JDBC drivers starts with "jdbc". Then, for MySQL drivers, the subprotocol is "mysql". After that, the database URL specifies the host machine and the name of the database.

In this first example, the URL specifies that the MySQL database named murach is running on the same machine as the servlet engine. Then, the username is the default of "root" and the password is an empty string. However, if the database is secure, you need to supply a valid username and password.

Since the forName method of the Class class throws a ClassNotFoundException and the getConnection method of the DriverManager class throws an SQLException, you must either throw or catch these exceptions when you write the code that connects to your database. That's why this example catches both of these errors and displays messages about the exceptions. That way, you can tell whether the exception is due to the driver (ClassNotFoundException) or the connection (SQLException).

The second example shows two statements that can be used to connect to an Oracle database. This shows that the syntax for connecting to a database is similar no matter what type of driver you use. To load the driver, you specify the name of the driver class. To connect to the database, you provide a valid database URL, username, and password.

In practice, connecting to the database is often frustrating because it's hard to figure out what driver name, URL name, username, and password you need to use. So if your colleagues have already made a connection to the database that you need to use, by all means try to get this information from them.

Database URL syntax

```
jdbc:subprotocolName:databaseURL
```

How to connect to a MySQL database named murach

```
Connection connection = null;
try{
    Class.forName("org.gjt.mm.mysql.Driver");
    String dbURL = "jdbc:mysql://localhost/murach";
    String username = "root";
    String password = "";
    connection = DriverManager.getConnection(
        dbURL, username, password);
}
catch(ClassNotFoundException e){
    message = "Database driver not found.";
}
catch(SQLException e){
    message = "Error loading database driver: " + e.getMessage();
}
```

How to load a driver for an Oracle database

```
Class.forName("oracle.jdbc.driver.OracleDriver");
connection = DriverManager.getConnection(
        "jdbc:oracle:thin@localhost/murach", "scott", "tiger");
```

Description

- Before you can get or modify the data in a database, you need to connect to it. To do that, you use the forName method of the Class class to load the driver. Then, you use the getConnection method of the DriverManager class to return a Connection object.

- When you use the forName method of the Class class, you must supply the driver name. This method throws a ClassNotFoundException.

- When you use the getConnection method of the DriverManager class, you must supply a URL for the database, a username, and a password. This method throws a SQLException.

- Although the connection string for each driver is different, the documentation for the driver should explain how to write a connection string for that driver.

- Typically, you only need to connect to one database for an application. However, it's possible to load multiple database drivers and establish connections to multiple types of databases.

Figure 11-2   How to connect to a database

How to return a result set and move the cursor through it

Once you connect to a database, you're ready to retrieve data from it as shown in figure 11-3. Here, the first two examples show how to use Statement objects to create a *result set*, or *result table*. Then, the next two examples show how to move the *row pointer*, or *cursor*, through the result set.

Both of the result sets in this figure are read-only, forward-only result sets. This means that you can only move the cursor forward through the result set, and you can only read records from the result set. Although versions 2.0 and 3.0 of JDBC support other types of scrollable, updateable result sets, these features require some additional overhead, and they aren't necessary for most types of web applications.

In the first example, the createStatement method is called from a Connection object to return a Statement object. Then, the executeQuery method is called from the Statement object to execute an SQL SELECT statement that's coded as a string. This returns a ResultSet object that contains the result set for the SELECT statement. In this case, the SELECT statement only retrieves a single column from a single row (the user ID for a specific email address) so that's what the ResultSet object contains. This object can be used to check whether a record exists.

The second example works like the first example. However, it returns all of the rows and columns for the Product table and puts this result set in a ResultSet object named products. This object can be used to display all products.

The third example shows how to use the next method of the ResultSet object to move the cursor to the first row of the result set that's created by the first example. When you create a result set, the cursor is positioned before the first row in the result set so the first use of the next method attempts to move the cursor to the first row in the result set. If the row exists, the cursor will be moved to that row and the next method will return a true value. Otherwise, the next method will return a false value. In the next figure, you'll learn how to retrieve values from the row that the cursor is on.

The fourth example shows how to use the next method to loop through all of the records in the result set that's created in the second example. Here, the while loop calls the next method. If the next row is a valid row, the next method will move the cursor to the row and return a true value. As a result, the code within the while loop will be executed. Otherwise, the next method will return a false value and the code within the while loop won't be executed.

Since all of the methods described in this figure throw an SQLException, you either need to throw or catch this exception when you're working with these methods. The applications that you'll see later in this chapter show how this works.

Although there are other ResultSet methods, the one you'll use the most with a forward-only, read-only result set is the next method. In this figure, though, three other methods are summarized that you may occasionally want to use for this type of result set.

How to create a result set that contains 1 row and 1 column

```
Statement statement = connection.createStatement();
ResultSet userIDResult = statement.executeQuery(
    "SELECT UserID FROM User " +
    "WHERE EmailAddress = 'jsmith@hotmail.com'");
```

How to create a result set that contains multiple columns and rows

```
Statement statement = connection.createStatement();
ResultSet products = statement.executeQuery(
    "SELECT * FROM Product ");
```

How to move the cursor to the first record in the result set

```
boolean userIDExists = userIDResult.next();
```

How to loop through a result set

```
while (products.next()) {
    // do statements
}
```

ResultSet methods for forward-only, read-only result sets

Method	Description
next()	Moves the cursor to the next row in the result set.
last()	Moves the cursor to the last row in the result set.
close()	Releases the result set's JDBC and database resources.
getRow()	Returns an int value that identifies the current row of the result set.

Description

- To return a *result set* to a class, you use the createStatement method of a Connection object to create a Statement object. Then, you use the executeQuery method of the Statement object to execute a SELECT statement that returns a ResultSet object.

- By default, the createStatement method creates a forward-only, read-only result set. This means that you can only move the *cursor* through it from the first record to the last and that you can't update it. Although you can pass arguments to the createStatement method that create other types of result sets, the default is appropriate for most web applications.

- When a result set is created, the cursor is positioned before the first row. Then, you can use the methods of the ResultSet object to move the cursor. To move the cursor to the next row, for example, you call the next method. If the row is valid, this method moves the cursor to the next row and returns a true value. Otherwise, it returns a false value.

- The createStatement, executeQuery, and next methods throw an SQLException. As a result, any code that uses these methods needs to catch or throw this exception.

Figure 11-3   How to return a result set and move the cursor through it

How to retrieve data from a result set

When the cursor is positioned on the row that you want to get data from, you can use the methods in figure 11-4 to get that data. Although the examples show how to use the getString and getDouble methods of the ResultSet object to return String values and double values, you can use similar get methods to return other types of data.

The methods in this figure show the two types of arguments accepted by the get methods. The first method accepts an int value that specifies the index number of the column in the result set, where 1 is the first column, 2 is the second column, and so on. The second method accepts a string value that specifies the name of the column in the result set. Although the get methods with column indexes run slightly faster and require less typing, the get methods with column names lead to code that's easier to read and understand.

The first example shows how to use column indexes to return data from a result set named products. Here, the first two statements use the getString method to return the code and description for the current product while the third statement uses the getDouble method to return the price of the product. Since these methods use the column index, the first column in the result set must contain the product code, the second column must contain the product description, and so on.

The second example shows how to use column names to return data from the products result set. Since this code uses the column name, the order of the columns in the result set doesn't matter. However, the column names must exist in the result set or an SQLException will be thrown that indicates that a column wasn't found.

The third example shows how you can use the get methods to create a Product object. Here, the constructor for the Product object uses three values that are returned by the get methods to create a new product. Since objects are often created from data that's stored in a database, code like this is commonly used.

If you look up the ResultSet interface in the java.sql package of the documentation for the Java API, you'll see that get methods are available for all of the primitive types and for other types of data too. For example, get methods exist for the Date, Time, and Timestamp classes that are a part of the java.sql package. For many purposes, though, like displaying numbers and dates, you can use the getString method to return a string representation of the data type.

Methods of a ResultSet object that return data from a result set

Method	Description
getXXX(intColumnIndex)	Returns data from the specified column number.
getXXX(StringColumnName)	Returns data from the specified column name.

Code that uses column indexes to return fields from the products result set

```
String code = products.getString(1);
String description = products.getString(2);
double price = products.getDouble(3);
```

Code that uses column names to return the same fields

```
String code = products.getString("ProductCode");
String description = products.getString("ProductDescription");
double price = products.getDouble("ProductPrice");
```

Code that creates a Product object from the products result set

```
Product product = new Product(products.getString(1),
                              products.getString(2),
                              products.getDouble(3));
```

Description

- The getXXX methods can be used to return all eight primitive types. For example, the getInt method returns the int type and the getLong method returns the long type.
- The getXXX methods can also be used to return strings, dates, and times. For example, the getString method returns any object of the String class, and the getDate, getTime, and getTimestamp methods return objects of the Date, Time, and Timestamp classes of the java.sql package.

Figure 11-4   How to retrieve data from a result set

How to insert, update, and delete data

Figure 11-5 shows how to use JDBC to modify the data in a database. To do that, you use the executeUpdate method of a Statement object to execute SQL statements that add, update, and delete data. Since this method has been a part of Java since version 1.0 of JDBC, it should work for all JDBC drivers.

When you work with the executeUpdate method, you just pass an SQL statement to the database. In these examples, the code adds, updates, and deletes a product in the Product table. To do that, the code combines data from a Product object with the appropriate SQL statement. For the UPDATE and DELETE statements, the SQL statement uses the product's code in the WHERE clause to select a single product.

How to use the executeUpdate method to modify data

How to add a record

```
String query =
    "INSERT INTO Product (ProductCode, ProductDescription, ProductPrice) " +
    "VALUES ('" + product.getCode() + "', " +
            "'" + product.getDescription() + "', " +
            "'" + product.getPrice() + "')";
Statement statement = connection.createStatement();
int rowCount = statement.executeUpdate(query);
```

How to update a record

```
String query = "UPDATE Product SET " +
    "ProductCode = '" + product.getCode() + "', " +
    "ProductDescription = '" + product.getDescription() + "', " +
    "ProductPrice = '" + product.getPrice() + "' " +
    "WHERE ProductCode = '" + product.getCode() + "'";
Statement statement = connection.createStatement();
int rowCount = statement.executeUpdate(query);
```

How to delete a record

```
String query = "DELETE FROM Product " +
                "WHERE ProductCode = '" + productCode + "'";
Statement statement = connection.createStatement();
int rowCount = statement.executeUpdate(query);
```

Description

- The executeUpdate method is an older method that works with most JDBC drivers. Although there are some newer methods that require less SQL code, they may not work properly with all JDBC drivers.

- The executeUpdate method returns an int value that identifies the number of records that were affected by the SQL statement.

Figure 11-5   How to insert, update, and delete data

How to work with prepared statements

Each time a Java application sends a new SQL statement to the database server, the server checks the statement for syntax errors, prepares a plan for executing the statement, and executes the statement. If the same statement is sent again, though, the database server checks to see whether it has already received one exactly like it. If so, the server doesn't have to check its syntax and prepare an execution plan for it so the server just executes it. This improves the performance of the database operations.

To take advantage of this database feature, Java provides for the use of *prepared statements* as shown in figure 11-6. This feature lets you send statements to the database server that get executed repeatedly by accepting the parameter values that are sent to it. That improves the database performance because the database server only has to check the syntax and prepare the execution plan once for each statement.

To illustrate, the first example in this figure shows how to use a prepared statement to create a result set that contains a single product. Here, the first statement uses a question mark (?) to identify the parameter for the SELECT statement, which is the product code for the book, and the second statement uses the prepareStatement method of the Connection object to return a PreparedStatement object. Then, the third statement uses a set method (the setString method) of the PreparedStatement object to set a value for the first parameter in the SELECT statement, and the fourth statement uses the executeQuery method of the PreparedStatement object to return a ResultSet object.

The result is that the prepared statement is the same each time the query is executed, which improves database performance, even though the product code changes each time based on the parameter value that's sent to the SQL statement. In contrast, if you don't use a prepared statement, the database server treats each statement as a new statement, which degrades database performance. For this reason, you should consider the use of prepared statements whenever performance is an issue and the SQL statements that you're using are complex.

The second example shows how to use a prepared statement to execute an UPDATE query that requires four parameters. Here, the first statement uses four question marks to identify the four parameters of the UPDATE statement, and the second statement creates the PreparedStatement object. Then, the next four statements use set methods to set the four parameters in the order that they appear in the UPDATE statement. The last statement uses the executeUpdate method of the PreparedStatement object to execute the UPDATE statement.

The third and fourth examples show how to insert and delete records with prepared statements. Here, you can see that the type of SQL statement that you're using determines whether you use the executeQuery method or the executeUpdate method. If you're using a SELECT statement to return a result set, you use the executeQuery method. But if you're using an INSERT, UPDATE, or DELETE statement, you use the executeUpdate method. This holds true whether you're using a Statement object or a PreparedStatement object.

How to use a prepared statement

To return a result set

```
String preparedSQL = "SELECT ProductCode, ProductDescription, ProductPrice "
                   + "FROM Product WHERE ProductCode = ?";
PreparedStatement ps = connection.prepareStatement(preparedSQL);
ps.setString(1, productCode);
ResultSet product = ps.executeQuery();
```

To modify data

```
String preparedSQL = "UPDATE Product SET "
                   + "    ProductCode = ?, "
                   + "    ProductDescription = ?, "
                   + "    ProductPrice = ?"
                   + "WHERE ProductCode = ?";
PreparedStatement ps = connection.prepareStatement(preparedSQL);
ps.setString(1, product.getCode());
ps.setString(2, product.getDescription());
ps.setDouble(3, product.getPrice());
ps.setString(4, product.getCode());
ps.executeUpdate();
```

To insert a record

```
String preparedQuery =
      "INSERT INTO Product (ProductCode, ProductDescription, BookPrice) "
    + "VALUES (?, ?, ?)";
PreparedStatement ps = connection.prepareStatement(preparedQuery);
ps.setString(1, product.getCode());
ps.setString(2, product.getDescription());
ps.setDouble(3, product.getPrice());
ps.executeUpdate();
```

To delete a record

```
String preparedQuery = "DELETE FROM Product "
                     + "WHERE ProductCode = ?";
PreparedStatement ps = connection.prepareStatement(preparedQuery);
ps.setString(1, productCode);
ps.executeUpdate();
```

Description

- When you use *prepared statements* in your Java programs, the database server only has to check the syntax and prepare an execution plan once for each SQL statement. This improves the efficiency of the database operations.

- To specify a parameter for a prepared statement, type a question mark (?) in the SQL statement.

- To supply values for the parameters in a prepared statement, use the set methods of the PreparedStatement interface. For a complete list of set methods, look up the PreparedStatement interface of the java.sql package in the documentation for the Java API.

- To execute a SELECT statement, use the executeQuery method. To execute an INSERT , UPDATE, or DELETE statement, use the executeUpdate method.

Figure 11-6   How to work with prepared statements

The SQL Gateway application

This topic presents the SQL Gateway application that allows you to use a JSP interface to execute any type of SQL statement. An application like this makes it easy to view and modify the data in a database. For example, you can cut and paste SQL scripts into this application and execute them. In addition, if you enter an SQL statement with incorrect syntax, this application will display an error message when you try to execute it. Then, you can edit the SQL statement and attempt to execute it again.

When working with a database, you'll usually want to use an application like this one instead of a command-line interface like the one shown in the last chapter. If you're working with a database that's hosted by an ISP, the ISP will usually include a web-based way to work with the database that's similar to this tool. If not, you can upload this application to work with the database.

The user interface

Figure 11-7 shows the user interface for the SQL Gateway application. To use this application, you enter an SQL statement in the SQL Statement text area. Then, you click on the Execute button to run the SQL statement. When you do that, the result will be displayed at the bottom of the page.

If the SQL statement is a SELECT statement that runs successfully, the result set will be displayed within an HTML table as in the second page in this figure. For other types of statements, the result will be a message that indicates the number of rows that were affected by the statement as in the first page in this figure. Of course, if the SQL statement doesn't execute successfully, the result will be a message that displays information about the SQLException that was thrown.

The SQL Gateway application after executing an INSERT statement

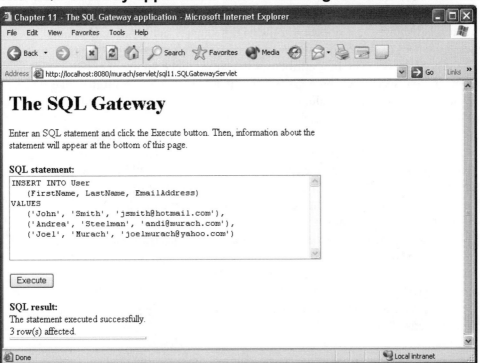

The SQL Gateway application after executing a SELECT statement

Figure 11-7   The user interface for the SQL Gateway application

The code for the JSP

Figure 11-8 shows the JSP code for the SQL Gateway application. Here, the scriptlet at the start of this JSP contains Java code that retrieves two attributes from the session object. The first attribute is the string that contains the SQL statement, and the second attribute is the string that contains the result message. If these attributes contain null values, they haven't been set yet so this code sets the sqlStatement and message variables to empty strings.

The form for this JSP contains a text area and a submit button. Here, the text area allows the user to enter the SQL statement. This code creates a text area that's approximately 60 characters wide and 8 lines tall. Within this area, the sqlStatement variable is displayed, which is empty the first time this JSP is run. Then, when the user clicks the submit button, this JSP calls the SQLGatewayServlet that's shown in the next figure.

The table near the end of this JSP displays the message string that contains the result of the SQL statement. Since this message might contain the rows for an HTML table, it's coded within the Table tags. Then, if the message string contains the HTML tags that define rows and columns, the message that's displayed uses the Table tags. Otherwise, the message that's displayed doesn't use the Table tags.

The JSP code (sql_gateway.jsp)

```
<!doctype html public "-//W3C//DTD HTML 4.0 Transitional//EN">
<%
    String sqlStatement = (String) session.getAttribute("sqlStatement");
    if (sqlStatement == null)
        sqlStatement = "";
    String message = (String) session.getAttribute("message");
    if (message == null)
        message = "";
%>

<html>

<head>
    <title>Chapter 11 - The SQL Gateway application</title>
</head>


<body>

<h1>The SQL Gateway</h1>

<p>Enter an SQL statement and click the Execute button. Then, information
    about the <br> statement will appear at the bottom of this page.</p>

<form action="../servlet/sql11.SQLGatewayServlet" method="post">
    <b>SQL statement:</b><br>
    <textarea name="sqlStatement" cols=60 rows=8>
      <%= sqlStatement %>
    </textarea><br>
    <br>
    <input type="submit" value="Execute">
</form>

<p>
<b>SQL result:</b><br>
<table cellpadding="5" border="1">
    <%= message %>
</table>
</p>

</body>

</html>
```

Figure 11-8   The code for the JSP of the SQL Gateway application

The code for the servlet

Figure 11-9 shows the code for the SQLGatewayServlet. To start, this servlet imports the java.sql package so it can use the JDBC classes. Then, it imports the util package so it can use the SQLUtil class that's presented in the next figure. In addition, it declares a Connection object so the connection can be used by all of the methods in the servlet.

When the servlet engine places this servlet into service, the init method opens the connection to the database. Usually, this occurs when the first user uses the application. That way, the database connection will be open and available for all subsequent users. Then, a new thread is spawned for each user that uses this servlet.

Conversely, before the servlet engine takes a servlet out of service, the destroy method closes the database connection and frees up the resources required by the connection. If any of these operations throws an exception, this servlet displays an appropriate message.

The SQLGatewayServlet class

```
package sql11;

import java.io.*;
import javax.servlet.*;
import javax.servlet.http.*;
import java.sql.*;
import util.*;

public class SQLGatewayServlet extends HttpServlet{

    private Connection connection;

    public void init() throws ServletException{
        try{
            Class.forName("org.gjt.mm.mysql.Driver");
            String dbURL = "jdbc:mysql://localhost/murach";
            String username = "root";
            String password = "";
            connection = DriverManager.getConnection(
                dbURL, username, password);
        }
        catch(ClassNotFoundException e){
            System.out.println("Database driver not found.");
        }
        catch(SQLException e){
            System.out.println("Error opening the db connection: "
                                + e.getMessage());
        }
    }

    public void destroy() {
        try{
            connection.close();
        }
        catch(SQLException e){
            System.out.println("Error closing the db connection: "
                                + e.getMessage());
        }
    }
```

Figure 11-9   The code for the SQLGatewayServlet (part 1 of 2)

When the JSP in the last figure calls the doPost method, this method calls the doGet method. Within the doGet method, the first statement gets the SQL statement that the user entered in the JSP, and the second statement declares the message variable. Then, within the try block, the first statement uses the Connection object to create a Statement object, and the next two statements use the trim and substring methods of a String object to return the first six letters of the SQL statement that the user entered.

If the first six letters of the SQL statement are "select", the executeQuery method of the Statement object returns a ResultSet object. Then, this object is passed to the getHtmlRows method of the SQLUtil class that's shown in the next figure, and it returns the result set formatted with the HTML tags for rows and columns.

However, if the first six letters of the SQL statement aren't "select", the executeUpdate method of the Statement object is called, which returns the number of rows that were affected. If the number of rows is 0, the SQL statement was a DDL statement like a DROP TABLE or CREATE TABLE statement. Otherwise, the SQL statement was an INSERT, UPDATE, or DELETE statement. Either way, the code sets the message variable to an appropriate message.

If any of the statements within the try block throw an SQLException, the catch block sets the message variable to display information about the SQLException. If, for example, you enter an SQL statement that contains incorrect syntax, this message will help you troubleshoot your syntax problem.

After the catch block, the next three statements get the session object and set the sqlStatement and message variables as attributes of that object. Then, the last two statements return a RequestDispatcher object that forwards the request and response objects to the JSP shown in the last figure.

The SQLGatewayServlet class (continued)

```java
public void doGet(HttpServletRequest request,
                  HttpServletResponse response)
                  throws IOException, ServletException{

    String sqlStatement = request.getParameter("sqlStatement");
    String message = "";

    try{
        Statement statement = connection.createStatement();
        sqlStatement = sqlStatement.trim();
        String sqlType = sqlStatement.substring(0, 6);
        if  (sqlType.equalsIgnoreCase("select")){
            ResultSet resultSet = statement.executeQuery(sqlStatement);
            // create a string that contains a HTML-formatted result set
            message = SQLUtil.getHtmlRows(resultSet);
        }
        else
        {
            int i = statement.executeUpdate(sqlStatement);
            if (i == 0) // this is a DDL statement
                message = "The statement executed successfully.";
            else        // this is an INSERT, UPDATE, or DELETE statement
                message = "The statement executed successfully.<br>"
                    + i + " row(s) affected.";
        }
        statement.close();
    }
    catch(SQLException e){
        message = "Error executing the SQL statement: <br>"
                + e.getMessage();
    }

    HttpSession session = request.getSession();
    session.setAttribute("message", message);
    session.setAttribute("sqlStatement", sqlStatement);

    RequestDispatcher dispatcher =
        getServletContext().getRequestDispatcher(
            "/sql11/sql_gateway.jsp");
    dispatcher.forward(request, response);

}

public void doPost(HttpServletRequest request,
                   HttpServletResponse response)
                   throws IOException, ServletException{
    doGet(request, response);
}
}
```

Figure 11-9   The code for the SQLGatewayServlet (part 2 of 2)

The code for the utility class

Figure 11-10 shows the code for the utility class named SQLUtil. This class contains two static methods: the getHtmlRows method that is called by the servlet in the last figure and the encode method that is used by the Email List application that's presented later in this chapter. Like the other utility classes presented in this book, this class is stored in the util package.

The getHtmlRows method accepts a ResultSet object and returns a String object that contains the HTML code for all of the column headings and rows in the result set. To build the information for that String object, the getHtmlRows method declares a StringBuffer object named htmlRows and appends data to it as the method is executed. At the end of the method, the toString method is used to convert the StringBuffer object to the String object that is returned to the servlet.

To get the column headings that are returned, the getHtmlRows method uses the getMetaData method of the ResultSet object to create a ResultSetMetaData object. This type of object contains information about the result set including the number of columns and the names of the columns. To get that information, the getHtmlRows method uses the getColumnCount and getColumnName methods of the ResultSetMetaData object.

To get the data from the result set, the getHtmlRows method uses a for loop within a while loop to get the data for each column in each row. Within these loops, the code uses the getString method of the result set to get the data for each field. That converts the data to a string no matter what data type the field is.

The second method in this class is the encode method that's used by the Email List application that's presented later on. This method accepts a String object and returns a String object. What this method does is to add a single quote (') after each single quote in the string that's passed to it. You can use this when you use SQL statements that work with string data that includes one or more single quotes. By adding the extra quotes, you prevent syntax errors when you try to execute the SQL statements. You'll see how this works in the Email List application.

Please note that both of the methods in this class are declared with the synchronized keyword. This prevents two or more threads of a servlet from executing the same method at the same time.

The SQLUtil class

```
package util;

import java.util.*;
import java.sql.*;

public class SQLUtil{

    public static synchronized String getHtmlRows(ResultSet results)
    throws SQLException{
        StringBuffer htmlRows = new StringBuffer();
        ResultSetMetaData metaData = results.getMetaData();
        int columnCount = metaData.getColumnCount();

        htmlRows.append("<tr>");
        for (int i = 1; i <= columnCount; i++)
            htmlRows.append("<td><b>" + metaData.getColumnName(i) + "</td>");
        htmlRows.append("</tr>");

        while (results.next()){
            htmlRows.append("<tr>");
            for (int i = 1; i <= columnCount; i++)
                htmlRows.append("<td>" + results.getString(i) + "</td>");
        }
        htmlRows.append("</tr>");
        return htmlRows.toString();
    }

    public static synchronized String encode(String s){
        if (s == null) return s;
        StringBuffer sb = new StringBuffer(s);
        for (int i = 0; i < sb.length(); i++){
            char ch = sb.charAt(i);
            if (ch == 39){   // 39 is the ASCII code for an apostrophe
                sb.insert(i++, "'");
            }
        }
        return sb.toString();
    }

}
```

Description

- The getHtmlRows method in this utility class is a static method that accepts a ResultSet object and returns a String object that contains the HTML code for the result set so it can be displayed by a browser.

- The getHtmlRows method uses the getMetaData method of the result set to return a ResultSetMetaData object. This object contains information about the result set.

- The getHtmlRows method uses the getColumnCount method of the ResultSetMetaData object to return the number of columns in the result set and the getColumnName method to get the name of each column as a String object.

Figure 11-10   The code for the SQLUtil class

How to work with connection pooling

Opening a connection to a database is a time-consuming process that can degrade an application's performance. As a result, it's a common programming practice to create a collection of Connection objects and store them in another object that's commonly known as a *connection pool*. Then, the Connection objects in the pool are shared by all the users of a web application. This limits the number of times that connections are opened as well as the total number of Connection objects.

How connection pooling works

Figure 11-11 shows how connection pooling works. To start, when the servlet engine places a servlet that uses connection pooling into service, it creates a ConnectionPool object that contains multiple Connection objects. Then, when a user accesses the servlet, the servlet spawns a thread. This thread gets a Connection object from the ConnectionPool object, uses that Connection object to access the database, and returns the Connection object to the connection pool.

Typically, you create a single connection pool for a web application. Then, all of the servlets in the application use the same connection pool to access the database. In the next two figures, you'll learn how to install, customize, and share a connection pool among all of the servlets in an application.

How connection pooling works

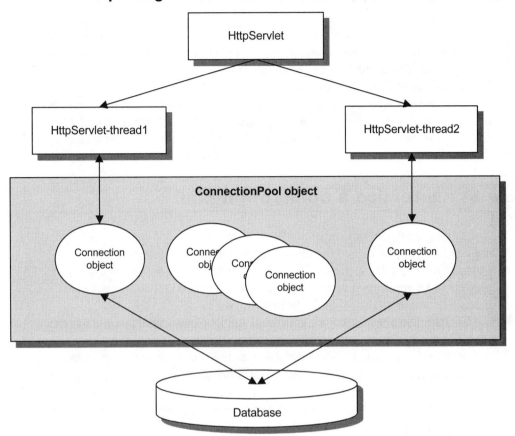

Description

- When *connection pooling* is used, a limited number of connections are opened for a database and these connections are shared by the users who connect to the database. This improves the performance of the database operations.

- When one of the threads of a servlet needs to perform a database operation, the thread gets a Connection object from the ConnectionPool object and uses that Connection object to do the operation. When it is finished, it returns the Connection object to the pool.

Figure 11-11   How connection pooling works

How to install a connection pool

Although you could write the Java code for your own ConnectionPool class, classes like this are already available from third-party sources. As a result, it's usually better to get one of these than it is to write your own. Then, you can install and customize that connection pool.

To make this easy for you, the CD for this book includes a connection pool class named DbConnectionBroker. This class is available for free from the Java Exchange website (*www.javaexchange.com*). To install this class, you can copy it to the WEB-INF\classes directory as described in figure 11-12.

How to customize a connection pool

To customize the DbConnectionBroker class so it's appropriate for your application, you can extend the class and customize it as shown by the MurachPool class in this figure. This class provides code that allows all of the servlets in an application to access the connection pool that connects to the murach database on the MySQL database server.

To start, the MurachPool class extends the DbConnectionBroker class that's stored in the com.javaexchange.dbConnectionBroker package. Then, this class declares a private static instance variable that holds the connection pool. After this declaration, the MurachPool class uses a private constructor to pass all of the connection parameters to the super class, which is the DbConnectionBroker class. Since this constructor is private, only a single instance of the MurachPool class can be created. As a result, this type of class is known as a *singleton class*.

After the constructor, the static getInstance method returns a reference to this single instance of the MurachPool object. To start, this method checks to see if the MurachPool object exists. For all but the first thread that uses this method, the object will exist so this method will just return a reference to the MurachPool object. However, if the MurachPool object hasn't been created, this method will create the MurachPool object and return a reference to this object.

Within the getInstance method, the code for creating the MurachPool object provides values for the eight arguments required by the MurachPool constructor. For the first four, you can use the same values that you use for creating a Connection object. For the last four, you can use the values shown in this figure because they are adequate for most small- to medium-sized web sites.

In the example in this figure, the minConns parameter specifies that the MurachPool object will contain 10 connections when it's first created. The maxConns parameter specifies that the MurachPool object will, if necessary, add 40 more connections for a maximum of 50 connections. The logFilename parameter specifies the file that the connection pool will write its log data to. And the maxConnTimeInDays parameter specifies the maximum number of days before the connection pool will reset itself. Although the path and filename for the log file work fine if you're running Tomcat locally, you may need to modify it if you upload your servlets to a remote computer.

How to install the DbConnectionBroker class

1. Put the CD that comes with this book in your CD driver and navigate to the ConnectionPool directory.

2. Copy the com\javaexchange\dbConnectionBroker subdirectory to the WEB-INF\classes directory if it's not already there.

The MurachPool class that extends the DbConnectionBroker class

```
package util;

import com.javaexchange.dbConnectionBroker.*;
import java.io.*;

public class MurachPool extends DbConnectionBroker{

    private static MurachPool pool = null;

    private MurachPool(String driverName,
                       String dbUrl, String username,
                       String password, int minConns, int maxConns,
                       String logFilename, double maxConnTimeInDays)
                       throws IOException{
        super(driverName,
              dbUrl, username,
              password, minConns, maxConns,
              logFilename, maxConnTimeInDays);
    }

    public synchronized static MurachPool getInstance(){
        try{
            if (pool == null){
                pool = new MurachPool(
                    "org.gjt.mm.mysql.Driver",
                    "jdbc:mysql://localhost/murach", "root",
                    "", 10, 50,
                    "../webapps/murach/WEB-INF/etc/connectPool.log", 1.0);
            }
        }
        catch(IOException ioe){
            System.err.println("MurachPool IOException: " + ioe.getMessage());
        }
        return pool;
    }
}
```

Description

*   The DbConnectionBroker class is available for free from the Java Exchange web site (*www.javaexchange.com*). It can be used to create and implement a connection pool. For more information about it, you can use your web browser to view the documentation that comes on this book's CD or you can go to that web site.

*   Since the MurachPool class uses a private constructor, only a single instance of this class can be created. As a result, this type of class is known as a *singleton class*.

Figure 11-12   How to implement a connection pool

How to use a connection pool

Figure 11-13 shows the code that a servlet can use to get a Connection object from the connection pool that's created by the MurachPool class in the last figure. To start, the init method calls the static getInstance method of the MurachPool class. This returns a reference to the one and only instance of the connection pool object, and it stores this reference as an instance variable. That way, this variable will be available to all of the methods in the servlet class.

After the init method, the destroy method of the servlet calls the destroy method of the connection pool object. This will remove the connection pool and its connections from memory when the servlet engine removes the servlet from service.

Within the doGet method, the first statement calls the getConnection method of the connection pool object to return a Connection object that can be used to access the database. Then, after all the code that uses the Connection object has been executed, the doGet method calls the freeConnection method of the connection pool to return the Connection object to the pool. Since a typical database operation takes only a fraction of a second, a relative low number of Connection objects can handle a high volume of user requests.

How to use a connection pool

```
package email11;

import java.io.*;
import javax.servlet.*;
import javax.servlet.http.*;
import java.sql.*;
import business.User;
import data.UserDB;
import util.MurachPool;

public class EmailServlet extends HttpServlet{

    private MurachPool connectionPool;

    public void init() throws ServletException{
        connectionPool = MurachPool.getInstance();
    }

    public void destroy() {
        connectionPool.destroy();
    }

    public void doGet(HttpServletRequest request,
                      HttpServletResponse response)
                      throws IOException, ServletException{

        Connection connection = connectionPool.getConnection();

        // code that uses the connection

        connectionPool.freeConnection(connection);
    }

    public void doPost(HttpServletRequest request,
                       HttpServletResponse response)
                       throws ServletException, IOException {
        doGet(request, response);
    }
}
```

Description

- You can use the init method of a servlet to get an instance of the connection pool, and you can use the destroy method of the servlet to remove that instance of the connection pool from memory.

- Within the doGet or doPost methods of a servlet, you can get a connection from the connection pool. Then, you can use that connection to access the database. When you're done accessing the database, you can return the connection to the connection pool.

Figure 11-13   How to use a connection pool

The Email List application

In section 2 of this book, you learned how to code an Email List application that uses a class named UserIO to write the User data to a text file. Now, you'll learn how to code an Email List application that uses a class named UserDB to write the User data to a database. This application also uses the connection pool described in the last topic so it quickly connects its threads to the database. This illustrates how easy it is to modify an application when you use the MVC pattern and keep the presentation, business, and data layers independent of each other.

The user interface

Figure 11-14 shows the user interface for the new Email List application. This is like the interface that you've seen in earlier versions of this application, but it displays an error message if a user enters an email address that already exists in the database.

The code for the JSP

Since you already know how to code JSPs like the one for this interface, this figure shows only a small portion of the JSP code. In particular, it shows the code that displays the error message if the corresponding servlet sets a message as a session attribute.

The Email List application as it displays an error message

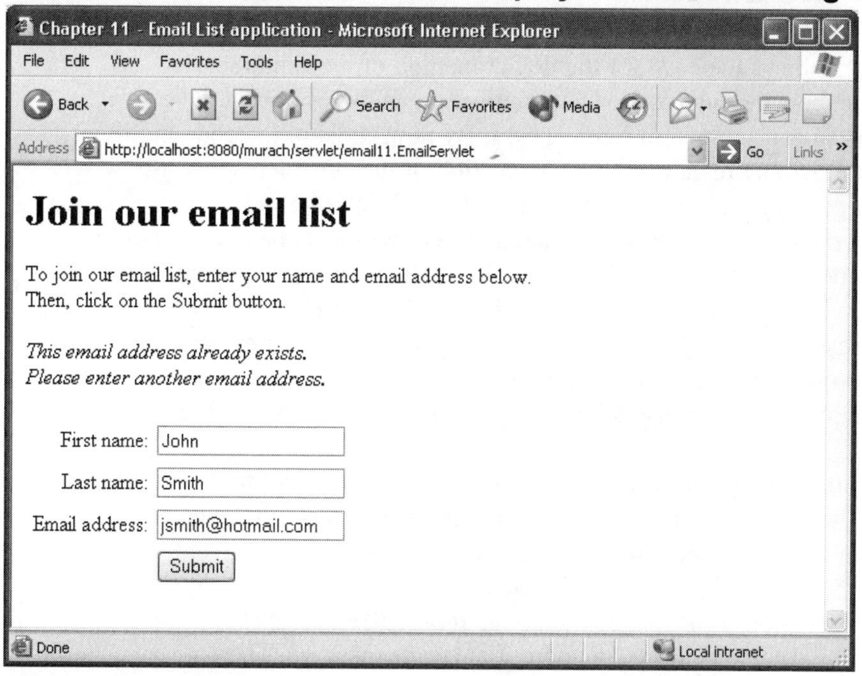

Some JSP code

```
<%
    String message = (String) session.getAttribute("message");
    if (message == null) message = "";
%>
```

```
<body>
```

```
<h1>Join our email list</h1>
```

```
<p>To join our email list, enter your name and email address below. <br>
    Then, click on the Submit button.
</p>
```

```
<p><i><%= message %></i></p>
```

Figure 11-14   The Email List application interface and JSP code

The code for the servlet

Figure 11-15 shows the code for the doGet method of the EmailServlet class. It doesn't show the init, destroy, and doPost methods for this class because they were already shown in figure 11-13. By now, most of the code in this doGet method should be review, with the exception of the statements that use the connection pool and call methods from the UserDB class.

Within this doGet method, the first statement retrieves a connection from the connection pool. Within the try block, the first statement passes the connection and the email address to the isMatch method of the UserDB class to see if that email address has already been stored in the database. If so, the code assigns an appropriate message, stores the message in the session object, and forwards the request and response to the join_email_list JSP shown in the last figure.

Otherwise, the code passes the connection and the User object to the addRecord method of the UserDB class to store that User object in the database. Then, it sets the message to an empty string, and forwards the request and response to the show_email_list JSP that you've seen in chapter 6.

If an SQLException is thrown by the isMatch or addRecord method in the UserDB class, the catch block sets an appropriate error message. Then, it forwards the request and response to the join_email_list JSP, which will display the message to the user.

The last statement in the doGet method frees the connection object in the connection pool so it can be used by other servlets or threads. Although this looks like an essential statement for the effective use of the connection pool by this servlet, the connection is automatically freed whenever a thread ends. Nevertheless, it's good to get in the habit of coding this statement because there are times when you should free the connection before the thread ends. If, for example, a lengthy servlet gets some data from a database at its start and doesn't need the database again, you should free the connection as soon as the database operation is completed.

The doGet method of the EmailServlet class

```java
public void doGet(HttpServletRequest request,
                  HttpServletResponse response)
                  throws IOException, ServletException{

    Connection connection = connectionPool.getConnection();

    String firstName = request.getParameter("firstName");
    String lastName = request.getParameter("lastName");
    String emailAddress = request.getParameter("emailAddress");
    User user = new User(firstName, lastName, emailAddress);

    HttpSession session = request.getSession();
    session.setAttribute("user", user);

    String message = "";
    try{
        //check that email address doesn't already exist
        boolean emailExists = UserDB.isMatch(connection, emailAddress);
        if (emailExists){
            message = "This email address already exists. <br>"
                    + "Please enter another email address.";
            session.setAttribute("message", message);
            RequestDispatcher dispatcher =
                getServletContext().getRequestDispatcher(
                    "/email11/join_email_list.jsp");
            dispatcher.forward(request, response);
        }
        else{
            UserDB.addRecord(connection, user);
            session.setAttribute("message", "");
            RequestDispatcher dispatcher =
                    getServletContext().getRequestDispatcher(
                        "/email11/show_email_entry.jsp");
            dispatcher.forward(request, response);
        }
    }
    catch(SQLException sqle){
        message = "EmailServlet SQLException: " + sqle;
        session.setAttribute("message", message);
        RequestDispatcher dispatcher =
            getServletContext().getRequestDispatcher(
                "/email11/join_email_list.jsp");
        dispatcher.forward(request, response);
    }
    connectionPool.freeConnection(connection);
}
```

Figure 11-15   The code for the EmailList class

The code for the UserDB class

Figure 11-16 shows the code for the UserDB class. Although this class provides five static methods, the EmailServlet uses only the first two: the isMatch and addRecord methods. The other methods, though, can be used by other servlets. These are the getUser, updateRecord, and deleteRecord methods.

The five methods in this class map the User object to the User table in the murach database. In particular, the addRecord method stores a User object in the User table while the getUser method creates a User object from a row in the User table. This is known as *object-to-relational mapping, or OR mapping*.

Although writing all of the OR mapping for an application gives you complete control over how it works, this can also be tedious and time-consuming. As a result, for larger projects, you may want to try using a commercial package like Webgain's Toplink, which automatically generates the OR mapping code from your database tables. That, however, is another subject since most of these packages are designed to work with EJBs (see chapter 17).

In the UserDB class, all of the methods accept a Connection object that allows them to connect to the database. Typically, a servlet will get the Connection object from a connection pool and pass it to the UserDB class.

To prevent two threads of a servlet from executing the same method at the same time, all of the methods in the UserDB class are declared with the synchronized keyword. As a result, if one thread starts executing the addRecord method and a second thread calls that method, the second thread has to wait until the first thread finishes. Because a method like the addRecord method executes in a fraction of a second, though, two threads will rarely call the same method at exactly the same time.

When you code SQL statements, you enclose all string and date values in single quotes. However, this can cause a problem if the data in a string contains a single quote. If, for example, you want to execute an SQL statement that updates a user's last name to O'Neil, the resulting SQL statement will look like this:

```
UPDATE User SET LastName = 'O'Neil' WHERE UserID = 1
```

But this will throw an SQLException that indicates that the SQL statement contains a syntax error.

To fix this, you need to modify the SQL statement so it looks like this:

```
UPDATE User SET LastName = 'O''Neil' WHERE UserID = 1
```

That's why the methods in the UserDB class call the encode method of the SQLUtil class for all string values that are passed to it. This method, which is shown in figure 11-10, searches each string for single quotes and replaces any single quotes that it finds with two single quotes, which prevents any syntax errors.

The isMatch method of the UserDB class checks to see if the specified email address already exists in the User table. To do that, this method executes a SELECT statement that searches for the specified email address. If this method finds the address, it will return a true value. Otherwise, it will return a false value.

The UserDB class

```java
package data;

import java.sql.*;
import util.*;
import business.User;

public class UserDB{

    public static synchronized boolean isMatch(Connection connection,
    String emailAddress) throws SQLException{
        String query = "SELECT EmailAddress FROM User " +
                        "WHERE EmailAddress = '"
                            + SQLUtil.encode(emailAddress) + "'";
        Statement statement = connection.createStatement();
        ResultSet results = statement.executeQuery(query);
        boolean emailExists = results.next();
        results.close();
        statement.close();
        return emailExists;
    }

    public static synchronized int addRecord(Connection connection,
    User user) throws SQLException{
        String query =
            "INSERT INTO User " +
                "(EmailAddress, FirstName, LastName) " +
            "VALUES ('" + SQLUtil.encode(user.getEmailAddress()) + "', " +
                    "'" + SQLUtil.encode(user.getFirstName()) + "', " +
                    "'" + SQLUtil.encode(user.getLastName()) + "')";
        Statement statement = connection.createStatement();
        int status = statement.executeUpdate(query);
        statement.close();
        return status;
    }

    public static synchronized int updateRecord(Connection connection,
    User user) throws SQLException{
        String query =
            "UPDATE User "
            + "SET EmailAddress = '"
                + SQLUtil.encode(user.getEmailAddress()) + "',"
            + "    FirstName = '" + SQLUtil.encode(user.getFirstName()) + "', "
            + "    LastName = '" + SQLUtil.encode(user.getLastName()) + "'"
            + "WHERE EmailAddress = '"
                + SQLUtil.encode(user.getEmailAddress()) + "'";
        Statement statement = connection.createStatement();
        int status = statement.executeUpdate(query);
        statement.close();
        return status;
    }
```

Figure 11-16   The code for the UserDB class (part 1 of 2)

The addRecord method adds a new row to the User table. To do that, it executes an INSERT statement that includes the data from the User object that was passed to the method. If this method executes successfully, it returns an integer value of 1 to the calling method. Otherwise, it will throw an SQLException.

The updateRecord method works like the addRecord method, but it uses an UPDATE statement instead of an INSERT statement. Within the UPDATE statement, the WHERE clause uses the email address to find the record to be updated.

The deleteRecord method also works like the addRecord method, but it uses the DELETE statement instead of the INSERT statement. In addition, the deleteRecord method only accepts an email address as a parameter. That's because this method only needs to identify the user that should be deleted.

The getUser method creates a User object that receives the data from the row in the User table that corresponds with the email address that's passed to the method. If the email address is found in the User table, this method uses the set methods of the User class to fill the User object with values from the database. Then, this method returns the User object to the calling method. Otherwise, this method returns a User object that doesn't contain any values.

So far in this book, the User and UserDB classes have only worked with three fields: first name, last name, and email address. In the real world, though, a single business class or database table may contain dozens of fields. To give you some idea of this complexity, section 5 presents a more realistic application. When you code an application like that, the good news is that all the skills you've just learned still apply. The bad news is that you have to write many more lines of code as you develop typical business and database classes.

The UserDB class (continued)

```java
    public static synchronized int deleteRecord(Connection connection,
    String emailAddress) throws SQLException{
        String query =
            "DELETE FROM User " +
            "WHERE EmailAddress = '"
                + SQLUtil.encode(emailAddress) + "'";
        Statement statement = connection.createStatement();
        int status = statement.executeUpdate(query);
        statement.close();
        return status;
    }

    public static synchronized User getUser(Connection connection,
    String emailAddress) throws SQLException{
        String query = "SELECT * FROM User " +
                        "WHERE EmailAddress = '"
                            + SQLUtil.encode(emailAddress) + "'";
        Statement statement = connection.createStatement();
        ResultSet results = statement.executeQuery(query);
        User user = new User();
        if (results.next() == true){
            user.setEmailAddress(results.getString("EmailAddress"));
            user.setFirstName(results.getString("FirstName"));
            user.setLastName(results.getString("LastName"));
        }
        results.close();
        statement.close();
        return user;
    }
}
```

Figure 11-16   The code for the UserDB class (part 2 of 2)

Perspective

The goal of this chapter has been to show you how to use JDBC and connection pooling within the context of a web application. Although there's a lot more to database programming than that, this should get you off to a good start. In fact, the skills in this chapter are adequate for most small- to medium-sized web sites.

For large web sites, though, performance becomes more of an issue. In addition, you may want to use third-party software that makes it easier to design and create a database, to map objects to a database, and to manage a connection pool. Often, that means using tools that are designed to work with EJBs. In chapter 17, then, you'll be introduced to EJBs so you can get a better idea of how they can be used.

Summary

- To write Java code that works with a database, you use *Java Database Connectivity*, or *JDBC*. To do that, you use the classes in the JDBC API.

- Before you can access a database, you must install a *database driver* on the database server. Then, before you can work with the database, you must load the driver and create a Connection object that connects to the database.

- You use the createStatement method of the Connection object to create a Statement object that contains the SQL statement that you want to run. Then, you use the executeQuery or executeUpdate method to run the SQL statement.

- When you run a SELECT statement, it returns a *result set* to your program. Then, you can use the methods of the ResultSet object to move the *cursor* through the rows of the result set and to get the data from the rows.

- *Prepared statements* can improve the performance of database operations because the database server only checks their syntax and prepares execution plans for them the first time they are executed. To use them, you create PreparedStatement objects that contain SQL statements, and you use the methods of these objects to pass parameters to them and run them.

- A ResultSetMetaData object contains information about a result set like the number and names of the columns.

- *Connection pooling* can improve the performance of a web application by sharing the connections to a database between all of the users of the database.

Terms

Java Database Connectivity (JDBC)
database driver
result set
result table
row pointer
cursor

prepared statement
connection pool
singleton class
object-to-relational mapping
OR mapping

Objectives

- Develop data classes that provide OR mapping and all of the database methods that your servlets need.

- Develop servlets that use connection pooling and the methods of your data classes.

- In general terms, describe what your program has to do to get data from a database.

- Explain how prepared statements can improve the performance of database operations.

- Describe the use of a ResultSetMetaData object.

- Explain how connection pooling can improve the performance of a web application.

Exercise 11-1   Implement connection pooling

In this exercise, you'll enhance the SQL Gateway application shown in this chapter so that it uses connection pooling.

1. Run the SQL Gateway application and execute SELECT statements to see how this application works.
2. Open the SQLGatewayServlet class that's located in the sql11 package. Then, modify this servlet so that it uses the MurachPool class to implement connection pooling.
3. Run the application and make sure it works as before.

Exercise 11-2   Create an Administration application

In this exercise, you'll create an application that allows you to view all users, update existing users, and delete users in the User table in the murach database. The HTML files and JSPs for this exercise are located in the user11 directory. You should save all servlets in the user11 package. As you code the classes for this exercise, you should implement connection pooling when appropriate.

1. Open the UserDB class that's located in the data package. Add a method named readRecords that accepts a Connection object and returns a Vector object of all users in the User table. Be sure to save and compile this class.

2. Create a servlet named UsersServlet in the user11 package that retrieves a Vector of all users from the User table, sets the Vector in the session, and calls the users JSP that's located in the user11 directory to display the data as shown below:

3. Open the users JSP and notice that the Update hyperlink requests the ShowUserServlet class and the Delete hyperlink requests the DeleteUserServlet.

4. Create the ShowUserServlet class that retrieves the request parameter for email address, retrieves the user from the User table, stores this object in the session, and calls the show_user JSP that's located in the user11 directory as shown below:

5. Open the show_user JSP and notice that it submits all data to the UpdateUserServlet class.

6. Create an UpdateUserServlet class that retrieves all request parameters from the show_user JSP and updates the user in the User table. This servlet should forward the request to the UsersServlet that you created in step 2 so that the list of users is displayed after an update is made.

7. Create a DeleteUserServlet class that retrieves the request parameter for email address and deletes the selected user. This servlet should forward the request to the UsersServlet that you created in step 2.

Section 4

Advanced servlet and JSP skills

This section contains six chapters that present other servlet and JSP skills that you may need for some of your web applications. Chapter 12 shows you how to send email from a servlet. Chapters 13 and 14 show you how to use a secure connection for sensitive data and how to restrict access to portions of a web application. Chapter 15 tells you more about working with the request and response objects of HTTP. Chapter 16 shows you how to use XML in your web applications. And chapter 17 provides a brief introduction to Enterprise JavaBeans.

Because each of these chapters is written as an independent module, you can read these chapters in whatever sequence you prefer. If, for example, you want to learn more about Enterprise JavaBeans, you can skip to chapter 17. Or, if want to learn how to work with a secure connection, you can skip to chapter 13. Eventually, though, you should read all of the chapters in this section because they all provide useful capabilities.

12

How to use JavaMail to send email

When you create a web application, you sometimes need to send email responses to the users of the application. For example, when a user makes a purchase from an e-commerce site, the web application usually sends a confirmation email that contains the order number and other data about the order. In this chapter, you'll learn how to use the JavaMail API to send an email from a servlet.

An introduction to the JavaMail API **376**
How email works 376
Protocols for working with email 376
How to install the JavaMail API 378
Code that uses the JavaMail API to send an email message 380
How to create and send an email message **382**
How to create a mail session 382
How to create a message 384
How to address a message 386
How to send a message 388
How to send an email message from a servlet **390**
A helper class that can be used to send a message 390
A servlet that uses a helper class to send a message 392
Perspective **394**

An introduction to the JavaMail API

The *JavaMail API* is a programming interface that makes it easy for Java developers to write code that automatically sends an email. It depends on another API known as the JavaBeans Activation Framework API, or the JAF API. Figure 12-1 introduces you to these APIs and several of the protocols for working with email messages that these APIs use.

How email works

You're probably familiar with *mail client* software such as Microsoft Outlook or Eudora that allows you to send and retrieve messages. This type of software communicates with the *mail server* software that actually sends and retrieves your email messages. Most likely, your mail server software is provided by your Internet Service Provider (ISP) or through your company.

The diagram in this figure shows how this works. When you send an email message to a friend, for example, it is first sent from the mail client software on your client computer to your mail server. Next, it is sent from your mail server to the mail server of your friend. And last, it is sent from that mail server to the client machine of your friend. To make this work, the mail clients and the mail servers use the protocols presented in this figure.

Protocols for working with email

The *Simple Mail Transfer Protocol*, or *SMTP*, is the most commonly used protocol for delivering email messages. When you send an email message, the message is sent to your SMTP mail server. Then, your SMTP server relays the message to the mail server of the recipient.

Once the message has been sent to the recipient's mail server, the mail client software retrieves the message. Typically, this software either uses the *Post Office Protocol* (*POP*) or the *Internet Message Access Protocol* (*IMAP*). In general, POP is used with email clients like Outlook or Eudora, and IMAP is used with web-based email clients like Yahoo or Hotmail accounts.

Unlike the SMTP, POP, and IMAP protocols, the *Multipurpose Internet Message Extension*, or *MIME*, protocol isn't used to transfer email messages. Instead, it defines the content type of an email message and its attachments. In this chapter, you'll learn how to send a simple email that contains plain text. Remember, though, that it's also possible to use the MIME type to send other types of messages such as a message that contains an attachment.

How email works

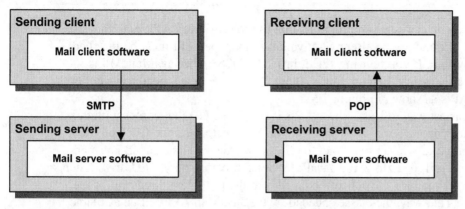

Three protocols for sending and retrieving email messages

Protocol	Description
SMTP	*Simple Mail Transfer Protocol* is used to send a message from one mail server to another.
POP	*Post Office Protocol* is used to retrieve messages from a mail server. This protocol transfers all messages from the mail server to the mail client. Currently, POP is in version 3 and is known as POP3.
IMAP	*Internet Message Access Protocol* is used by web-based mail services such as Hotmail and Yahoo. This protocol allows a web browser to read messages that are stored in the directories of the mail server. Currently, IMAP is in version 4 and is known as IMAP4.

Another protocol that's used with email

Protocol	Description
MIME	The *Multipurpose Internet Message Extension* type, or *MIME* type, specifies the type of content that can be sent as a message or attachment.

The JAR files for the JavaMail API

mail.jar	Contains the Java classes for the JavaMail API.
activation.jar	Contains the Java classes for the JavaBean Activation Framework. These classes are necessary for the JavaMail API to run.

Description

- When an email message is sent, it goes from the sender's *mail client* to its *mail server* to the receiver's mail server to the receiver's mail client.

- SMTP, POP, and IMAP are the protocols that are commonly used for sending and receiving email messages.

- The *JavaMail API* is a high level API that allows you to use a mail protocol to communicate with a mail server. It depends upon another API known as the JavaBeans Activation Framework API, or the JAF API.

Figure 12-1   An introduction to the JavaMail API

How to install the JavaMail API

Before you can compile programs that use the JavaMail API, both the JavaMail API and the JavaBeans Activation Framework API must be installed on your system. If you're using J2EE, instead of J2SE, the JavaMail API is probably already installed on your system. Otherwise, you'll need to install both of these APIs as shown in figure 12-2.

The easiest way to install these APIs is to use the CD that comes with this book. After you navigate to the JavaExtensions directory on the CD, you use a zip program like WinZip to extract the files from the zip files named javamail-1_3.zip and jaf1_0_2.zip to the JavaExtensions directory on your C drive. Then, you copy the mail.jar and activation.jar files to the jre\lib\ext directory for the Java SDK. That way, the classes needed by the JavaMail API will be available to your system.

If you want to install a different version of these APIs, you can download the zip files for the current versions of the JavaMail and JAF APIs from the Java web site. Then, you can follow steps 2 and 3 to unzip and install these APIs.

When you unzip the zip file for the JavaMail API, the documentation for that API is installed on your system. To view this documentation, you can navigate to the directory that contains the index.html file for the JavaMail API and view that page in your web browser. For example, if you unzipped the JavaMail API into the C:\JavaExtensions directory, the index file for the documentation will be in this directory:

```
C:\JavaExtensions\javamail-1.2\docs\javadocs
```

Once you open the index file in a web browser, you'll be able to get more information about the interfaces and classes that make up the JavaMail API.

How to install the JavaMail API

1. Put the CD that comes with this book into your CD drive, and navigate to the JavaExtensions directory.

2. Use a zip program such as WinZip to extract the files from the zip file named javamail-1_3 to the directory named C:\JavaExtensions (you may need to create this directory).

3. Copy the mail.jar file from the C:\JavaExtensions\javamail-1.3 directory to the C:\j2sdk1.4.0\jre\lib\ext directory.

How to install the JavaBeans Activation Framework API

1. Put the CD that comes with this book into your CD drive, and navigate to the JavaExtensions directory.

2. Use a zip program such as WinZip to extract the files from the zip file named jaf1_0_2 to the directory named C:\JavaExtensions (you may need to create this directory).

3. Copy the activation.jar file from the C:\JavaExtensions\jaf-1.0.2 directory to the C:\j2sdk1.4.0\jre\lib\ext directory.

Description

- If you're using J2EE, not J2SE, both the JavaMail and JavaBeans Activation Framework APIs are automatically installed for you.

- If you want to be able to compile and test applications that use the JavaMail API on your local computer, you'll need to install the JavaMail API and the JavaBeans Activations Framework API.

- If you want to use different versions of these APIs, you can download the zip files for the APIs from the Java web site (*www.java.sun.com*). Then, you can follow steps 2 and 3 above to unzip these files and install the APIs.

- If you unzip the JavaMail API into the C:\JavaExtensions directory, you can view the documentation for the API by opening the index.html page in the C:\JavaExtensions\javamail-1.3\docs\javadocs directory.

Figure 12-2   How to install the JavaMail API

Code that uses the JavaMail API to send an email message

Figure 12-3 shows some Java code that creates and sends an email message that contains plain text. Although you may not understand every line in this example, you can see how the Java API makes it easy to create and send an email. In the next four figures, you'll learn the details for writing code like this.

This figure also shows what this simple email will look like when viewed by a mail client. In this case, the mail client is a web browser that's accessing a Yahoo email account. However, the mail client could also be a software program such as Microsoft Outlook, Eudora, America Online, and so on. Regardless, the mail client will display the From address, the To address, the Subject line, and the body of the message.

Code that uses the JavaMail API to send an email

```
// 1 - get the mail session
Properties props = new Properties();
props.put("mail.smtp.host", "localhost");
Session session = Session.getDefaultInstance(props);

// 2 - create the message
MimeMessage message = new MimeMessage(session);
message.setSubject("Order Confirmation");
message.setText("Thanks for your order!");

// 3 - address the message
InternetAddress addressFrom = new InternetAddress("cds@murach.com");
message.setFrom(addressFrom);
InternetAddress addressTo = new InternetAddress("andi@yahoo.com");
message.setRecipient(Message.RecipientType.TO, addressTo);

// 4 - send the message
Transport.send(message);
```

An email that's sent from a servlet when viewed by a client

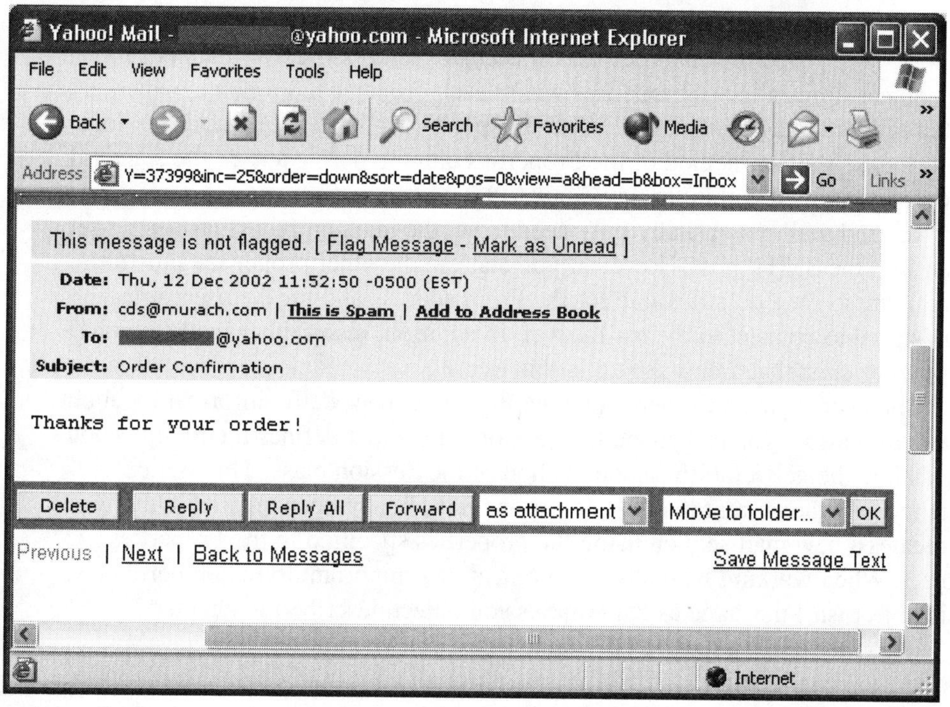

Figure 12-3   Code that uses the JavaMail API to send an email message

How to create and send an email message

Now that you have a general idea of how to use the JavaMail API to create and send an email message, you'll learn the coding details for creating and sending an email message.

How to create a mail session

Figure 12-4 shows how to get a *mail session* so that you can create and send an email message. To get one, you have to identify the host of your SMTP mail server. If your Java application is running on the same server as your SMTP mail server software, you can use the localhost keyword to identify the host of your SMTP mail server. Otherwise, you may be able to use an Internet address to identify the host of your SMTP mail server. To get a valid Internet address, you may need to contact your network administrator or your ISP.

Before you create a mail session, you need to create a Properties object that contains any properties that the session needs to send or receive mail. A Properties object stores a list of properties where each property has a name, which is often referred to as a *key*, and a value. To specify properties for a mail session, you can use the put method of the Properties class to define any of the standard properties defined within the JavaMail API.

To send mail, you usually only need to set the mail.smtp.host property so it identifies the SMTP host. However, you can use the other properties shown in this figure to set a default value for the From address and for the username that's used to connect to the mail server. In addition, many other mail session properties exist that aren't shown in this figure.

Once you create a Properties object that contains specific information about the mail session, you can create the Session object that defines the mail session by calling the getDefaultInstance method of the Session class. This static method gets the current mail session if one has already been created. Otherwise, it creates a new mail session using the properties specified in the Properties object. When working with a Session object, it's important to remember that this object isn't the same as the HttpSession object described in chapter 7.

If you're running stand-alone Tomcat and you want to test how JavaMail works, you can identify your SMTP host through your mail client. To do this in Outlook Express, for example, select Tools, Accounts, and your internet host in the mail accounts. Then select Properties and the Servers tab. There, you'll find the name of the SMTP host that you should use when creating the mail session. If you use Microsoft Outlook with Microsoft Exchange, your SMTP host is the server name or IP address that is running Microsoft Exchange. For other clients, you may have to contact your ISP to get the name of the host.

How to get a mail session

```
Properties props = new Properties();
props.put("mail.smtp.host", "localhost");
Session session = Session.getDefaultInstance(props);
```

How to get a mail session and set the default From address

```
Properties props = new Properties();
props.put("mail.smtp.host", "mail.lemoorenet.com");
props.put("mail.from", "webmaster@murach.com");
Session session = Session.getDefaultInstance(props);
```

A few standard properties that can be set for a Session object

Property name	Description
mail.smtp.host	Specifies the default outgoing host for SMTP protocol.
mail.from	Specifies the default return email address.
mail.user	Specifies the default username to use when connecting to the mail server.

Description

- A Session object contains information about the *mail session*. For example, it contains information about the host and protocol for the mail server, the return address, the username, and so on. This is not the same as the HttpSession object that you use for session management.

- The getDefaultInstance method of the Session class returns the default Session object for the application. If one hasn't been created yet, this constructor creates a Session object and installs it by using the default properties stored in the Properties object.

- To supply default values for the properties of a Properties object, you can create a Properties object and use the put method to specify each property name and value.

- To specify the SMTP server for a session, you can use the mail.smtp.host property to specify the host name of the SMTP server.

- If the Java application is running on the same server as the mail server, you can usually use the localhost keyword to specify the host address of the mail server.

- If the Java application isn't running on the same server as the mail server, you may need to contact your network administrator or your Internet Service Provider to get a valid host address for the mail server.

- The Session class is stored in the javax.mail package. The Properties class is stored in the java.util package. As a result, you must import these packages when working with Session and Properties objects.

Figure 12-4   How to create a mail session

How to create a message

Once you've created the Session object, you can create an object that defines an email message as shown in figure 12-5. To do that, you pass a Session object to the constructor of the MimeMessage class to create a MimeMessage object. Then, you can set the subject, body, and addresses for the message. To set the subject, you use the setSubject method. To set the message body as plain text, you use the setText method. Then, you use the methods shown in the next figure to set the addresses for the message.

When you use the setText method to set the body of the message, the MIME type for the message is automatically set to text/plain. For most text messages, this is adequate. However, since most modern mail clients can display text that's formatted with HTML tags, it's also common to use the setContent method to change the MIME type for a message to text/html. Then, the body of the message can include HTML tags that format the text, display images, and provide links to web resources.

How to create a message

```
MimeMessage message = new MimeMessage(session);
```

How to set the subject line of a message

```
message.setSubject("Order Confirmation");
```

How to set the body of a plain text message

```
message.setText("Thanks for your order!");
```

How to set the body of an HTML message

```
message.setContent("<H1>Thanks for your order!</H1>", "text/html");
```

Description

- You can use the MimeMessage class that's stored in the javax.mail.internet package to create a message. This message extends the Message class that's stored in the java.mail package.

- To create a MimeMessage object, you supply a valid Session object to the MimeMessage constructor.

- Once you've created a MimeMessage object, you can use the setSubject and setText methods to set the subject line and body of the email message. This automatically sets the MIME type to text/plain.

- You can use the setContent method to include an HTML document as the body of the message. To do that, the first argument specifies a string for the HTML document, and the second argument specifies text/html as the MIME type.

- All of the methods in this figure throw a javax.mail.MessagingException. As a result, you must handle this exception when using these methods.

Figure 12-5   How to create a message

How to address a message

Figure 12-6 shows how to address a MimeMessage object like the one in the last figure. This allows you to specify the From address as well as the To, CC (*carbon copy*), and BCC (*blind carbon copy*) addresses. When you send a carbon copy, the CC addresses will appear in the message, but when you send a blind carbon copy, the BCC addresses won't appear in the message.

Before you can set an address within a MimeMessage object, though, you must create an Address object that defines at least an email address. To do that, you create an object from the InternetAddress subclass of the Address class. When you create this object, the first argument specifies the email address. If you want to associate a name with the email address, you can include the second argument.

To set the From address, you can use the setFrom method of the MimeMessage object. When you use this method, you must supply an Address object that defines the email address you wish to be displayed in the From attribute of the email message.

To set the To, CC, and BCC addresses, you can use the setRecipient method of the MimeMessage object. With this method, the first argument specifies the type of recipient for the address. Then, the second argument specifies an Address object. To specify the recipient type, you use one of the fields defined in the Message.RecipientType class.

If you want to send your message to multiple recipients, you can use the setRecipients method of the MimeMessage class. This method allows you to send a message to an array of Address objects. When you use this method, it replaces any recipients that were already set in the message. However, if you want to add recipients to an existing message, you can use the addRecipient or addRecipients methods. These methods work like the setRecipient and setRecipients methods, but they add recipients to an existing list.

Since the methods of the MimeMessage class throw a MessagingException, you must handle this exception in any code that uses these methods. In addition, the InternetAddress constructor throws an AddressException when an illegally formatted address is found. However, since the AddressException class extends the MessagingException, you can catch both exceptions by catching the MessagingException.

How to set the From address

```
InternetAddress fromAddress = new InternetAddress("cds@murach.com");
message.setFrom(fromAddress);
```

How to set the To address

```
InternetAddress toAddress = new InternetAddress("andi@yahoo.com");
message.setRecipient(Message.RecipientType.TO, toAddress);
```

How to set the CC address

```
InternetAddress ccAddress = new InternetAddress("ted@yahoo.com");
message.setRecipient(Message.RecipientType.CC, ccAddress);
```

How to set the BCC address

```
InternetAddress bccAddress = new InternetAddress("msmith@hotmail.com");
message.setRecipient(Message.RecipientType.BCC, bccAddress);
```

How to include an email address and a name

```
InternetAddress toAddress =
    new InternetAddress("andi@yahoo.com", "Andrea Steelman");
```

How to send a message to multiple recipients

```
Address[] mailList ={ new InternetAddress("andi@hotmail.com"),
                      new InternetAddress("joelmurach@yahoo.com"),
                      new InternetAddress("msmith@hotmail.com") };
message.setRecipients(Message.RecipientType.TO, mailList);
```

Description

* To define an email address, you can use the InternetAddress class that's stored in the javax.mail.internet package. This class is a subclass of the Address class that's stored in the javax.mail package.
* You can use the setFrom method of the MimeMessage object to set the From address.
* You can use the setRecipient and setRecipients methods of the MimeMessage object to set the To, CC (*carbon copy*), and BCC (*blind carbon copy*) addresses. If you specify a BCC, the recipients with To and CC addresses won't be able to view the recipients with BCC addresses.
* To include a name that's associated with an email address, you can add a second argument to the InternetAddress constructor. Then, the name will be displayed next to the email address like this: andi@yahoo.com (Andrea Steelman). When you do this, though, you must handle a java.io.UnsupportedEncodingException type.
* To send an email message to multiple recipients, you can pass an array of Address objects to the setRecipients method.
* If you want to add email addresses to a message instead of replacing any existing addresses, you can use the addFrom, addRecipient, and addRecipients methods instead of the setFrom, setRecipient, and setRecipients methods.
* All of the methods in this figure throw a javax.mail.MessagingException. As a result, you must handle this exception when using these methods.

Figure 12-6   How to address a message

How to send a message

Once you've created and addressed a MimeMessage object as shown in the last two figures, you can send the message as shown in figure 12-7. To do that, you just call the static send method of the Transport class with the MimeMessage object as the argument.

If the message can't be sent, the send method will throw an exception of the SendFailedException type. This exception contains a list of (1) invalid addresses to which the message could not be sent, (2) valid addresses to which the message wasn't sent, and (3) valid addresses to which the message was sent. If necessary, you can use this exception to write these addresses to a log file.

How to send a message

```
Transport.send(message);
```

Description

- You can use the static send method of the Transport class to send a message to the specified email server, which is almost always a SMTP server.

- The send method throws a SendFailedException object when a message can't be sent. You can use this object to return the invalid addresses, the valid addresses that have been sent, and the valid addresses that haven't been sent.

- If the SMTP host is incorrect in the session object, the send method will throw a SendFailedException object.

- The SendFailedException class inherits the MessagingException class. As a result, you can handle both of these exceptions by handling the MessagingException.

Figure 12-7   How to send a message

How to send an email message from a servlet

Now that you know the coding details for creating and sending an email message, here are two classes that put that code into use. The first is a helper class that can be used to send a message. The second is a servlet that uses the helper class to send a message.

A helper class that can be used to send a message

Figure 12-8 shows a helper class named MailUtil that can make it easier to send a message from a servlet, or any other Java class for that matter. This class contains a static method named sendMail that creates and sends a simple plain text message from a single email address to a single email address. Since this method throws an exception of the MessagingException type, any servlet that calls this method must catch this exception.

Although this MailUtil class is simple, it provides a useful function. To enhance it, you can add sendMail methods that provide for CC and BCC addresses. You can also add a method named sendHtmlMail that sets the body of the message to the text/html MIME type.

A helper class with a method that sends an email

```
package util;

import javax.mail.*;
import javax.mail.internet.*;
import java.util.*;

public class MailUtil{

    public static void sendMail(String to, String from,
                                String subject, String messageText)
                                throws MessagingException{

        // 1 - get a mail session
        Properties props = new Properties();
        props.put("mail.smtp.host", "localhost");
        Session session = Session.getDefaultInstance(props);

        // 2 - create a message
        MimeMessage message = new MimeMessage(session);
        message.setSubject(subject);
        message.setText(messageText);

        // 3 - address the message
        InternetAddress fromAddress = new InternetAddress(from);
        InternetAddress toAddress = new InternetAddress(to);
        message.setFrom(fromAddress);
        message.setRecipient(Message.RecipientType.TO, toAddress);

        // 4 - send the message
        Transport.send(message);
    }
}
```

Description

- You can use the static sendMail method of this MailUtil class to send an email message with a from address and a to address.

- Since the sendMail method throws the MessagingException, any class that uses this method must handle the exception.

Figure 12-8   A helper class that can be used to send a message

A servlet that uses a helper class to send a message

Figure 12-9 presents the code for the EmailServlet class. Since you've seen variations of this class throughout this book, you shouldn't have any trouble understanding how it works. This time, though, the servlet uses the MailUtil class in the last figure to send an email message to the email address that the user enters into the calling JSP.

Once the servlet writes the User object to a file, the servlet creates four strings that contain the information for the email message. First, it sets the To address to the email address that was passed with the request. Then, it sets the From address, the subject line, and the text for the body of the message.

To create and send the message, the servlet calls the sendMail method of the MailUtil class. Since this method throws a MessagingException, the servlet catches that exception. Then, it writes the exception to a log file.

If you can't send an email message with a servlet like this one, there are several possible causes. First, you might not be connected to the SMTP mail server. To solve this problem, you might need to log on to the Internet. Second, you might not have the correct name for the SMTP host. To solve this problem, you might need to contact your network administrator or ISP. This usually isn't a problem after you've deployed the servlet to an Internet server, but it can be a problem when you're testing a servlet on your own computer.

A servlet that sends an email

```java
package email12;

import java.io.*;
import javax.servlet.*;
import javax.servlet.http.*;
import javax.mail.*;
import business.User;
import data.UserIO;
import util.MailUtil;

public class EmailServlet extends HttpServlet{

    public void doGet(HttpServletRequest request,
                      HttpServletResponse response)
                      throws IOException, ServletException{

        String firstName = request.getParameter("firstName");
        String lastName = request.getParameter("lastName");
        String emailAddress = request.getParameter("emailAddress");

        User user = new User(firstName, lastName, emailAddress);
        UserIO.addRecord(user,
            "../webapps/murach/WEB-INF/etc/UserEmail.txt");

        String to = emailAddress;
        String from = "emaillist@murach.com";
        String subject = "Welcome to our email list";
        String message = "Dear " + firstName + ",\n" +
            "Thanks for joining our email list. We'll make sure to send " +
            "you announcements about new products and promotions.\n" +
            "Have a great day and thanks again!";

        try{
            MailUtil.sendMail(to, from, subject, message);
        }
        catch (MessagingException me){
            log("MessagingException: " + emailAddress);
            log(me.toString());
        }

        RequestDispatcher dispatcher =
                    getServletContext().getRequestDispatcher(
                        "/email12/show_email_entry.jsp");
        dispatcher.forward(request, response);
    }
}
```

Figure 12-9   A servlet that uses a helper class to send a message

Perspective

The goal of this chapter has been to show you how to use the JavaMail API to send email messages from your servlets. So if you can get servlets like the one in figure 12-9 to work on your system, this chapter has accomplished its goal.

Keep in mind, though, that you can use the JavaMail API to do more than just that. For instance, you can use that API to send messages that have attachments and to retrieve messages. If you need to do tasks like that, you should be able to use the documentation for the JavaMail API to build on the skills you've learned in this chapter.

Summary

- When an email message is sent it goes from the *mail client* software to that client's *mail server* software to the receiving client's mail server and then to the receiving mail client.

- To send email messages from server to server, the *Simple Mail Transfer Protocol* (*SMTP*) is commonly used. Then, to retrieve messages from a server, *Post Office Protocol* (*POP*) and *Internet Message Access Protocol* (*IMAP*) are commonly used.

- To send email messages from your Java programs, you use the classes of the *JavaMail API*. In particular, you create a Session object that contains information about the *mail session* including the protocol that's used.

Terms

JavaMail API	Multipurpose Internet Message
mail client	Extension (MIME)
mail server	mail session
Simple Mail Transfer Protocol (SMTP)	carbon copy
Post Office Protocol (POP)	blind carbon copy
Internet Message Access Protocol (IMAP)	

Objectives

- Develop servlets that send email messages to the users of the application.

- In general terms, describe how an email message is sent from one client to another.

Exercise 12-1   Send a message from a servlet

1. Create a servlet named SendMailServlet in the email12 package that sends a plain text message to yourself. To do that, you'll need to make sure that you've installed the JavaMail API, and you'll need to find the host name for your SMTP mail server. (Don't use the MailUtil class for this exercise).

2. Test the servlet in a browser by requesting it. Or, you can create HTML pages to test the servlet.

3. Modify the servlet so the message is sent as HTML rather than plain text. Be sure to include some HTML tags so you can verify that this works.

Exercise 12-2   Enhance the MailUtil class

1. Open the MailUtil class that's located in the util package. Then, modify this class so it contains an additional sendMail method that allows the user to specify multiple To, CC, and BCC addresses. To do this, the method should contain a declaration similar to this one:

```
public static void sendMail(String[] to, String[] cc, String[] bcc,
                            String from, String subject,
                            String messageText) throws MessagingException{
```

2. Open the EmailServlet class in the email12 package. Then, modify it so it uses the new sendMail method to send a test message to yourself and a friend. (Use known addresses, though, so you don't send email to people who don't know you!)

13

How to use SSL to work with a secure connection

If your application requires users to enter sensitive data such as credit card numbers and passwords, you should use a secure connection when you send data between the client and the server. Otherwise, a hacker might be able to intercept and view this data. In this chapter, you'll learn how to transfer data over a secure connection.

An introduction to SSL **398**
How SSL works 398
How TLS works 398
When to use a secure connection 398
How SSL authentication works 400
How to obtain a digital secure certificate 402
How to configure a testing environment for SSL **404**
How to install the JSSE API 404
How to create a certificate for testing 406
How to enable SSL in Tomcat 406
How to test a local SSL connection 408
How to work with a secure connection **410**
How to request a secure connection 410
A page that uses a secure connection 412
How to return to a regular HTTP connection 412
How to switch from a local system to an Internet server 412
Perspective **414**

An introduction to SSL

To prevent others from reading data that is transmitted over the Internet, you can use the *Secure Sockets Layer*, or *SSL*. This is the protocol that lets you transfer data between the server and client over a secure connection.

How SSL works

Figure 13-1 shows a web page that uses SSL to transfer data between the server and client over a *secure connection*. To determine if you're transmitting data over a secure connection, you can read the URL. If it starts with https rather than http, then you're transmitting data over a secure connection. In addition, a small lock icon appears in the lower right of the browser when you're using a secure connection.

With a regular HTTP connection, all data is sent as unencrypted plain text. As a result, if a hacker intercepts this data, it is easy to read. With a secure connection, though, all data is encrypted before it's transferred between the client and server. Although a hacker can still intercept this data, he won't be able to read it unless he can break the encryption code.

How TLS works

Transport Layer Security, or *TLS*, is another protocol that's used for working with secure connections. This protocol is more advanced that SSL, but it works similarly. As a user, it's hard to tell whether you're using an SSL connection or a TLS connection. Although TLS is only supported by newer browsers, any server that implements TLS also implements SSL. That way, the newer browsers can use TLS, and the older browsers can still use SSL.

When you're working with secure connections, you'll find that SSL is often used to describe the connection instead of TLS. That's because SSL is the older, more established protocol for working with secure connections. In this chapter, the term SSL is used even though the connection could also be a TLS connection.

When to use a secure connection

Due to the time it takes to encrypt and decrypt the data that's sent across a secure connection, secure connections are noticeably slower than regular HTTP connections. As a result, you usually use secure connections only when your application passes sensitive data between the client and the server.

A request made with a secure connection

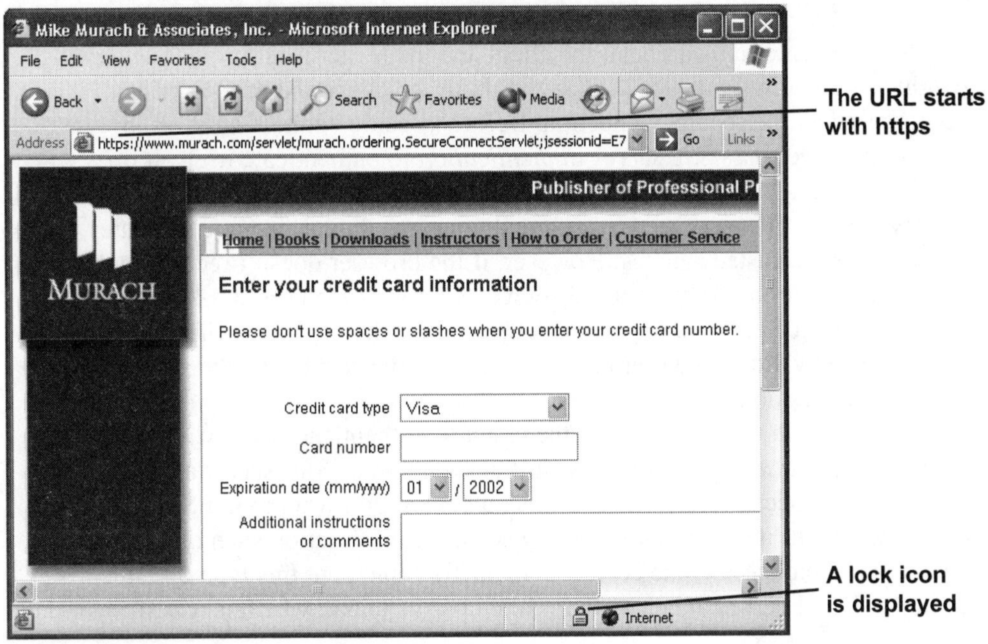

The URL starts with https

A lock icon is displayed

How SSL works

- *Secure Sockets Layer*, or *SSL*, is the protocol used by the World Wide Web that allows clients and servers to communicate over a *secure connection*.
- With SSL, both the client and browser encrypt all data that's sent and decrypt all data that's received.
- SSL is able to determine if data has been tampered with during transit.

How TLS works

- The *Transport Layer Security*, or *TLS*, is the protocol that's the successor to SSL.
- Only newer browsers support TLS.
- If a server implements TLS, the newer browsers will use TLS, but the older browsers will use SSL.

Description

- The URL for a secure connection starts with https.
- A web browser that is using a secure connection displays a lock in the lower right corner.

Figure 13-1   An introduction to SSL

How SSL authentication works

To use SSL to transmit data, the client and the server must provide *authentication* as shown in figure 13-2. That way, both the client and the server can accept or reject the secure connection. Before a secure connection is established, the server uses *SSL server authentication* to authenticate itself. It does this by providing a *digital secure certificate* to the browser.

By default, browsers are programmed to accept digital secure certificates that come from trusted sources. However, if the browser doesn't recognize the certificate as coming from a trusted source, it informs the user and lets the user view the certificate. Then, the user can determine whether the certificate should be considered valid. If the user chooses to accept the certificate, the secure connection is established.

Sometimes, a server may want the client to authenticate itself with *SSL client authentication*. Although this isn't as common as SSL server authentication, it is used occasionally. For example, a bank might want to use SSL client authentication to make sure it's sending sensitive information such as account numbers and balances to the correct person. To implement this type of authentication, a digital certificate must be installed on the client, which is usually a browser.

How authentication works

- *Authentication* is the process of determining whether a server or client is who and what it claims to be.
- When a browser makes an initial attempt to communicate with a server over a secure connection that uses SSL, the server authenticates itself by providing a *digital secure certificate*. In some instances, the server may also request that your browser authenticate itself by presenting its own digital secure certificate.

Types of SSL Authentication

Authentication	Description
SSL server authentication	Allows a client to confirm a server's identity by checking a digital secure certificate that's installed on the server.
SSL client authentication	Allows a server to confirm a client's identity by checking a digital secure certificate that's installed on the client.

A digital secure certificate

Description

- An SSL-enabled server authenticates itself to the user of a site by providing a *digital secure certificate*.
- If the digital secure certificate is registered with the browser, the browsers won't display the certificate by default. However, the user still has the option to view the certificate.

Figure 13-2   How SSL authentication works

How to obtain a digital secure certificate

If you want to establish a secure connection with your clients, you must obtain a digital secure certificate from a trusted source such as those listed in figure 13-3. These *certification authorities*, or *CAs*, verify that the person or company requesting the certificate is a valid person or company by checking with a *registration authority*, or *RA*. To obtain a digital secure certificate, you'll need to provide an RA with information about yourself or your company. Once the RA approves the request, the CA can issue the digital secure certificate.

A digital secure certificate from a trusted source is not free, and the cost of the certificate will depend on a variety of factors such as the level of security. As a result, when you purchase a digital certificate, you want one that fits the needs of your web site. In particular, you'll need to decide what *SSL strength* you want the connection to support. SSL strength refers to the level of encryption that the secure connection uses when it transmits data.

If you use a 40-bit SSL strength, it might be possible for a determined hacker to break the encryption code. On the other hand, most browsers support 40-bit strength, that security level is appropriate for most sites, and these certificates are reasonably priced.

If your site requires a higher level of security, you can purchase a certificate that uses 128-bit SSL strength. Although these certificates are more expensive than 40-bit certificates, it's almost impossible for a hacker to break the encryption code.

Once you purchase a secure certificate, you typically send it to your web host who installs it for your site. Once the certificate is installed, you can use SSL to transmit data over a secure connection.

Common certificate authorities that issue digital secure certificates

```
www.verisign.com
www.geotrust.com
www.entrust.com
www.equifaxsecure.com
```

SSL strength

- *SSL strength* refers to the length of the generated key that is created during the encryption process. The longer the key, the more difficult to break the encryption code.

The pros and cons of SSL strengths

Strength	Pros and Cons
40-bit	It's less expensive, but it's easier to break the encryption code.
128-bit	It's trillions of times stronger than 40-bit, but it's more expensive.

Description

- To use SSL in your web applications, you must first purchase a digital secure certificate from a trusted *certificate authority*, or *CA*. Once you obtain the certificate, you send it to the people who host your web site so they can install it on the server.

- A CA is a company that issues and manages security credentials. To verify information provided by the requestor of the secure certificate, a CA must check with a *registration authority*, or *RA*. Once the RA verifies the requestor's information, the CA can issue a digital secure certificate.

- Since SSL is built into all major browsers and web servers, installing a digital secure certificate enables SSL.

Figure 13-3   How to obtain a digital secure certificate

How to configure a testing environment for SSL

If you're using a commercial web server that supports servlet and JSP development, you probably won't need to configure the server for SSL. To implement SSL, you just purchase a secure certificate and provide it to the web hosting company. Then, your web hosting company should configure SSL for you.

However, if you want to be able to test secure connections before you deploy them to your web server, you'll need to configure a testing environment. To do that, you don't need to purchase a digital secure certificate from a trusted source. Instead, you can create and install a self-signed digital secure certificate for free.

Since a self-signed certificate doesn't come from a trusted source, it will cause a warning dialog box to be displayed when you use it. However, it will allow you to configure SSL for your local testing environment as described in this topic. Although this topic shows how to work with Tomcat 4.0, similar skills apply to other versions of Tomcat.

How to install the JSSE API

The *Java Secure Socket Extension API*, or *JSSE API*, is a collection of Java classes that let you use secure connections within your Java programs. Without it, your application won't be able to connect to the server that transmits data over a secure connection. This means that this API must be installed on any server that uses Java to transmit data over a SSL connection.

If you're using version 1.4 or higher of the SDK, then the JSSE API should already be installed on your system. However, if you're using an older version of the SDK, you may need to install the JSSE API as described in figure 13-4.

How to configure a local testing environment for SSL

1. Make sure the JSSE API is installed as shown in this figure.

2. Create a self-signed digital secure certificate as shown in the next figure.

3. Open the server.xml file that's in Tomcat's conf directory and remove the comments from the Connector element that defines an SSL connector on port 8443 as shown in the next figure.

4. Restart Tomcat.

How JSSE works

- The *Java Secure Socket Extension* API, or *JSSE*, is a collection of Java classes that enable secure connections within Java programs by implementing a version of the SSL and TLS protocols.

- If you want to use a secure connection with your servlets and JSPs, you must have the JSSE API installed on the server.

- If you're using a commercial web server that supports servlet and JSP development, the JSSE API should already be installed.

- If you're working in a local testing environment and you're using version 1.3.1 of the SDK or earlier, you may need to install the JSSE API. However, this API is included with version 1.4 of the SDK and later.

How to install JSSE

- To install the JSSE API, you can copy the jsse.jar file that's included on the CD that comes with this book from the JavaExtension directory to the SDK's jre\lib\ext directory. Or, you can download the jsse.jar file from the Java web site (*www.java.sun.com*) and move it to the jre\lib\ext directory.

Figure 13-4   How to install the JSSE API

How to create a certificate for testing

Figure 13-5 shows how to create a self-signed digital secure certificate for your system. To create a self-signed certificate, you must create a *keystore file*. To do this, you can open a command prompt window and use the cd command to change the current directory to the bin directory of your SDK. Then, you can enter the keytool command with the parameters shown in this figure. After you enter this command, the keytool program will prompt you to enter some passwords and other information.

When you enter the keystore password, you must enter "changeit". If you don't, the certificate won't work properly. Later, when the keytool program asks for the key password for Tomcat, you press Enter to keep the password the same as the keystore password.

For the rest of the prompts, you can enter any information about yourself and your company that you want. This information will be displayed on the secure certificate that's used for testing purposes.

Once you finish responding to the prompts, the keytool program creates a keystore file named

`.keystore`

and it stores this file in your home directory. For Windows XP, this directory is C:\Documents and Settings\Owner, but this directory will vary depending on your operating system.

How to enable SSL in Tomcat

Once you've created a keystore file, you need to enable SSL in Tomcat by editing the server.xml file located in Tomcat's conf directory. To do this, you open this file in TextPad or any other text editor and remove the comments from the SSL Connector element that's shown in this figure. This Connector element defines a secure connection on port 8443, and it specifies the TLS protocol. As a result, newer browsers will use the TLS protocol, and older browsers will use the SSL protocol.

How to create a secure certificate for testing purposes

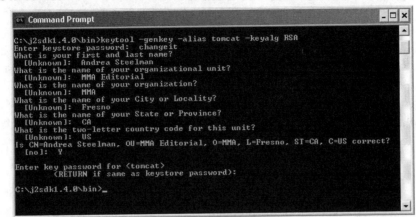

How to define an SSL connection in Tomcat's server.xml file

```
<!-- Define an SSL HTTP/1.1 Connector on port 8443 -->
<Connector className="org.apache.catalina.connector.http.HttpConnector"
           port="8443" minProcessors="5" maxProcessors="75"
           enableLookups="true"
    acceptCount="10" debug="0" scheme="https" secure="true">
    <Factory className="org.apache.catalina.net.SSLServerSocketFactory"
             clientAuth="false" protocol="TLS"/>
</Connector>
```

Description

- To test SSL connections in a local environment, you can create a self-signed certificate. However, you'll need to purchase a valid certificate before you deploy the application to a commercial web server.

- To create a self-signed certificate, you must create a *keystore file*. To do this, you open a commmand prompt window, use the cd command to navigate to the bin directory of your SDK, execute the keytool command, and enter some information about yourself.

- When you create a keystore file, you must use "changeit" as the keystore password, and you should press Enter to use the same password for the key password.

- The keystore file is named .keystore and it's stored in your operating system's home directory.

- To define an SSL connection, you can open the server.xml file that's stored in Tomcat's conf directory. Then, you can remove the comments from the Connector element as shown above.

- By default, Tomcat's server.xml file defines the protocol as TLS, not SSL. As a result, newer browsers will use TLS, and older browsers will use SSL.

Note

- When you enable an SSL connection on an older computer, it may take Tomcat a long time to start.

Figure 13-5   How to configure SSL on a local system

How to test a local SSL connection

Once you've configured your testing environment as described in the last two figures, you can test your local SSL connection by starting Tomcat and entering this URL:

```
https://localhost:8443/index.html
```

Notice that this URL begins with https and includes the port number for the SSL connection. Although it's possible to change the SSL port to another value when you're using a testing environment, you must specify the number of a valid SSL port.

If you've successfully set up SSL, you should be able to view the page shown in figure 13-6. Otherwise, you'll need to troubleshoot your local SSL connection. To do that, you can check the problems described in this figure, and you can review the previous two figures. If there's a problem with the keystore file, you may need to find the keystore file, delete it, and create a new one.

How to determine if SSL is set up correctly in the testing environment

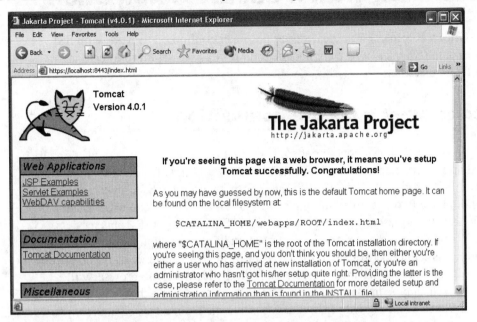

The URL you can enter to test the local SSL connection

```
https://localhost:8443/index.html
```

Common problems when configuring the local SSL connection

Problem 1

Problem: Java can't find the jsse.jar file. This will cause a java.security.NoSuchAlgorithmException to be thrown.

Solution: Make sure the jsse.jar file is located in the SDK's jre\lib\ext directory.

Problem 2

Problem: Tomcat can't find the keystore file. When you start Tomcat, it will throw a java.io.FileNotFoundException.

Solution: Make sure the .keystore file is located in your home directory, which will vary from system to system. For Windows XP, the home directory is C:\Documents and Settings\Owner.

Problem 3

Problem: The keystore password and key passwords that you used to create the keystore file don't match. When you start Tomcat, it will display a java.io.FileNotFoundException that says, "keystore was tampered with" or "password was incorrect."

Solution: Create a new keystore file.

Figure 13-6   How to test a local SSL connection

How to work with a secure connection

Once a commercial or local server has been configured to work with SSL, it's easy to request a secure connection, and it's easy to return to a regular HTTP connection.

How to request a secure connection

Figure 13-7 shows how to code a URL that requests a secure connection. To do that, you code an absolute URL that begins with https. If you're using a local server, you need to include the port number that's used for SSL connections. Although the two examples show how to request a JSP, you can use the same technique to request secure connections for HTML pages, JSPs, and servlets.

When a secure connection is requested, the server authenticates itself by sending its secure certificate to the browser. If the certificate doesn't come from a certification authority that's registered with the browser, the browser will probably display a dialog box like the first dialog box that's shown in this figure. Since a self-signed certificate doesn't come from a trusted source, you will probably see a dialog box like this when you request a secure connection in your local testing environment.

Even if the certificate does come from a certification authority that's registered with the browser, you may get a dialog box like the second dialog box in this figure. However, this depends on the security settings for the browser. When you begin working with secure connections, this dialog box is helpful since it tells you when you're about to use a secure connection and when you're about to return to a regular HTTP connection.

A URL that requests a secure connection over the Internet

```
https://www.murach.com/murach/email13/join_email_list.jsp
```

A URL that requests a secure connection from a local system

```
https://localhost:8443/murach/email13/join_email_list.jsp
```

A dialog box that may be displayed for secure connections

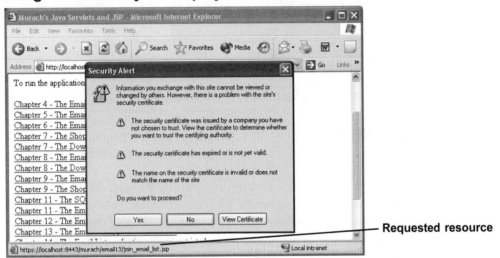

Requested resource

Another dialog box that may be displayed for secure connections

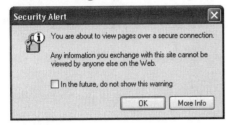

Description

- To request a secure connection, you use an absolute URL that starts with https. If you're requesting a resource from a local system, you also need to specify the port that's used for secure connections. For Tomcat, that port is usually 8443.

- Once you establish a secure connection, you can use relative URLs to continue using the secure connection.

- If you're using a self-signed certificate, your browser will probably display a dialog box similar to the first dialog box above before it establishes a secure connection. If you purchased a secure certificate from a registered certificate authority, this dialog box shouldn't appear.

- Depending on the security settings in your browser, you may get a dialog box like the second dialog box above.

Figure 13-7   How to request a secure connection

A page that uses a secure connection

Once the authentication process is complete, the server sends the response to the browser. For example, figure 13-8 shows the join_email_list.jsp page when it's displayed over a secure connection. This means that when the user submits data in this page, the data is encrypted before it's sent to the server.

You can tell that this page uses a secure connection since the URL starts with https. In addition, since this page is running on the local server, it uses port 8443 for the secure connection. If this page were running on the Internet, though, it wouldn't need the port number.

How to return to a regular HTTP connection

Once you establish a secure connection, you can use relative paths to request web resources. In fact, the only way to return to a regular HTTP connection is to use an absolute URL that begins with http.

To view the secure certificate for a secure connection, you can double-click the lock button in the bottom right corner of the browser. When you view a certificate for a local testing environment, the browser will display the information that was entered when the self-signed certificate was created. When you view a certificate on the web, you'll see a certificate similar to the one in figure 13-2.

How to switch from a local system to an Internet server

When you transfer a web site from a local testing environment to a web server on the Internet, you need to modify the absolute URLs used in the application so they refer to the web site. If, for example, your web site is named *www.trout.com*, then you need to change all URLs that begin with

```
https://localhost:8443
```

to

```
https://www.trout.com
```

You also need to change all URLs that begin with

```
http://localhost:8080
```

to

```
http://www.trout.com
```

To make this switch easier, you can store variables that refer to the secure connection and the regular HTTP connection in a central location. Then, you only need to make two changes when you switch to an Internet server. Or, you can use your text editor to find and replace these strings.

A JSP that uses a secure connection

Double-click the lock icon to view the certificate

A URL that returns to a regular connection over the Internet

```
http://www.murach.com/murach/index.htm
```

A URL that returns to a regular connection from a local system

```
http://localhost:8080/murach/email13/join_email_list.jsp
```

Description

- Once you establish a secure connection, the application will continue using that connection as long as you use relative URLs.

- To return to a regular HTTP connection after using a secure connection, you code an absolute URL that starts with http.

Figure 13-8   How to return to a connection that isn't secure

Perspective

The goal of this chapter has been to show you how to use SSL to work with a secure connection. Now, if you can modify your applications so they use a secure connection whenever that's needed, this chapter has done its job.

In the next chapter, you'll learn how to restrict access to certain portions of your web site by requiring the user to supply a username and a password. This is another form of security that is often used in conjunction with SSL.

Summary

- *Secure Sockets Layer*, or *SSL*, is the protocol used by the World Wide Web that allows clients and servers to communicate over a *secure connection*. When SSL is used, the data that's passed between client and server is encrypted.

- When a browser attempts to communicate with a server using SSL, the server *authenticates* itself by providing a *digital secure certificate*. This is referred to as *SSL server authentication*. In some cases, the server asks the client to authenticate itself, which is referred to as *SSL client authorization*.

- To get a digital secure certificate, you go to a *certificate authority* that uses a *registration authority* to authorize your certificate. This certificate specifies the *SSL strength* of the encryption that's used. When you get the certificate, you install it on your web site.

- To use SSL, you need to install the *Java Secure Socket Extension API*, or *JSSE API*. You also need to define an SSL connection in the server.xml file.

- To request a secure connection from a web application, you use a URL that starts with https. Then, the secure connection is retained as long as you use relative URLs. To return to a regular connection, you use a URL that starts with http.

Terms

Secure Sockets Layer (SSL)
secure connection
Transport Layer Security (TLS)
authentication
SSL server authentication
digital secure certificate
SSL client authentication

certificate authority (CA)
registration authority (RA)
SSL strength
Java Secure Socket Extension API
JSSE API
keystore file

Objectives

- Develop web applications that use secure connections whenever that's needed.

- In general terms, explain how the use of secure connections secures the data that's used in an application.

- In terms of your Java servlets and the server.xml file, describe what you have to do to implement the use of secure connections.

Exercise 13-1   Test a secure connection

1. Create a local testing environment by implementing SSL on your computer.

2. Run the Email List application for chapter 13 using a secure connection. To do this, you can either request the application from the Index page or use https in the browser when you request this page. Be sure to view the secure certificate.

3. Open the join_email_list JSP that's located in the email13 directory and modify it so it always uses a secure connection.

4. Open the show_email_entry JSP that's located in the email13 directory and modify it so it uses a regular HTTP connection when the user clicks the Return button.

5. Test the application and notice how it switches back and forth from SSL to regular HTTP connections.

14

How to restrict access to a web resource

In this chapter, you'll learn how to restrict access to parts of a web site. Then, you'll learn how to allow a user to access the restricted parts of the web site. For example, many web sites have an administrative section that can only be accessed by a user who logs in to the site with a valid username and password.

An introduction to authentication **418**
How container-managed authentication works 418
Three types of authentication 420
How to restrict access to web resources **422**
How to create a security constraint 422
How to implement the JDBC realm 424
How to create the tables for the JDBC realm 426
How to use basic authentication **428**
The login dialog box 428
The XML tags 428
How to use form-based authentication **430**
The login page 430
The XML tags 430
The code for the login page 432
Perspective **434**

An introduction to authentication

Restricting access to certain parts of an application to certain users is often referred to as *authentication*. In other words, a browser must authenticate itself by supplying a valid username and password before it can access a restricted resource.

Although you can implement authentication by writing servlets and JSPs, doing that can be tedious. That's why most modern servlet containers such as Tomcat provide a way to work with authentication. Then, the servlet container handles the authentication, which is known as *container-managed security*.

How container-managed authentication works

Figure 14-1 shows what happens when a user requests a resource that has been restricted. Here, the user requests the application for chapter 14 by clicking the hyperlink. Since this resource has been restricted, though, a dialog box appears that requests a username and password. Then, if the user enters a valid username and password, the user will be able to access the requested resource. Otherwise, the user won't be able to access the requested resource.

To restrict access to this resource, a *security constraint* must be coded in the web.xml file for the application. This constraint restricts access to all files in the admin14 directory. As a result, when a browser requests a JSP that's in this directory, Tomcat notifies the browser that authentication is required to access this directory. Then, the browser displays a dialog box that requests a username and password. Once the user clicks the Submit button, the username and password are sent to the server so the server can attempt to validate the user. If the user is valid, the browser can access the requested resource.

To validate the username and password, the server usually uses two database tables. One table contains the usernames and the roles they are authorized for; the other contains the usernames and valid passwords. These tables are identified by the server.xml file, which you'll soon learn more about.

A restricted web resource

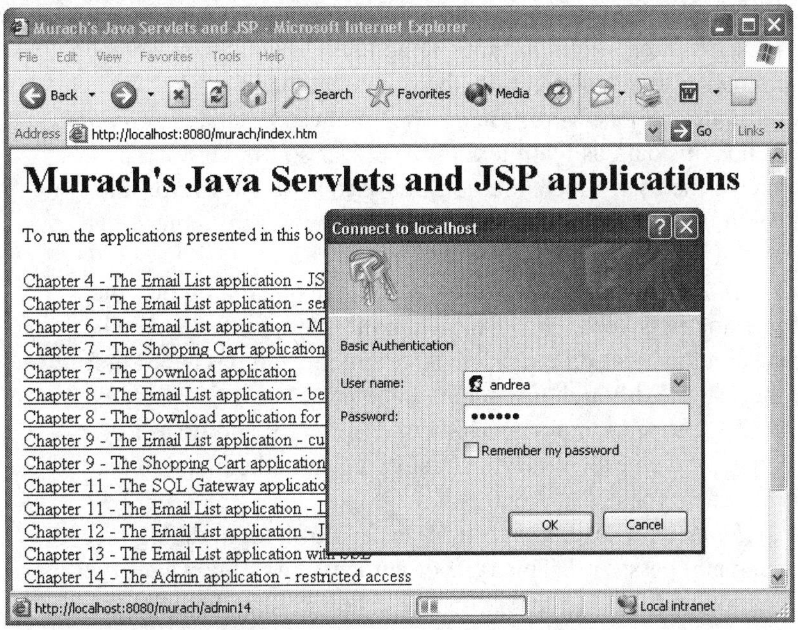

The security constraint and authentication type in the web.xml file

```
<security-constraint>
  <web-resource-collection>
    <web-resource-name>Protected Area</web-resource-name>
    <url-pattern>/admin14/*</url-pattern>
  </web-resource-collection>
  <auth-constraint>
    <role-name>service</role-name>
    <role-name>admin</role-name>
  </auth-constraint>
</security-constraint>

<login-config>
  <auth-method>BASIC</auth-method>
  <realm-name>Basic Authentication</realm-name>
</login-config>
```

Description

- One way to restrict access to specific directories or files is to use Tomcat to implement *container-managed security*. Although you can write servlets and JSPs that implement security, it's usually easier to let Tomcat manage authentication for you.

- To restrict access to a web resource, you can code a *security constraint* in the application's web.xml file that specifies the files or directories that you want to restrict.

- To allow certain users to access a web resource, you can specify what type of *authentication* the web application can use to authenticate users by checking a username and a password.

Figure 14-1   An introduction to authentication

Three types of authentication

Figure 14-2 presents three common types of authentication. *Basic authentication* causes the browser to display a dialog box like the one in the last figure that requests a username and password. Then, when the user enters a username and password, it sends this data as plain text to the server so the server can attempt to authenticate the user. Since you don't have to code a form for this type of authentication, it is easy to implement. However, you can't control the appearance of this dialog box.

Digest authentication also causes the browser to display a dialog box that requests a username and password. However, when the user enters a username and password, digest authentication encrypts the username and password before it sends them to the server. Although this seems to be more secure, it's not as secure as using an SSL connection as described in chapter 13, and it isn't supported by all types of web browsers. As a result, digest authentication isn't used as often as the other types of authentication.

Form-based authentication uses a web form instead of a login dialog box to request the username and password. This type of authentication allows a developer to control the look and feel of the web page. Although form-based authentication doesn't encrypt the username and password, you can use a secure connection to transfer the username and password when security is an issue.

Since basic authentication and form-based authentication transmit the username and password as plain text, a hacker can possibly intercept an unencrypted username and password and gain access to a restricted web resource. As a result, if the resource you want to restrict requires a high level of security, you can use a secure connection as described in chapter 13. That way, the username and password will be encrypted.

Basic authentication

- Causes the browser to display a dialog box like the one shown in the previous figure.
- Doesn't encrypt the username and password before sending them to the server.
- Is supported by most browsers.

Digest authentication

- Causes the browser to display a dialog box like the one shown in the previous figure.
- Encrypts the username and password before sending them to the server, but still isn't as secure as using an SSL connection as described in chapter 13.
- Is only supported by the Internet Explorer browser.

Form-based authentication

- Allows the developer to code a login form that gets the username and password.
- Doesn't encrypt the username and password before sending them to the server.
- Is supported by most browsers.

Description

- Although *basic authentication* and *form-based authentication* don't automatically encrypt the username and password before sending them to the server, the username and password will be encrypted if you use an SSL connection as described in chapter 13.
- Since *digest authentication* isn't supported by all browsers, it's not used as often as basic authentication or form-based authentication.

Figure 14-2 Three types of authentication

How to restrict access to web resources

Now that you understand the general concept of how container-managed authentication works, you're ready to learn how to use Tomcat to create a constraint that restricts access to web resources. Although this topic uses Tomcat 4.0 to create a constraint, similar concepts should apply to other versions of Tomcat and to other servlet containers.

How to create a security constraint

To restrict access to a web resource, you add a security constraint to the web.xml file for the application as shown in figure 14-3. To do that, you add a Security-Constraint element. This XML element specifies the files that are restricted and it specifies who can access these files.

To specify the web resource that you want to restrict access to, you must specify a URL pattern that specifies one or more files. To specify one file, you can enter a URL that's relative to the document root that specifies the file. In addition, you can use the asterisk character to restrict access to multiple files. For example, it's common to use the asterisk to restrict access to all files in a directory as shown in this figure. Although this figure shows how to restrict access to HTML documents and JSPs, you can also restrict access to servlets.

When you restrict access to a resource, you can restrict access only for specified HTTP methods. If, for example, you want to restrict access for requests that use the Get method, you can use the HTTP-Method element to specify the Get method. In this figure, both the Get and Post methods are restricted. If you want to restrict access for all requests, regardless of the HTTP method, you can omit the HTTP-Method element entirely.

To define who can access a restricted web resource, you use an Auth-Constraint element. Within this element, you define the user *roles* that can access the restricted resource. For instance, the example in this figure allows any user associated with the admin role or the service role to access the files in the admin14 directory.

To restrict access to multiple files or directories, you can define several URL-Pattern elements within a single Security-Constraint element. However, if you define more than one URL pattern in the same Web-Resource-Collection element, all of those web resources can be accessed by the same roles. As a result, if you have several web resources that you need to restrict access to and if you need to specify different levels of security for each resource, you should create one Security-Constraint element for each resource.

How to set a security constraint in web.xml file

```
<security-constraint>

    <web-resource-collection>
        <web-resource-name>Protected Area</web-resource-name>
        <url-pattern>/admin14/*</url-pattern>
        <http-method>GET</http-method>
        <http-method>POST</http-method>
    </web-resource-collection>

    <auth-constraint>
        <role-name>service</role-name>
        <role-name>admin</role-name>
    </auth-constraint>

</security-constraint>
```

The elements used to create a security constraint

Element	Description
`<security-constraint>`	Creates a security constraint for one or more web resources.
`<web-resource-collection>`	Specifies a collection of web resources that the security constraint restricts access to.
`<web-resource-name>`	Specifies a name for the collection of web resources.
`<url-pattern>`	Specifies the URL pattern for the web resources that you wish to restrict access to.
`<http-method>`	Specifies the HTTP methods that require authentication. If no HTTP method is specified, the constraint will restrict access to all HTTP methods.
`<auth-constraint>`	Specifies the users that are permitted to access a restricted web resource.
`<role-name>`	Specifies a valid user role that's permitted access to the web resource.

Description

- When coding the web.xml file, you should add the Security-Constraint element after all Servlet, Servlet-Mapping, and Error-Page elements.
- When specifying the URL-Pattern element, you can use the asterisk character (*) to specify several files at once.

Figure 14-3   How to create a security constraint

How to implement the JDBC realm

When you use Tomcat to manage security, you need to determine what type of *realm* you want to implement. A realm is the mechanism that identifies valid users. In Tomcat, you can choose between three types of security realms.

When Tomcat is first installed, for example, the *memory realm* stores usernames and passwords in memory. Since this type of realm should only be used for testing, though, we won't discuss it here. Instead, figure 14-4 shows how to implement the *JDBC realm*. This realm lets you store valid user names, passwords, and roles in a relational database.

To implement the JDBC realm, you need to edit the server.xml file that's stored in Tomcat's conf directory. In particular, you need to locate the part of the server.xml file that contains the Realm elements. When you first install Tomcat, the Realm element for the memory realm is active and the Realm element for the JDBC realm is inactive. Then, you can deactivate the memory realm by coding comments around its Realm element, and you can activate the JDBC realm by removing any comments from around its Realm element.

After you uncomment the Realm element for the JDBC realm, you may need to modify some of its attributes. For example, you may need to modify the name of the database driver and the database connection URL. If you're using a MySQL database as described in chapters 10 and 11, the attribute values supplied in this figure should work. Here, the JDBC realm uses a standard MySQL driver to connect to a MySQL database named murach with a username of root and an empty password.

The rest of the attributes in the JDBC realm element define the names of the tables and columns that are used to store the user's name, password, and role. In this figure, these attributes are the default names that are supplied by Tomcat. In the next figure, you'll see how you can create these tables and fill them with data. However, if you already have a table that contains usernames and passwords, you can use these attributes to specify the name of that table and its columns.

The Realm elements in the server.xml file

```
<!-- <Realm className="org.apache.catalina.realm.MemoryRealm" />-->

<!-- Replace the above Realm with one of the following to get a Realm
     stored in a database and accessed via JDBC -->

<Realm   className="org.apache.catalina.realm.JDBCRealm"
         debug="99"
         driverName="org.gjt.mm.mysql.Driver"
         connectionURL="jdbc:mysql://localhost/murach?user=root;password="
         userTable="users" userNameCol="user_name" userCredCol="user_pass"
         userRoleTable="user_roles" roleNameCol="role_name" />
```

How to set the Realm element in the server.xml file

- Comment out the Realm element that specifies MemoryRealm.
- Remove the comments from the Realm element that specifies JDBCRealm.
- If necessary, modify the driverName attribute so it specifies the database driver that you're using.
- If necessary, modify the connection URL to the URL of your database and provide a username and password value that have read-access to the database.
- If necessary, modify the attributes for the table and column names so they match the tables and columns that your database will use. In the next figure, you'll see how to create the tables with the column names shown above.

Description

- A *realm* is a mechanism that's used to authenticate users so they can access web resources that have been restricted.
- Although Tomcat provides for three types of realms, the *JDBC realm* is the one that's used the most. In contrast, the *memory realm* should only be used for testing purposes.
- Tomcat's JDBC realm uses a database to check a user's name and password against a table of valid user names and passwords. In addition, the JDBC realm associates a *role* with each user that allows you to grant access to any user that's associated with a certain role.
- For the JDBC realm to work, the database driver that's specified in the server.xml file must be stored in Tomcat's common\lib directory. To learn more about database drivers, databases, and connecting to databases, please refer back to chapter 11.

Figure 14-4   How to implement the JDBC realm

How to create the tables for the JDBC realm

If the tables for the JDBC realm don't already exist, you need to create a table of users that contains a username and password for each user, and you need to create a table of roles that can be associated with each user. To show how you can create those tables, figure 14-5 presents the SQL statements that you can use to create them. For the JDBC realm to work, of course, the table and column names in these statements must match the table and column names specified in the server.xml file.

Once you create the table that stores the users of the application, you need to create a table that stores the roles that can be associated with each user. For example, this figure defines one role named admin and another role named service. Then, when you write data to this table, you can associate a username with one or more roles, or you can choose to not associate any roles with a username. In this figure, Andrea belongs to both the service and admin roles, Joel belongs to the admin role, and Doug doesn't belong to any roles. As a result, Doug won't be able to access any restricted resources.

The SQL statement that creates the users table

```
CREATE TABLE users (
  user_name VARCHAR(15) NOT NULL,
  user_pass VARCHAR(15) NOT NULL,
  PRIMARY KEY (user_name)
)
```

The SQL statement that creates the user_roles table

```
CREATE TABLE user_roles (
  user_name VARCHAR(15) NOT NULL,
  role_name VARCHAR(15) NOT NULL,
  PRIMARY KEY (user_name, role_name)
)
```

The SQL statement that inserts three users

```
INSERT INTO users
VALUES ('andrea', 'dime10'),
       ('joel', '86band'),
       ('doug', 'lowe1')
```

The SQL statement that assigns three roles to two users

```
INSERT INTO user_roles
VALUES ('andrea', 'service'),
       ('andrea', 'admin'),
       ('joel', 'admin')
```

Description

- The table and column names must match the table and column names specified in the JDBC realm in the server.xml file.

- A user can have zero roles, one role, or multiple roles.

- A users table can contain columns other than the ones for username and password.

Figure 14-5   How to create the tables for the JDBC realm

How to use basic authentication

Figure 14-6 shows how to use basic authentication to provide access to a restricted resource. In particular, it shows how to use basic authentication to provide access to the application for chapter 14, which is the Admin application.

The login dialog box

If you request a restricted web resource that uses basic authentication, your browser will display an authentication dialog box like the one in this figure. This box requests a username and password. Then, when the user selects the OK button, the username and password are sent to the server.

If you're using the JDBC realm, the server checks the related database to see whether the username and password are valid, and it checks whether the user is associated with a role that allows the user to access the resource. If so, the user will be allowed to access the resource.

The XML tags

Since basic authentication is the simplest type of authentication, the web.xml file only requires a few XML elements. To start, you code the Login-Config element. Within this element, you specify that you want to use basic authentication. Then, you specify a name for the realm. This name will be displayed in the dialog box. When you add the XML tags for the Login-Config element to the web.xml file, they must immediately follow the Security-Constraint element that they relate to as shown in figure 14-1.

Basic authentication

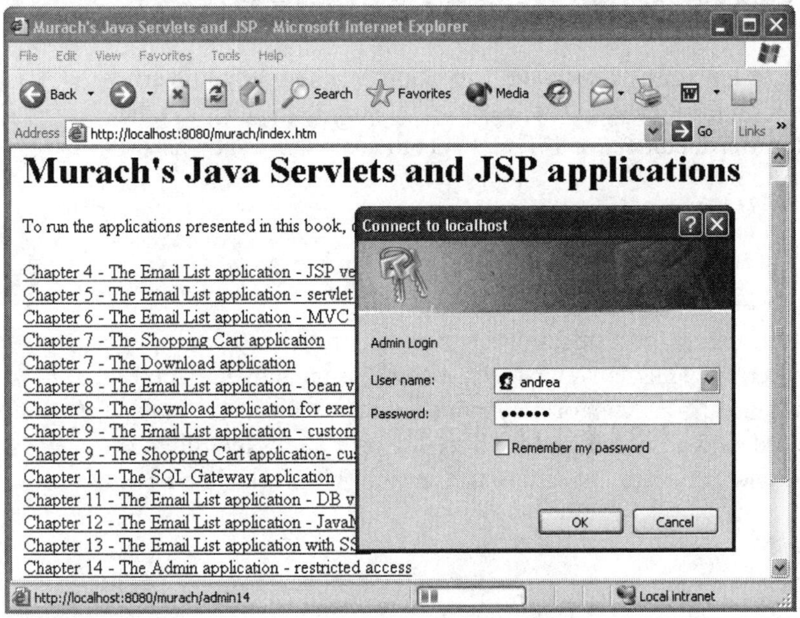

The web.xml elements for basic authentication

```
<login-config>
   <auth-method>BASIC</auth-method>
   <realm-name>Admin Login</realm-name>
</login-config>
```

The Login-Config elements

Element	Description
`<login-config>`	Tells the servlet engine what authentication type to use.
`<auth-method>`	Specifies the authentication type like BASIC or FORM. However, it's also possible to use DIGEST for digest authentication or CLIENT-CERT for SSL client authentication (see figure 13-2 in chapter 13 for more on client authentication).
`<realm-name>`	Specifies the text that's displayed in the dialog box.

Description

- To use basic authentication, you code a security constraint in the web.xml file as shown in figure 14-3. Then, you code a Login-Config element immediately after the security constraint.

- If the user enters an invalid username or password, the browser will prompt the user three times for valid entries. Then, the server will return an error page that indicates that the request was unauthorized.

- If the user enters a valid username and password, the browser stores the authentication information for the current session so the user can access all web resources specified by the constraint without having to re-enter the username and password for each page.

Figure 14-6   How to use basic authentication

How to use form-based authentication

Now that you know how to use basic authentication, you're ready to learn how to use form-based authentication. This works like basic authentication, but it lets you code an HTML document or JSP that gets the username and password.

The login page

When you use form-based authentication, requesting a restricted resource will cause your browser to display a web page that contains an authentication form like the one in figure 14-7. This form contains a text box for a username, a text box for a password, and a Submit button. Once the user clicks the Submit button, the username and password are sent to the server. This works like basic authentication.

The XML tags

This figure also shows how to code the Form-Login-Config element for form-based authentication. Within this element, you use the Auth-Method element to specify that you want to use form-based authentication. Then, you can specify the name of the HTML or JSP file that defines the form. You can also specify the name of the HTML or JSP file that will be displayed if the user enters an invalid username or password.

Form-based authentication

The web.xml elements for form-based authentication

```
<login-config>
  <auth-method>FORM</auth-method>
  <form-login-config>
      <form-login-page>/admin14/login.html</form-login-page>
      <form-error-page>/admin14/login_error.html</form-error-page>
  </form-login-config>
</login-config>
```

The Form-Login-Config elements

Element	Description
`<form-login-config>`	Specifies the login and error pages that should be used for form-based authentication. If form-based authentication isn't used, these elements are ignored.
`<form-login-page>`	Specifies the location of the login page that should be displayed when a restricted resource that's set in the security constraint is accessed. This page can be an HTML page, JSP, or servlet.
`<form-error-page>`	Specifies the location of the page that should be displayed when an invalid username and/or password is entered in the login form.

Description

- When you use form-based authentication, you can use HTML to code the login form that's displayed when someone attempts to access a restricted resource. This form can be coded within an HTML document or a JSP.
- To use form-based authentication, you can code a security constraint in the web.xml file as shown in figure 14-3. Then, you can code a Form-Login-Config element.
- If you want the login page to be displayed again when the user enters an invalid username or password, you can specify the same page for both the login page and the error page.

Figure 14-7   The login page and XML tags used with form-based authentication

The code for the login page

Figure 14-8 shows the code for the login page that's shown in the previous figure. Although you can place any HTML or JSP tags in a login page, this page must at least provide an HTML form that contains a submit button and two text boxes, and this form must use the three highlighted attributes shown in this figure. Here, the action attribute for the form must be j_security_check. The name of the text box that gets the username must be j_username. And the name of the text box that gets the password must be j_password.

In this example, the text box that requests the password uses the password type. As a result, the password won't be displayed on the screen when the user types it. Instead, this text box will display a special character such as a bullet or an asterisk for each character. You can see how this works by looking at the previous figure.

The code for a login web page

```
<!DOCTYPE HTML PUBLIC "-//W3C//DTD HTML 4.0 Transitional//EN">
<html>
<head>
    <title>Chapter 14 - The Admin application</title>
</head>
<body>

<h1>Admin Login Form</h1>

<p>Please enter your username and password to continue.</p>

<table cellspacing="5" border="0">
    <form action="j_security_check" METHOD="get">
    <tr>
        <td align="right">Username</td>
        <td><input type="text" name="j_username"></td>
    </tr>
    <tr>
        <td align="right">Password</td>
        <td><input type="password" name="j_password"></td>
    </tr>
    <tr><td><input type="submit" value="Login"></td></tr>
    </form>
</table>

</body>
</html>
```

Description

- The login form for form-based authentication must contain the three elements highlighted above.
- The login form can be stored in any directory where HTML and JSP files can be stored.

Figure 14-8   The code for a login page

Perspective

The goal of this chapter has been to show you how to restrict access to web resources. Now, if this chapter has been successful, you should be able to use Tomcat 4.0 to implement container-managed security in your applications. Since this allows Tomcat to handle the HTTP responses for you, it shields you from having to write code that interacts more directly with HTTP. In the next chapter, though, you can learn more about working with HTTP.

Summary

- To restrict access to HTML documents, JSPs, and servlets, you can use *container-managed security*.

- When you use container-managed security, *basic authentication* displays default dialog boxes, while *form-based authentication* can be used to display custom web forms.

- You use the web.xml file to identify the directories and files that should have restricted access, the *roles* that can be used to access them, and the type of authentication to be used. Then, you use the server.xml file to identify the database that contains the usernames, roles, and passwords that are used for authentication.

- In the database that's used for authentication, one table provides usernames and roles, while another table provides usernames and valid passwords.

- When you use form-based authentication, the HTML code for the login page must include a form and two text boxes that use the required names for specific attributes.

Terms

authentication
container-managed security
security constraint
basic authentication
digest authentication
form-based authentication
role
realm
memory realm
JDBC realm

Objectives

- Use container-managed security and the JDBC realm to restrict access to specific portions of your web applications.

- In general terms, describe the use of the web.xml file, the server.xml file, and the database tables for container-managed security that uses the JDBC realm.

- Distinguish between basic authentication and form-based authentication.

Exercise 14-1   Implement the JDBC realm

1. Implement the JDBC Realm for Tomcat. To do this, create the users and user_roles tables as shown in figure 14-5 in the murach database. Then, modify the server.xml file so the JDBC Realm is activated.

2. Open the web.xml file and make sure access is restricted to the Admin application located in the admin14 directory.

3. Test the Admin application to make sure the JDBC realm is implemented. This means that access should only be granted to roles specified in the web.xml file. Enter an invalid username and password to see how this application reacts. Then, enter a valid username and password.

Exercise 14-2   Work with authentication types

1. Modify the web.xml file so the Admin application for chapter 14 uses basic authentication instead of form-based authentication.

2. Test the Admin application by entering an invalid username and password. Then, enter a valid username and password.

15

How to work with HTTP requests and responses

When you write servlets and JSPs, the classes and methods of the servlet API shelter you from having to work directly with HTTP. Sometimes, though, you need to know more about HTTP requests and responses, and you need to use the methods of the servlet API to work with them. So that's what you'll learn in this chapter. Along the way, you'll get a better idea of how HTTP works.

An introduction to HTTP **438**
An HTTP request and response 438
Common MIME types 440
Common HTTP request headers 442
Common HTTP status codes 444
Common HTTP response headers 446

How to work with the request **448**
How to get request headers 448
How to display all request headers 450
The request headers for the IE and Netscape browsers 452

How to work with the response **454**
How to set status codes 454
How to set response headers 454

Practical skills for working with HTTP **456**
How to return a tab-delimited file as an Excel spreadsheet 456
How to control caching 456
How to encode the response with GZIP compression 458
How to require the File Download dialog box 460

Perspective **462**

An introduction to HTTP

This topic introduces you to some of the most common headers and status codes that make up *Hypertext Transfer Protocol*, or *HTTP*. This protocol can be used to request a resource from a server, and it can be used to return a response from a server.

An HTTP request and response

Figure 15-1 shows the components of a typical HTTP request and a typical HTTP response. As you learn more about these components, you'll get a better idea of how HTTP requests and responses work.

The first line of an HTTP request is known as the *request line*. This line contains the request method, the request URL, and the request protocol. Typically, the request method is a Get or Post method, but other methods are also supported by HTTP. Similarly, the request protocol is usually HTTP 1.1, but some older browsers use HTTP 1.0.

After the request line, an HTTP request contains the *request headers*. These headers contain information about the client that's making the request. In this figure, the HTTP request contains eight request headers with one header per line, but a request can include more headers than that. Each request header begins with the name of the request header, followed by a colon and a space, followed by the value of the request header.

After the request headers, an HTTP request that uses the Post method may include a blank line followed by the parameters for the request. Unlike a Get request, a Post request doesn't include its parameters in the URL.

The first line of an HTTP response is known as the *status line*. This line specifies the version of HTTP that's being used, a *status code*, and a message that's associated with the status code.

After the status line, an HTTP response contains the *response headers*. These headers contain information about the server and about the response that's being returned to the client. Like request headers, each response header takes one line. In addition, each line begins with the name of the header, followed by a colon and a space, followed by the value of the header.

After the response headers, an HTTP response contains a blank line, followed by the *response entity*, or *response body*. In this figure, the response entity is an HTML document, but it could also be plain text, tab-delimited text, and so on.

To learn more about HTTP 1.1, you can use Adobe Acrobat to open the PDF file that's stored in the HTTPSpec directory of the CD that comes with this book. This PDF file contains a highly technical description of HTTP 1.1 including a list of headers and status codes. Or, you can view this document by going to *www.rfc-editor.org* and searching for 2616. Then, you can follow the links to other related HTTP documents, which may contain updated information.

An HTTP request

```
GET http://www.murach.com/email/join_email_list.html HTTP/1.1
referer: http://www.murach.com/murach/index.html
connection: Keep-Alive
user-agent: Mozilla/4.61 [en] (Win98; I)
host: www.murach.com
accept: image/gif, image/x-xbitmap, image/jpeg, image/pjpeg, image/png, */*
accept-encoding: gzip
accept-language: en
cookie: emailCookie=jsmith%40hotmail.com; userID=39210
```

An HTTP response

```
HTTP/1.1 200 OK
date: Sat, 17 Aug 2002 10:32:54 GMT
server: Apache/1.3.6 (Unix) PHP/3.0.7
content-type: text/html
content-length: 201
last-modified: Fri, 16 Aug 2002 12:52:09 GMT

<!DOCTYPE HTML PUBLIC "-//W3C//DTD HTML 4.01 Transitional//EN">
<html>
<head>
  <title>Chapter 4 - Email List application</title>
</head>
<body>
  <h1>Join our email list</h1>
</body>
</html>
```

Description

- *Hypertext Transfer Protocol*, or *HTTP*, is the primary protocol that's used to transfer data between a browser and a server. Two versions of HTTP exist: 1.0 and 1.1. Since HTTP 1.1 is a superset of the HTTP 1.0, all HTTP 1.0 request headers are also available in HTTP 1.1.

- The first line of an HTTP request is known as the *request line*. This line specifies the request method, the URL of the request, and the version of HTTP.

- After the first line of a request, the browser sends *request headers* that give information about the browser and its request.

- The first line of an HTTP response is known as the *status line*. This line specifies the HTTP version, a *status code*, and a brief description associated with the status code.

- After the first line of a response, the server sends *response headers* that give information about the response. Then, it sends the *response entity*, or *response body*. The body of a response is typically HTML, but it can also be other types of data.

- To view a technical description of the HTTP 1.1 specification, you can use Adobe Acrobat to open the PDF file that's stored in the HTTPSpec directory of the CD that comes with this book. This PDF file includes a list of headers and status codes. Or, you can view this document by going to *www.rfc-editor.org* and searching for 2616.

Figure 15-1   An HTTP request and response

Common MIME types

Figure 15-2 shows some of the most common *Multipurpose Internet Mail Extension*, or *MIME*, types that are used by HTTP. You can use them in the accept header of a request or the content-type header of a response.

To specify an officially registered MIME type, you can use this format:

```
type/subtype
```

To specify a MIME type that isn't officially registered, you can use this format:

```
type/x-subtype
```

Although the "text/plain" MIME type is the default MIME type for a servlet, the most commonly used MIME type is the "text/html" type. Later in this chapter, you'll see examples of how MIME types can be used in HTTP requests and responses.

If you want to learn more about MIME types, you can use Adobe Acrobat to open the PDF file that's stored in the MIMESpec directory on the CD that comes with this book. This PDF file contains a highly technical description of MIME types. Or, you can go to *www.rfc-editor.org* and search for 1341. Then, you can follow the links to newer MIME types.

Common MIME types

Type/Subtype	Description
text/plain	Plain text document
text/html	HTML document
text/css	HTML cascading style sheet
text/xml	XML document
image/gif	GIF image
image/jpeg	JPEG image
image/png	PNG image
image/tiff	TIFF image
image/x-xbitmap	Window bitmap image
application/msword	Microsoft Word document
application/vnd.ms-excel	Microsoft Excel spreadsheet
application/pdf	Adobe Acrobat file
application/postscript	PostScript file
application/zip	Zip file
application/x-java-archive	Jar file
application/x-gzip	Gzip file
application/octet-stream	Binary data
audio/basic	A sound file (usually in the *.au or *.snd format)
video/mpeg	MPEG video clip

Two web sites that have lists of other MIME types

```
www.isi.edu/in-notes/iana/assignments/media-types/media-types
www.ltsw.se/knbase/internet/mime.htp
```

Description

- The *Multipurpose Internet Mail Extension* types, or *MIME* types, provide standards for the various types of data that can be transferred across the Internet.
- MIME types can be included in the accept header of a request or the content-type header of a response.
- For more technical information about MIME types, you can check *www.rfc-editor.org* and search for RFC 1341.

Figure 15-2   MIME types

Common HTTP request headers

Figure 15-3 lists some of the most common HTTP request headers. When you work with HTTP, you should be aware that some older browsers don't support HTTP 1.1. So if your web application needs to support these older browsers, you should only use headers that were specified in the HTTP 1.0 version. Today, however, most web browsers support HTTP 1.1 so you can usually use HTTP 1.1 headers.

Most of the time, a web browser automatically sets these request headers when it makes a request. Then, when the server receives the request, it can check these headers to learn about the browser. In addition, though, you can write servlets that set some of these request headers. For example, chapter 7 shows how to use the servlet API to set the cookie header. And chapter 14 shows how to use the servlet container to automatically set the authorization header.

Common HTTP request headers

Name	Description
accept	Specifies the preferred order of MIME types that the browser can accept. The "*/*" type indicates that the browser can handle any MIME type.
accept-encoding	Specifies the types of compression encoding that the browser can accept.
accept-charset	Specifies the character sets that the browser can accept. Although the Internet Explorer doesn't usually return this header, Netscape usually does.
accept-language	Specifies the standard language codes for the languages that the browser prefers. The standard language code for English is "en" or "en-us".
authorization	Identifies the authorization level for the browser. When you use container-managed security as described in chapter 14, the servlet container automatically sets this header.
connection	Indicates the type of connection that's being used by the browser. In HTTP 1.0, a value of "keep-alive" means that the browser can use a persistent connection that allows it to accept multiple files with a single connection. In HTTP 1.1, this type of connection is the default.
cookie	Specifies any cookies that were previously sent by the current server. In chapter 7, you learned how to use the servlet API to work with this header.
host	Specifies the host and port of the machine that originally sent the request. This header is optional in HTTP 1.0 and required in HTTP 1.1.
pragma	A value of "no-cache" indicates that any servlet that's forwarding requests shouldn't cache this page.
referer	Indicates the URL of the referring web page. The spelling error was made by one of the original authors of HTTP and is now part of the protocol.
user-agent	Indicates the type of browser. Although both Internet Explorer and Netscape identify themselves as "Mozilla", the Internet Explorer always includes "MSIE" somewhere in the string.

Figure 15-3   HTTP request headers

Common HTTP status codes

Figure 15-4 summarizes the five categories of status codes. Then, this figure lists some of the most common status codes. For successful requests, the server typically returns a 200 (OK) status code. However, if the server can't find the requested file, it typically returns the infamous 404 (Not Found) status code. Or, if the server encounters an error while trying to retrieve the file, it may return the equally infamous 500 (Internal Server Error) status code.

Status code summary

Number	Type	Description
100-199	Informational	The request was received and is being processed.
200-299	Success	The request was successful.
300-399	Redirection	Further action must be taken to fulfill the request.
400-499	Client errors	The client has made a request that contains an error.
500-599	Server errors	The server has encountered an error.

Status codes

Number	Name	Description
200	OK	The default status indicating that the response is normal.
301	Moved Permanently	The requested resource has been permanently moved to a new URL.
302	Found	The requested resource resides temporarily under a new URL.
400	Bad Request	The request could not be understood by the server due to bad syntax.
401	Unauthorized	The request requires authentication. The response must include a www-authenticate header. If you use container-managed security as described in chapter 14, the web server automatically returns this status code when appropriate.
404	Not Found	The server could not find the requested URL.
405	Method Not Allowed	The method specified in the request line is not allowed for the requested URL.
500	Internal Server Error	The server encountered an unexpected condition that prevented it from fulfilling the request.

Figure 15-4   HTTP status codes

Common HTTP response headers

Figure 15-5 lists some of the most common HTTP response headers. Most of the time, the web server automatically sets these response headers when it returns the response. However, there are times when you may want to use Java code to set response headers that control the response sent by your web server.

For example, you can use the cache-control header to control how your web server caches a response. To do that, you can use the cache-control values specified in this figure to turn off caching, to use a private cache, to use a public cache, to specify when a response must be revalidated, or to increase the duration of the cache. You'll see an example of this later on in this chapter.

Common HTTP response headers

Name	Description
cache-control	Controls when and how a browser caches a page. For more information, see figure 15-10 and the list of possible values shown below.
content-disposition	Can be used to specify that the response includes an attached binary file. For an example, see figure 15-12.
content-length	Specifies the length of the body of the response in bytes. This allows the browser to know when it's done reading the entire response and is necessary for the browser to use a persistent, keep-alive connection.
content-type	Specifies the MIME type of the response document. You can use the "maintype/subtype" format shown earlier in this chapter to specify the MIME type.
content-encoding	Specifies the type of encoding that the response uses. Encoding a document with GZIP can enhance performance. For an example, see figure 15-11.
expires	Specifies the time that the page should no longer be cached.
last-modified	Specifies the time when the document was last modified.
location	Works with status codes in the 300s to specify the new location of the document.
pragma	Turns off caching for older browsers when it is set to a value of "no-cache".
refresh	Specifies the number of seconds before the browser should ask for an updated page.
www-authenticate	Works with the 401 (Unauthorized) status code to specify the authentication type and realm. If you use container-managed security as described in chapter 14, the servlet container automatically sets this header when necessary.

Values for the cache-control header

Name	Description
public	The document can be cached in a public, shared cache.
private	The document can only be cached in a private, single-user cache.
no-cache	The document should never be cached.
no-store	The document should never be cached or stored in a temporary location on the disk.
must-revalidate	The document must be revalidated with the original server (not a proxy server) each time it is requested.
proxy-revalidate	The document must be revalidated on the proxy server but not on the original server.
max-age=x	The document must be revalidated after x seconds for private caches.
s-max-age=x	The document must be revalidated after x seconds for shared caches.

Figure 15-5   HTTP response headers

How to work with the request

This topic shows how to use the methods of the request object to get the data that's contained in an HTTP request.

How to get request headers

You can use the first group of methods in figure 15-6 to get any of the headers in an HTTP request. The getHeader method lets you return the value of any header. The getIntHeader and getDateHeader methods make it easier to work with headers that contain integer and date values. And the getHeaderNames method returns an Enumeration object that contains the names of all of the headers for the request.

You can use the second group of methods to get the request headers more easily. For example, this statement:

```
int contentLength = request.getIntHeader("Content-Length");
```

returns the same value as this statement:

```
int contentLength = request.getContentLength();
```

The first example uses the getHeader method to return a string that includes all of the MIME types supported by the browser that made the request. Then, it uses the indexOf method within an if statement to check if a particular MIME type exists in the string. If it does, the code calls a method that returns a PNG image if the browser supports that type. Otherwise, the code calls a method that returns a GIF image.

The second example uses the getHeader method to return a string that identifies the type of browser that made the request. Since the Internet Explorer always includes the letters "MSIE" in its string, this example uses an indexOf method within an if statement to check if the string contains the letters "MSIE". If so, it calls a method that executes some code that's specific to the Internet Explorer. Otherwise, it calls a method that executes some code that's specific to the Netscape browser.

Although you may never need to write code that checks the MIME types or the browser type, these examples illustrate a general concept that you can use to check any request header. First, you use the getHeader, getIntHeader, or getDateHeader methods to return a header. Then, you can use an if statement to check the header. For a String object, you can use the indexOf method to check if a substring exists within the string. For int values and Date objects, you can use other comparison operators.

General methods for working with request headers

```
String getHeader(String headerName)
int getIntHeader(String headerName)
Date getDateHeader(String headerName)
Enumeration getHeaderNames()
```

Convenience methods for working with request headers

```
String getContentType()
int getContentLength()
Cookie[] getCookies()
String getAuthType()
String getRemoteUser()
```

An example that checks the MIME types accepted by the browser

```
String mimeTypes = request.getHeader("Accept");
if (mimeTypes.indexOf("image/png") > -1)
    returnPNG();
else
    returnGIF();
```

An example that checks the browser type

```
String browser = request.getHeader("User-Agent");
if (browser.indexOf("MSIE") > -1)
    doIECode();
else
    doNetscapeCode();
```

Description

- All of these methods can be called from the request object to return information about the HTTP request.

- The general header methods provide a generic way to access any HTTP header.

- The convenience header methods provide a specialized way to access commonly used HTTP headers.

- For more information about using the getCookies method to work with the cookie header, see chapter 7.

- For more information about using the servlet container to automatically check the authorization header, see chapter 14.

- For more information about any of these methods, you can look up the HttpServletRequest interface in the documentation for the servlet API.

Figure 15-6 Methods and examples for working with request headers

How to display all request headers

Figure 15-7 shows a JSP that displays all of the request headers for a request. If you're developing a web application that needs to check other request headers, you can use this JSP to quickly view the request headers for all of the different browsers that your web application supports. Then, you can write the code that checks the request headers and works with them.

This JSP begins by defining the table that will contain the request headers. In the first row of the table, the first column is the Name column, and the second column is the Value column.

After the first row of the table, this page imports the java.util package, so the page can work with the Enumeration class. Then, it uses the getHeaderNames method of the request object to return an Enumeration object that contains the names of all of the request headers. After that, a while loop cycles through all of the header names. To do that, this loop uses the hasMoreElements method to check if more elements exist, and it uses the nextElement method to return the current header name and move to the next header name. Once the loop has returned the name of the header, the getHeader method of the request object uses this name to return the value of the header. Last, the loop displays the name and value for the current header in a row.

The JSP code that displays all request headers

```
<!doctype html public "-//W3C//DTD HTML 4.0 Transitional//EN">
<html>
<head>
  <title>Chapter 14 - HTTP requests and responses</title>
</head>
<body>

<h1>Request Headers</h1>

<table cellpadding="5" border="1">

  <tr>
    <td align="right"><b>Name</td>
    <td><b>Value</td>
  </tr>
<%@ page import="java.util.*" %>
<%
  Enumeration headerNames = request.getHeaderNames();
  while (headerNames.hasMoreElements()){
    String name = (String) headerNames.nextElement();
    String value = request.getHeader(name);
%>
  <tr>
    <td align="right"><%= name %></td>
    <td><%= value %></td>
  </tr>
<% } %>

</table>

</body>
</html>
```

Description

- This JSP displays all the request headers for a request.
- In the next figure, you can see how this JSP is rendered for two different browsers.

Figure 15-7   How to display all request headers

The request headers for the IE and Netscape browsers

Since the request headers and their values vary depending on the client that makes the request, figure 15-8 shows how the JSP in the last figure looks when displayed by different clients. First, it shows how the JSP will look when requested by version 6.0 of the Internet Explorer. Then, it shows how the JSP will look when requested by version 7.0 of the Netscape browser. If you compare the values sent by each of these browsers, you'll see some of the differences between them.

For example, the accept header for IE6 indicates that it prefers documents in Microsoft Word or Microsoft Excel formats. Of course, this is what you would expect from a Microsoft product. Since the Netscape browser supports the */* type, it also support these formats. However, by not specifying these formats in its accept header, the Netscape browser indicates that it doesn't prefer the Microsoft formats.

If you compare the user-agent headers, you'll see that the Netscape browser identifies itself as a "Mozilla" browser while the IE browser identifies itself as being compatible with "Mozilla". However, the IE browser includes the "MSIE" string that indicates that it's the Microsoft Internet Explorer. In addition, if you check the accept-charset header, you'll see that the Netscape browser sends this header while the IE browser doesn't.

All request headers sent by Internet Explorer 6.0

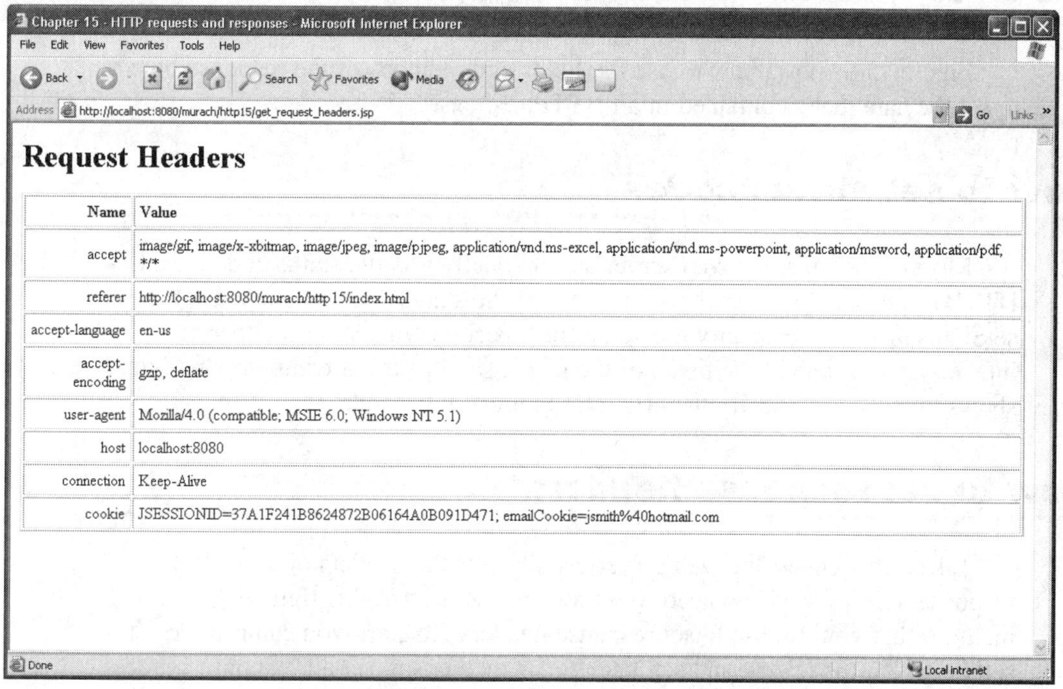

Request Headers

Name	Value
accept	image/gif, image/x-xbitmap, image/jpeg, image/pjpeg, application/vnd.ms-excel, application/vnd.ms-powerpoint, application/msword, application/pdf, */*
referer	http://localhost:8080/murach/http15/index.html
accept-language	en-us
accept-encoding	gzip, deflate
user-agent	Mozilla/4.0 (compatible; MSIE 6.0; Windows NT 5.1)
host	localhost:8080
connection	Keep-Alive
cookie	JSESSIONID=37A1F241B8624872B06164A0B091D471; emailCookie=jsmith%40hotmail.com

All request headers sent by Netscape 7.0

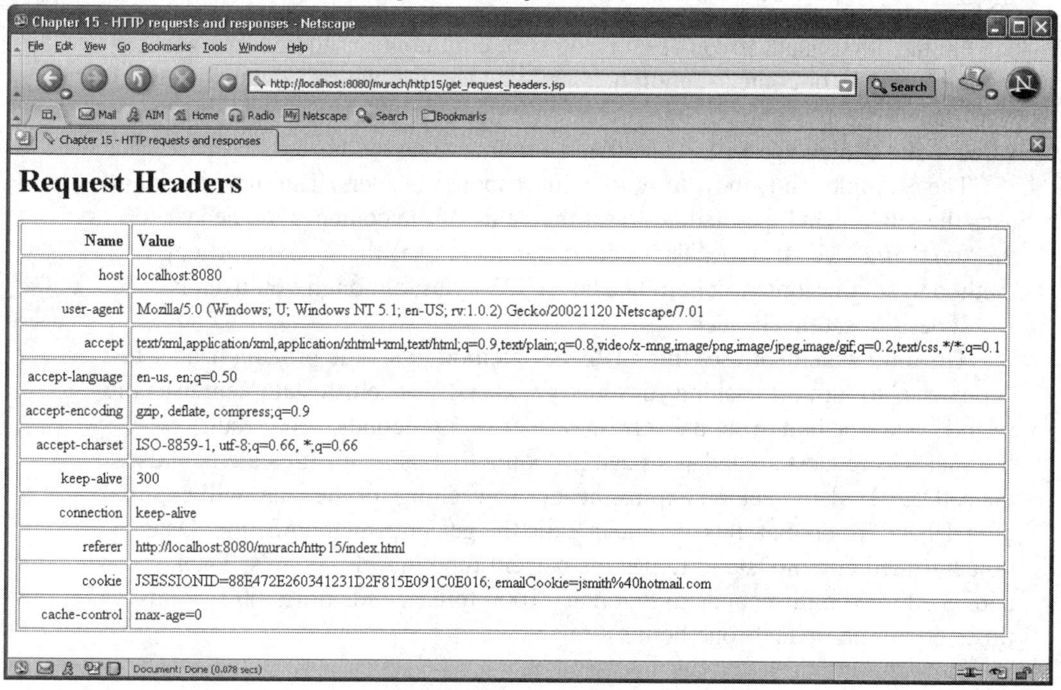

Request Headers

Name	Value
host	localhost:8080
user-agent	Mozilla/5.0 (Windows; U; Windows NT 5.1; en-US; rv:1.0.2) Gecko/20021120 Netscape/7.01
accept	text/xml,application/xml,application/xhtml+xml,text/html;q=0.9,text/plain;q=0.8,video/x-mng,image/png,image/jpeg,image/gif;q=0.2,text/css,*/*;q=0.1
accept-language	en-us, en;q=0.50
accept-encoding	gzip, deflate, compress;q=0.9
accept-charset	ISO-8859-1, utf-8;q=0.66, *;q=0.66
keep-alive	300
connection	keep-alive
referer	http://localhost:8080/murach/http15/index.html
cookie	JSESSIONID=88E472E260341231D2F815E091C0E016; emailCookie=jsmith%40hotmail.com
cache-control	max-age=0

Figure 15-8 Typical request headers for the IE and Netscape browsers

How to work with the response

Figure 15-9 shows how to use the fields and methods of the response object to set the data that's contained in an HTTP response.

How to set status codes

Most of the time, the web server automatically sets the status code for an HTTP response. However, if you need to set the status code, you can use the setStatus method. To specify the value for this code, you can use either an integer value or one of the fields of the response object. For example, this figure shows two ways to specify the 404 (Not Found) status code.

How to set response headers

Like status codes, the web server usually sets the headers of an HTTP response. However, if you need to set a response header, this figure shows six methods that you can use to set response headers. To start, you can use the setHeader, setIntHeader, and setDateHeader methods to set all response headers that accept strings, integers, or dates. Here, the setDateHeader accepts a long value that represents the date in milliseconds since January 1, 1970 00:00:00 GMT.

On the other hand, if you're working with commonly used headers, such as the content-type or content-length headers, you can use the setContentType and setContentLength methods. And you can use the addCookie method to add a value to the cookie header as described in chapter 7.

The examples show how to work with response headers. The first statement uses the setContentType method to set the value of the content-type header to the "text/html" MIME type. The second statement uses the setContentLength method to set the content-length header to 403 bytes, although you usually won't need to set this header.

The third statement uses the setHeader method to set the pragma header to "no-cache" to turn off caching for older browsers. The fourth statement uses the setIntHeader method to set the refresh header to 60 seconds. As a result, the browser will request an updated page in 1 minute. Last, the fifth statement uses the setDateHeader to set the expires header so caching for the page will expire after 1 hour. To do that, this statement calls the getTime method from a Date object named currentDate to return the current time in milliseconds. Then, it adds 3,600,000 milliseconds to that date (1000 miliseconds times 60 seconds times 60 minutes equals one hour).

The main method for setting the status codes

```
void setStatus(int code)
```

How status codes map to fields of the response object

Code	HttpServletResponse field
200 (OK)	SC_OK
404 (Not Found)	SC_NOT_FOUND
XXX (Xxx Xxx)	SC_XXX_XXX

Examples that set the status code

```
response.setStatus(404);
response.setStatus(response.SC_NOT_FOUND);
```

General methods for setting response headers

```
void setHeader(String headerName, String headerValue)
void setIntHeader(String headerName, int headerValue)
void setDateHeader(String headerName, long headerValue)
```

Convenience methods for setting response headers

```
void setContentType(String mimeType)
void setContentLength(int lengthInBytes)
void addCookie(Cookie cookie)
```

Examples that set response headers

```
response.setContentType("text/html");
response.setContentLength(403);
response.setHeader("pragma", "no-cache");
response.setIntHeader("refresh", 60);
response.setDateHeader("expires", currentDate.getTime() + 60 * 60 * 1000);
```

Description

* For more information about these methods and fields, you can look up the
  HttpServletResponse interface in the documentation for the servlet API.

Figure 15-9   Methods and examples for working with responses

Practical skills for working with HTTP

Now that you understand how to use the servlet API to work with HTTP requests and responses, you're ready to learn some practical skills for working with HTTP. These will illustrate when you might want to work directly with the requests and responses.

How to return a tab-delimited file as an Excel spreadsheet

Most modern browsers can use Microsoft Excel to read tab-delimited text. To display tab-delimited text as a spreadsheet, then, you can create some tab-delimited text, set the Content-Type response header to the "application/vnd.ms-excel" MIME type, and return the tab-delimited text to the browser. Then, the browser will open the tab-delimited text in Excel as shown in figure 15-10.

The code in this figure starts by storing the column headings for the spreadsheet in a StringBuffer object named report. Then, it retrieves all of the columns and rows from the User table in the Murach database and stores this data in tab-delimited format in the StringBuffer object.

When the code finishes storing the tab-delimited data in the StringBuffer object, the first statement in the highlighted code uses the setContentType method to set the content-type header of the response object. Here, the value in the header indicates that the response body contains data that's intended to be opened with Microsoft Excel. Then, the last two statements get a PrintWriter object that's used to return the StringBuffer object to the client.

How to control caching

The second statement in the highlighted code uses the setHeader method to set the cache-control response header so the document that's returned won't be cached. Otherwise, the server might automatically cache the response. Although it's usually more efficient to allow a document to be cached, preventing caching makes sure that the user updates the data with every visit.

An Excel spreadsheet displayed within the Internet Explorer

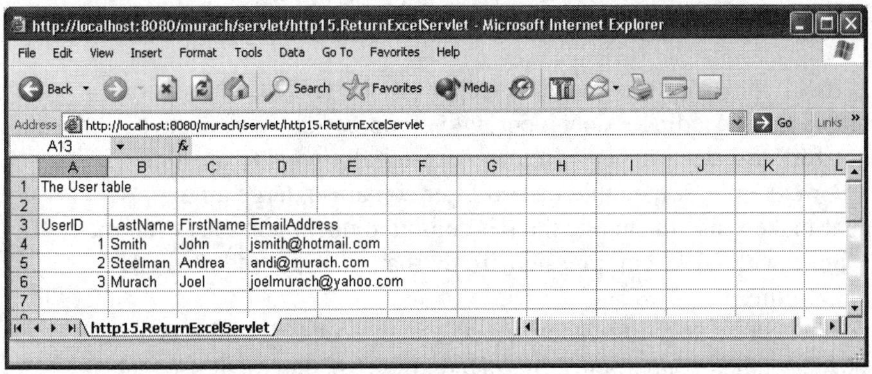

Code that returns a tab-delimited file as an Excel spreadsheet

```
String query = "SELECT * FROM User ORDER BY UserID";
String d = "\t";
StringBuffer report = new StringBuffer("The User table\n\n"
                + "UserID" + d
                + "LastName" + d
                + "FirstName" + d
                + "EmailAddress" + "\n");
try{
    Statement statement = connection.createStatement();
    ResultSet results = statement.executeQuery(query);
    while (results.next()){
        report.append(results.getInt("UserID") + d
                    + results.getString("LastName")+ d
                    + results.getString("FirstName") + d
                    + results.getString("EmailAddress") + "\n");
    }
    results.close();
    statement.close();
}
catch(SQLException e){
    System.out.println("SQLException: " + e.getMessage());
}
response.setContentType("application/vnd.ms-excel");
response.setHeader("cache-control", "no-cache");

PrintWriter out = response.getWriter();
out.println(report);
```

Description

- To view the complete code for this servlet, open the ReturnExcelServlet class that's stored in the murach\WEB-INF\classes\http15 directory.

Figure 15-10   How to return a tab-delimited file as an Excel spreadsheet

How to encode the response with GZIP compression

Figure 15-11 shows how to encode a response with GZIP compression. Since encoding and decoding a document with compression can improve performance for large documents, you may occasionally want to use this technique. For example, if the table named User contains a large amount of data, it might make sense to encode the tab-delimited document that's returned in the last figure with GZIP compression. To do that, you just add the code shown in this figure.

This code checks a request header named accept-encoding and sets a response header named content-encoding. Here, the first statement uses the getHeader method to return the accept-encoding request header. This request header is a string that contains the types of encoding that the browser supports. Then, the second statement declares a PrintWriter object.

If the browser supports GZIP encoding, the statements within the if block create a PrintWriter object that uses a GZIPOutputStream to compress the output stream. In addition, the third statement uses the setHeader method to set the content-encoding response header to GZIP. That way, the browser knows to use GZIP to decompress the stream before trying to read it. On the other hand, if the browser doesn't support GZIP encoding, the getWriter method of the response object is used to return a normal PrintWriter object. Either way, the PrintWriter object is used to return the report to the browser.

Version 1.4 of the J2SE API includes the GZIPOutputStream class in the java.util.zip package. So to use this class, you need to import this package. You can get more information about this class by looking it up in the documentation for the J2SE API.

How to encode a response with GZIP compression

```
String encodingString = request.getHeader("accept-encoding");
PrintWriter out;

if ((encodingString != null)
    && (encodingString.indexOf("gzip") > -1)){

        OutputStream outputStream = response.getOutputStream();
        out = new PrintWriter(
                new GZIPOutputStream(outputStream), false);
        response.setHeader("content-encoding", "gzip");
}
else{
        out = response.getWriter();
}
out.println(report);
```

Description

- The GZIPOutputStream class is included in the java.util.zip package of version 1.4 of the J2SE.

- The getOutputStream method of the response object returns a binary output stream. The getWriter method of the response object returns a text output stream.

- To view the complete code for this servlet, open the ReturnGZIPServlet class that's stored in the murach\WEB-INF\classes\http15 directory.

Figure 15-11   How to encode the response with GZIP compression

How to require the File Download dialog box

When coding a web application, you can code an HTML link that points to a downloadable file. For example, let's say you code a link that points to a *Portable Document Format*, or *PDF* file. When a user clicks on this link, most systems will automatically start Adobe's Acrobat Reader and attempt to display the PDF file within the Acrobat Reader.

Although this is adequate for some applications, the Acrobat Reader doesn't indicate how long it will take to open the file. As a result, for a large PDF file, the user may be left staring at a blank screen for several minutes while the document downloads. In that case, you might want to display a File Download dialog box like the one shown in figure 15-12. That way, the user will have the choice of opening the PDF file or saving the file to disk, and the user will see a dialog box that indicates the progress of the download.

The code in this figure begins by showing how to code an HTML link to a MP3 sound file. On many systems, clicking on a link like this automatically launches an audio player that plays the sound file. If that's not what you want, you can code an HTML link to a JSP that forces the File Download dialog box to be displayed by setting a content-disposition header.

The code for the JSP sets two response headers and creates a FileInputStream that's used to read the specified file and convert it into a binary stream. To start, the JSP uses a page directive to import the java.io package. Then, the first two statements within the scriptlet get the path and name of the file that were sent as request parameters. After that, the third statement in the scriptlet sets the content-type response header to indicate that the response will contain generic binary data, and the fourth statement sets the content-disposition header to indicate that the response contains an attached file. This will force the File Download dialog box to be displayed. Once the response headers have been set, the scriptlet uses a PrintWriter object to read each byte of the specified file and write it to the response.

When using a JSP like this, you must make sure that the response doesn't include any bytes besides the binary data that's stored in the file. That's why the ending tag for the page directive ends on the same line as the beginning tag of the scriptlet like this:

```
%><%
```

Otherwise, the response would begin with the new line character that separates the page directive from the scriptlet, and the browser wouldn't be able to understand the response.

The File Download dialog box

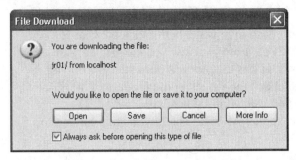

An HTML link to an MP3 sound file

```
<a href="c:/tomcat/webapps/murach/sound/jr01/filter.mp3">Filter</a>
```

An HTML link to the download.jsp file

```
<a href=
"download.jsp?name=filter.mp3&path=c:/tomcat/webapps/murach/sound/jr01/">
Filter</a><br>
```

The download.jsp file

```
<%@ page import="java.io.*"
%><%
String path = request.getParameter("path");
String name = request.getParameter("name");

response.setContentType("application/octet-stream");
response.setHeader("content-disposition", "attachment; filename=" + name);

FileInputStream in = new FileInputStream(path + name);
int i;
while ((i = in.read()) != -1)
    out.write(i);
in.close();

%>
```

Description

- To force a File Download dialog box to be displayed, set the content-disposition header as shown above.
- To view the code for this JSP, open the download.jsp file that's stored in the murach\http15 directory.

Note

- If the File Download dialog box is displayed twice on your system, you can deselect the "Always ask before opening this type of file" option. Then, the File Download dialog box will only be displayed once.

Figure 15-12   How to require the File Download dialog box

Perspective

The goals of this chapter have been (1) to give you a better idea of what HTTP requests and responses consist of, and (2) to show you how you can use Java to work with HTTP requests and responses. If this chapter has been successful, you should now be able to use Java code to check the values in the headers of an HTTP request and also to set the status code and values of the headers of an HTTP response. Most of the time, though, the servlet API will shield you from having to work directly with HTTP.

Summary

- An HTTP request consists of a *request line* followed by *request headers*, while an HTTP response consists of a *status line* followed by *response headers* and then by a *response body*. The headers specify the attributes of a request or a response.

- The *Multipurpose Internet Mail Extension* (*MIME*) types provide standards for various types of data that can be transferred across the Internet.

- You can use the get methods of the request object to get the values of request headers, and you can use the set methods of the response object to set the values of response headers. This is useful for some applications.

Terms

Hypertext Transfer Protocol (HTTP)	response entity
request line	response body
request header	Multipurpose Internet Mail Extension
status line	(MIME)
status code	Portable Document Format (PDF)
response header	

Objectives

- Use the get and set methods of the request and response objects whenever you need them.

- Describe the components of an HTTP request and an HTTP response.

- Describe a case in which you would need to know the values of one or more request headers.

- Describe a case in which you would need to set the values of one or more response headers.

Exercise 15-1   Run the sample applications

1. Run the first three applications in the http15 directory to see how the request headers can be returned in different formats. Then, view the code for each of the JSPs that return the request headers so you can see how the different MIME types are returned.

2. Run the application that displays the users in the User table in an Excel spreadsheet. Then, compare this with the application that uses GZIP compression to return the spreadsheet. View the servlet code for these applications in the http15 package to see how these applications work.

3. Run the application that uses an HTML link to download a MP3 file. Then, run the application that uses a JSP to download the same file. This time, the application should display a dialog box similar to the one in figure 15-12. Perform the same task for the last two applications that download PDF files.

Exercise 15-2   Enhance the Download application

Enhance the Download application presented in chapter 7 so it displays a File Download dialog box for all sound files. To do this, modify each of the product download JSPs so the hyperlinks refer to the download JSP in the http15 directory.

How to work with XML

XML is a markup language that's similar to HTML. However, it is used for storing and transferring the data in web applications. In this chapter, you'll learn how to work with XML in your web applications.

An introduction to XML **466**
An XML document 466
Common uses of XML 466
XML declarations and comments 468
XML elements 468
XML attributes 470
An introduction to DTDs 472
An introduction to XML APIs 474

How to work with DOM **476**
The DOM tree 476
Interfaces for working with the DOM tree 478
How to create an empty DOM tree 480
How to add nodes to a DOM tree 482
How to write a DOM tree to a file 484
How to read a DOM tree from a file 486
How to read the nodes of a DOM tree 488
How to add, update, and delete nodes 490

The Email List application **492**
The code for the XMLUtil class 492
The code for the UserXML class 494
The code for the EmailServlet class 496

How to return an XML document via HTTP **498**
The code for the XMLServlet class 498
The XML document displayed in a browser 498

Perspective **500**

An introduction to XML

Before you begin using Java to work with XML, you must learn some background concepts and terms. To start, *XML* stands for *Extensible Markup Language*.

An XML document

Figure 16-1 shows an *XML document* that uses *XML tags* to identify the data for three users. When you use XML, you define the names and structure of the XML tags that you use. Then, you use these tags as you add data to the XML document. When you're done, you can save the document in an *XML file*, which usually has an extension of XML.

Because you've already seen how Tomcat uses the web.xml and server.xml files, you should already understand the basic design and structure of an XML document. That's why this chapter goes quickly over the coding details. One point to note, though, is that XML tags are case-sensitive.

Common uses of XML

In the last few years, XML has received much hype about its many potential uses. Because it is a general-purpose markup language, it's true that it can be used in many ways. In practice, though, you're likely to see it used in just the three ways that are summarized in this figure.

First, XML works well for control files like the web.xml and server.xml files. Similarly, many applications require control files that keep track of the next invoice number to be used, the next payroll check number to be used, special account numbers, and so on. When you use XML for this type of file, it's easy to see what the data in the file represents.

Second, XML works well for transferring data from one platform or system to another. If, for example, you want to transfer some data from a MySQL database that's used by Java on a Unix platform to a SQL Server database that's used by Visual Basic .NET on the Windows platform, you can use XML as the exchange medium. To do that, you first use Java to get the data from the database and convert it to an XML file. Then, the Visual Basic programmer can open the XML document and save it in the SQL Server database. In a case like this, neither the Java programmer or the Visual Basic programmer needs to know the details of the other programmer's system because XML is the common language.

Third, you can use XML for storing business data. The benefit of this is that it can easily be used by more than one type of system. The shortcoming is that this isn't efficient because an XML file requires much more storage than a file that just contains the data. Later in this chapter, you'll see how an XML file can be used to store the user data in the Email application so you can judge this for yourself.

Tabular data for three users

First name	Last name	Email address	Contact
Andrea	Steelman	andi@yahoo.net	no
Joel	Murach	joel@murach.com	yes
Alexandra	White	allie@lemoorenet.com	yes

The same data stored in an XML document

```
<?xml version="1.0" encoding="UTF-8"?>
<!--User Information-->
<Users>
    <User contact="no">
        <firstName>Andrea</firstName>
        <lastName>Steelman</lastName>
        <emailAddress>andi@yahoo.net</emailAddress>
    </User>
    <User contact="yes">
        <firstName>Joel</firstName>
        <lastName>Murach</lastName>
        <emailAddress>joel@murach.com</emailAddress>
    </User>
    <User contact="yes">
        <firstName>Alexandra</firstName>
        <lastName>White</lastName>
        <emailAddress>allie@lemoorenet.com</emailAddress>
    </User>
</Users>
```

Common uses of XML

- Control files
- Files for exchanging data between two different systems
- Business data files that contain small amounts of data, especially if they are used by two different types of systems.

Description

- *XML*, which stands for *Extensible Markup Language*, is a method of structuring information.
- An *XML document* uses *XML tags* to identify the data elements. When an XML document is stored in an *XML file*, the file usually has an extension of XML.
- Unlike HTML tags, XML tags are case-sensitive.

Figure 16-1   An introduction to XML

XML declarations and comments

The first tag in any XML document is an *XML declaration* as shown in figure 16-2. This declaration identifies the document as an XML document, indicates the XML version of the document, and provides other information. In this example, the XML declaration identifies the document version as 1.0 and the character set for the document as UTF-8, which is the most common character set used for XML documents in English-speaking countries.

An XML document can also contain *XML comments*. These are coded and work like HTML comments as illustrated by the second line in the first example in this figure.

XML elements

An XML document uses *XML elements* to store data with the *content* of each element between the opening and closing tags. For example, the firstName element in this figure contains text that identifies the user's first name.

Note, however, that an element can also contain other XML elements. For example, the User element contains the firstName, lastName, and emailAddress elements, which can be referred to as *child elements* of the User element. To say this another way, the User element is the *parent element* of the firstName, lastName, and emailAddress elements.

An element can also occur more than once within an XML document. For example, the XML document in figure 16-1 contains three User elements within the Users element. Since each User element contains the firstName, lastName, and emailAddress elements, these elements also appear three times in the document.

If necessary, you can take this nesting to other levels. If, for example, you want to be able to store one or more email addresses per user, you can use an emailAddresses element that contains one or more emailAddress elements as shown by the second example in figure 16-2.

The highest-level element in an XML document is known as the *root element*, and an XML document can have one and only one root element. In this figure, the root element is the Users element. For XML documents that contain repeating information, it's common to use a plural name for the root element to indicate that it contains multiple child elements.

A User element and its child elements

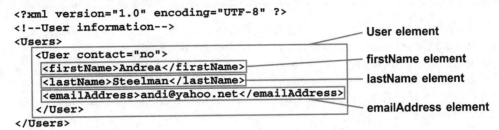

```
<?xml version="1.0" encoding="UTF-8" ?>
<!--User information-->
<Users>
    <User contact="no">
        <firstName>Andrea</firstName>
        <lastName>Steelman</lastName>
        <emailAddress>andi@yahoo.net</emailAddress>
    </User>
</Users>
```

User element

firstName element

lastName element

emailAddress element

A User element that adds another level of child elements

```
<User contact="no">
    <firstName>Andrea</firstName>
    <lastName>Steelman</lastName>
    <emailAddresses>
        <emailAddress>andi@yahoo.net</emailAddress>
        <emailAddress>andi@lemoore.com</emailAddress>
    </emailAddresses>
</User>
```

XML declarations and comments

- The first line in an XML document is an *XML declaration* that indicates which version of the XML standard is being used for the document. In addition, this declaration usually identifies the standard character set that's being used (UTF-8 is the character set that's commonly used for XML documents in English-speaking countries).

- *XML comments* are coded the same way HTML comments are coded.

XML elements

- An *XML element* begins with a starting tag and ends with an ending tag. The starting tag provides the name of the element and contains any attributes assigned to the element (see the next figure for details on attributes). The ending tag repeats the element name, but is prefixed with a slash (/).

- The *content* for an element is coded within the element's starting and ending tags.

- An element can contain one or more other elements. An element that's contained within another element is the *child element*. An element that contains a child element is a *parent element*.

- The highest-level parent element in an XML document is the *root element*. An XML document must have one and only one root element.

Figure 16-2   XML declarations, comments, and elements

XML attributes

An XML document can also use *XML attributes* to store data. To illustrate, figure 16-3 shows an attribute named contact that's defined for each User element. This attribute provides a value that indicates whether the user wants to be contacted. As you can see, the coding for an XML attribute is the same as the coding for an HTML attribute, although quotation marks are required around the attribute value.

When you design an XML document, you can create as many attributes as necessary, using names that describe the data that's stored in each attribute. If an element has more than one attribute, you can list the attributes in any order you want. However, you must separate each attribute with one or more spaces.

When you design an XML document, you need to decide whether to use elements or attributes for your data items. In many cases, either approach will work. In this figure, for example, the contact data item could have been stored in an element named contact. Conversely, the emailAddress element could have been stored in an attribute.

Since attributes require less code than elements, it's often tempting to store data in attributes rather than elements. However, an element that contains multiple attributes soon becomes unwieldy. As a result, most programmers who work with XML documents limit their use of attributes. One of the common uses of an attribute, though, is to store a number or code that uniquely identifies the element.

An attribute of the User element

```
<?xml version="1.0" encoding="UTF-8" ?>
<!--User information-->
<Users>
  <User contact="no">                       ──── the contact attribute
    <firstName>Andrea</firstname>
    <lastName>Steelman</lastname>
    <emailAddress>andi@yahoo.net</emailAddress>
  </User>
</Users>
```

XML attributes

- You can include one or more *XML attributes* in the starting tag for an element. An attribute consists of an attribute name, an equals sign, and a string value in single or double quotes. Unlike HTML, the quotes around the attribute are required.

- If an element has more than one attribute, the attributes must be separated by one or more spaces.

When to use attributes instead of child elements

- When you design an XML document, you can use child elements or attributes to identify the data items of an element. The choice of whether to implement a data item as an attribute or as a child element is often a matter of preference.

- Although attributes require less code, an element that contains too many attributes can become unwieldy.

- Although child elements require more code, they're usually easier to read, they're better for working with long string values, and they can store additional child elements.

Figure 16-3   XML attributes

An introduction to DTDs

To define a list of conditions that an XML document must follow, you can use a *schema language* to create a document known as a *schema*. Two schema languages that are supported by the XML standards are *Document Type Definition*, or *DTD*, and *XML Schema Definition*, or *XSD*. Because DTD is supported by SDK 1.4 and XSD isn't, figure 16-4 shows an example of DTD.

In this figure, you can see the DTD for a document that is defined by the rules at the start of this figure. Although a DTD is optional, the use of one helps ensure that an XML document has the proper format when it is used by a Java program.

To code a DTD, you start with the DOCTYPE declaration. Within this declaration, you code the name of the root element. This establishes that this element appears once and only once. After that, you code brackets that hold the body of the DTD.

In the body of a DTD, each XML element is declared in an ELEMENT declaration. If an element has children, that element must declare the children by listing their names in order, separated by commas. For example, the User element contains firstName, lastName, and emailAddress elements in that order.

To specify that a child element is optional, you can code a question mark after the element name. To specify that a child element may occur zero or more times, you can code an asterisk after the element name. And to specify that an element must occur one or more times, you can code a plus sign after the element name.

To specify the attributes for an element, you can use the ATTLIST declaration. This declaration specifies the element to which the attribute belongs, the name of the attribute, possible values for the attribute, and the default value for the attribute. In this example, the contact attribute of the User element can only store yes and no values, and the default value is yes. To require an attribute, you can use the #REQUIRED keyword.

To declare that an element contains text, you can use the #PCDATA keyword. When you use this keyword, the element can contain text data, but it can't contain any child elements.

To use a DTD when you create an XML file, you use a DOCTYPE declaration to refer to the file that contains the DTD. This is illustrated by second example in this figure. You can also code the DTD directly in the XML document that uses it. In that case, the entire DTD replaces the DOCTYPE declaration.

The rules for an XML document

- The document must contain one and only one Users element.
- The document can contain multiple User elements. Each of these User elements must contain three elements named firstName, lastName, and emailAddress.
- Each User element can contain one attribute named contact that can hold either a "yes" value or a "no" value. The default value is "yes".
- The firstName, lastName, and emailAddress elements can contain any text data. They can't contain child elements.

A DTD the implements these rules

```
<!DOCTYPE Users [
    <!ELEMENT User (firstName, lastName, emailAddress)>
    <!ATTLIST User contact (yes|no) "yes">
    <!ELEMENT firstName (#PCDATA)>
    <!ELEMENT lastName (#PCDATA)>
    <!ELEMENT emailAddress (#PCDATA)>
]>
```

How to refer to a DTD file in an XML document

```
<?xml version="1.0" encoding="UTF-8" ?>
<!DOCTYPE Users SYSTEM "c:/tomcat/webapps/murach/web-inf/etc/users.dtd">
<!--User information-->
<Users>
  <User contact="no">
    <firstName>Andrea</firstName>
    <lastName>Steelman</lastName>
    <emailAddress>andrea@murach.com</emailAddress>
  </User>
</Users>
```

DTD declarations

Keyword	Defines
DOCTYPE	The root element
ELEMENT	The names of the child elements or the element name and the type of data it will contain
ATTLIST	The names of the attributes and the types of data they will contain

Description

- To define the conditions of an XML document, you use a *schema language* to create a *schema*. These conditions can then be enforced for any XML document that's based on the schema.
- *Document Type Definition*, or *DTD*, is a schema language that's part of standard XML. It is supported by SDK 1.4.
- *XML Schema Definition*, or *XSD*, is a newer schema language that's part of standard XML. It is more flexible than DTD, but it is also more difficult to work with and it isn't supported by SDK 1.4.
- An XML document can refer to a DTD that's stored in a file or it can contain an inline DTD at the start of the XML document.

Figure 16-4   An introduction to DTDs

An introduction to XML APIs

Figure 16-5 presents the pros and cons of the two major APIs for working with XML documents in Java. Both of these APIs are included with version 1.4 of the SDK, and both contain a *parser* that makes it relatively easy to read an XML document. If the XML document uses a DTD, the parser also validates the document against the DTD.

The *Simple API for XML*, or *SAX*, is fast and memory efficient. It allows an application to respond to events as the parser reads the tags, text, and comments in one XML line at a time. This API is commonly used to work with large XML documents. Note, however, that you can't use SAX to write an XML document to a file.

The *Document Object Model*, or *DOM*, isn't as fast or memory efficient as SAX. Unlike SAX, DOM begins by reading the entire XML document into memory and storing the document as a collection of objects. This makes it easy to use object-oriented programming techniques to access the data stored in the XML document. In addition, you can use DOM to write an XML document to a file. As a result, DOM is commonly used to work with short XML documents.

In this chapter, you'll learn how to use DOM to work with XML documents. However, you can find more information about working with SAX and other XML APIs on the Java web site.

SAX is

*   Memory efficient
*   Read-only
*   Typically used for working with documents larger than 10 megabytes

DOM is

*   Memory intensive
*   Read-write
*   Typically used for working with documents smaller than 10 megabytes

Description

*   Version 1.4 of the SDK includes two APIs that you can use to *parse* XML documents to get the data you want. Although earlier versions of the SDK don't contain any APIs for working with XML, you can download these APIs from the Java web site.

*   Two types of APIs exist for processing XML documents with Java. The *Simple API for XML (SAX)* and the *Document Object Model (DOM)*. In addition to these APIs, there are several others including JDOM, dom4j, and ElectricXML.

*   SAX reads one line at a time and lets you access the tags in the line immediately.

*   DOM reads an entire XML document before you can access the individual tags.

*   You can find more information about these and other XML APIs on the Java web site.

Figure 16-5   An introduction to XML APIs

How to work with DOM

Now that you've learned some basic concepts about XML, this topic will show you how to use DOM to work with an XML document. But first, you need to learn how a DOM tree works.

The DOM tree

Figure 16-6 presents a *DOM tree* for the XML document presented in figure 16-1. This tree is a collection of objects that represent the XML document after it has been read into memory.

The DOM tree is a collection of related *nodes*. Each node can have a *parent node*, zero or more *child nodes*, and zero or more *sibling nodes*. For example, Node B in this figure has one sibling node (Node C), two child nodes (Nodes D and E) and one parent node (Node A). Similarly, node J has one parent node (Node G), no child nodes, and no sibling nodes.

Each node has a *node type*. For example, Node D is an element type and Node F is an attr type. In the next figure, you'll learn that these types correspond to Java objects. Remember, though, that DOM is an object model that can be used by any object-oriented language.

Every DOM tree contains one document node that defines the DOM tree. This node must contain one and only one child element node, but it can contain other type of nodes such as a comment node. Any other element node in a DOM tree can contain multiple child elements. For example, Node D contains three child elements. Unlike element nodes, comment nodes and text nodes can't contain children.

In a DOM tree, any element node that contains text contains a text node that stores the text data. A common error in DOM processing is to navigate to an element node and expect it to contain the data that is stored in that element. For example, Node G is the node for the firstName element, but this node doesn't hold the value for first name. Instead, it contains a child text node (Node J) that holds that value. .

The structure of the DOM tree for the User XML document

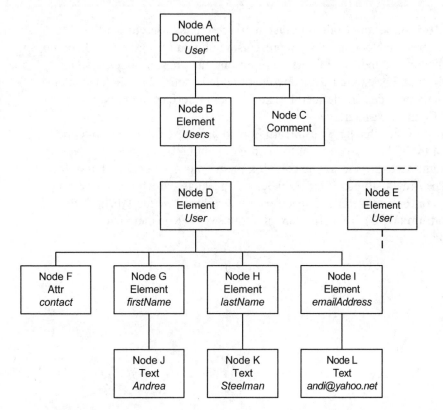

Description

- You can use the DOM API to load an XML document into a *DOM tree*. Then, you can use the DOM API to work with the data in the DOM tree.

- A DOM tree is a collection of *nodes*. Each node may have a *parent node*, one or more *child nodes*, and one or more *sibling nodes*.

- Each node has a *node type* that indicates whether the node represents the document, an element, a comment, an attribute, or a text value.

Figure 16-6   The DOM tree

Interfaces for working with the DOM tree

Figure 16-7 shows the Node interface hierarchy that's used to work with a DOM tree. Here, the Node interface represents a node on a DOM tree. Then, the interfaces that extend the Node interface represent the types of nodes available from a DOM tree. For example, the document node is defined by the Document interface, element nodes are defined by the Element interface, and text nodes are defined by the Text interface.

In the rest of this chapter, you'll learn how to use these interfaces to work with a DOM tree. Then, if you want to learn more about the methods that are available from these interfaces, you can look them up in the documentation for the SDK. They're all stored in the org.w3c.dom package, which contains Java classes that conform to the DOM specification developed by the World Wide Web Consortium (W3C). To learn more about the W3C, you can visit *www.w3c.org*.

The Node interface hierarchy

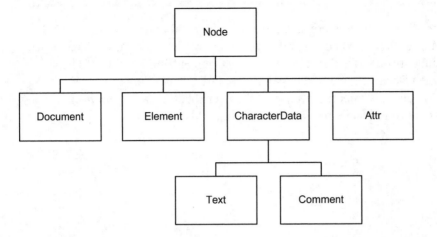

Description

- The Node interface represents a single node in the DOM tree.
- The Document, Element, Text, Comment, and Attr interfaces represent the different types of nodes available in a DOM tree.
- You can use the methods of these interfaces to work with the nodes of a DOM tree.
- Since the Document, Element, CharacterData, Attr, Text, and Comment interfaces inherit the Node interface, you can use any of the methods in the Node interface to work with nodes.
- These interfaces are located in the org.w3c.dom package.

Figure 16-7   Interfaces for working with the DOM tree

How to create an empty DOM tree

Figure 16-8 shows how to create a Document object that represents an empty DOM tree. Before you can get the Document object, though, you need to use the DocumentBuilderFactory class to get a DocumentBuilder object. Then, you call the newDocument method to get an empty Document object. For this code to work, you must import the javax.xml.parsers and org.w3c.dom packages. You also need to handle the ParserConfigurationException.

Code that creates an empty DOM tree

```
DocumentBuilderFactory dbf = DocumentBuilderFactory.newInstance();
DocumentBuilder db = dbf.newDocumentBuilder();
Document doc = db.newDocument();
```

Packages

```
javax.xml.parsers
org.w3c.dom
```

Exceptions

```
javax.xml.parsers.ParserConfigurationException
```

Description

- To create an empty DOM tree, you must use the DocumentBuilderFactory class and DocumentBuilder classes to create a Document object.

- The newDocumentBuilder method in the DocumentBuilderFactory class throws a ParserConfigurationException.

- The DocumentBuilderFactory and DocumentBuilder classes are located in the javax.xml.parsers package.

Figure 16-8   How to create an empty DOM tree

How to add nodes to a DOM tree

Once you have a Document object that represents a DOM tree, you can create nodes and add them to the tree as shown in figure 16-9. To do this, you can use the methods from the Document, Element, and Node interfaces.

The first example shows how to create the root element (Users) and append it to the document node. The second example shows how to create a comment and append it to a node. In this case, the comment is appended to the document node so it's displayed before the root element in the XML document. This works the same if you want to display a comment before any other node.

The third example shows how to create a User element and append it to the Users element. The fourth example shows how to create an attribute, set its value, and add it to the User element. To do that, you call the setAttribute method from the User element and specify the name and value of the attribute.

The fifth example shows how to create an element that contains text. To do that, this code creates the firstName element and appends it to the User element. Then, it creates a text node and appends it to the firstName element.

Whenever you create a comment or element node, you must append the node to another node or it won't be placed in the DOM tree. To do that, you use the appendChild method that's defined in the Node interface. However, if you call the appendChild method from a node that can't have children, such as a text node or a comment node, the appendChild method will throw a DOMException. As a result, you must handle this exception when you work with this method.

Code that creates and appends the root element

```
Element rootElement = doc.createElement("Users");
doc.appendChild(rootElement);
```

Code that creates and appends a comment

```
Comment comment = doc.createComment("User Information");
doc.appendChild(comment);
```

Code that creates and appends an element

```
Element userElement = doc.createElement("User");
rootElement.appendChild(userElement);
```

Code that sets an attribute

```
userElement.setAttribute("contact", "yes");
```

Code that creates and appends an element that contains text

```
Element firstNameElement = doc.createElement("firstName");
userElement.appendChild(firstNameElement);
Text firstNameText = doc.createTextNode("firstName");
firstNameText.setNodeValue("Alexandra");
firstNameElement.appendChild(firstNameText);
```

Packages

```
org.w3c.dom
```

Exceptions

```
org.w3c.dom.DOMException
```

Description

- You can use the createComment, createElement, and createTextNode methods to create comment, element, and text nodes.
- Once you create a node, you can use the appendChild method to append any node to another node.
- You can use the setNodeValue method to set the value for a text node.
- You can use the setAttribute method to create an attribute, set its value, and append it to its element.
- The createElement, setNodeValue, and appendChild methods throw a DOMException.

Figure 16-9   How to add nodes to a DOM tree

How to write a DOM tree to a file

After you create a Document object that contains a DOM tree, you're ready to *transform* that document into an input stream that can be written to an output stream. To illustrate, figure 16-10 shows how to write a DOM tree to a file. Although this code may seem complex, you can use similar code whenever you need to write an XML document to a file. And you can use a similar procedure to write an XML document to other types of output streams.

To write a DOM tree to a file, you must follow three steps. First, you must define the DOM tree as the input source. To do that, you can create a DOMSource object by providing the name of the Document object in the constructor. Second, you must define the File object to be used as the output destination. To do that, you can create a File object for the XML file, and you can use that File object to create a StreamResult object. Third, you must use the transform method of the Transformer object to write the input source to the output destination.

To obtain a Transformer object, you can use the newInstance and newTransformer methods of the TransformerFactory class. Before you call the transform method, though, you may want to set some properties that affect the output of the XML document. To specify that the document should use indentation, for example, you can use the setOutputProperty method as shown in this figure. To specify the number of indentation spaces, you can supply values like the ones shown in this figure. In this case, the indentation is set to 4 spaces.

When the code in this figure is executed, the DOM tree in the Document object is written to an XML file. Then, you can use any text editor to open and edit this file. In addition, you can use any web browser to view the contents of this file. To do that, you can use the Explorer to navigate to the file and double-click on it. If the file has an extension of XML, this will open the web browser and the browser will display the XML document.

To use the code in this figure, you need to import the javax.xml.transform, javax.xml.transform.dom, and the javax.xml.transform.stream packages. In addition, you have to handle a TransformerException that may be thrown by the newTransformer and transform methods.

Code that writes a DOM tree to a file

```
//Prepare the DOM document as the input source
DOMSource in = new DOMSource(doc);

//Prepare the output file
File xmlFile = new File("C:/tomcat/webapps/murach/WEB-INF/etc/users.xml");
StreamResult out = new StreamResult(xmlFile);

// Write the DOM document to the file
Transformer transformer =
    TransformerFactory.newInstance().newTransformer();
transformer.setOutputProperty(OutputKeys.INDENT, "yes");
transformer.setOutputProperty(
    "{http://xml.apache.org/xslt}indent-amount", "4");
transformer.transform(in, out);
```

Packages

```
javax.xml.transform
javax.xml.transform.dom
javax.xml.transform.stream
```

Exceptions

```
javax.xml.transform.TransformerException
```

Description

- To specify the DOM tree as the input source, you create a DOMSource object from the Document object.
- To specify an XML file as the output, you create a StreamResult object that points to an XML file.
- To write the DOM tree to the XML file, you create a Transformer object by calling the newTransformer method of the TransformerFactory class. Then, you can call the transform method of the Transformer object.
- If you don't specify any output properties in the Transformer object, the XML document will appear as one continuous string and may be difficult to read. To specify indentation and other formatting, you can use the setOutputProperty methods.
- The DOMSource class is located in the javax.xml.transform.dom package, the StreamResult interface is located in the javax.xml.transform.stream package, and the Tranformer and TransformerFactory classes are located in the javax.xml.transform package.
- Both the newTransformer method of the TransformerFactory class and the transform method of the Transformer class throw a TransformerException.

Figure 16-10 How to write a DOM tree to a file

How to read a DOM tree from a file

Figure 16-11 shows how to read a Document object that represents a DOM tree from an XML document that's stored in a file. When you use this code, you must create an InputSource object that refers to the XML file. To do that, you can code a string that refers to the XML file in the constructor for the InputSource class.

Then, you create a DocumentBuilder object that will hold the DOM tree. Before you do that, you can use the methods of the DocumentBuilderFactory class to set conditions for the DOM tree that's returned. For example, you can use the three set methods in this figure to tell the parser that's created by the DocumentBuilderFactory to ignore comments, eliminate white space within an element, and to validate the document against a schema. By default, these three methods use false values, but the second example shows how you can use the setIgnoringComments method to turn this option on so comments are ignored.

If you ignore comments, the parser won't include any XML comments in the DOM tree. As a result, you should only use this method when you want to read an XML document, but you don't need to update it. Otherwise, the comments will be lost when you write the updated XML document to the file. This is true for the white space option too.

After you create the DocumentBuilder object, you use the parse method to parse the input file into the DOM tree. Although this method throws a SAXException, you don't need to know how to work with SAX to handle this exception. However, you will need to import the org.xml.sax package, and you will need to throw or catch this exception.

Code that reads a DOM tree from a file

```
InputSource in = new InputSource(
    "c:/tomcat/webapps/murach/web-inf/etc/users.xml");
DocumentBuilderFactory dbf = DocumentBuilderFactory.newInstance();
DocumentBuilder db = dbf.newDocumentBuilder();
Document doc = db.parse(in);
```

Code that reads a DOM tree and validates it against its DTD schema

```
InputSource in = new InputSource(
    "c:/tomcat/webapps/murach/web-inf/etc/users.xml");
DocumentBuilderFactory dbf = DocumentBuilderFactory.newInstance();
dbf.setValidating(true);
DocumentBuilder db = dbf.newDocumentBuilder();
Document doc = db.parse(in);
```

Common methods of the DocumentBuilderFactory class

setIgnoringComments(boolean b)

Specifies whether the parser will ignore comments.

setIgnoringElementContentWhitespace(boolean b)

Specifies whether the parser will eliminate white space within the content of elements.

setValidating(boolean b)

Specifies whether the parser will validate the XML document against a schema.

Packages

```
javax.xml.parsers
org.w3c.dom
```

Exceptions

```
java.io.IOException
org.xml.sax.SAXException
```

Description

- To get a Document object for an existing XML document, you can call the parse method of the DocumentBuilder object with an InputSource object that points to the XML file as its argument.
- By default, the three set methods above are set to false. If that's not what you want, you can call them from the DocumentBuilder object and change them so they're true.
- The three set methods above have corresponding is methods that return a boolean value.
- The parse method of the DocumentBuilder class throws a SAXException and an IOException.

Figure 16-11   How to read a DOM tree from a file

How to read the nodes of a DOM tree

Figure 16-12 shows how to read the nodes of a Document object that represents a DOM tree. To start, it shows how to use the getDocumentElement method to return the root element of a Document object directly as an Element object. Then, this figure shows how to read all element nodes named emailAddress and add them to a vector of String objects. Last, this figure shows how to read all element nodes named User and add them to a vector of User objects. If the Document object contains an XML document like the one in figure 16-1, both of these vectors will store three objects.

To obtain a NodeList object that contains a collection of element nodes, you can use the getElementsByTagName method of the Document object. Once you get a NodeList object, you can use its methods to loop through all of the Node objects contained within the NodeList object. To do that, you use the item method to return a specified item in the list, and you use the getLength method to return the number of nodes in the list. Since the item method returns a Node object, you must cast the Node object to an Element object for this code to work.

Once you have an Element object, you can use the methods in this figure to get its child elements and its attributes. To get an attribute value, you call the getAttribute method of the Element interface. However, getting the value of a child element that contains a text value requires more steps. First, you must use the getElementsByTagName method and the item method to return the child element. Then, you use the getFirstChild method to return the text node. And last, you use the getNodeValue method to return the value of the node.

The code in this figure assumes that you know the structure of the XML document and that it's acceptable to hard code the names of the XML elements and attributes. However, for many types of applications, you may not know the exact structure of the DOM tree so you can't hard code the names of the elements. In that case, you can use other methods of the Node interface to determine the structure of an XML document and to retrieve values from this structure. To learn more about these methods, you can look up the Node interface in the org.w3c.dom package of the documentation for the SDK.

Code that reads the root element of the DOM tree

```
Element root = doc.getDocumentElement();
```

Code that reads all EmailAddress elements into a vector

```
Vector emailVector = new Vector();
NodeList emailList = doc.getElementsByTagName("emailAddress");

for (int i = 0; i < emailList.getLength(); i++){
    Element emailElement = (Element) emailList.item(i);
    Text emailText = (Text) emailElement.getFirstChild();
    String emailAddress = emailText.getNodeValue();
    emailVector.add(emailAddress);
}
```

Code that reads all User elements into a vector

```
Vector users = new Vector();
NodeList usersList = doc.getElementsByTagName("User");

for (int i = 0; i < usersList.getLength(); i++){
    Element userElement = (Element) usersList.item(i);

    String contact = userElement.getAttribute("contact");

    NodeList firstList = userElement.getElementsByTagName("firstName");
    Element firstElement = (Element) firstList.item(0);
    Text firstText = (Text) firstElement.getFirstChild();
    String firstName = firstText.getNodeValue();

    NodeList lastList = userElement.getElementsByTagName("lastName");
    Element lastElement = (Element) lastList.item(0);
    Text lastText = (Text) lastElement.getFirstChild();
    String lastName = lastText.getNodeValue();

    NodeList emailList = userElement.getElementsByTagName("emailAddress");
    Element emailElement = (Element) emailList.item(0);
    Text emailText = (Text) emailElement.getFirstChild();
    String emailAddress = emailText.getNodeValue();

    User user = new User(firstName, lastName, emailAddress);
    users.add(user);
}
```

Description

- The NodeList interface stores a collection of Node objects. You can use the getLength and item methods to loop through the Node objects stored in a NodeList object.

- You can use the getElementsByTagName method to return a NodeList object that contains a collection of nodes for the specified tag, and you can use the getDocumentElement method to return the root element of the XML document.

- You can use the getAttribute method to return the value of the specified attribute, you can use the getFirstChild method to return the first child node, and you can use the getNodeValue method to return the value of a text node.

- For more information about these and other methods for reading nodes, you can look up the Node and NodeList interfaces in the org.w3c.dom package.

Figure 16-12   How to read the nodes of a DOM tree

How to add, update, and delete nodes

You can use the methods shown in figure 16-13 to add, update, and delete the nodes of a DOM tree. In this figure, the examples work with child elements of the root element. To return an Element object for the root element, you use the getDocumentElement method that you saw in the last figure.

To add a new element, you start by creating the Element object. Then, you can use the appendChild method to add that element to the end of the list of child elements for that element. However, if you want to add an element somewhere else in the list of child elements, you can use the insertBefore method. When you use this method, you supply two arguments: a Node object that represents the element that you want to insert, and a Node object that represents the reference node. Then, this method will add the new node before the reference node. If you supply a null value for the second argument, though, this method will add the element to the end of the list of child elements, just as it would if you used the appendChild method.

To update an element, you can use the replaceChild method. To do that, you create the new Element object and specify the element to be replaced. If you only want to update the value of a text node, though, you can use the setNodeValue method to update the value that's stored in the element instead of creating a new element and replacing the old element with the new one.

To delete an element, you call the removeChild method from the parent node and specify the element that you want to delete as the argument. However, before you delete a node, you usually need to search through the DOM tree to find the node that you want to delete. For example, to delete a User element, your code may need to first find the User element that has a specific emailAddress.

Code that appends an element after all other child nodes

```
root.appendChild(userElement);
```

Code that inserts an element before another child node

```
root.insertBefore(userElement1, userElement2);
```

Code that updates an element

```
root.replaceChild(userElement1, userElement2);
```

Code that removes an element

```
root.removeChild(userElement);
```

Methods of the Node interface for adding, updating, and deleting elements

appendChild(Node child)

Inserts the new node at the end of any existing child nodes.

insertBefore(Node newChild, Node refChild)

Inserts the new node before the reference node. If you code a null value for the reference node, this method inserts the new child at the end of any existing child nodes.

replaceChild(Node newChild, Node oldChild)

Replaces the specified child node with a new child node.

removeChild(Node child)

Removes the specified child node.

Description

- The appendChild, insertBefore, removeChild, and replaceChild methods throw a DOMException.
- If you want to modify one or more values stored in a node instead of replacing the entire node, you can use the setAttribute and setNodeValue methods described in figure 16-9.

Figure 16-13   How to add, update, and delete nodes

The Email List application

Now that know the details for writing Java code that uses DOM to work with an XML document, you're ready to see how that code fits within an application. That's why this topic presents a class that makes it easier to work with XML, and that's why this topic presents a version of the Email List application that uses an XML file instead of a database or text file.

The code for the XMLUtil class

As you use Java to work with XML, you find yourself repeating the same blocks of code over and over. That's why figure 16-14 presents a helper class named XMLUtil that can make it easier to work with XML. This class contains static methods for reading a DOM tree from a file and writing a DOM tree to file. It also contains methods for getting and setting the values of an element's text node.

To get a Document object from an XML file, this class provides a method name getDocumentFromFile. To use this method, you must supply a String argument that provides the filename and location of the XML document. In addition, you must handle the three exceptions that are thrown by this code.

To get the value of an element's text node, you can use the getTextNodeValue method of this utility class. To use this method, you must supply the parent element and the tag name of the element. Then, this method searches for the child element and retrieves the value of the child's text node.

To add an element that contains a child text node to a DOM tree, you can use the addTextNodeElement method. To use this method, you must supply the Document object, the parent element, the name of the element you wish to add, and the value of its text node.

To write a Document object to a file, you can use the writeDocumentToFile method. To use this method, you must supply the name and location of the XML file and the Document object.

The XMLUtil class

```
package util;

import org.xml.sax.*;
import org.w3c.dom.*;
import javax.xml.transform.*;
import javax.xml.transform.dom.*;
import javax.xml.transform.stream.*;
import javax.xml.parsers.*;
import java.io.*;

public class XMLUtil{

    public static Document getDocumentFromFile(String xmlFile)
            throws IOException, ParserConfigurationException, SAXException{
        DocumentBuilderFactory dbf = DocumentBuilderFactory.newInstance();
        DocumentBuilder db = dbf.newDocumentBuilder();
        InputSource in = new InputSource(xmlFile);
        Document doc = db.parse(in);
        return doc;
    }

    public static String getTextNodeValue(Element parent, String tagName){
        NodeList list = parent.getElementsByTagName(tagName);
        Element element = (Element) list.item(0);
        Text text = (Text) element.getFirstChild();
        String value = text.getNodeValue();
        return value;
    }

    public static void addTextNode(Document doc, Element parent,
            String elementName, String elementValue){
        Element element = doc.createElement(elementName);
        parent.appendChild(element);
        Text text = doc.createTextNode(elementName);
        text.setNodeValue(elementValue);
        element.appendChild(text);
    }

    public static void writeDocumentToFile(String xmlFile, Document doc)
            throws TransformerException {
        DOMSource in = new DOMSource(doc);
        File xmlFileObj = new File(xmlFile);
        StreamResult out = new StreamResult(xmlFileObj);
        Transformer transformer =
            TransformerFactory.newInstance().newTransformer();
        transformer.setOutputProperty(OutputKeys.INDENT, "yes");
        transformer.setOutputProperty(
            "{http://xml.apache.org/xslt}indent-amount", "4");
        transformer.transform(in, out);
    }
}
```

Figure 16-14   The code for the XMLUtil class

The code for the UserXML class

Figure 16-15 presents the code for the UserXML class. This class makes it easy to map a User object to a User element that's stored in an XML file. To accomplish this, this class uses methods from the XMLUtil class presented in the last figure.

The first method in this class determines whether an email address already exists in the XML file. This method begins by using the getDocumentFromFile method of the XMLUtil class to return a Document object. Then, it returns a NodeList object that contains all elements named "emailAddress". Next, it loops through each of those element nodes to see if the value of the child text node is equal to the emailAddress argument. If so, this method returns a true value. Otherwise, it returns a false value.

The second method in this class adds a User object to the specified XML file as a User element. This method begins by using the getDocumentFromFile method to return a Document object. Then, it creates a User element that contains the data that's stored in the User object, and it adds that element to the DOM tree. To accomplish this, this method uses the addTextNode method of the XMLUtil class. Last, this method uses the writeDocumentToFile method of the XMLUtil class to write the DOM tree to the specified XML file.

The UserXML class that's on the CD that comes with this book contains additional methods. In particular, it contains methods that allow you to delete a User element from an XML file, to update a User element in an XML file, and to return a vector that contains one User object for each User element within an XML file. If you want to see how these methods work, you can open the code for this class in a text editor.

The UserXML class

```
package data;

import org.xml.sax.*;
import org.w3c.dom.*;
import javax.xml.transform.*;
import javax.xml.transform.dom.*;
import javax.xml.transform.stream.*;
import javax.xml.parsers.*;
import java.io.*;
import java.util.Vector;
import business.User;
import util.XMLUtil;

public class UserXML{

    public synchronized static boolean isMatch(String emailAddress,
        String xmlFile) throws IOException, ParserConfigurationException,
        SAXException {

        Document doc = XMLUtil.getDocumentFromFile(xmlFile);

        NodeList emailElements = doc.getElementsByTagName("emailAddress");
        for (int i = 0; i < emailElements.getLength(); i++){
            Text textNode = (Text) emailElements.item(i).getFirstChild();
            if (textNode.getNodeValue().equalsIgnoreCase(emailAddress)){
                return true;
            }
        }
        return false;
    }

    public synchronized static void addRecord(User user, String xmlFile)
        throws IOException, SAXException, ParserConfigurationException,
        TransformerException {

        Document doc = XMLUtil.getDocumentFromFile(xmlFile);

        Element userElement = doc.createElement("User");
        userElement.setAttribute("contact", "yes");
        XMLUtil.addTextNode(
            doc, userElement, "firstName", user.getFirstName());
        XMLUtil.addTextNode(
            doc, userElement, "lastName", user.getLastName());
        XMLUtil.addTextNode(
            doc, userElement, "emailAddress", user.getEmailAddress());
        Element root = doc.getDocumentElement();
        root.appendChild(userElement);

        XMLUtil.writeDocumentToFile(xmlFile, doc);
    }

    // other methods that delete and update records

}
```

Figure 16-15   The code for the UserXML class

The code for the EmailServlet class

Figure 16-16 presents the code for the doGet method of the EmailServlet class. The first highlighted statement in this servlet uses the isMatch method of the UserXML class to determine whether the email address for the current user already exists in the XML file. If it doesn't, the second highlighted statement uses the addRecord method of the UserXML file to add the user's data to the XML file.

If you look at the previous figure, you can see that the isMatch method throws three exceptions and the addRecord method throws four exceptions. To catch all of these exceptions, this servlet uses a single catch block that catches the Exception object. This works because all exceptions extend the Exception class. However, if you want to take different actions depending on the type of exception, you can code multiple catch blocks to catch the specific exceptions that are thrown by the isMatch and addRecord methods.

At this point, you may want to consider whether storing user data in an XML file is a good use of XML. If you look back to figure 16-1, you can see that storing the data for three records requires more than twice as many characters in an XML file as it does in a text file and that ratio holds true no matter how many records are stored in the file. Worse, when you use the DOM methods, you have to read the entire file into a DOM tree before you can read any of the records and you have to write the entire DOM tree back to the file after you update the records. Imagine, then, how inefficient the use of an XML file that contains 10,000 records is. In contrast, you can use the SQL statements of a database to read and update just one record at a time.

With that in mind, you can see why XML is more commonly used for control files and data transfer than it is for business data. But no matter what the use is, the techniques that are illustrated by this Email List application still apply.

The doGet method of the EmailServlet class

```
public void doGet(HttpServletRequest request,
                  HttpServletResponse response)
                  throws IOException, ServletException{

    String file = "../webapps/murach/WEB-INF/etc/users.xml";

    String firstName = request.getParameter("firstName");
    String lastName = request.getParameter("lastName");
    String emailAddress = request.getParameter("emailAddress");
    User user = new User(firstName, lastName, emailAddress);

    HttpSession session = request.getSession();
    session.setAttribute("user", user);

    String message = "";
    try{
        //check whether the email address already exist
        boolean emailExists = UserXML.isMatch(emailAddress, file);
        if (emailExists){
            message = "This email address already exists. <br>"
                    + "Please enter another email address.";
            session.setAttribute("message", message);
            RequestDispatcher dispatcher =
                getServletContext().getRequestDispatcher(
                    "/email16/join_email_list.jsp");
            dispatcher.forward(request, response);
        }
        else{
            UserXML.addRecord(user, file);
            session.setAttribute("message", "");
            RequestDispatcher dispatcher =
                    getServletContext().getRequestDispatcher(
                        "/email16/show_email_entry.jsp");
            dispatcher.forward(request, response);
        }
    }
    catch(Exception e){
        message = "EmailServlet Exception: " + e;
        session.setAttribute("message", message);
        RequestDispatcher dispatcher =
            getServletContext().getRequestDispatcher(
                "/email16/join_email_list.jsp");
        dispatcher.forward(request, response);
    }
}
```

Figure 16-16   The code for the EmailServlet class

How to return an XML document via HTTP

The Email List application that you just saw writes an XML document to a file that's stored in the murach\WEB-INF\etc directory. Since this directory isn't web accessible, you can't use an HTTP URL to view this document in a web browser. To provide for that, though, you can code a servlet like the one that's described next.

The code for the XMLServlet class

Figure 16-17 shows the code for the XMLServlet class. Here, the doGet method begins by using the setContentType method of the response object to set the content type to "text/xml". Next, this method creates an input stream from the XML file, and it gets an output stream from the response object. Then, it uses a while loop to send each byte of data stored in the XML file to the browser.

The XML document displayed in a browser

The browser in this figure displays the XML document that's contained in the file sent by the XMLServlet class. This shows that a browser is able to read the XML tags and display an XML document in a structured format that's easy to read. When you view an XML document in a browser, you can click on the minus sign (-) to the left of an element to collapse the element. Then, you can click on the plus sign (+) to the right of an element to expand the element.

The code for the XMLServlet class

```
package email16;

import java.io.*;
import javax.servlet.*;
import javax.servlet.http.*;

public class XMLServlet extends HttpServlet{

    public void doGet(HttpServletRequest request,
                      HttpServletResponse response)
                      throws IOException, ServletException{

        response.setContentType("text/xml");

        File file = new File("../webapps/murach/WEB-INF/etc/users.xml");
        FileInputStream in = new FileInputStream(file);
        PrintWriter out = response.getWriter();

        int i;
        while ((i = in.read()) != -1)
            out.write(i);
        in.close();
    }
}
```

The XML file displayed in a browser

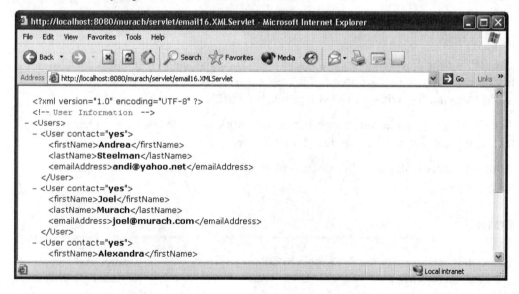

Description

- To use HTTP to return an XML document to a browser, you must use the setContentType method of the response object to set the content type to "text/xml".

- When you view an XML document in the Internet Explorer, you can collapse an element by clicking on its minus sign (-) and expand an element by clicking on its plus sign (+).

Figure 16-17   How to return an XML document via HTTP

Perspective

In this chapter, you learned the basic concepts and terms for working with an XML file. You also learned some specific skills for using Java to work with DOM trees that represent XML documents. Keep in mind, though, that there's more to XML than just that, including other XML APIs like SAX. To find out more, you can go to *www.xml.org* and *www.java.sun.com*.

Summary

- An *XML document* uses *XML tags* to define its *elements* in a structure that consists of a *root element*, *parent elements*, and *child elements*.

- XML documents are commonly used for control files and for transferring data from one system to another. They can also be used for storing limited amounts of business data.

- Data in an XML document can be stored as the *content* of an element or as an *attribute* of an element.

- A *Document Type Definition (DTD)* is a *schema* that defines the structure of an XML document. This schema can be enforced when a document is read or written.

- The *Simple API for XML (SAX)* can be used for reading an XML document, one line at a time.

- The API for the *Document Object Model (DOM)* can be used for creating a DOM tree, for working with the nodes of the tree, for reading an XML document into a DOM tree, and for writing a DOM tree into an XML file.

- The DOM API provides interfaces that let you work with the document, element, text, comment, and attribute nodes of a DOM tree.

- A browser can display an XML document in a form that's easy to read, expand, and collapse.

Terms

Extensible Markup Language (XML)	root element	Document Object Model (DOM)
XML document	XML attribute	DOM tree
XML tag	schema language	node
XML file	schema	parent node
XML declaration	Document Type Definition (DTD)	child node
XML comment	XML Schema Definition (XSD)	sibling node
XML element	XML parser	node type
element content	Simple API for XML (SAX)	transform
child element		
parent element		

Objectives

- Use servlets to work with XML files whenever you need to do that.
- Describe two common types of uses for XML files.
- Distinguish between storing data in an attribute and storing data as content for an element.
- In general terms, describe the use of a Document Type Definition.
- In general terms, describe the use of the API for the Document Object Model.

Exercise 16-1   Create and view an XML document

In this exercise, you'll create an XML document that represents the data found in the products.txt file located in the murach\WEB-INF\etc directory. For consistency, you should save the data access class in the data package, other Java classes in a package named product16, and the JSPs in a directory named product16.

1. Create a Java application that writes a vector of Product objects to an XML file. Each Product element should contain an attribute named code and two child elements named description and price.
2. View the XML file in a web browser.
3. Create a JSP named products that reads the Product XML file and displays its information in an HTML table. To do this, you should create a data access class named ProductXML that contains a method that returns a vector of Product objects based on the data in the Product XML file.

Exercise 16-2   Modify an XML document

In this exercise, you'll create a JSP and servlet that lets you add elements to the Product XML file that you created in exercise 16-1.

1. Modify the ProductXML class that you created in exercise 16-1 so it contains a method that adds a Product object to the Product XML file.
2. Create a JSP named add_product that allows a user to add a product to the Product XML file. For this to work, this JSP should have at least three text input fields for code, description, and price, and one submit button that calls the ProductServlet class.
3. Write a servlet named ProductServlet that retrieves the request parameters from the add_product JSP, creates a Product object, adds the Product to the Product XML file, and calls another JSP to display the data.

17

An introduction to Enterprise JavaBeans

So far, this book has shown you how to build web applications with servlets, JSPs, and JavaBeans. With these components, you can build and maintain web applications for most small- to medium-sized web sites.

For large web sites, though, some companies use Enterprise JavaBeans instead of JavaBeans for the business logic and data access layers of the applications. Since this has a significant affect on web development, this chapter introduces you to Enterprise JavaBeans. Then, you can decide whether they're right for your applications and whether you need to learn more about them.

How Enterprise JavaBeans work 504
The components of a web application that uses EJBs 504
What EJBs can provide 506
The pros and cons of EJBs 506
Typical EJB developer roles 506

How to implement EJBs 510
How to implement an entity bean 510
How to code the remote and home interfaces 512
How to code the bean implementation class 514
How to implement BMP 516
How to access an EJB in an application 518

Perspective 520

How Enterprise JavaBeans work

Enterprise JavaBeans, or *EJBs*, are server-side components that contain the code for the business logic and data access layers of an application. To use an EJB, your application must use a type of *application server* known as an *EJB server*, or *EJB container*.

The components of a web application that uses EJBs

Figure 17-1 shows how an EJB server can extend the web application architecture that you've used throughout the rest of this book. In this diagram, the EJB container sits between the servlet and JSP engine and the database server. In a web application, the EJB server provides services to EJBs that can be accessed by the servlets and JSPs.

When you use EJBs in a web application, the browser can request a servlet or JSP that calls a method from an EJB. Then, the EJB server presents the EJB to the servlet so it can access the data and code that's stored in the EJB. In some cases, the EJB server may communicate with a third-party database server such as MySQL or Oracle. In other cases, the EJB server may use an internal database.

The components of a web application that uses EJBs

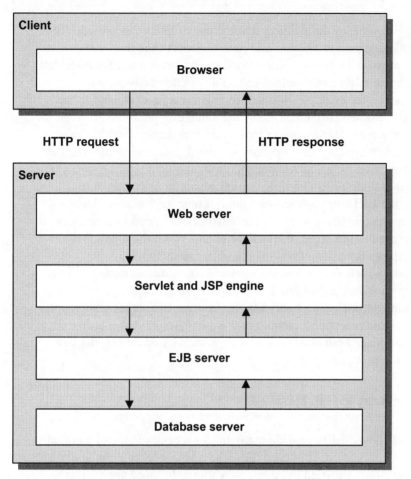

Description

- An *Enterprise JavaBean*, or *EJB*, is a server-side component that contains the code for the business logic and data access layers of an application.

- An *EJB server*, or *EJB container*, is an *application server* that presents EJBs to the rest of the application. In addition, an EJB server automatically provides many services for EJBs. This can improve the performance of an application.

- Some EJB servers have a built-in mechanism for providing persistence while other EJB servers can be configured to work with a database management system like MySQL or Oracle.

- JBoss is an open-source, industry-leading EJB container that's distributed for free. For more information about this EJB container, check *www.jboss.org*.

- The *Java 2 Platform, Enterprise Edition*, or *J2EE*, provides the classes necessary for working with EJBs. For more information about these classes, check *www.java.sun.com*.

Figure 17-1   The components of a web application that uses EJBs

What EJBs can provide

Figure 17-2 lists some of the features that the use of EJBs can provide. To start, it can provide connection pooling and persistence. Although you've already learned how to provide connection pooling and persistence for a servlet/ JSP application, using EJBs can standardize and automate persistence and connection pooling. If, for example, you use an EJB for a Product object, the EJB container can automatically take care of the database operations for that object. It can insert a new Product object into a row in a database table, create a Product object from an existing row, update that row if you modify the Product object, and remove that row if you remove the Product object.

EJBs can also provide *object pooling*, which is similar to connection pooling. To start, the EJB container keeps a pool of objects available. Then, when a client requests an object, the EJB container doesn't need to create one; it just passes a reference to the object back to the client. When the client is done using the object, the EJB container returns the object to the pool.

Last, EJBs can provide for the use of *transactions*. A transaction is a group of operations that must succeed or fail as a group. If, for example, you want to subtract an amount from one object and add that amount to another object, you don't want to complete one operation but not the other. To prevent that from happening, you can place both operations within a transaction and let the EJB container handle the processing.

The pros and cons of EJBs

As figure 17-2 shows, EJBs provide many useful services that can automate and standardize an application. However, they also add a level of complexity to an application that's only justified in large applications. In those applications, the cost of configuring the EJB container and developing the EJBs is offset by the improvements in application development, system performance, and administration.

Typical EJB developer roles

One of the advantages of EJB development is that it allows developers to specialize as summarized in this figure. To start, the *EJB container provider* is the organization or vendor who writes the code for the EJB container. For example, the JBoss group is an EJB container provider.

To develop the web applications that use the EJB container, programmers called *bean developers* develop the beans that are used by the web applications. This is a difficult phase of application development. In contrast, the *application assemblers* are the programmers who assemble the beans created by other programmers as they create the applications. This is made easier by the use of the EJBs. Then, after an application has been deployed, a *system administrator* monitors and maintains it.

What EJBs can provide

- **Connection pooling.** An EJB container can create a connection pool that provides access to your database.
- **Persistence.** An EJB container can automatically handle saving and retrieving enterprise beans from a database.
- **Object pooling.** An EJB container can create a pool of EJBs that can be used by your application.
- **Transactions.** An EJB container can manage transactions.

The pros of EJBs

- Once the EJB container is configured properly, it provides many services that can be used by the EJBs.
- Once the EJBs have been developed, the application programming is easier than it is in an equivalent servlet/JSP application.
- Once you deploy an EJB application, it may be easier to administer than an equivalent servlet/JSP application.
- EJBs are also available from third-party vendors. This can help you develop applications more rapidly.
- When you use EJBs, your programmers can specialize in certain aspects of application development.

The cons of EJBs

- EJB applications are significantly more difficult to configure and develop than the equivalent servlet/JSP applications.

Typical EJB developer roles

- **EJB container provider.** The organization or vendor that provides the EJB server and container.
- **Bean developer.** A programmer who writes EJBs. For a large application, there may be several enterprise bean developers.
- **Application assembler.** A programmer who assembles the enterprise beans written by in-house or third party bean developers to create an application.
- **System administrator.** The administrator who monitors and maintains an EJB application after it has been deployed.

Figure 17-2   The pros and cons of EJBs

Two types of entity EJBs

Figure 17-3 describes the two types of EJBs that are commonly used. *Session beans* are used to implement the business logic of the application. Since these beans exist as long as a client has a session with the server, they're similar in some ways to the session objects that are used by servlets and JSPs. In contrast, *entity beans* are used to implement the data access layer of the application. Typically, an entity bean is an object that represents the data that's stored in one row of a table.

This figure also describes the two types of session beans. A *stateless session bean* isn't associated with a specific client. As a result, if the EJB container creates a pool of stateless beans, any client can use any instance of the bean. On the other hand, a *stateful session bean* maintains state with a specific client. As a result, if the EJB container creates a pool of stateful beans, the EJB container must return the appropriate bean to the client when the client requests the bean.

Last, this figure describes two types of persistence that can be used by entity beans. If you use *bean-managed persistence*, or *BMP*, you must write SQL code within the entity bean to handle all of the database operations. That way, you can save the data for each bean in the database. Then, you can find the bean in the database, you can update the bean in the database, you can delete the bean from the database, and so on. Although it can be tedious to write the SQL code for these operations, this approach gives you complete control over the database operations.

If you use *container-managed persistence*, or *CMP*, the EJB container automatically takes care of all of the database operations for the bean. Although this saves you the trouble of having to write and maintain the SQL code, it requires more setup and reduces the amount of control you have over the database operations. In some cases, though, you can use *EJB Query Language*, or *EJB QL*, to gain control over some of these database operations.

Two types of EJBs

- **Session beans.** Session beans implement the business logic of the application. These beans exist for a client as long as the client has an active session.

- **Entity beans.** Entity beans implement the data access layer of an application.

Two types of session beans

- **Stateless session beans.** The EJB container doesn't associate a stateless bean with a specific client. As a result, any client can call any instance of this type of bean.

- **Stateful session beans**. The EJB container associates a stateful bean with a specific client. This is similar to how servlets and JSPs associate a session object with a specific client.

Two types of persistence for entity beans

- **Bean-managed persistence (BMP)**. To use BMP, each bean must contain SQL code for creating, finding, storing, and removing itself from the database.

- **Container-managed persistence (CMP)**. When you use CMP, the EJB container can automatically create, find, store, and remove each bean from the database.

Figure 17-3   Session and entity beans

How to implement EJBs

Although you've now been introduced to the concepts and terms for EJBs, it can be difficult to understand how they work and why they're beneficial without seeing a code example. That's why this topic presents the code for a User entity bean that can be used in an application similar to the Email List application that you've seen throughout this book.

How to implement an entity bean

Figure 17-4 shows how to implement an EJB. To start, you need to create a table in the database that represents all the data in the bean. Typically, the properties of the bean match the data that's stored in one row of a table. For the User bean, that's the last name, first name, and email address.

Then, to create an EJB, you need to code at least two interfaces and one bean class. First, you must code a *remote interface* that extends the EJBObject interface. For the user entity bean, this is an interface named User. Second, you must code a *home interface* that extends the EJBHome interface. For the user entity bean, this is an interface named UserHome. And finally, you must code a *bean implementation class* that implements either the SessionBean or EntityBean class. For the user bean, which is an entity bean, this is a class named UserBean that implements the EntityBean class.

So how do two interfaces and a class communicate with the EJB container and the client? To do that, you must create an XML file known as a *deployment descriptor* that tells the EJB container about the two interfaces and the class for the bean. Then, the EJB container can present the bean to the client. As you'll see in figure 17-8, the client accesses beans through references of the remote and home interfaces, rather than through the bean class.

The components of a User entity bean

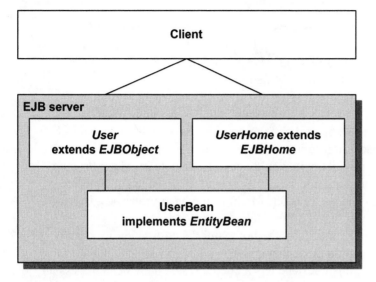

How to implement a User entity bean

1. Create a table in the database that corresponds to the data in the entity bean.
2. Code the remote interface (User) that defines the business methods of the bean.
3. Code the home interface (UserHome) that defines the methods for creating, locating, and destroying the bean.
4. Code the entity bean implementation class (UserBean).
5. Package the interfaces and class in a JAR file by using a deployment descriptor that comes with the EJB container.

Description

- An Enterprise JavaBean is composed of one class and two interfaces. The *remote interface* extends the EJBObject interface. The *home interface* extends the EJBHome interface. And the *bean class* implements the SessionBean or EntityBean interface.
- An XML file known as the *deployment descriptor* lets the EJB container communicate with the client, the bean, and the two interfaces for the bean.
- The EJBHome and EJBObject interfaces and the SessionBean and EntityBean classes are stored in the javax.ejb package.

Figure 17-4   How to implement an entity bean

How to code the remote and home interfaces

As you just learned, every EJB consists of a remote interface and a home interface. Now, in figure 17-5, you'll learn how to code these interfaces for the User entity bean. As you read this figure, keep in mind that the client accesses the bean solely through the methods defined in these interfaces.

Since the remote interface is responsible for declaring methods that perform the business logic of the bean, it's a common practice to name the interface as you would name a business object. For example, the remote interface in this figure is named User because it represents a user. Similarly, if you were creating a bean that represents a product, you would name the remote interface Product.

When you code the remote interface, you extend the EJBObject interface. Then, you define the set and get methods for all of the bean properties. For each of these methods, you must throw a RemoteException.

In contrast to the remote interface, the home interface for an entity bean is responsible for defining the methods that create, locate, and destroy bean instances. In other words, this interface lets a client create a new bean, access an existing bean, or destroy a bean.

When you code the home interface, you extend the EJBHome interface. Then, you define zero or more create methods that instantiate a new bean. Typically, one of these create methods accepts the property that's used as the primary key in the database table. In this example, the primary key in the User table is the email address. As a result, the create method in this figure accepts an email address as a parameter. Since each create method must return the bean's remote interface type, this method returns a User object. When you define a create method, you must throw a RemoteException and a CreateException.

To allow a client to access existing beans, you define find methods in the home interface that return the remote interface type. Typically, one of the find methods is named findByPrimaryKey that accepts the primary key value as a parameter. You can also define find methods that search for existing beans by other properties. For example, you can define a method named findByLastName that accepts the lastName parameter. When you define a find method, you must throw a RemoteException and a FinderException.

To allow a client to destroy a bean, you can use any of the remove methods defined in the EJBHome interface. However, if you want some other processing to occur before a bean is destroyed, you can override a remove method in the home interface.

The remote interface for the User bean

```
import javax.ejb.*;
import java.rmi.RemoteException;

public interface User extends EJBObject {

    public String getFirstName() throws RemoteException;
    public void setFirstName(String first) throws RemoteException;

    public String getLastName() throws RemoteException;
    public void setLastName(String last) throws RemoteException;

    public String getEmailAddress() throws RemoteException;
    public void setEmailAddress(String email) throws RemoteException;
}
```

The home interface for the User bean

```
import javax.ejb.*;
import java.rmi.RemoteException;

public interface UserHome extends EJBHome {

    public User create(String emailAddress)
                       throws RemoteException, CreateException;

    public User findByPrimaryKey(String emailAddress)
                                 throws RemoteException, FinderException;
}
```

Description

- To create a remote interface for a bean, you extend the EJBObject interface. Then, you define the set and get methods for the bean.

- It's a common coding practice to name the remote interface as you would name the object in an application.

- To create the home interface for a bean, you extend the EJBHome interface. Then, you define methods that create, locate, and destroy beans.

- The home interface can define create methods that create a new entity bean. Each create method returns the remote interface data type.

- The home interface can define find methods that locate a specific instance of a bean. Each find method returns the remote interface data type.

- Every home interface inherits a set of remove methods from the EJBHome interface that destroy a bean instance.

Figure 17-5   How to code the remote and home interfaces

How to code the bean implementation class

Once you code the remote and home interfaces, you can code the bean implementation class as shown in figure 17-6. To start, the bean class for an entity bean implements the EntityBean interface. Therefore, you must code all methods that are defined in this interface. In addition, you should code all methods defined in the remote interface.

Note, however, that the bean class doesn't implement this interface or the home interface. In fact, it's recommended that you don't implement these interfaces since the parent interfaces define other methods that are implemented automatically by the EJB container.

As this figure shows, an entity bean class should declare, set, and get the bean properties. For example, the UserBean class declares the first name, last name, and email address instance variables. After that, the class contains the set and get methods for each of these variables as defined in the remote interface.

For each create method defined in the home interface, the bean implementation class must contain corresponding ejbCreate and ejbPostCreate methods. For example, the bean class in this figure contains an ejbCreate method that accepts the email address parameter. If you compare this declaration to the create method in the home interface, you'll see that both accept the same type and number of parameters and return the same type. On the other hand, the ejbPostCreate method accepts the same parameter but has no return type.

When a create method is invoked in the home interface, the EJB container calls the corresponding ebjCreate and ejbPostCreate methods. The ejbCreate method is used to initialize the bean before the record is inserted in the database. In this figure, the ejbCreate method initializes the emailAddress property and returns null since this class is using CMP. At this point, the EJB exists and can be accessed by the client. The ejbPostCreate method can be used to perform any processing after the bean is created but before it's accessed by a client. For simple beans, though, this method will be empty.

The last seven methods in the class are *callback methods* that are defined in the EntityBean interface. These methods are used by the container to notify the bean class when certain events take place. To learn more about events, you can use the EntityContext object that's defined as a *transient* instance variable, which means it isn't included in the persistent state of the bean. Although this object isn't used in this class, you'll see how it can be used in the next figure.

The ejbLoad and ejbStore methods are invoked by the container when the entity bean is being synchronized with the database. First, the ejbLoad method is called after the container has refreshed all bean data with data stored in the database. Second, the ejbStore method is called before the container writes the bean data to the database.

If you want processing performed before a bean is associated with a remote reference, you can provide code in the ejbActivate method. And if you want processing performed before a bean is dereferenced from a remote interface, you can provide code in the ejbPassivate method.

Note that the find methods in the home interface aren't coded in this class. That's because the container implements them automatically when CMP is used.

The User bean class

```
import javax.ejb.*;
import java.rmi.RemoteException;

public class UserBean implements EntityBean {
    //variable that holds information about the bean context
    transient private EntityContext ejbContext;

    public String firstName;
    public String lastName;
    public String emailAddress;

    //business methods defined in the remote interface
    public String getFirstName() { return firstName; }
    public void setFirstName(String first) { firstName = first; }

    public String getLastName() { return lastName; }
    public void setLastName(String last) { lastName = last; }

    public String getEmailAddress() { return emailAddress; }
    public void setEmailAddress(String email) { emailAddress = email; }

    public User ejbCreate(String email) {
        emailAddress = email;
        return null;
    }

    public void ejbPostCreate(String email) { }

    //callback methods defined in the EntityBean interface
    public void setEntityContext(EntityContext ctx) { ejbContext = ctx; }
    public void unsetEntityContext() { ejbContext = null; }
    public void ejbActivate() {}
    public void ejbPassivate() {}
    public void ejbLoad() {}
    public void ejbStore() {}
    public void ejbRemove() {}
}
```

Description

- To code an entity bean class, you implement the EntityBean interface. In addition to the methods defined in the EntityBean interface, the bean class must implement all methods defined in the remote interface.

- The bean implementation class must contain an ejbCreate method for each create method defined in the home interface. Each ebjCreate method should contain the same number and type of parameters as the corresponding create method.

- To learn about the context of the bean, such as transaction status or remote references, you can use the EntityContext object. Since it's declared as *transient*, this variable isn't part of the persistent state of the bean.

- The code shown above uses CMP. Therefore, all data access logic is handled by the EJB container so the callback methods for the EntityBean interface don't have to provide that logic.

Figure 17-6   How to code the bean implementation class

How to implement BMP

In the last figure, you learned how to code a bean class that uses container-managed persistence. Now, figure 17-7 shows how to modify that class so that it uses bean-managed persistence. Although this bean class is now responsible for accessing the database, the container is still responsible for calling the methods in the bean class whenever that's appropriate.

To implement BMP, you code the first five methods shown in this figure to access the database. In the ejbCreate method, you must provide code that writes a new record to the database. In the case of the User bean, the ejbCreate method only has access to the primary key, which is the email address. Therefore, this method must create a record in the database table that consists of the primary key value. To get the primary key, the ejbCreate method can use the getPrimaryKey method of the EntityContext object as shown in the ejbLoad method in this figure.

With BMP, the ejbLoad method contains code that reads data from the database and stores it in the bean instance variables, the ejbStore method contains code that writes the bean to the database, and the ejbRemove method contains code that deletes the bean from the database. Although you must provide the database access logic for these operations, the EJB container is responsible for calling these methods. Usually, though, the ejbLoad method is called before a business method is invoked on the bean, the ejbStore method is called before the container commits all changes to the database, and the ejbRemove method is called when a bean is destroyed.

For each find method defined in the home interface, a bean class that implements BMP must contain a corresponding ejbFind method. Each ejbFind method should read the appropriate record from the database and return the primary key value for that record. For example, the ejbFindByPrimaryKey method in this figure should perform a SELECT statement on the User table with a WHERE clause that matches the email address parameter. Then, it should return the value of the primary key for that record. In this case, the return value should be the same value as the value sent in or, if the record doesn't exist, an ObjectNotFoundException should be thrown. On the other hand, an ejbFindByLastName method should receive a parameter that contains the last name, and it should return the email address value.

Finally, since all methods that access the database require a database connection, most bean classes that implement BMP contain a getConnection method that obtains a database connection. With CMP, of course, this is handled automatically.

Now, if you now look more closely at the ejbLoad method in this figure, you can see how it reads a record from the User table. To do that, it needs to provide an email address in the WHERE clause, but this method doesn't accept any parameters. That's why it uses the EntityContext object to obtain the primary key value. Once it has that value, it can execute the SELECT statement and set the instance variables of the bean to the values returned in the result set.

Methods used in bean-managed persistence

```
public void ejbCreate() {
    // writes a new record to the database
}
public void ejbLoad() {
    // reads data from the database
}
public void ejbStore() {
    // writes data to the database
}
public void ejbRemove() {
    // deletes data from the database
}
public String ejbFindByPrimaryKey(String primaryKey)
                                throws ObjectNotFoundException{
    //locates a record in the database and returns the primary key
}
private Connection getConnection() {
    //a helper method that returns a connection object
}
```

An example of an ejbLoad method for BMP

```
public void ejbLoad()
    Connection connection;
    try {
        String primaryKey = (String)ejbContext.getPrimaryKey();
        connection = this.getConnection();
        Statement statement =
            connection.createStatement("SELECT * FROM User " +
                "WHERE emailAddress = " + primaryKey);
        ResultSet result = statement.executeQuery();
        if (result.next()) {
            //set instance variables
            firstName = result.getString("FirstName");
            lastName = result.getString("LastName");
            emailAddress = result.getString("EmailAddress");
        }
    }
    catch (SQLException sqle) {
        throw new EJBException(sqle);
    }
    finally {
        if (connection != null)
            connection.close();
    }
}
```

Description

- To implement bean-managed persistence, the bean class must code the methods presented above so that they perform the database access logic.

- For each find method defined in the home interface, you must code an ejbFind method in the bean class that locates the bean in the database and returns the primary key.

- Since many of these methods don't accept or return data types, you must use the EntityContext object to obtain the primary key for the bean.

Figure 17-7   How to implement BMP

How to access an EJB in an application

Once the EJBs have been implemented, the JSPs and servlets of an application can use the beans as shown in figure 17-8. To create new beans, access existing beans, or destroy beans, you use a reference to the home interface. Then, since the methods in the home interface return remote interface data types, you use the methods of the remote interface to access and manipulate bean properties.

The first example in this figure shows how to create an EJB. To do this, you obtain a reference to the home interface, which is UserHome for a User bean. Since obtaining this reference requires networking topics that are beyond the scope of this book, however, the method that obtains this reference isn't presented here.

After you obtain the home interface reference, you can obtain a remote interface reference by invoking a create or find method. For instance, the first example in this figure uses the create method to obtain a new User bean. It then invokes two business methods that are defined in the remote interface for that bean.

To access existing beans, you can use a find method of the home interface as shown in the second example. Then, you can use the remote interface to manipulate the properties of that bean.

Since the examples in this figure use EJBs, you don't have to worry about coding database classes. This is all done for you behind the scenes. As you can see, this can make your Java applications easier to code, which is one of the major benefits that you get from using EJBs.

Code that creates an EJB

```
UserHome home = //get reference to home interface
User user = home.create("andi@yahoo.com");
user.setFirstName("Andrea");
user.setLastName("Steelman");
```

Code that accesses an existing EJB

```
User previousUser = home.findByPrimaryKey("joel@murach.com");
String lastName = previousUser.getLastName();
```

Description

- To use an EJB in an application, you must obtain a reference to the home interface. To do this, you use networking methods that aren't presented in this book.

- To create a new bean, you use one of the create methods defined in the home interface to return an object of the remote interface type.

- To access an existing bean, you use one of the find methods defined in the home interface to return an object of the remote interface type.

- With EJBs, you can create and manipulate the beans without worrying about updating the database. This is automatically done for you.

Figure 17-8 How to access an EJB in an application

Perspective

The primary goal of this chapter has been to introduce you to EJBs so you have a general idea of how they work, what benefits they provide, and how you code them. Now, if you want to learn more about using EJBs, you can start with the tutorials that are available from the Java web site (*www. java.sun.com*).

Summary

- *Enterprise JavaBeans* (or *EJBs*) are server-side components that contain the code for the business logic and data access layers of an application. This requires the classes in the *Java 2 Platform, Enterprise Edition* (or *J2EE*).

- An *EJB server* (or *EJB container*) presents the EJBs to the rest of the application. It also provides services like connection and object pooling.

- When you use *container-managed persistence* (*CMP*) with *entity beans*, the EJB container creates, finds, stores, and removes each bean in the database.

- When you use *bean-managed persistence* (*BMP*), each bean class must provide SQL statements that create and manage the beans in the database.

- To implement an entity bean, you create a *remote interface*, a *home interface*, and a *bean implementation class*. You also create a *deployment descriptor* that lets the EJB container use the bean and the two interfaces.

- To use an EJB, you get a reference to the home interface. Then, you use a find or create method in the home interface to return an object of the remote interface type and you use its methods to work with the bean data.

Terms

Enterprise JavaBean (EJB)	session bean
EJB server	entity bean
EJB container	bean-managed persistence (BMP)
Java 2 Platform, Enterprise Edition (J2EE)	container-managed persistence (CMP)
object pooling	home interface
transaction	remote interface
EJB container provider	bean implementation class
bean developer	deployment descriptor
application assembler	callback method
system administrator	transient

Objectives

- Describe the benefits that you get from using EJBs.

- Describe the difficulties that are associated with using EJBs.

Section 5

The Music Store web site

One of the best ways to improve your web programming skills is to study web sites and applications that have been developed by others. That's why the CD that comes with this book includes a complete Music Store web site. And that's why this section presents some of the key components of that web site.

In chapter 18, you'll be introduced to this web site and to the components that are common to all three of its applications. In chapters 19 and 20, you'll learn more about the Download and Shopping Cart applications that let users download songs and order albums. And in chapter 21, you'll learn about the Admin application that lets the employees of the company process the orders and prepare reports.

Although the Music Store web site isn't a real web site, it illustrates all of the skills that you need for developing a real site. As you study it, though, you'll see that it requires only the skills that are presented in the first 15 chapters of this book. In other words, this book presents everything you need to know for developing a complete e-commerce web site.

18

An introduction to
the Music Store web site

The Music Store web site is a web site for a fictional record company that
allows a user to navigate between several web applications. This chapter shows
how the Music Store web site works, and it describes the common resources
that are used by its web applications.

The user interface **524**
The Home and Catalog pages 524
The HTML for the home page 524

The structure **528**
The structure of the web site 528
The directory structure 530

The business layer **532**
The class diagrams 532
The Product class 534

The database **536**
The database diagram 536
The SQL script for the database 536

The data layer **540**
The class diagrams 540
The ProductDB class 540

Perspective **544**

The user interface

The Music Store application uses HTML pages and JSPs to present the user interface of the application. Although these pages are more complex than the web pages you've seen so far in this book, they don't use any HTML tags that aren't described in chapter 3.

The Home and Catalog pages

Figure 18-1 shows two HTML pages of the Music Store application: the Home page and the Catalog page. Both of these pages use the same header and footer, and both use left and right columns. The left column contains five links that let the user navigate through the site, and the right column displays a new release. If, for example, the user clicks on the "Browse through our catalog" link in the left column, the Catalog page is displayed in the middle column, but the right column remains the same.

The HTML for the Home page

Figure 18-2 shows the HTML document for the Home page. This code divides the page into a table that contains five main parts: the header row, the left column, the middle column, the right column, and the footer row. Although this is more complex than the code in earlier chapters, it's actually simpler than the code for most real-world applications. Nevertheless, it's common for a real-world application to use nested tables to control the layout of its pages. And that's how the HTML and JSP pages in the Music Store web site are coded.

The Home page

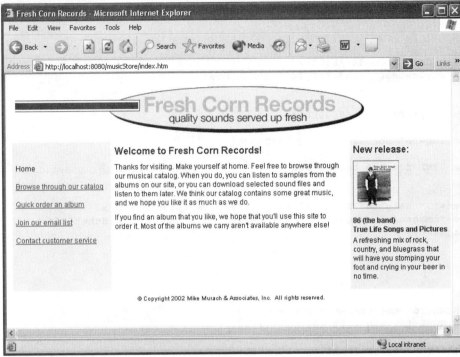

The Catalog page

Figure 18-1   The Home and Catalog pages

The HTML for the Home page

```
<!doctype html public "-//W3C//DTD HTML 4.0 Transitional//EN">

<html>
<head>
    <title>Fresh Corn Records</title>
    <link rel="stylesheet" href="styles/murach.css">
</head>

<body bgcolor="#FFFFFF" text="#000000">

<table cellpadding="5" border="0" width="756">

<!-- start the HTML for the header row -->

  <tr>
    <td colspan="3" height="79" bgcolor="#FFFFFF" cellpadding="0">
      <img src="images/storelogo.gif" alt="Fresh Corn Records" width="606"
          height="79">
    </td>
  </tr>

  <tr>

<!-- end the HTML for the header row -->
<!-- start the HTML for the left column -->

    <td width="160"  valign="top" bgcolor="#FFFFCC">
        <p>
        <br><br>
        Home<br><br>
        <a href="catalog.htm">Browse through our catalog</a><br><br>
        <a href="cart">Quick order an album</a><br><br>
        <a href="email/join_email_list.jsp">Join our email list</a><br><br>
        <a href="customer_service.htm">Contact customer service</a>
        </p>
    </td>

<!-- end the HTML for the left column -->
<!-- start the HTML for the middle column -->

    <td width="404" valign="top">
      <h1>Welcome to Fresh Corn Records!</h1>
      <p>
      Thanks for visiting. Make yourself at home. Feel free to browse through
      our musical catalog. When you do, you can listen to samples from the albums
      on our site, or you can download selected sound files and listen to them
      later. We think our catalog contains some great music, and we hope you
      like it as much as we do.
      </p>
      <p>
      If you find an album that you like, we hope that you'll use this site
      to order it. Most of the albums we carry aren't available anywhere else!
      </p>
    </td>

<!-- end the HTML for the middle column -->
```

Figure 18-2   The HTML for the Home page (part 1 of 2)

The HTML for the Home page (continued)

```
<!-- start the HTML for the right column -->

    <td width="166" valign="top" bgcolor="#FFFFCC">
      <h1>New release:</h1>
      <img src="images/8601_cover_t.jpg" width="80" height="80"><br>
      <p>
      <h4>86 (the band)<br>
      True Life Songs and Pictures</h4>
      <p>A refreshing mix of rock, country, and bluegrass that will have you
         stomping your foot and crying in your beer in no time.</p>
      </p>
    </td>

<!-- end the HTML for the left column -->

  </tr>

<!-- start the HTML for the footer row -->

  <tr>
    <td colspan="3"><center>
      <p class="copyright">
        &copy; Copyright 2002 Mike Murach &amp; Associates, Inc. 
        All rights reserved.</p></center>
    </td>
  </tr>


</table>

</body>
</html>
```

Figure 18-2   The HTML for the Home page (part 2 of 2)

The structure

This topic shows the overall structure of the Music Store web site. That includes the structure of the web site and its applications as well as the structure of the directories used by the web site.

The structure of the web site

Figure 18-3 shows how the pages of the Music Store web site lead to three of the applications for this web site. In particular, it shows how you can start the Download application that's described in chapter 19 and how you can start the Shopping Cart application that's described in chapter 20. In addition, it shows that you can use the "Join our email list" link to start an Email application that's similar to the Email List application in chapter 11. As you will see in chapter 21, the Admin application is an employee application that's started in another way.

The structure

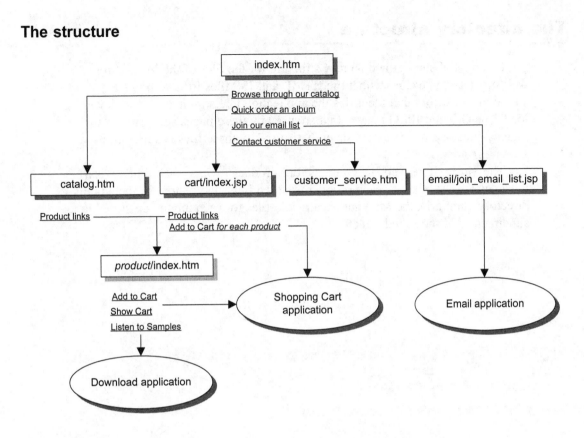

Description

- You can start the Download application by clicking on the Listen to Samples button from any Product page.
- You can start the Shopping Cart application by clicking on the Add to Cart button from any Product page or from the Index page for the Shopping Cart application.
- You can start the Email List application by clicking on the Join Our Email List link from the Home page.

Figure 18-3   The structure of the web site

The directory structure

Figure 18-4 shows the directory structure for the files of the Music Store web site. Here, you can see that the HTML and JSP files for a web site are stored in a directory that identifies the application like admin, cart, and download. The GIF and JPEG images that are used by these pages are stored in the images directory, and the style sheet that's used by these files is stored in the styles directory.

The Music Store web site contains four products, where each product is a music album. As a result, each product is stored in a subdirectory of the albums directory. Similarly, the MP3 and RealAudio files for each album are stored in a subdirectory of the sound directory.

The directory structure

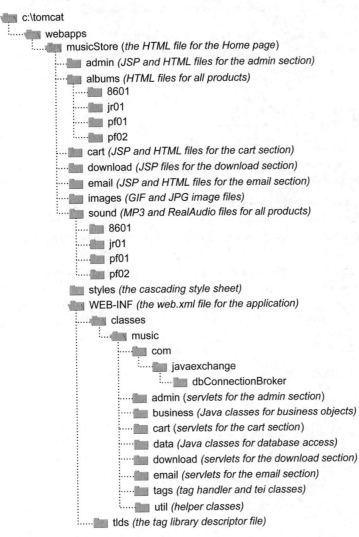

c:\tomcat
  webapps
    musicStore *(the HTML file for the Home page)*
      admin *(JSP and HTML files for the admin section)*
      albums *(HTML files for all products)*
        8601
        jr01
        pf01
        pf02
      cart *(JSP and HTML files for the cart section)*
      download *(JSP files for the download section)*
      email *(JSP and HTML files for the email section)*
      images *(GIF and JPG image files)*
      sound *(MP3 and RealAudio files for all products)*
        8601
        jr01
        pf01
        pf02
      styles *(the cascading style sheet)*
      WEB-INF *(the web.xml file for the application)*
        classes
          music
            com
              javaexchange
                dbConnectionBroker
            admin *(servlets for the admin section)*
            business *(Java classes for business objects)*
            cart *(servlets for the cart section)*
            data *(Java classes for database access)*
            download *(servlets for the download section)*
            email *(servlets for the email section)*
            tags *(tag handler and tei classes)*
            util *(helper classes)*
        tlds *(the tag library descriptor file)*

Description

- The HTML documents and JSPs are stored in a directory that identifies the name of the application.
- The servlet classes are stored in a directory that identifies the name of the application.
- The business classes for all applications are stored in the music.business package.
- The data access classes for all applications are stored in the music.data package.
- The utility classes for all applications are stored in the music.util package.
- The classes that define the custom JSP tags that can be used by all applications are stored in the music.tags package (see chapter 9).
- The web.xml file is stored in the WEB-INF directory.

Figure 18-4   The directory structure of the web site

The business layer

The business objects that make up the business layer of the Music Store web site are stored in the music.business package. All of these business objects are coded as JavaBeans.

The class diagrams

Figure 18-5 shows the class diagrams for the six business objects that can be used by any application in the Music Store web site. These diagrams show that the User class that's used by the Music Store web site is more complex than the User class that was used in chapters 4 through 15. However, the same concepts still apply to this object.

In addition, these class diagrams show that a business object can contain another business object as an instance variable. For example, the Download and Invoice objects can set and get a User object. Similarly, the LineItem object can get and set a Product object. And the Invoice and Cart items can get and set a vector that can contain zero or more LineItem objects.

The business objects

User
-firstName : String
-lastName : String
-emailAddress : String
-companyName : String
-address1 : String
-address2 : String
-city : String
-state : String
-zip : String
-country : String
-creditCardType : String
-creditCardNumber : String
-creditCardExpirationDate : String
+User()
+User(first : String,
last : String, email :
String, company :
String, address1 :
String, address2 : String,
city : String,
state : String,
zip : String,
country : String)
+setFirstName(f : String)
+getFirstName() : String
+setLastName(l : String)
+getLastName() : String
+setEmailAddress(e : String)
+getEmailAddress() : String
+setCompanyName(c : String)
+getCompanyName() : String
+setAddress1(a : String)
+getAddress1() : String
+setAddress2(a : String)
+getAddress2() : String
+setCity(c : String)
+getCity() : String
+setState(s : String)
+getState() : String
+setZip(z : String)
+getZip() : String
+setCountry(c : String)
+getCountry() : String
+setCreditCardType(c : String)
+getCreditCardType() : String
+setCreditCardNumber(n : String)
+getCreditCardNumber() : String
+setCreditCardExpirationDate(d : String)
+getCreditCardExpirationDate() : String

Download
-user : User
-downloadDate: Date
-productCode : String
+Download()
+Download(user : User,
date : Date,
code : String)
+setUser(user : User)
+getUser() : User
+setDownloadDate(date : Date)
+getDownloadDate() : Date
+setProductCode(code : String)
+getProductCode() : String

Invoice
-user : User
-lineItems : Vector
-invoiceDate : Date
-invoiceNumber : int
+Invoice()
+Invoice(user : User,
items : Vector,
date : Date,
num : int)
+setUser(user : User)
+getUser() : User
+setLineItems(items : Vector)
+getLineItems() : Vector
+setInvoiceDate(date : Date)
+getInvoiceDate() : Date
+setInvoiceNumber(num : int)
+getInvoiceNumber() : int

Cart
-items : Vector
+Cart()
+Cart(lineItems : Vector)
+setItems(lineItems: Vector)
+getItems() : Vector
+addItem(item : LineItem)
+removeItem(item : LineItem)

Product
-code : String
-description: String
-price : double
+Product()
+Product(code : String,
description : String,
price : double)
+seCode(c: String)
+getCode() : String
+setDescription(d : String)
+getDescription() : String
+setPrice(p : double)
+getPrice() : double

LineItem
-item : Product
-quantity: int
+LineItem()
+LineItem(product : Product,
quantity: int)
+setProduct(product: Product)
+getProduct() : Product
+setQuantity(qty : int)
+getQuantity() : int
+getTotalPrice() : double

Description

- These business classes are stored in the music.business package. These classes are all coded as JavaBeans (see chapter 8).
- Some of these business objects can get and set other business objects.

Figure 18-5   The class diagrams for the business objects

The Product class

Figure 18-6 shows the code for the Product class that implements the Product diagram in the last figure. Although this class is one of the simpler classes used by the Music Store web site, all of the other classes have the same structure. That is, they all provide private instance variables, get and set methods for each instance variable, and one zero-argument constructor. In other words, they all follow the rules for creating a JavaBean.

If you want to view the code for the other business classes, you can open them in a text editor. They're all stored in the music.business package. In fact, due to the highlighting and color-coding that's provided by a text editor, you may find it easier to read these classes when they're opened in a text editor. If not, you can use your text editor to print the code for the classes that you want to review.

The Product class

```
package music.business;

public class Product{
    private String code;
    private String description;
    private double price;

    public Product(){}

    public Product(String code, String description, double price){
        this.code = code;
        this.description = description;
        this.price = price;
    }

    public void setCode(String code){
        this.code = code;
    }
    public String getCode(){ return code; }

    public void setDescription(String description){
        this.description = description;
    }
    public String getDescription(){ return description; }

    public void setPrice(double price){
        this.price = price;
    }
    public double getPrice(){ return price; }

}
```

Description

- Like all the business classes for this application, the Product class is defined by a class diagram in figure 18-5 and it is coded as a JavaBean.

Figure 18-6   The Product class

The database

The Music Store web site uses a MySQL database named music to store the data for the web site in five tables. For more information about working with MySQL, you can refer to chapter 10.

The database diagram

Figure 18-7 shows the database diagram for the Music Store database. This diagram shows that this database stores the bulk of its data in five tables that correspond to five of the business objects. The asterisk used in this diagram shows that one User record can have multiple Download or Invoice records. Similarly, an Invoice record can have multiple LineItem records. However, a Download record and a LineItem record can have one and only one Product record.

In addition to these five tables, the Music Store database provides two more tables that are used to store the usernames, passwords, and roles. These tables are used by the Admin application that's described in chapter 21.

The SQL script for the database

Figure 18-8 shows the SQL script that you can use to create the Music Store database. This script creates a database named music, and it creates the seven tables in the database diagram. To do that, it uses seven CREATE TABLE statements that identify the column names, data types, primary keys, and so on. In addition, this script uses three INSERT INTO statements to insert data into the Product, users, and user_roles tables. If you want to use your own usernames and passwords for the Admin application, you can modify the INSERT INTO statements for the users and user_roles tables before you run this script.

The database diagram

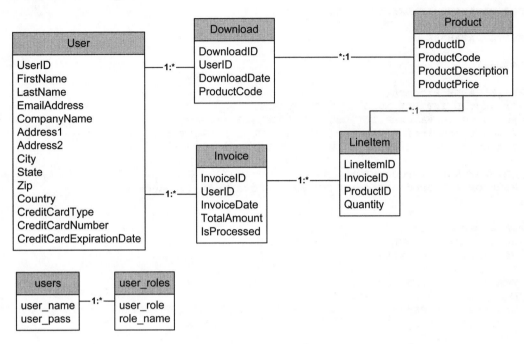

Description

- This database diagram shows the tables that are used to store the data for the Music Store web site.

- The User, Invoice, LineItem, Download, and Product tables correspond to the business classes that are defined in figure 18-5.

- The users and user_roles tables are used to store the usernames and passwords that can be used to access the Admin application that's shown in chapter 21.

Figure 18-7   The database diagram

The SQL script for the database

```
DROP DATABASE IF EXISTS music;

CREATE DATABASE music;

USE music;

CREATE TABLE Product(
  ProductID INT NOT NULL AUTO_INCREMENT,
  ProductCode VARCHAR(10) NOT NULL DEFAULT '',
  ProductDescription VARCHAR(100) NOT NULL DEFAULT '',
  ProductPrice DECIMAL(7,2) NOT NULL DEFAULT '0.00',

  PRIMARY KEY  (ProductID),
  FOREIGN KEY(ProductCode) REFERENCES Downloads (ProductCode)
);

CREATE TABLE User (
  UserID INT NOT NULL AUTO_INCREMENT,
  FirstName VARCHAR(50),
  LastName VARCHAR(50),
  EmailAddress VARCHAR(50),
  CompanyName VARCHAR(50),
  Address1 VARCHAR(50),
  Address2 VARCHAR(50),
  City VARCHAR(50),
  State VARCHAR(50),
  Zip VARCHAR(50),
  Country VARCHAR(50),
  CreditCardType VARCHAR(50),
  CreditCardNumber VARCHAR(50),
  CreditCardExpirationDate VARCHAR(50),

  PRIMARY KEY (UserID)
);

CREATE TABLE LineItem(
  LineItemID INT NOT NULL AUTO_INCREMENT,
  InvoiceID INT NOT NULL DEFAULT '0',
  ProductID INT NOT NULL DEFAULT '0',
  Quantity INT NOT NULL DEFAULT '0',

  PRIMARY KEY  (LineItemID),
  FOREIGN KEY(UserID) REFERENCES User (UserID)
);

CREATE TABLE Invoice(
  InvoiceID INT NOT NULL AUTO_INCREMENT,
  UserID INT NOT NULL,
  InvoiceDate DATETIME NOT NULL DEFAULT '0000-00-00 00:00:00',
  TotalAmount FLOAT NOT NULL DEFAULT '0',
  IsProcessed enum('y','n') DEFAULT NULL,

  PRIMARY KEY  (InvoiceID),
  FOREIGN KEY(UserID) REFERENCES User (UserID)
);
```

Figure 18-8   The SQL script for the database (part 1 of 2)

The SQL script for the database (continued)

```
CREATE TABLE Download (
  DownloadID INT NOT NULL AUTO_INCREMENT,
  UserID INT NOT NULL,
  DownloadDate DATETIME NOT NULL,
  ProductCode VARCHAR(10)  NOT NULL,

  PRIMARY KEY(DownloadID),
  FOREIGN KEY(UserID) REFERENCES User (UserID)
);

INSERT INTO Product VALUES
('1', '8601', '86 (the band) - True Life Songs and Pictures', '14.95'),
('2', 'pf01', 'Paddlefoot - The first CD', '12.95'),
('3', 'pf02', 'Paddlefoot - The second CD', '14.95'),
('4', 'jr01', 'Joe Rut - Genuine Wood Grained Finish', '14.95');

CREATE TABLE users (
  user_name varchar(15) not null primary key,
  user_pass varchar(15) not null
);

INSERT INTO users VALUES ('andrea', 'dime10'),
                         ('joel', '87band'),
                         ('doug', 'lowe1');

CREATE TABLE user_roles (    user_name varchar(15) not null,
    role_name varchar(15) not null,
    primary key (user_name, role_name)
);

INSERT INTO user_roles VALUES ('andrea', 'service'),
                              ('andrea', 'admin'),
                              ('joel', 'admin');
```

Description

- You can use this SQL script to create the tables needed by the Music Store application. This SQL script is provided on the CD that comes with this book, and appendix A shows how to use it.

Figure 18-8   The SQL script for the database (part 2 of 2)

The data layer

The data access classes that let the Music Store web site access the database are stored in the music.data package. In addition, these classes use a connection pool class that's stored in the music.util package. For more information about coding these classes, you can refer to chapter 11.

The class diagrams

Figure 18-9 shows the class diagrams for five data access classes. These classes use static methods to read and write business objects to a database. As a result, they don't contain instance variables or constructors.

Each method in this figure accepts two arguments. The first argument is a Connection object, and the second argument is usually a business object. However, the second argument can also be a String object or a primitive type that uniquely identifies the row for a business object.

The ProductDB class

Figure 18-10 shows the code for the ProductDB class. This code implements the ProductDB class diagram in the previous figure. If you understand this code, you shouldn't have much trouble understanding how the other classes in the data access layer work since they all follow the same principles.

If you want to view the code for the other data access classes, you can open them in a text editor. They're all stored in the music.data package.

Class diagrams for the data access classes

ProductDB
+readProduct(connection : Connection, productCode : String) : Product +readProductID(connection : Connection, product : Product) : int +readRecord(connection : Connection, code: String) : Product

UserDB
+writeRecord(connection : Connection, user : User) +overwriteRecord(connection: Connection, user : User) : boolean +isMatch(connection : Connection, emailAddress : String) : boolean +readUserID(connection : Connection, user : User) : int +readRecord(connection : Connection, emailAddress : String) : User

InvoiceDB
+writeRecord(connection : Connection, invoice : Invoice)

LineItemDB
+writeRecord(connection : Connection, invoiceID : int, lineItem : LineItem) +readRecords(connection : Connection, invoiceID : int) : Vector

DownloadDB
+addRecord(connection : Connection, download : Download)

Description

- These data access classes are stored in the music.data package. You can use them to read business objects from the database and write them to the database. To do that, you must pass a Connection object and the name of the appropriate business object.
- The Admin application uses two more data access classes that aren't shown here: the OrderDB class and the ReportDB class. You can learn about them in chapter 21.

Figure 18-9   The class diagrams for the data access classes

The ProductDB class

```java
package music.data;

import java.sql.*;
import music.business.*;

public class ProductDB{
    public static Product readRecord(Connection connection, String productCode)
                                    throws SQLException{
        //This method returns null if a product isn't found.
        String query = "SELECT * FROM Product " +
                       "WHERE ProductCode = '" + productCode + "'";
        Statement statement = connection.createStatement();
        ResultSet record = statement.executeQuery(query);
        Product product = null;
        boolean exists = record.next();
        if (exists){
            int id = record.getInt("ProductID");
            String code = record.getString("ProductCode");
            String description = record.getString("ProductDescription");
            double price = record.getDouble("ProductPrice");
            product = new Product(code, description, price);
        }
        record.close();
        statement.close();
        return product;
    }

    public static int readProductID(Connection connection, Product product)
                                    throws SQLException{
        //This method will return 0 if productID isn't found.
        String query = "SELECT ProductID FROM Product " +
                       "WHERE ProductCode = '" + product.getCode() + "'";
        Statement statement = connection.createStatement();
        ResultSet record = statement.executeQuery(query);
        record.next();
        int productID = record.getInt("ProductID");
        record.close();
        statement.close();
        return productID;
    }
```

Figure 18-10   The ProductDB class (part 1 of 2)

The ProductDB class (continued)

```
public static Product readRecord(Connection connection, int productID)
                            throws SQLException{
    //This method returns null if a product isn't found.
    String query = "SELECT * FROM Product " +
                   "WHERE ProductID = '" + productID + "'";
    Statement statement = connection.createStatement();
    ResultSet record = statement.executeQuery(query);
    Product product = null;
    boolean exists = record.next();
    if (exists){
        String code = record.getString("ProductCode");
        String description = record.getString("ProductDescription");
        double price = record.getDouble("ProductPrice");
        product = new Product(code, description, price);
    }
    record.close();
    statement.close();
    return product;
}
}
```

Figure 18-10   The ProductDB class (part 2 of 2)

Perspective

Once you understand the components of the Music Store web site that are described in this chapter, you're ready to learn more about the Download, Shopping Cart, and Admin applications that are presented in the next three chapters. If you had trouble understanding the components in this chapter, though, you may want to review some of the earlier chapters in this book.

To get the most from the Music Store web site, you should of course install it on your computer as described in appendix A. Then, you can review the figures in any of the chapters in this section as you run the related pages on your computer. If at any time you want to review the code for a component, you can find the component in its directory, open it in a text editor, and review it.

The Download application

Users browsing through the Music Store web site can download and listen to the sound files that are available. But first, they must use the Download application to register with the web site by providing a name and email address. This chapter describes how this Download application works.

The Download application **546**
The user interface 546
The structure 546
The code 550
Perspective **556**

The Download application

The Download application presented in this topic is an expanded version of the Download application presented in chapter 7. This version uses more sophisticated graphics, and it writes a record for each download to the database for the Music Store web site.

The user interface

Figure 19-1 shows the web pages that make up the user interface of the download application. The Product page contains a "Listen to Samples" link that the user can click on to start the Download application. If the user has already registered with this web site, the Download application displays a Sound page that lets the user download Real Audio or MP3 sound files by clicking on a link. Otherwise, the Shopping Cart application displays the Register page. Then, the user must register by entering a name and email address.

The structure

Figure 19-2 shows how the HTML pages, JSPs, and servlets that are used by the Download application are structured and organized. This diagram shows that the servlet files for the Download application are stored in the music.download package. In addition, it shows that most servlets forward the response to a corresponding JSP. However, if a user has already registered for downloads, the DownloadServlet class skips the RegisterServlet and the Register page by calling the DownloadWriteServlet class.

A Product page

The Register page

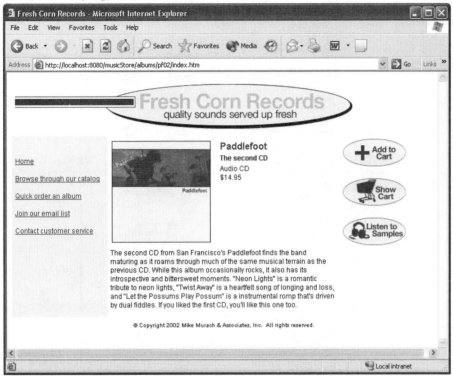

Figure 19-1   The user interface (part 1 of 2)

A Sound page

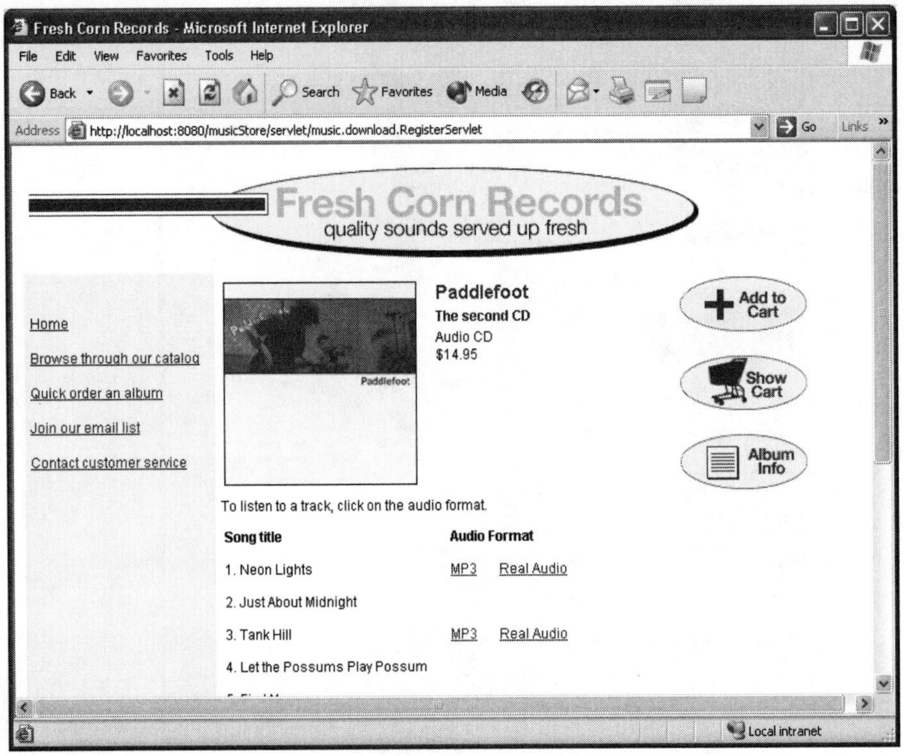

Description

- The Register page will only be displayed if the user hasn't already registered with the web site. A user can register with the web site by using this Register page or by using the Shopping Cart application described in the next chapter to make a purchase.

Figure 19-1   The user interface (part 2 of 2)

The structure of the Download application

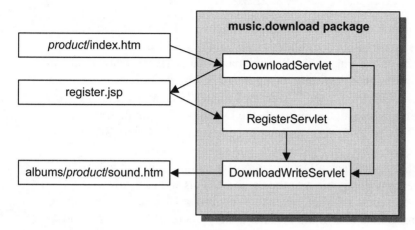

Description

- The JSPs for this application are stored in the musicStore\download directory.
- The servlet classes for this application are stored in the music.download package.
- The DownloadServlet checks to see if the user has registered. If so, it proceeds to the DownloadWriteServlet. Otherwise, it displays the Register page.
- The RegisterServlet gets the data entered in the Register page, creates a User object from that data, writes the User object to the database, stores the User object in a session, and returns a cookie to the user's browser so the user won't have to register again.
- The DownloadWriteServlet creates a Download object, writes the Download object to the database, and returns the appropriate Sound page to the user.

Figure 19-2   The structure of the Download application

The code

In this application, the Product and Sound pages are HTML pages. Since the code for these pages is easy to understand, figures 19-3 through 19-6 don't show them. However, the link on the Product page that starts the Download application is shown at the beginning of figure 19-3. This link contains an image tag that specifies a GIF file for the "Listen to Samples" image. As a result, when the user clicks on this image, the link calls the DownloadServlet class.

In figures 19-4 and 19-5, you can see the code for the Register JSP and the RegisterServlet class. Then, in figure 19-6, you can see that the DownloadWriteServlet creates a Download object and uses the DownloadDB class to write the Download object to the database. This writes a row to the Download table that includes a reference to a row in the User table, the current date, and a reference to a row in the Product table. As a result, the Download database stores information for each user download.

All of the servlet classes for this application catch the SQLException that is thrown if the data access classes can't access the database for the Music Store web site. If this exception is thrown, these servlets use the log method to write the exception to a log file, and they throw a ServletException object that's created from the SQLException so the exception is displayed in the browser. If the web.xml page for the Music Store web site has enabled error pages, the browser will display a custom error page. Otherwise, the browser will display the details for the exception.

Since the code for the business objects and data access classes was described in chapter 18, this chapter doesn't show any of those classes. In addition, this chapter doesn't show any of the utility classes stored in the music.util package. However, these classes are included on the CD that comes with this book. So once you've installed the Music Store web site, you can view these files by opening them in a text editor.

The Product page link that calls the DownloadServlet

```
<a href="../../servlet/music.download.DownloadServlet?productCode=8601">
  <img src="../../images/listen.gif" width="113" height="47" border="0">
</a>
```

The DownloadServlet class

```
package music.download;

import java.io.*;
import javax.servlet.*;
import javax.servlet.http.*;
import java.sql.*;
import music.business.*;
import music.data.*;
import music.util.*;

public class DownloadServlet extends HttpServlet{

    private MurachPool connectionPool;

    public void init() throws ServletException{
        connectionPool = MurachPool.getInstance();
    }

    public void destroy() {
        connectionPool.destroy();
    }

    public void doGet(HttpServletRequest request,
                      HttpServletResponse response)
                      throws IOException, ServletException {

        String productCode = request.getParameter("productCode");
        HttpSession session = request.getSession();
        session.setAttribute("productCode", productCode);
        User user = (User) session.getAttribute("user");
        Connection connection = null;

        // if the User object doesn't exist, check for the email cookie
        if (user == null){
            Cookie[] cookies = request.getCookies();
            String emailAddress =
                CookieUtil.getCookieValue(cookies, "emailCookie");

            // if the email cookie doesn't exist, go to the registration page
            if (emailAddress == null || emailAddress.equals("")){
                RequestDispatcher dispatcher =
                    getServletContext().getRequestDispatcher(
                        "/download/register.jsp");
                dispatcher.forward(request, response);
            }
```

Figure 19-3   The code for the DownloadServlet class (part 1 of 2)

The DownloadServlet class

```
            // if the email cookie does exist, create the User object
            // from the email cookie and skip the registration page
            else{
                connection = connectionPool.getConnection();
                try{
                    user = UserDB.readRecord(connection, emailAddress);
                    session.setAttribute("user", user);
                }
                catch(SQLException e){
                    log("DownloadServlet SQLException: " + e);
                    throw new ServletException(e);
                }
                finally{
                    connectionPool.freeConnection(connection);
                }
                RequestDispatcher dispatcher =
                    getServletContext().getRequestDispatcher(
                        "/servlet/music.download.DownloadWriteServlet");
                dispatcher.forward(request, response);
            }
        }

        // if the User object exists, skip the registration page
        else{
            RequestDispatcher dispatcher =
                getServletContext().getRequestDispatcher(
                    "/servlet/music.download.DownloadWriteServlet");
            dispatcher.forward(request, response);
        }
    }

    public void doPost(HttpServletRequest request,
                       HttpServletResponse response)
                       throws IOException, ServletException {
        doGet(request, response);
    }
}
```

Note

- This class uses the CookieUtil class that's stored in the music.util package to retrieve a cookie from the browser. For more information about working with this class, see chapter 7.

Figure 19-3   The code for the DownloadServlet class (part 2 of 2)

The main column of the Register page

```
<!-- begin main column -->

    <td width="404" valign="top">
      <h1>Download registration</h1>

      <p>Before you can download and listen to these sound files,
      you must register with us by entering your name and email
      address below.</p>

      <form action="<%= response.encodeURL(
            "/musicStore/servlet/music.download.RegisterServlet")%>"
          method="post">
        <table cellpadding="5" border="0">
          <tr>
            <td align="right"><p>First name:</td>
            <td><input type="text" name="firstName"></td>
          </tr>
          <tr>
            <td align="right"><p>Last name:</td>
            <td><input type="text" name="lastName"></td>
          </tr>
          <tr>
            <td align="right"><p>Email address:</td>
            <td><input type="text" name="emailAddress"></td>
          </tr>
          <tr>
            <td></td>
            <td><input type="button" value="Submit"
                      onClick="validate(this.form)"></td>
          </tr>
        </table>
      </form>
    </td>

<!-- end main column -->
```

Note

- This JSP uses JavaScript code that isn't shown in this figure to validate the entries made by the user.

Figure 19-4   The register.jsp file

The RegisterServlet class

```
package music.download;
import java.io.*;
import javax.servlet.*;
import javax.servlet.http.*;
import java.sql.*;
import music.business.*;
import music.data.*;
import music.util.*;

public class RegisterServlet extends HttpServlet{
    private MurachPool connectionPool;

    public void init() throws ServletException{
        connectionPool = MurachPool.getInstance();
    }
    public void destroy() {
        connectionPool.destroy();
    }

    public void doPost(HttpServletRequest request,
                       HttpServletResponse response)
                       throws IOException, ServletException {

        String firstName = request.getParameter("firstName");
        String lastName = request.getParameter("lastName");
        String emailAddress = request.getParameter("emailAddress");
        User user = new User();
        user.setFirstName(firstName);
        user.setLastName(lastName);
        user.setEmailAddress(emailAddress);

        Connection connection = connectionPool.getConnection();
        try{
            UserDB.writeRecord(connection, user);
        }
        catch(SQLException e){
          log("RegisterServlet SQLException: " + e);
          throw new ServletException(e);
        }
        finally{ connectionPool.freeConnection(connection); }

        HttpSession session = request.getSession(true);
        session.setAttribute("user", user);

        Cookie emailCookie = new Cookie("emailCookie", emailAddress);
        emailCookie.setMaxAge(60*60*24*365*2);
        emailCookie.setPath("/");
        response.addCookie(emailCookie);

        RequestDispatcher dispatcher =
            getServletContext().getRequestDispatcher(
                "/servlet/music.download.DownloadWriteServlet");
        dispatcher.forward(request, response);
    }
}
```

Figure 19-5   The code for the RegisterServlet class

The DownloadWriteServlet class

```
package music.download;
import java.io.*;
import javax.servlet.*;
import javax.servlet.http.*;
import java.sql.*;
import music.util.*;
import music.business.*;
import music.data.*;

public class DownloadWriteServlet extends HttpServlet{

    private MurachPool connectionPool;

    public void init() throws ServletException{
        connectionPool = MurachPool.getInstance();
    }

    public void destroy(){
        connectionPool.destroy();
    }

    public void doGet(HttpServletRequest request,
                      HttpServletResponse response)
                      throws IOException, ServletException{

        HttpSession session = request.getSession(true);

        User user = (User) session.getAttribute("user");
        String productCode = (String)session.getAttribute("productCode");
        Download download = new Download(user, new java.util.Date(),
                                         productCode);

        Connection connection = connectionPool.getConnection();
        try{
            DownloadDB.addRecord(connection, download);
        }
        catch(SQLException e){
            log("DownloadWriteServlet SQLException: " + e);
            throw new ServletException(e);
        }
        finally{
            connectionPool.freeConnection(connection);
        }
        RequestDispatcher dispatcher =
            getServletContext().getRequestDispatcher(
                "/albums/" + productCode + "/sound.htm");
        dispatcher.forward(request, response);
    }

    public void doPost(HttpServletRequest request,
                       HttpServletResponse response)
                       throws IOException, ServletException{
        doGet(request, response);
    }
}
```

Figure 19-6   The code for the DownloadWriteServlet class

Perspective

If you study the code for this application, you may notice a couple of minor flaws. For example, since the Sound pages are HTML pages, it's possible for a user to access these pages without registering by entering a URL that points directly to the page. However, to do this, the user would have to know the URL for the sound page. As a result, it's unlikely that a first time user would be able to guess the URL. Besides, since the worst case scenario is that a user will be able to download a sound file without registering, this isn't a critical security issue. To solve this problem, though, you can use a security constraint as shown in chapter 14.

In addition, you may notice that the record that's written to the database for each download isn't as complete as it could be. Specifically, the Download object contains only a User object, a date, and a product code. In a more complete application, this object could also contain the name and type of the sound file for each download.

Despite these flaws, this Download application is adequate for instructional purposes. In particular, you can see how the Download application writes a record to the database. Then, in chapter 21, you'll see how you can create an administrative application that lets selected users view reports that summarize this download data.

The Shopping Cart application

A user browsing through the Music Store web site can add any album on the site to a virtual shopping cart. Then, the user can use the Shopping Cart application to buy the items in the shopping cart. This chapter describes how this e-commerce application works.

The Shopping Cart application **558**
The user interface 558
The structure 564
The code 566
Perspective **578**

The Shopping Cart application

Although some aspects of the Shopping Cart application have been simplified for instructional purposes, this application introduces all of the elements of a real e-commerce application. As a result, if you ever need to build an e-commerce site, you can use the code that's on the CD that comes with this book as a starting point.

The user interface

Figure 20-1 presents some of the key pages of the Shopping Cart application. The first two pages provide links that start the Shopping Cart application. For example, the Product page provides a link that surrounds the "Add to Cart" graphic. This link adds the current product to the cart and displays the cart. In addition, the Product page contains a link that surrounds the "Show Cart" graphic. This link displays the items that are already in the cart. In contrast, the Index page for the Shopping Cart application shows a list of the four albums available from the site. Each of these albums contains an "Add To Cart" link. Like the "Add to Cart" graphic, this link adds the related product to the cart and displays the cart.

The Cart page displays the items that have been added to the cart. To change the quantity for an item, the user can enter a new quantity and click on the Update button. To remove an item, the user can change the quantity to 0 and click on the Update button. To add more items to the cart, the user can select the Continue Shopping button, which returns the user to the Index page. To proceed to checkout, the user can click on the Checkout button.

If the user has a valid cookie, and a record for the user exists in the database, the Shopping Cart application skips the User page and proceeds directly to the Invoice page. Otherwise, the Shopping Cart application displays the User page.

No matter how the user gets to the Invoice page, the user can verify that the shipping and order data is correct. To modify the shipping data, the user can select the Edit Address button to display the User page again. Then, the application displays the User page with the current data in its text boxes so the user can modify the current data.

When the user clicks on the Continue button from the Invoice page, the application uses a secure SSL connection to display the Credit Card page. On this page, the user selects a payment type, enters a credit card number, and chooses an expiration date. To submit the order, the user can click on the Submit Order button. This should display another page that informs the user that the order was successful.

A Product page

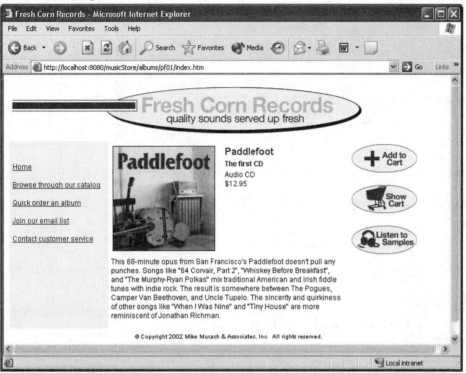

The Index page

Figure 20-1   The user interface (part 1 of 3)

The Cart page

The User page

Figure 20-1   The user interface (part 2 of 3)

The Invoice page

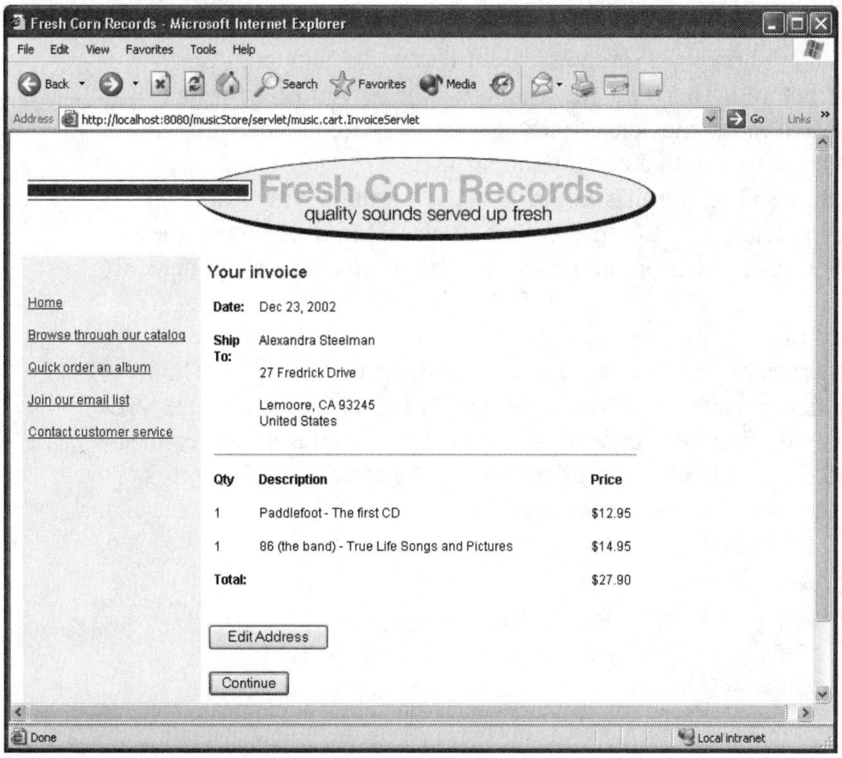

The Credit Card page

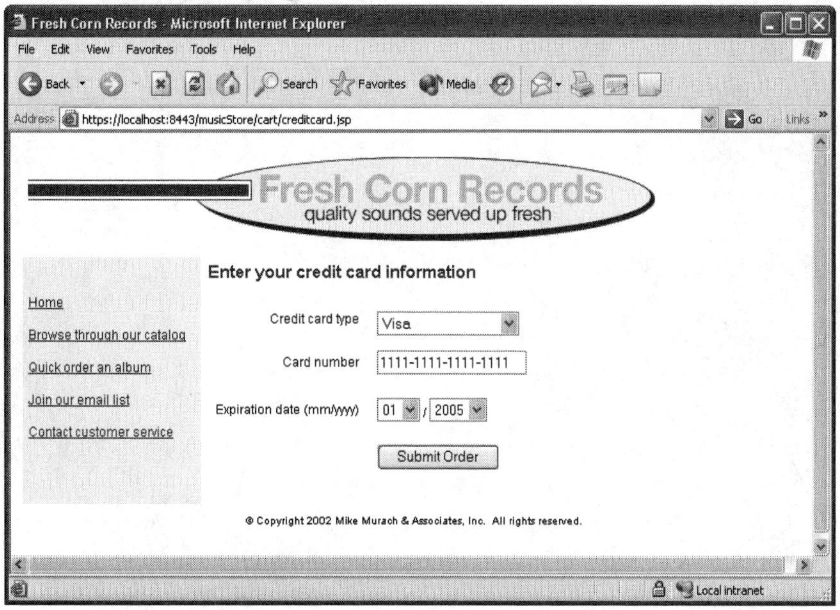

Figure 20-1   The user interface (part 3 of 3)

The structure

Figure 20-2 shows how the JSP and servlet files for the Shopping Cart application are structured. This diagram shows that the servlet files for this application are stored in the music.cart package. In addition, it shows that most servlets forward the response to a corresponding JSP.

However, if a user already exists in the database for the Music Store web site, the UserServlet class calls the InvoiceServlet class. Similarly, when the user clicks on the Continue button on the JSP for the invoice, the Shopping Cart application forwards the response to the JSP that gets the credit card data.

Since the start of the Shopping Cart application doesn't transmit any sensitive data, it uses a regular HTTP connection. However, before the Shopping Cart application transmits the credit cart data, it begins using a secure SSL connection. When you first install the Music Store web site, this secure connection isn't enabled. To enable it, you need to modify the server.xml file and create a self-signed digital certificate as described in chapter 13.

The structure of the Shopping Cart application

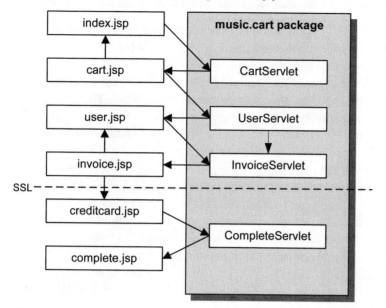

Description

- The JSPs for this application are stored in the musicStore\cart directory.
- The servlets for this application are stored in the music.cart package.
- The JSPs and servlets that transmit the credit card data use an SSL connection.
- The CartServlet finds the user's cart and displays it. If the user's cart doesn't contain any items, this servlet displays the Index page for the Shopping Cart application.
- The UserServlet checks if a user has already entered his personal information. If so, this servlet creates a User object from the database and skips the User page.
- The InvoiceServlet creates the Invoice object and displays the Invoice page. From the Invoice page, the user can call the User page to edit any personal information that isn't correct.
- The CompleteServlet writes the data for the user and the invoice to the database, sends a confirmation email, and displays the Complete page.

Figure 20-2 The structure of the Shopping Cart application

The code

Figures 20-3 through 20-11 show some of the code for the JSPs and servlets used by this application. By now, you shouldn't have much trouble understanding this code, but here are a few notable points.

The servlets and JSPs in figures 20-7 and 20-8 use a session attribute named updateUserFields. To start, the User page sets this attribute to "yes". Then, the InvoiceServlet checks this parameter. If it has been set to "yes", the InvoiceServlet gets the parameters from the request object and updates the User object accordingly. Otherwise, the InvoiceServlet uses the User object that was created from the database by the UserServlet.

All of the servlet classes for this application catch the SQLException that is thrown if the data access classes can't access the database for the Music Store web site. If this exception is thrown, these servlets use the log method to write the exception to a log file, and they throw a ServletException object that's created from the SQLException so the exception is displayed in the browser. If the web.xml page for the Music Store web site has enabled error pages, the browser will display a custom error page. Otherwise, the browser will display the details for the exception.

Since the code for the business objects and data access classes are described in chapter 18, these figures don't show any of those classes. In addition, these figures don't list the code for the custom tags and helper classes that are used by the Shopping Cart application. If you're interested in them, though, you can use your text editor to open and review them.

The links from a Product page that call the CartServlet class

```
<a href="../../servlet/music.cart.CartServlet?productCode=8601">
    <img src="../../images/addtocart.gif" width="113" height="47" border="0">
</a><br><br>

<a href="../../servlet/music.cart.CartServlet">
    <img src="../../images/showcart.gif" width="113" height="47" border="0">
</a><br><br>
```

The index.jsp file

```
<h1>Quick order an album</h1>

<table cellpadding="5" border="0">
  <tr valign="bottom">
    <th align="left"><p>Description</th>
    <th align="left"><p>Price</th>
    <th align="left"><p> </th>
  </tr>

  <tr valign="top">
    <td><p><a href="../albums/8601">
        86 (the band) - True Life Songs and Pictures</a></td>
    <td><p>$14.95</td>
    <td><p><a href="../servlet/music.cart.CartServlet?productCode=8601">
          Add To Cart</a></td>
  </tr>

  <tr valign="top">
    <td><p><a href="../albums/pf01">Paddlefoot - The first CD</a></td>
    <td><p>$12.95</td>
    <td><p><a href="../servlet/music.cart.CartServlet?productCode=pf01">
          Add To Cart</a></td>
  </tr>
```

.
.
.

Note

- Each Product page contains two links that call the CartServlet class. These links surround a tag that specifies a GIF file. As a result, when the user clicks on the graphic, the CartServlet is called.

Figure 20-3   The index.jsp file

The CartServlet class

```
package music.cart;

import javax.servlet.*;
import javax.servlet.http.*;
import java.io.*;
import java.sql.*;
import music.business.*;
import music.data.*;
import music.util.*;

public class CartServlet extends HttpServlet{
    private MurachPool connectionPool;

    public void init() throws ServletException{
        connectionPool = MurachPool.getInstance();
    }

    public void destroy() {
        connectionPool.destroy();
    }

    public void doPost(HttpServletRequest request,
                       HttpServletResponse response)
                       throws IOException, ServletException{

        String productCode = request.getParameter("productCode");
        String quantityAsString = request.getParameter("quantity");
        HttpSession session = request.getSession(true);

        Cart cart = (Cart) session.getAttribute("cart");
        if (cart == null){
            cart = new Cart();
            session.setAttribute("cart", cart);
        }
        int quantity = 1;
        // If the user enters a negative or invalid number in the
        // Update text box, the quantity is automatically reset to 1.
        try{
            quantity = Integer.parseInt(quantityAsString);
            if (quantity < 0) throw new NumberFormatException();
        }
        catch(NumberFormatException nfe){
            quantity = 1;
        }
```

Figure 20-4   The CartServlet class (part 1 of 2)

The CartServlet class (continued)

```
        Connection connection = connectionPool.getConnection();
        try{
            Product product = ProductDB.readRecord(connection, productCode);
            if (product != null){
                LineItem lineItem = new LineItem(product, quantity);
                if (quantity > 0)
                    cart.addItem(lineItem);
                else
                    cart.removeItem(lineItem);
            //throw new SQLException("test");
            }
        }
        catch(SQLException e){
            log("CartServlet SQLException: " + e);
            throw new ServletException(e);
        }
        finally{
            connectionPool.freeConnection(connection);
        }
        session.setAttribute("cart", cart);

        // If no items exist in cart, forward to the Index page.
        String url = "";
        if (cart.getItems().size() <= 0){
            url = "/cart/index.jsp";
        }
        // Otherwise, forward to the Cart page.
        else{
            url = "/cart/cart.jsp";
        }
        RequestDispatcher dispatcher =
            getServletContext().getRequestDispatcher(url);
        dispatcher.forward(request, response);
    }

    public void doGet(HttpServletRequest request,
                      HttpServletResponse response)
                      throws IOException, ServletException{
        doPost(request, response);
    }
}
```

Figure 20-4   The CartServlet class (part 2 of 2)

The cart.jsp file

```
<%@ taglib uri="../WEB-INF/tlds/music.tld" prefix="msc" %>

<h1>Your shopping cart</h1>
<table cellspacing="5" border="0">
  <tr>
    <th align="left"><p>Qty</th>
    <th align="left"><p>Description</th>
    <th align="left"><p>Price</td>
    <th align="left"><p>Amount</td>
  </tr>


<msc:cart>
  <tr valign="top">
    <td><p>
      <form action="<%=response.encodeURL(
          "../servlet/music.cart.CartServlet")%>" method="post">
        <input type="hidden" name="productCode" value="<%=productCode%>">
        <input type=text size=2 name="quantity" value="<%=quantity%>">
        <input type="submit" value="Update">
      </form>
    </td>
    <td><p><%=productDescription%></td>
    <td><p><%=productPrice%></td>
    <td><p><%=total%></td>
  </tr>
</msc:cart>


  <tr>
    <td colspan="3">
      <p><b>To change the quantity for an item</b>, enter the new quantity
          and click on the Update button.</p>
      <p><b>To remove an item</b>, set the quantity to zero
          and click on the Update button.</p>
    </td>
  </tr>
</table>

<form action="<%=response.encodeURL("../cart/index.jsp")%>" method="post">
  <input type="submit" value="Continue Shopping">
</form>

<form action="<%=response.encodeURL(
    "../servlet/music.cart.UserServlet")%>" method="post">
  <input type="submit" value="Checkout">
</form>
```

Note

- This page uses the custom msc:cart tag to display the items in the cart. The classes that define this tag are stored in the music.tag package. For more information about custom tags, see chapter 9.

Figure 20-5   The cart.jsp file

The UserServlet class

```
package music.cart;

import java.io.*;
import javax.servlet.*;
import javax.servlet.http.*;
import java.sql.*;
import music.business.*;
import music.data.*;
import music.util.*;

public class UserServlet extends HttpServlet{
    private MurachPool connectionPool;

    public void init() throws ServletException{
        connectionPool = MurachPool.getInstance();
    }

    public void destroy() {
        connectionPool.destroy();
    }

    public void doGet(HttpServletRequest request,
                      HttpServletResponse response)
                      throws IOException, ServletException{

        HttpSession session = request.getSession(true);

        // Get the emailAddress from the emailCookie.
        // If no cookie is found, this code returns an empty string
        Cookie[] cookies = request.getCookies();
        String emailAddress = CookieUtil.getCookieValue(cookies,
            "emailCookie");

        // If the emailAddress cookie exists, try to get the User object
        // from the database
        User user = null;
        if (!(emailAddress == "")){
            Connection connection = connectionPool.getConnection();
            try{
                user = UserDB.readRecord(connection, emailAddress);
                // If the user exists, go to the Invoice page
                if ( (user != null) && (!(user.getAddress1().equals("")) ) ){
                    session.setAttribute("user", user);
                    session.setAttribute("updateUserFields", "no");
                    RequestDispatcher dispatcher =
                        getServletContext().getRequestDispatcher(
                            "/servlet/music.cart.InvoiceServlet");
                    dispatcher.forward(request, response);
                }
```

Figure 20-6   The UserServlet class (part 1 of 2)

The UserServlet class (continued)

```java
                    // Otherwise, go to the User page
                    else{
                        session.setAttribute("user", user);
                        RequestDispatcher dispatcher =
                            getServletContext().getRequestDispatcher(
                                "/cart/user.jsp");
                        dispatcher.forward(request, response);
                    }
                }
                catch(SQLException e){
                    log("UserServlet SQLException: " + e);
                    throw new ServletException();
                }
                finally{
                    connectionPool.freeConnection(connection);
                }
            }

            // If the emailAddress doesn't exist, create a new User object
            // and go to the User page
            else{
                user = new User();
                session.setAttribute("user", user);
                RequestDispatcher dispatcher =
                    getServletContext().getRequestDispatcher("/cart/user.jsp");
                dispatcher.forward(request, response);
            }
        }

        public void doPost(HttpServletRequest request,
                           HttpServletResponse response)
                           throws ServletException, IOException {
            doGet(request, response);
        }
    }
```

Note

- The CookieUtil class used in this figure is stored in the music.util package. For more information about this class, see chapter 7.

Figure 20-6   The UserServlet class (part 2 of 2)

The user.jsp file

```
<jsp:useBean id="user" class="music.business.User" scope="session" />
<%
    /*
       Set a session attribute that lets the InvoiceServlet know if fields in
       the User object need to be updated
    */
    session.setAttribute("updateUserFields", "yes");
%>
<h1>Enter your name and contact information</h1>

<form action="../servlet/music.cart.InvoiceServlet" method=post>
<table border="0" cellpadding="5">
  <tr>
    <td></td>
    <td align=left><p>Required <font color=red>*</font></td>
  </tr>
  <tr>
    <td align=right><p>First Name</td>
    <td><input type="text" name="firstName"  size="20" maxlength=20
             value="<jsp:getProperty name="user" property="firstName"/>">
             <font color=red>*</font></td>
  </tr>
  <tr>
    <td align=right><p>Last Name</td>
    <td><input type=text name="lastName" size=20
             value="<jsp:getProperty name="user" property="lastName"/>">
             <font color=red>*</font></td>
  </tr>
    .
    .
    .
  <tr>
    <td align=right><p>Zip Code</td>
    <td><input type=text name="zip" size=20
             value="<jsp:getProperty name="user" property="zip"/>">
             <font color=red>*</font></td>
  </tr>
  <tr>
    <td align=right><p>Country</td>
    <td><input type=text name="country" size=20
             value="<jsp:getProperty name="user" property="country"/>">
             <font color=red>*</font></td>
  </tr>
  <tr>
    <td align=right><p> </td>
    <td><input type="button" value="Continue" onClick="validate(this.form)"></td>
  </tr>
</table>

</form>
```

Note

- Although it isn't shown in this figure, this page uses JavaScript to validate the entries.
  For more information about using JavaScript, see chapter 6.

Figure 20-7   The user.jsp file

The InvoiceServlet class

```
package music.cart;

import java.io.*;
import javax.servlet.*;
import javax.servlet.http.*;
import java.text.*;
import java.util.*;
import music.business.*;
import music.data.*;
import music.util.*;

public class InvoiceServlet extends HttpServlet{

    public void doGet(HttpServletRequest request,
                      HttpServletResponse response)
                      throws IOException, ServletException{

        HttpSession session = request.getSession(true);
        Cart cart = (Cart)session.getAttribute("cart");
        User user = (User)session.getAttribute("user");
        String updateUserFields =
            (String)session.getAttribute("updateUserFields");

        /*
            If the User page was displayed,
            get and set the data for the User object.
            Otherwise, leave the User object as it is.
        */
        if (updateUserFields != null && updateUserFields.equals("yes")){
            String firstName = request.getParameter("firstName");
            String lastName = request.getParameter("lastName");
            String companyName = request.getParameter("companyName");
            String emailAddress = request.getParameter("emailAddress");
            String address1 = request.getParameter("address1");
            String address2 = request.getParameter("address2");
            String city = request.getParameter("city");
            String state = request.getParameter("state");
            String zip = request.getParameter("zip");
            String country = request.getParameter("country");
            user.setFirstName(firstName);
            user.setLastName(lastName);
            user.setEmailAddress(emailAddress);
            user.setCompanyName(companyName);
            user.setAddress1(address1);
            user.setAddress2(address2);
            user.setCity(city);
            user.setState(state);
            user.setZip(zip);
            user.setCountry(country);
            session.setAttribute("user", user);
        }
```

Figure 20-8   The InvoiceServlet class (part 1 of 2)

The InvoiceServlet class (continued)

```
        // Get the current date and format it for the Invoice page
        java.util.Date today = new java.util.Date();
        DateFormat dateFormat = DateFormat.getDateInstance();
        String invoiceDateAsString = dateFormat.format(today);
        session.setAttribute("invoiceDateAsString", invoiceDateAsString);

        // Create an Invoice object and set the attributes.
        Invoice invoice = new Invoice();
        invoice.setUser(user);
        invoice.setInvoiceDate(today);
        Vector lineItems = cart.getItems();
        invoice.setLineItems(lineItems);

        // Get the invoice total and format it for the Invoice page
        double total = invoice.getInvoiceTotal();
        NumberFormat currency = NumberFormat.getCurrencyInstance();
        session.setAttribute("invoiceTotalAsString", currency.format(total));

        session.setAttribute("invoice", invoice);
        String url = response.encodeURL("/cart/invoice.jsp");
        RequestDispatcher dispatcher =
            getServletContext().getRequestDispatcher(url);
        dispatcher.forward(request, response);
    }

    public void doPost(HttpServletRequest request,
                       HttpServletResponse response)
                       throws IOException, ServletException{
        doGet(request, response);
    }
}
```

Figure 20-8   The InvoiceServlet class (part 2 of 2)

The invoice.jsp file

```jsp
<%@ taglib uri="../WEB-INF/tlds/music.tld" prefix="msc" %>
<jsp:useBean id="user" class="music.business.User" scope="session" />

<h1>Your invoice</h1>

<table border="0" cellspacing="5">
  <tr><td><p><b>Date:</td>
      <td width="400"><p><%=session.getAttribute("invoiceDateAsString")%></td>
      <td></td>
  </tr>
  <tr valign="top">
    <td><p><b>Ship To:</td>
    <td><p><jsp:getProperty name="user" property="firstName"/>
           <jsp:getProperty name="user" property="lastName"/><br>
           <jsp:getProperty name="user" property="companyName"/><br>
           <jsp:getProperty name="user" property="address1"/><br>
           <jsp:getProperty name="user" property="address2"/><br>
           <jsp:getProperty name="user" property="city"/>,
           <jsp:getProperty name="user" property="state"/>
           <jsp:getProperty name="user" property="zip"/><br>
           <jsp:getProperty name="user" property="country"/></td>
    <td></td>
  </tr>
  <tr><td colspan="3"><hr></td></tr>
  <tr><td><p><b>Qty</td>
      <td><p><b>Description</td>
      <td><p><b>Price</b></p></td>
  </tr>
<msc:cart>
  <tr>
    <td><p><%=quantity%></td>
    <td><p><%=productDescription%></td>
    <td><p><%=total%></td>
  </tr>
</msc:cart>
  <tr>
    <td><p><b>Total:</td>
    <td></td>
    <td><p><%=(String)session.getAttribute("invoiceTotalAsString")%></td>
  </tr>
</table>

<form action="<%=response.encodeURL("../cart/user.jsp")%>" method="post">
    <input type="submit" value="Edit Address">
</form>

<form action="<%=response.encodeURL("../cart/creditcard.jsp")%>" method="post">
    <input type="submit" value="Continue">
</form>
```

Note

- This page uses the custom msc:cart tag to display the items in the cart. The classes that define this tag are stored in the music.tag package. For more information about custom tags, see chapter 9.

Figure 20-9   The invoice.jsp file

The creditcard.jsp file

```
<h1>Enter your credit card information</h1>

<form action="<%=response.encodeURL(
        "../servlet/music.cart.CompleteServlet")%>" method="post">
   <table border="0" cellpadding="5">
   <tr>
      <td align="right"><p>Credit card type</td>
      <td><select name="creditCardType" size="1">
            <option value="Visa">Visa</option>
            <option value="Mastercard">Mastercard</option>
            <option value="AmEx">American Express</option>
         </select>
      </td>
   </tr>
   <tr>
      <td align="right"><p>Card number</td>
      <td><p><input type="text" size="20" name="creditCardNumber" maxlength="25"></td>
   </tr>
   <tr>
      <td align="right"><p>Expiration date (mm/yyyy)</td>
      <td><p><select name="creditCardExpirationMonth">
               <option value="01">01
               <option value="02">02
               <option value="03">03
               <option value="04">04
               <option value="05">05
               <option value="06">06
               <option value="07">07
               <option value="08">08
               <option value="09">09
               <option value="10">10
               <option value="11">11
               <option value="12">12
            </select>
            /
            <select name="creditCardExpirationYear">
               <option value="2003">2003
               <option value="2004">2004
               <option value="2005">2005
               <option value="2006">2006
               <option value="2007">2007
               <option value="2008">2008
               <option value="2009">2009
               <option value="2010">2010
            </select>
            </p>
      </td>
   </tr>
   <tr>
      <td> </td>
      <td align="left"><input type="submit" value="Submit Order"></td>
   </tr>
   </table>
</form>
```

Figure 20-10   The creditcard.jsp file

The CompleteServlet class

```
package music.cart;

import java.io.*;
import javax.servlet.*;
import javax.servlet.http.*;
import java.sql.*;
import java.text.DateFormat;
import javax.mail.*;
import music.business.*;
import music.data.*;
import music.util.*;

public class CompleteServlet extends HttpServlet{
    private MurachPool connectionPool;

    public void init() throws ServletException{
        connectionPool = MurachPool.getInstance();
    }

    public void destroy() {
        connectionPool.destroy();
    }

    public void doGet(HttpServletRequest request,
                      HttpServletResponse response)
                      throws IOException, ServletException{

        HttpSession session = request.getSession(true);
        User user = (User)session.getAttribute("user");
        Invoice invoice = (Invoice)session.getAttribute("invoice");

        String creditCardType = request.getParameter("creditCardType");
        String creditCardNumber = request.getParameter("creditCardNumber");
        String creditCardExpMonth = request.getParameter("creditCardExpirationMonth");
        String creditCardExpYear = request.getParameter("creditCardExpirationYear");
        user.setCreditCardType(creditCardType);
        user.setCreditCardNumber(creditCardNumber);
        user.setCreditCardExpirationDate(creditCardExpMonth
            + "/" + creditCardExpYear);
```

Figure 20-11   The CompleteServlet class (part 1 of 2)

The CompleteServlet class (continued)

```java
Connection connection = connectionPool.getConnection();
try{
    // If a record for the User object exists, update it
    boolean found = UserDB.overwriteRecord(connection, user);
    // Otherwise, write a new record for the User object
    if (!found)
        UserDB.writeRecord(connection, user);
    InvoiceDB.writeRecord(connection, invoice);
}
catch(SQLException e){
    log("CompleteServlet SQLException: " + e);
    throw new ServletException();
}
finally{
    connectionPool.freeConnection(connection);
}

// Set the emailCookie in the user's browser.
Cookie emailCookie = new Cookie("emailCookie",
    user.getEmailAddress());
emailCookie.setMaxAge(60*24*365*2*60);
emailCookie.setPath("/");
response.addCookie(emailCookie);

// Send an email to the user to confirm the order.
try{
    String to = user.getEmailAddress();
    String from = "confirmation@freshcornrecords.com";
    String subject = "Order Confirmation";
    String message = "Dear " + user.getFirstName() + ",\n\n" +
        "Thanks for ordering from us. You should receive your order \n" +
        "in 3-5 business days. Please contact us if you have any questions.";
    MailUtil.sendMail(to, from, subject, message);
}
catch(MessagingException e){
    System.out.println("CompleteServlet MessagingException: "
        + e.getMessage());
}
String url = response.encodeURL("/cart/complete.jsp");
RequestDispatcher dispatcher =
    getServletContext().getRequestDispatcher(url);
dispatcher.forward(request, response);
}

public void doPost(HttpServletRequest request,
                   HttpServletResponse response)
                   throws IOException, ServletException{
    doGet(request, response);
}
}
```

Note

- This class uses the MailUtil class that's stored in the music.util package to send a confirmation email. For more information about working with this class, see chapter 12.

Figure 20-11   The CompleteServlet class (part 2 of 2)

Perspective

The goal of this chapter has been to show you how all the skills taught in chapters 1 through 15 can be integrated into an e-commerce application. For instructional purposes, though, this application has been simplified. As a result, some real-world issues aren't completely resolved. Nevertheless, this application is a good starting point for any e-commerce application that you develop.

When you do develop your own applications, for example, you should certainly validate all user entries including credit card information. If you have many products, you will also want to generate the Product pages from data that's stored in the database. If you've mastered chapters 1 through 15, though, you have all the skills you need for making enhancements like that.

In the next chapter, you'll see how an administrative application lets employees with proper security clearance process the orders that the Shopping Cart application writes to the database. You'll also see how this application lets the users view reports that summarize the orders that have been written to the database. Once you read this chapter, you'll have a complete view of how you can use JSPs and servlets to create an e-commerce site.

21

The Admin application

In the last two chapters, you were introduced to the applications of the Music Store web site that allow anyone in the world with an Internet connection and a web browser to download sound files and order albums. Now, you'll learn about the Admin application. This application provides the administrative functions for the web site, but it's only available to a user who has a valid username and password.

An introduction to the Admin application **580**
The Index page 580
The structure 580
The security 580

The Collect Orders application **584**
The user interface 584
The code 584

The Reports application **592**
The user interface 592
The code 592

Perspective **598**

An introduction to the Admin application

The Admin application provides two main functions. The first one lets the user collect and process orders, and the second one lets the user view reports.

The Index page

Figure 21-1 shows the Index page for the Admin application. Each button on this page leads to a different part of this application. The Collect Orders button lets the user collect and process the orders that have been placed by users of the Shopping Cart application. The Reports button lets the user view reports that summarize data about users, orders, and downloads.

The structure

Figure 21-2 shows the JSPs and servlets that are used by the Admin application. To collect and process orders, this application calls the CollectServlet class. This class collects all orders that have not been processed yet. Then, the Orders page displays these orders. When the user of the application selects an order, the ShowOrderServlet displays the page for the order. This page shows the data for a specific order. Then, the user can choose to process the order or return to the Orders page.

To access reports, this application calls the Reports page. Depending on the report requested by the user, the application either calls the ReportServlet class or the Parameters page. Either way, the ReportServlet class is eventually called and the report is then displayed.

The security

Since the Admin application should only be available to employees of the Music Store web site, it uses a security constraint like the one in figure 21-3 to restrict access to all pages in the admin directory. When you first install the Music Store web site, this constraint won't be enabled. To enable it, you'll need to modify the server.xml and web.xml files as described in chapter 14.

Similarly, since this application transmits sensitive data, it uses a secure SSL connection. But when you first install the Music Store web site, this application will use a regular HTTP connection. To enable the secure connection, you'll need to modify the server.xml file and install a self-signed certificate as described in chapter 13.

The Index page for the Admin application

Description

- The Index page for the Admin application lets the user choose between the two main administrative functions: (1) collecting the unprocessed orders, and (2) viewing reports.

- When the Admin application is first installed, it doesn't use a secure connection. To learn how to configure a secure connection, see chapter 13.

- You can start the Admin application by entering the URL for the index page in your browser. If you have configured a secure connection, you can access this application with the URL shown above. Otherwise, you can use a regular HTTP connection to access the application.

Figure 21-1   The Index page for the Admin application

The structure of the Admin application

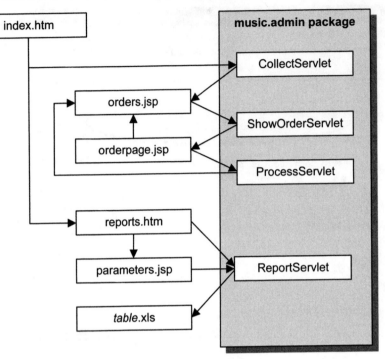

Description

- The JSP files for this application are stored in the musicStore\admin directory.
- The servlets for this application are stored in the music.admin package.
- The CollectServlet collects each unprocessed invoice and stores it as an Invoice object in a vector. Then, the Orders page can display a link to each unprocessed invoice.
- The ShowOrderServlet gets the selected invoice from the vector of invoices. Then, the Order page can display the invoice so the user can decide whether to process it.
- The ProcessServlet processes the selected invoice.
- The ReportServlet accepts the name of the report and its parameters and creates a tab-delimited string that contains the data of the report. Then, it returns that string as an Excel spreadsheet.

Figure 21-2   The structure of the Admin application

The security constraint defined in the web.xml file

```
<security-constraint>
  <web-resource-collection>
     <web-resource-name>Basic</web-resource-name>
        <url-pattern>/admin/*</url-pattern>
  </web-resource-collection>
  <auth-constraint>
     <role-name>service</role-name>
  </auth-constraint>
  <user-data-constraint>
     <transport-guarantee>NONE</transport-guarantee>
  </user-data-constraint>
</security-constraint>

<login-config>
  <auth-method>BASIC</auth-method>
</login-config>
```

The BASIC authentication dialog box in Internet Explorer

Description

- The security constraint causes a dialog box like the one above to be displayed the first time the user requests any page from the admin directory. To learn how to enable a security constraint, see chapter 14.

- The entire Admin application should use a secure connection so all data that's passed between the browser and server is encrypted. To learn how to configure and use a secure connection, see chapter 13.

Figure 21-3   The security for the Admin application

The Collect Orders application

The Collect Orders application allows a user with proper security access to view and process all unprocessed orders made by the Shopping Cart application.

The user interface

Figure 21-4 presents the two pages of the Collect Orders application. From the Orders page, the user can view a list of unprocessed orders. Then, to view the details of any unprocessed order, the user can click on the corresponding link to display the Order page.

If the user determines that the order is valid, the user can process the order by clicking on the Process Order button. Then, the application will process the order and return to the Orders page. However, the order that has been processed won't be displayed on this page anymore. If no unprocessed orders exist, the Admin application will display the main menu for the application.

The code

Figures 21-5 through 21-9 present the code for the JSPs and servlets of the Admin application. Although this code shows how JSPs and servlets are used in a practical application, they don't present any coding skills that haven't already been covered in chapters 3 through 15. As a result, you should be able to understand this code without any help.

In figure 21-9, the code for the ProcessServlet calls a method of the OrderDB class to set the IsProcessed column for the invoice in the database to 'y'. In this simple application, that's the only processing that's done. However, in a real application, the ProcessServlet could include code that sends an email to the user, processes the credit card data, or prints the order.

The Orders page

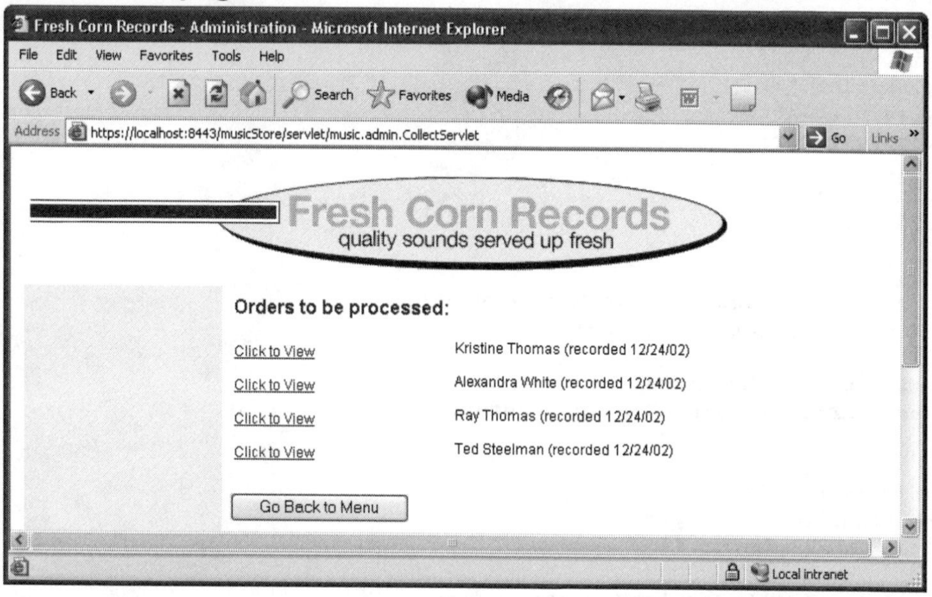

The Order page

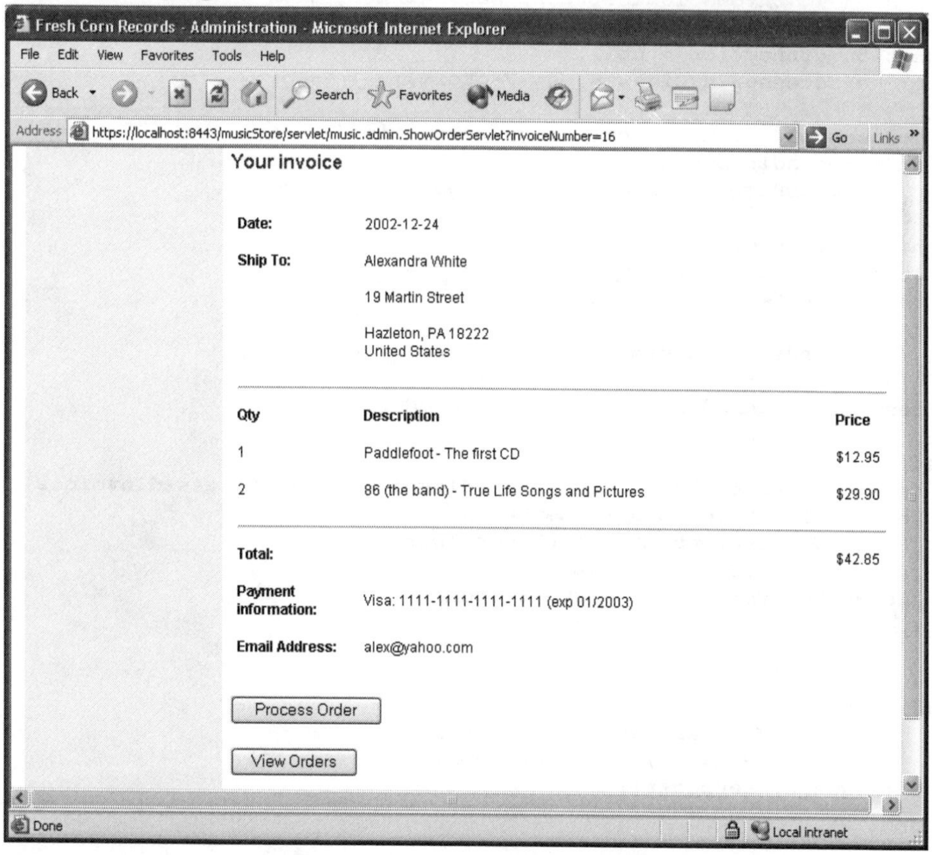

Figure 21-4   The user interface for the Collect Orders button

The CollectServlet class

```
package music.admin;
import java.io.*;
import javax.servlet.*;
import javax.servlet.http.*;
import java.util.Vector;
import java.sql.*;
import music.util.*;
import music.data.*;


public class CollectServlet extends HttpServlet{
    private MurachPool connectionPool;

    public void init() throws ServletException{
        connectionPool = MurachPool.getInstance();
    }

    public void destroy() {
        connectionPool.destroy();
    }

    public void doGet(HttpServletRequest request,
                      HttpServletResponse response)
                  throws IOException, ServletException{
        HttpSession session = request.getSession(true);
        Connection connection = null;
        Vector unProcessedInvoices = new Vector();
        try{
            connection = connectionPool.getConnection();
            unProcessedInvoices =
                OrderDB.readUnProcessedInvoices(connection);
        }
        catch(SQLException e){
            log("CollectServlet SQLException: " + e);
            throw new ServletException(e);
        }
        if ( (unProcessedInvoices == null) ||
             (unProcessedInvoices.size()<=0) ){
            response.sendRedirect("/musicStore/admin");
        }
        else{
            session.setAttribute("unProcessedInvoices", unProcessedInvoices);
            RequestDispatcher dispatcher =
                getServletContext().getRequestDispatcher(
                    "/admin/orders.jsp");
            dispatcher.forward(request, response);
        }
    }

    public void doPost(HttpServletRequest request,
                       HttpServletResponse response)
                   throws IOException, ServletException{
        doGet(request, response);
    }
}
```

Figure 21-5   The CollectServlet class

The orders.jsp file

```
<!-- begin main column -->

<%@ taglib uri="../WEB-INF/tlds/music.tld" prefix="msc" %>

<table>

<tr>
  <td><h1>Orders to be processed:</h1></td>
<tr>

<msc:order>
<tr>
  <td>
    <a href=
      "../servlet/music.admin.ShowOrderServlet?invoiceNumber=<%=invoiceNumber%>">
      Click to View
    </a>
  </td>
  <td><p><%=firstName%> <%=lastName%> (recorded <%=day%>)</td>
</tr>
</msc:order>

</table>
<form action="../admin/index.htm" method="post">
    <input type=submit value="Go Back to Menu">
</form>

<!-- end main column -->
```

Note

- This page uses the custom msc:order tag to display the unprocessed orders. The classes that define this tag are stored in the music.tag package, and the tag library descriptor is stored in the WEB-INF\tld directory. For more information about custom tags, see chapter 9.

Figure 21-6   The orders.jsp file

The ShowOrderServlet class

```
package music.admin;
import java.io.*;
import javax.servlet.*;
import javax.servlet.http.*;
import java.util.Vector;
import java.sql.*;
import java.text.NumberFormat;
import music.business.*;
import music.util.*;

public class ShowOrderServlet extends HttpServlet{
    private MurachPool connectionPool;

    public void init() throws ServletException{
        connectionPool = MurachPool.getInstance();
    }

    public void destroy() {
        connectionPool.destroy();
    }

    public void doGet(HttpServletRequest request,
                      HttpServletResponse response)
                      throws IOException, ServletException{

        HttpSession session = request.getSession(true);
        int invoiceNumber =
            Integer.parseInt(request.getParameter("invoiceNumber"));
        Vector unProcessedInvoices =
            (Vector) session.getAttribute("unProcessedInvoices");
        int i = 0;
        boolean found = false;
        Invoice orderInvoice = null;
        while ( (i<unProcessedInvoices.size()) && (!found) ){
            orderInvoice = (Invoice)unProcessedInvoices.get(i);
            if (orderInvoice.getInvoiceNumber() == invoiceNumber)
                found = true;
            i++;
        }
        User user = orderInvoice.getUser();
        Vector lineItems = orderInvoice.getLineItems();
        session.setAttribute("user", user);
        session.setAttribute("invoice", orderInvoice);
        Cart cart = new Cart(lineItems);
        session.setAttribute("cart", cart);
        NumberFormat currency = NumberFormat.getCurrencyInstance();
        session.setAttribute("invoiceTotalAsString",
            currency.format(orderInvoice.getInvoiceTotal()));

        RequestDispatcher dispatcher =
            getServletContext().getRequestDispatcher(
                "/admin/orderpage.jsp");
        dispatcher.forward(request, response);
    }
}
```

Figure 21-7   The ShowOrderServlet class

The orderpage.jsp file

```
<!-- begin main column -->

<%@ taglib uri="../WEB-INF/tlds/music.tld" prefix="msc" %>

<jsp:useBean id="user" class="music.business.User" scope="session" />
<jsp:useBean id="invoice" class="music.business.Invoice" scope="session" />

<h1>Your invoice</h1>

<table border="0" cellspacing="5">
  <tr>
    <td><p><b>Date:</td>
    <td width="400"><p>
        <jsp:getProperty name="invoice" property="invoiceDate"/></td>
    <td></td>
  </tr>
  <tr valign="top">
    <td><p><b>Ship To:</td>
    <td><p><jsp:getProperty name="user" property="firstName"/>
           <jsp:getProperty name="user" property="lastName"/><br>
           <jsp:getProperty name="user" property="companyName"/><br>
           <jsp:getProperty name="user" property="address1"/><br>
           <jsp:getProperty name="user" property="address2"/><br>
           <jsp:getProperty name="user" property="city"/>,
           <jsp:getProperty name="user" property="state"/>
           <jsp:getProperty name="user" property="zip"/><br>
           <jsp:getProperty name="user" property="country"/></td> <br>

    <td></td>
  </tr>
  <tr>
    <td colspan="3"><hr></td>
  </tr>
  <tr>
    <td><p><b>Qty</td>
    <td><p><b>Description</td>
    <td><p><b>Price</b></p></td>
  </tr>

<msc:cart>
  <tr>
    <td><p><%=quantity%></td>
    <td><p><%=productDescription%></td>
    <td><p><%=total%></td>
  </tr>
</msc:cart>

  <tr>
    <td colspan="3"><hr></td>
  </tr>
```

Figure 21-8   The orderpage.jsp file (part 1 of 2)

The orderpage.jsp file (continued)

```
<tr>
    <td><p><b>Total:</td>
    <td></td>
    <td><p><%=(String)session.getAttribute("invoiceTotalAsString")%></td>
  </tr>
  <tr>
  <td><p><b>Payment information:</td>
  <td><p><jsp:getProperty name="user"
          property="creditCardType"/>: <jsp:getProperty name="user"
          property="creditCardNumber"/> (exp <jsp:getProperty name="user"
          property="creditCardExpirationDate"/>)</td>
  </tr>
  <tr>
  <td><p><b>Email Address:</i></td>
  <td><p><jsp:getProperty name="user" property="emailAddress"/></td>
  </tr>
  </table>

<form action="<%=response.encodeURL(
                  "../servlet/music.admin.ProcessServlet")%>"
      method="post">
    <input type="submit" value="Process Order">
</form>
<form action="<%=response.encodeURL("../admin/orders.jsp")%>"
      method="post">
    <input type="submit" value="View Orders">
</form>

<!-- end main column -->
```

Note

- This page uses the custom msc:cart tag to display the line items of the order. The classes that define this tag are stored in the music.tag package. For more information about custom tags, see chapter 9.
- The page uses JSP tags to access the User and Invoice JavaBeans. For more information about working with JavaBeans, see chapter 8.

Figure 21-8   The orderpage.jsp file (part 2 of 2)

The ProcessServlet class

```
package music.admin;

import java.io.*;
import javax.servlet.*;
import javax.servlet.http.*;
import java.sql.*;
import music.util.*;
import music.data.*;
import music.business.*;

public class ProcessServlet extends HttpServlet{
    private MurachPool connectionPool;

    public void init() throws ServletException{
        connectionPool = MurachPool.getInstance();
    }

    public void destroy() {
        connectionPool.destroy();
    }

    public void doGet(HttpServletRequest request,
                      HttpServletResponse response)
                      throws IOException, ServletException{

        HttpSession session = request.getSession(true);
        Invoice orderInvoice = (Invoice)session.getAttribute("invoice");
        int invoiceID = orderInvoice.getInvoiceNumber();
        //get the Invoice object, set the IsProcessed field to "y"
        Connection connection = null;
        try{
            connection = connectionPool.getConnection();
            OrderDB.setIsProcessed(connection, invoiceID);
        }
        catch(SQLException e){
            log("ProcessServlet SQLException: " + e);
            throw new ServletException(e);
        }
        finally{
            connectionPool.freeConnection(connection);
        }
        RequestDispatcher dispatcher =
            getServletContext().getRequestDispatcher(
                "/servlet/music.admin.CollectServlet");
        dispatcher.forward(request, response);
    }

    public void doPost(HttpServletRequest request,
                       HttpServletResponse response)
                       throws ServletException, IOException {
        doGet(request, response);
    }
}
```

Figure 21-9   The ProcessServlet class

The Reports application

The Reports application lets the user view the data that's stored in the database for the Music Store web site. In particular, this application provides access to four reports that summarize data about users, orders, and downloads.

The user interface

Figure 21-10 shows the pages of the Reports application. To start, the Reports page displays a list of available reports. If the user selects the first report, the report is displayed. But if the user selects one of the next three reports, the Parameters page is displayed. This page lets the user enter a start date and end date for the report.

This figure also shows three of the reports that can be generated from the Admin application. This shows that the reports are returned as Excel spreadsheets. As a result, the user can view the data, or the user can save the data as an Excel spreadsheet. However, these reports could also be returned as HTML tables or XML documents.

The code

Figures 21-11 and 21-12 show the code for the Reports application. Although this code shows how JSPs and servlets are used in a practical application, they don't present any coding skills that haven't already been covered in chapters 3 through 15. As a result, you should be able to understand this code without any help.

Unlike most of the other applications, the Reports application doesn't use any business objects. Instead, the ReportServlet in figure 21-11 calls a method from the ReportDB class directly. Then, the ReportDB class gets a result set from the database and creates a tab-delimited string that contains the data in the result set. Here, the ReportDB class uses a StringBuffer object instead of a String object to create the string. This can make a large report run noticeably faster.

The Reports page

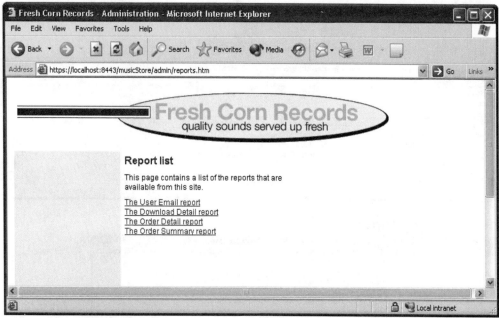

The Parameters page

Figure 21-10   The user interface for the Reports application (part 1 of 2)

The User Email report

	A	B	C	D	E	F	G	H	I	J	K
1	The User Email report										
2											
3	LastName	FirstName	EmailAddress	CompanyName	Address1	Address2	City	State	Zip	Country	UserID
4	Flinstone	Fred	freddie@yahoo.com		55 Pebble Lane		Bedrock	PA	92551	USA	12
5	Lewis	Robert	lewis@erob.edu	Edu. Systems	2000 Lotus Way	Bld. 87	Fresno	CA	93711	USA	14
6	Motors	Mike	cars@motors.com	Motors Inc.	4232 Railway Dr.	Suite A	Lemoore	CA	93245	USA	13
7	Murach	Ben	ben@murach.com		554 Easy Rd		Emmaus	ID	83669	USA	8

Address: https://localhost:8443/musicStore/servlet/music.admin.ReportServlet?reportTitle=The%20User%20Email%20report&reportName=userEmail

music.admin.ReportServlet

The Order Summary report

	A	B	C	D	E	F	G
1	The Order Summary report						
2							
3	Start Date: 2002-01-01						
4	End Date: 2002-12-31						
5							
6	ProductCode	ProductDescription	ProductPrice	Quantity	Total		
7	8601	86 (the band) - True Life Songs and Pictures	14.95	10	149.5		
8	pf01	Paddlefoot - The first CD	12.95	11	142.45		
9	pf02	Paddlefoot - The second CD	14.95	9	134.55		
10	jr01	Joe Rut - Genuine Wood Grained Finish	14.95	7	104.65		
11							

Address: https://localhost:8443/musicStore/servlet/music.admin.ReportServlet?reportName=orderSummary&reportTitle=The

music.admin.ReportServlet

The Order Detail report

	A	B	C	D	E	F	G	H	I
1	The Order Detail report								
2									
3	Start Date: 2002-01-01								
4	End Date: 2002-12-31								
5									
6	Date	Time	InvoiceID	EmailAddress	UserID	ProductCode	ProductPrice	Quantity	LineItemAmount
7									
8	12/24/2002	8:50:33	18	ted@net.com	25	pf01	12.95	1	12.95
9	12/24/2002	8:48:13	17	ray@thomas.com	24	pf02	14.95	1	14.95
10	12/24/2002	8:47:32	16	alex@yahoo.com	22	pf01	12.95	1	12.95
11	12/24/2002	8:42:43	12	alex@yahoo.com	22	pf02	14.95	2	29.9

Address: https://localhost:8443/musicStore/servlet/music.admin.ReportServlet?reportName=orderDetail&reportTitle=The+Order

music.admin.ReportServlet

Figure 21-10   The user interface for the Reports application (part 2 of 2)

The ReportServlet class

```
package music.admin;

import java.io.*;
import javax.servlet.*;
import javax.servlet.http.*;
import java.util.*;
import java.sql.*;
import music.util.*;
import music.data.*;

public class ReportServlet extends HttpServlet {
    private MurachPool connectionPool;

    public void init() throws ServletException{
        connectionPool = MurachPool.getInstance();
    }

    public void destroy() {
        connectionPool.destroy();
    }

    public void doGet(HttpServletRequest request,
                      HttpServletResponse response)
                      throws IOException, ServletException{

        response.setContentType("application/vnd.ms-excel");
        PrintWriter out = response.getWriter();

        String reportName = request.getParameter("reportName");
        String reportTitle = request.getParameter("reportTitle");
        String startDate = request.getParameter("startDate");
        String endDate = request.getParameter("endDate");

        Connection connection = null;
        String returnString = null;
        try{
            connection = connectionPool.getConnection();
            if (reportName.equalsIgnoreCase("userEmail")){
                returnString = ReportDB.getUserEmail(connection,
                    reportTitle);
            }
            else if (reportName.equalsIgnoreCase("downloadDetail")){
                returnString = ReportDB.getDownloadDetail(connection,
                    reportTitle, startDate, endDate);
            }
            else if (reportName.equalsIgnoreCase("orderSummary")){
                returnString = ReportDB.getOrderSummary(connection,
                    reportTitle, startDate, endDate);
            }
            else if (reportName.equalsIgnoreCase("orderDetail")){
                returnString = ReportDB.getOrderDetail(connection,
                    reportTitle, startDate, endDate);
            }
```

Figure 21-11   The ReportServlet class (part 1 of 2)

The ReportServlet class (continued)

```
            else{
                System.out.println("reportName not found: " + reportName);
                response.sendRedirect("/musicStore/admin/reports.htm");
            }
        }
        catch(SQLException e){
            log("ReportServlet SQLException: " + e);
            response.sendRedirect("/musicStore/admin/index.htm");
        }
        finally{
            connectionPool.freeConnection(connection);
        }
        out.println(returnString);
    }

    public void doPost(HttpServletRequest request,
                       HttpServletResponse response)
                       throws IOException, ServletException{
        doGet(request, response);
    }
}
```

Figure 21-11   The ReportServlet class (part 2 of 2)

The ReportDB class

```java
package music.data;

import java.util.Vector;
import java.util.StringTokenizer;
import java.sql.*;
import music.util.*;

public class ReportDB{

    // The Order Summary report
    public static String getOrderSummary(Connection connection,
                String reportTitle, String startDate, String endDate)
                throws SQLException{
        String query =
            "SELECT ProductCode, ProductDescription, "
          + "     ProductPrice, Quantity, "
          + "     SUM(Quantity) AS ProductQuantity, "
          + "     SUM(ProductPrice*Quantity) AS ProductTotal "
          + "FROM Invoice "
          + "     INNER JOIN LineItem ON Invoice.InvoiceID = LineItem.InvoiceID "
          + "     INNER JOIN Product ON LineItem.ProductID = Product.ProductID "
          + "WHERE InvoiceDate >= '" + startDate + "' "
          + "     AND InvoiceDate <= '" + endDate + "' "
          + "GROUP BY ProductCode, ProductDescription "
          + "ORDER BY ProductTotal DESC";
        Statement statement = connection.createStatement();
        ResultSet record = statement.executeQuery(query);
        String d = "\t";
        StringBuffer report = new StringBuffer(
                reportTitle + "\n\n"
              + "Start Date: " + startDate + "\n"
              + "End Date: " + endDate + "\n\n"
              + "ProductCode" + d
              + "ProductDescription" + d
              + "ProductPrice" + d
              + "Quantity" + d
              + "Total" + "\n");
        while (record.next()){
            report.append(record.getString("ProductCode") + d
                        + record.getString("ProductDescription") + d
                        + record.getDouble("ProductPrice") + d
                        + record.getInt("ProductQuantity") + d
                        + record.getDouble("ProductTotal") + "\n");
        }
        record.close();
        statement.close();
        return report.toString();
    }
    //methods that generate other reports
}
```

Note

- The code that generates the User Email, Order Detail, and Download Detail reports isn't shown in this figure. However, it is on the CD that comes with this book.

Figure 21-12   The ReportsDB class

Perspective

The goal of this chapter has been to show you how to provide administrative access to the Music Store web site. However, you should be able to use the principles illustrated here to provide administrative access to any web site.

Although the Admin application only provides two functions, it's common for an Admin application to provide many functions. For example, an Admin application can be used to add, update, or delete products from a Products table. This is useful in an application that generates the product pages from the data in the Products table.

Although this chapter shows how to return a report as an Excel spreadsheet, there are other options for implementing the reports of a web site. In fact, many companies use third-party software for creating reports. As a result, you may be able to save development time and create more professional looking reports by using this type of software.

Appendix A

How to install the software and applications for this book

Chapter 2 shows how to install Tomcat, a popular servlet and JSP engine. This appendix shows how to install and configure the rest of the software that you need for running the web applications that are presented in this book. It also shows how to install those web applications. All of this software and the web applications are available on the CD that comes with this book.

How to install the SDK and MySQL 600
How to install Java's SDK 600
How to install MySQL 602
How to configure Windows to work with Java 604
How to set the path 604
How to set the classpath 606
How to install the applications for this book 608
The applications for chapters 4 through 16 608
The applications for the Music Store web site 608
How to install and use two text editors 610
How to install and use TextPad 610
How to install and use HomeSite 612

How to install the SDK and MySQL

Chapter 2 of this book shows how to install and configure Tomcat so you can run servlets and JavaServer Pages. However, for Tomcat to work properly, Java's Software Development Kit (SDK) must also be installed on your system. In addition, if you want to develop web applications that access a database, a database management system like MySQL, must be installed on your system. That's why this topic shows how to install Java's SDK and MySQL.

How to install Java's SDK

If you've been using Java for a while, it is probably installed on your computer already. In that case, you can skip this topic. Otherwise, figure A-1 shows how to install version 1.4 of the SDK.

If you're using Windows, the easiest way to install Java is to use the CD that comes with this book. Just navigate to the WindowsSDK directory and run the exe file. Then, respond to the resulting dialog boxes. However, if you want to install a different version of Java, or if you need a version of Java for a non-Windows operating system, you can download that version from the Java web site as described in this figure.

Since Sun is continually updating the Java web site, the procedure in this figure may not be up-to-date by the time you read this. As a result, you may have to do some searching to find the current version of the SDK. In general, you can start by looking for products for the Java 2 Platform, Standard Edition. Then, you can find the most current version of the SDK for your operating system.

The Java web site address

www.java.sun.com

How to install the SDK from the CD that comes with this book

1. Navigate to the WindowsSDK directory that's on the CD.

2. Double-click on the exe file, and respond to the resulting dialog boxes. When you're prompted for the SDK directory, use the default directory and install all of the components unless disk space is a problem.

How to download and install the SDK from the Java web site

1. Go to the Java web site (*www.java.sun.com*).

2. Locate Java products and find the Java 2 Platform, Standard Edition.

3. Go to the download page for the most current SDK version that's available for your platform.

4. After clicking on the download button, follow the instructions. Note the name of the file and the download size.

5. Select one of the FTP download options, unless you're behind a firewall and you need to use the HTTP option.

6. Save the setup file to your hard disk. On a 56K modem, it takes about 2 hours to download this file.

7. Once the entire package has downloaded, check to make sure that you got the executable and that the size is correct. Otherwise, you will get an error when you try to run the executable.

8. Run the exe file, and respond to the resulting dialog boxes. When you're prompted for the SDK directory, use the default directory and install all of the components unless disk space is a problem.

How to configure the SDK for Tomcat

- Copy the servlet.jar file from Tomcat's common\lib directory to the SDK's jre\lib\ext directory. This will give the SDK access to the Java classes it needs to work with servlets.

Figure A-1   How to install Java's SDK

How to install MySQL

Some of the web applications presented in this book access a MySQL database. For example, the applications in chapter 11 use a MySQL database, and the Music Store web site presented in chapters 18 through 21 uses a MySQL database. Before you can run these applications, you need to install MySQL on your system and make sure that the MySQL server is running as described in figure A-2. Then, you need to install the appropriate databases as described in figure A-5.

This figure shows how to install version 3.23 of MySQL on a Windows machine. If you're using Windows, the easiest way to do that is to use the CD that comes with this book. Just navigate to the MySQL directory on the CD and run the setup.exe file. Then, you can usually accept the default values from the prompts. This should install MySQL in the mysql directory on your C drive.

If you want to install a different version of MySQL, or if you want to install MySQL on a different operating system, you can download that version from the MySQL web site (*www.mysql.com*) and use a zip program to extract the files from that zip file. Then, you can navigate to the folder that contains the un-zipped files and follow steps 2 and 3 of the installation procedure in this figure. If you're using a Unix system, you'll also need to run the mysql_install_db script that's stored in the mysql\scripts directory to initialize the data directory and install the database that keeps track of user priviledges.

When you install MySQL on most Windows systems, the MySQL database server starts every time you start your computer. On some systems, this displays the MySQL icon in the tray. This icon looks like a stoplight, and the light is green when this server is running. On other systems, the server is running but the icon isn't displayed in the tray.

To display the MySQL icon, you can run the winmysqladmin.exe file that's in MySQL's bin directory. Then, you can stop the database server by selecting the "Stop this Service" or the "ShutDown this Server" command from the icon. If you select the "Stop this Service" command, the light on the icon will become red, and you can restart the server by selecting the "Start this Service" command from the icon.

To be able to access a MySQL database, Tomcat needs to be able to access a database driver for MySQL. The easiest way to allow Tomcat to do that is to move the JAR file from the MySQL_Driver directory on the CD to Tomcat's common\lib directory. However, you can also modify your classpath so it includes the location of the database driver JAR file.

Since MySQL is continuously updating the JDBC database driver, the one we have on the CD isn't the latest version. To find a later version, you can go to *www.mysql.com* and look for MySQL Connector. For the purposes of this book, though, the driver on the CD is more than adequate.

How to install MySQL from the CD that comes with this book

1. Navigate to the MySQL directory that's on the CD.

2. Run the setup.exe file for MySQL.

3. Respond to the prompts to install MySQL on your computer. On most systems, you can accept all default options.

How to configure MySQL for Tomcat

- Copy the mm.mysql-2.0.8-bin.jar file from the MySQL_Driver directory that's located on the book's CD to c:\tomcat\common\lib. This will give Tomcat access to the MySQL driver it needs to be able to access a MySQL database.

The icon for the MySQL server

MySQL icon

How to start the MySQL server

- On most systems, the MySQL server starts every time you start your computer.

- If the MySQL server doesn't start when you start your computer, you can start the MySQL server by running the winmysqladmin.exe file in MySQL's bin directory.

- On some systems, the MySQL icon is displayed in the tray as shown above. On other systems, you must run the winmysqladmin.exe file to display the icon.

A DOS window that starts the MySQL server and displays the MySQL icon

How to stop the MySQL server

- To stop the server, you can click on the MySQL icon. Then, you can select the "Win 9x" and "ShutDown this Server" commands, or you can select the "Win NT" and "Stop this Service" commands.

Description

- For more information about installing and configuring MySQL, check the MySQL website at *www.mysql.com*, or the MySQL documentation in MySQL's docs directory.

- For more information about working with MySQL, see chapter 10.

Figure A-2   How to install MySQL

How to configure Windows to work with Java

Once you install the SDK on a Windows system, you'll probably want to add the SDK's home directory to the *command path*, or *path*, so Windows can find the commands that are available from the SDK. In addition, you may need to add some directories to the *classpath* so the compiler that comes as part of the SDK can find all of the Java classes it needs.

How to set the path

Figure A-3 shows you how to set the path so Windows will always be able to find the Java commands available from the SDK. To do that, you just need to add the SDK's bin directory to the path. If you're not using Windows, you can refer to the Java web site to see what, if anything, you need to do to configure Java for your system.

To update the path for Windows 95, 98, or ME, you can use the first procedure in this figure to edit the Path or Set Path command in the autoexec.bat file. This is the file that is automatically executed every time you start your computer. After you edit this file, you can restart your computer to run the autoexec.bat file and establish the new path. Then, you can start a DOS prompt and enter *path* to make sure that the bin directory is now in the command path.

When you edit the autoexec.bat file, be careful! Since this file may affect the operation of other programs on your PC, you don't want to delete or modify any of the commands that this file contains. You only want to add one directory to the command path. If that doesn't work, be sure that you're able to restore the autoexec.bat file to its original condition.

If you're using a later version of Windows, you can use the second procedure in this figure to set the command path. It is easier to use with less chance that you'll do something that will affect the operation of other programs.

If you don't configure Windows in this way, you can still compile and run Java programs, but it's more difficult. In particular, you need to enter the complete path for each command. For instance, you need to enter

```
\j2sdk1.4.0\bin\javac
```

instead of just

```
javac
```

to run the javac command that's stored in the c:\j2sdk1.4.0\bin directory. If you understand DOS, you should understand how this works.

A Path statement in the autoexec.bat file

```
C:\AUTOEXEC.BAT                                    _ □ ×
PATH=C:\WINDOWS;C:\WINDOWS\COMMAND;C:\J2SDK1.4.0\BIN;
```

The directory that you need to add to the path

`c:\j2sdk1.4.0\bin`

How to set the path for Windows 95/98/ME

1. Open the autoexec.bat file (usually c:\autoexec.bat) in a text editor.
2. If the file contains a Path or Set Path command, type a semicolon at the end of the command. Then, enter the SDK's bin directory as shown above. If the file doesn't contain a Path or Set Path command, enter a Path statement like the one shown above at the beginning of the file.
3. Save the file and exit the text editor.
4. To have the new path take effect, you can restart your computer (which runs the autoexec.bat file).

How to set the path for Windows NT/2000/XP

1. Go to the Start menu, point to Settings, and select the Control Panel.
2. Edit the environment variables for your system. For NT, select the System icon, and the Environment tab. For 2000, select the System icon, the Advanced tab, and the Environment Variables button. For XP, select the Performance and Maintenance icon, the System icon, the Advanced tab, and the Environment Variables button.
3. Add the SDK's bin directory to the far right side of the current path in System Variables and select OK.
4. To have the new environment variables take effect, you can shutdown and restart all programs that use Java.

How to check the current path

- To check the current path setting, you can start a DOS prompt and enter the set command. When you do, the DOS window will display various configuration data including the path and classpath (which you'll learn about in the next figure).

Description

- After you add the SDK's bin directory to the path, Windows is able to find the commands that it needs to compile and run Java programs.
- The Path statement is not case-sensitive. As a result, you can use uppercase or lowercase letters when coding this statement.

Figure A-3   How to set the path

How to set the classpath

To compile Java classes that depend on other classes that aren't bundled with the SDK, you must set the classpath so the Java compiler knows where to look for these classes. If you set the classpath correctly, Java will be able to find these classes when you attempt to compile a class. Otherwise, you'll get an error that indicates that the compiler can't find a class it needs.

To update the classpath for Windows 95, 98, or ME, you can use the first procedure in figure A-4 to edit the Classpath or Set Classpath command in the autoexec.bat file. This procedure is similar to the one in the previous figure for setting the command path. As always, when editing the autoexec.bat file, you should make sure that you're able to restore the autoexec.bat file to its original condition.

If you're using a later version of Windows, you can use the second procedure in this figure to set the classpath. It is easier to use with less chance that you'll do something that will affect the operation of other programs.

Either way, when you specify the classpath, you should include a period (.) to specify the current directory. That way, Java will always check the current directory for classes. Then, you can specify any other directories that you want to include. For example, if you want to use TextPad's Compile Java command to work with the Java classes presented on the CD that comes with this book, your classpath has to include the two directories shown in this figure. These directories assume that your Tomcat home directory is c:\tomcat.

In addition to directories that contain classes, you can specify JAR files that contain classes. For example, to specify the servlet.jar file, you can add this directory to your classpath:

```
c:\tomcat\common\lib\servlet.jar
```

Then, all classes contained within the JAR file will be available to the SDK. This is an alternative to copying the servlet.jar file into the SDK's jre\lib\ext directory as described in chapter 2.

When you enter directories or JAR files within the classpath, make sure to separate each entry with a semicolon. As you progress with your Java programming, you may need to add many directories or JAR files to the classpath and this statement may become quite long.

A Classpath statement in the autoexec.bat file

```
C:\AUTOEXEC.BAT
PATH=C:\WINDOWS;C:\WINDOWS\COMMAND;C:\J2SDK1.4.0\BIN;
SET CLASSPATH=.;c:\tomcat\webapps\murach\WEB-INF\classes;c:\tom
```

The directories that you need to add to the classpath

```
c:\tomcat\webapps\murach\WEB-INF\classes
c:\tomcat\webapps\musicStore\WEB-INF\classes
```

How to set the classpath for Windows 95/98/ME

1. Open the autoexec.bat file (usually c:\autoexec.bat) in a text editor.

2. If the file contains a Classpath or Set Classpath command, add the directories to the classpath. Make sure to separate all entries in the classpath with a semicolon. If the file doesn't contain a Classpath or Set Classpath command, enter one as shown above.

3. Save the file and exit the text editor.

4. To have the new classpath take effect, you can restart your computer (which runs the autoexec.bat file).

How to set the classpath for Windows NT/2000/XP

1. Go to the Start menu, point to Settings, and select the Control Panel.

2. Edit the environment variables for your system. For NT, select the System icon, and the Environment tab. For 2000, select the System icon, the Advanced tab, and the Environment Variables button. For XP, select the Performance and Maintenance icon, the System icon, the Advanced tab, and the Environment Variables button.

3. If you have a system variable named classpath, double-click on the variable and edit the existing classpath. If you don't have a classpath system variable, select the New button under System Variables. Then, create and set a classpath variable.

4. Click OK.

5. To have the new classpath take effect, you can shutdown and restart programs that compile Java classes.

Description

- To include the current directory in the classpath, you can use a single period to specify the current directory as shown in the Classpath command above.

- To be able to use TextPad to compile the classes provided on the CD, your classpath must include the WEB-INF\classes directory for the application. For the applications and exercises that come with this book, the classpath must include the directories shown above.

- The Classpath statement is not case-sensitive. As a result, you can use uppercase or lowercase letters when coding this statement.

Figure A-4   How to set the classpath

How to install the applications for this book

Figure A-5 shows how to install the applications that are included on the CD that comes with this book. Once you install these applications, you can use a web browser to run them, and you can use a text editor or IDE to view, modify, and recompile the source code.

To begin installing these applications, you can run the Install.exe file that's located in the root directory of the CD that comes with this book. Then, you respond to the resulting dialog boxes. Once you finish responding to these dialog boxes, the files for the applications should be installed in the c:\murach\webapps directory.

The applications for chapters 4 through 16

To install the applications for chapters 4 through 16, you can copy the murach subdirectory from c:\murach\webapps to c:\tomcat\webapps. When you do, the applications that don't rely upon a database should work correctly. However, the applications presented in chapter 11 use a MySQL database named murach.

To create the murach database, you must make sure the MySQL server is running as described in figure A-2. Then, you can use the CD command to change the current directory to the mysql\bin directory of your C drive, and you can execute the statement in this figure that runs the MurachMaster SQL script. This statement runs a SQL script that creates the database and its tables. When prompted for a password, just press the Enter key. When you do, the SQL script should create the database and its tables. At this point, if you start Tomcat and the MySQL server, you should be able to use a web browser to run all of the web applications for chapters 4 through 16 by entering this URL:

```
http://localhost:8080/murach
```

The applications for the Music Store web site

Chapters 18 through 21 present a complete web site that contains several web applications, including a Shopping Cart application. To install this web site and its applications, you can copy the musicStore subdirectory from c:\murach\webapps to c:\tomcat\webapps. Then, you can run the SQL script that creates the database for this web site. At this point, if you start Tomcat and the MySQL server, you should be able to use a web browser to browse through this web site. To do that, you can go to home page for the site by entering this URL:

```
http://localhost:8080/musicStore
```

For more information about this web site, see chapters 18 through 21.

How to install the applications for this book

- From the root directory of the CD, double-click on the file named Install.exe and respond to the dialog boxes that follow. This will install all applications into a directory structure that starts with c:\murach\webapps.

- Navigate to c:\murach\webapps\murach directory and copy this directory to c:\tomcat\webapps.

- Navigate to c:\murach\webapps\musicStore directory and copy this directory to c:\tomcat\webapps.

The MySQL command for creating the murach database

```
C:\mysql\bin>mysql -u root -p < c:\tomcat\webapps\murach\MurachMaster.sql
Enter password:
```

The MySQL command for creating the music database

```
C:\mysql\bin>mysql -u root -p < c:\tomcat\webapps\musicStore\MusicMaster.sql
Enter password:
```

How to create the databases

1. Install MySQL as described in figure A-2.
2. Make sure the MySQL server is running as described in figure A-2.
3. Use the CD command to navigate to the bin directory for MySQL.
4. Install the database named murach by executing the MurachMaster SQL script as shown above. Press Enter when prompted for the password.
5. Install the database named music by executing the MusicMaster SQL script as shown above. Press Enter when prompted for the password.

Notes

- Chapter 2 shows how to install Tomcat and run web applications, and it shows how to view and execute the applications that are on the CD that comes with this book.
- Chapters 18 through 21 describe the Music Store web site and its applications.

Figure A-5   How to install the applications for this book

How to install and use two text editors

If you're not using an IDE to enter and edit your source code, you can use a text editor. This topic shows how to install and use TextPad, a text editor that's designed for working with Java classes such as servlets. In addition, this topic shows how to install and use HomeSite, a text editor that's designed for working with HTML pages and JavaServer Pages.

How to install and use TextPad

You can use TextPad to save, edit, and compile Java classes. Unfortunately, though, TextPad only runs under Windows. So if you aren't using Windows, you have to use another text editor to save and edit your Java classes. In that case, you may have to use a command prompt to compile these classes.

Figure A-6 shows how to install a trial version of TextPad that's located on the book's CD. To do that, run the exe file located in the TextPad directory. Then, respond to the resulting dialog boxes.

Since this is a trial version of TextPad, you should pay for TextPad if you decide to use it beyond the initial trial period. Fortunately, this program is relatively inexpensive (about $27), especially when you consider how much time and effort it can save you.

This figure also shows some basic skills that you need when you use TextPad with Java. In general, you can use the standard Windows shortcut keystrokes and menus to enter, edit, and save your code. For instance, you can use the File menu to open and close files. You can use the Edit menu to cut, copy, and paste text. And you can use the Search menu to find and replace text. In addition, TextPad color codes the source files so it's easier to recognize the Java syntax, and TextPad makes it easy to save *.java files with the proper capitalization and extension.

Once your files are saved, you can compile them by pressing Ctrl+1, or selecting the Compile Java option from the Tool menu. If Java encounters any compile-time errors, it will display them in the Command Results window. Then, you can fix the errors and compile the class again.

Similarly, if you're developing a desktop application, you can test it by pressing Ctrl+2 or by selecting the Run Java Application command from the Tools menu. Then, the application will run in a console window.

Note, however, that this book shows you how to develop web-based applications. To run this type of application, you enter the appropriate URL in a web browser. You'll see how that works throughout this book.

TextPad with source code for a servlet

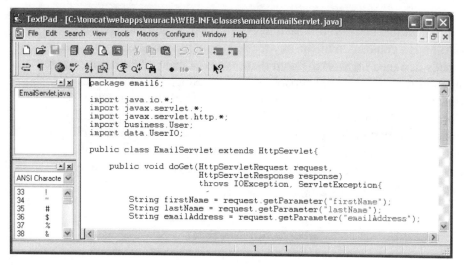

How to install TextPad on your PC

- Double-click on the exe file that's included on the CD that comes with this book. Then, respond to the resulting dialog boxes.

How to enter, edit, and save source code

- To enter and edit source code, you can use the same techniques that you use for working with any other Windows text editor.

- To save Java source code, select the Save command from the File menu (Ctrl+S). Then, enter the file name so it's exactly the same as the class name, and select the Java option from the Save As Type list so TextPad adds the four-letter java extension to the file name. (On earlier versions of Windows, you may need to enter the four-letter extension with the file name to prevent the extension from being truncated to jav.)

How to compile and execute source code

- To compile the current source code, press Ctrl+1 or select the Compile Java command from the Tools menu.

- To run a desktop application, press Ctrl+2 or select the Run Java Application command from the Tools menu. For web applications like those presented in this book, you won't use this command to run the applications.

- If you encounter compile-time errors, TextPad will print them to a window named Command Results. To switch between this window and the window that holds the source code, you can press Ctrl+F6 or use the Document Selector pane that's on the left side of the TextPad window.

Figure A-6   How to install and use TextPad

How to install and use HomeSite

Throughout this book, you'll need to code HTML pages and JavaServer Pages. Although you can do this in any text editor, it makes sense to use a text editor that's designed for working with these types of pages. That's why figure A-7 shows how to install a trial version of Macromedia's HomeSite 5.0.

To install Homesite, you should run the exe file that's located in the HomeSite directory on the CD and respond to the resulting dialog boxes. Since this version of HomeSite is a trial version, you should pay for HomeSite if you decide to use it beyond the initial trial period. Although this product is more expensive than TextPad (around $99), it is worth the cost if you code a lot of HTML pages and JSPs.

HomeSite 5.0 with the source code for an HTML document

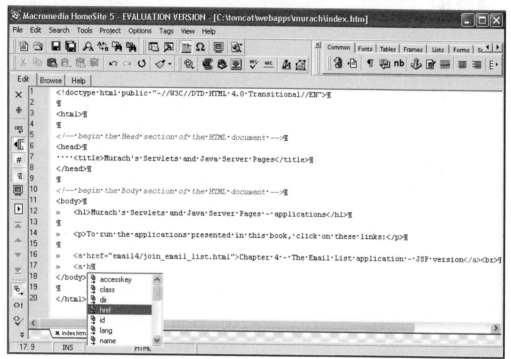

How to install HomeSite

*   Navigate to the HomeSite directory on the CD that comes with this book. Then, double-click on the exe file and respond to the resulting dialog boxes.

How to enter, edit, and save source code

*   To enter and edit source code, you can use the same techniques that you use for working with any other Windows text editor. When you enter HTML tags, HomeSite provides pop-up windows like the one shown above to help you enter tag attributes and closing tags.

*   To save the source code, select the Save command from the File menu (Ctrl+S). Then, enter the file name, and select the HTML Documents or JavaServer Pages option from the Save As Type list so HomeSite adds the appropriate extension to the file name.

Figure A-7   How to install and use HomeSite

Index

40-bit SSL, 402, 403
128-bit SSL, 402, 403
404 HTTP error, 46, 47, 132, 133, 444, 445
500 HTTP error, 132, 133, 444, 445

A

Absolute URLs, 72, 73
Abstract classes (JavaBeans), 256, 257
Accept request header, 443
Accept-encoding header, 458, 459
Action queries, 328, 329
Admin application, 580-597
Anchor tag, 72, 73
Apache server, 6, 7, 31
Applets, 12
Application assembler, 506, 507
Application scope, 248, 249
Application server (EJB), 504, 505
Applications, 4-7
Architecture, 20, 21
Attributes
    button, 86-89
    combo box, 90, 91
    custom tag, 278-283
    form, 82, 83
    HTML, 72, 73
    image, 78, 79
    list box, 90, 91
    style sheet, 80, 81
    table, 76, 77
    text area, 92, 93
    XML, 470, 471
Authentication, 400, 401
    basic, 418, 419, 428, 429
    client/server, 400, 401
    digest, 418, 419
    form-based, 418, 419, 430-433
    SSL, 400, 401
Authorization request header, 443

B

Basic authentication, 418, 419, 428, 429
BCC (Blind Carbon Copy), 386, 387
Bean developer, 506, 507
Bean-managed persistence, *see BMP*
Beans, *see JavaBeans or EJBs*
Blind Carbon Copy, 386, 387
BMP (bean-managed persistence), 508, 509, 516, 517
Body tags, 274, 275

BodyContent class, 288, 289, 300, 301
BodyTagSupport class, 286-289, 298, 299
Book applications
    Admin application, 580-597
    Collect Orders application, 584-591
    CookieUtil class, 224, 225
    Download application, 230-239
    Download application (Music Store), 546-555
    Email List application, 258-263
    Email List application (database version), 362-369
    Email List application (XML version), 492-497
    installing and running, 50, 51
    MailUtil class, 390, 391
    MurachPool class, 358, 359
    Music Store web site, *see Music Store web site*
    Reports application, 592-597
    Shopping Cart application, 207, 208
    Shopping Cart application (Music Store), 558-577
    SQL Gateway application, 346-355
    structure, 56, 57
    XMLUtil class, 492, 493
Browsers, 6, 7
    determining type, 449
    enabling/disabling cookies, 212, 213
    returning XML, 498, 499
Business classes, 172, 173
Business rules, 20, 21
Buttons, 82, 83
    JavaScript, 86, 87
    radio, 88, 89

C

Cache control header, 447, 456, 457
Callback methods (EJBs), 514, 515
CA (certificate authority), 402, 403
Cascading style sheets, 80, 81
Catalina, 34
CC (Carbon Copy), 386, 387
Certificate authorities, 402, 403
Certificates
    secure, 400-403
    self-signed, 404-407
CharacterData interface, 478, 479
Checkboxes, 88, 89
Child elements, 190, 191, 468, 469
    versus attributes, 470, 471
Child nodes, 476, 477
Classes
    abstract, 256, 257
    bean implementation, 510, 511, 514, 515

business, 172, 173
    singleton, 358, 359
    using in JSP, 120, 121
Client, 6, 7
Client authentication, 400, 401
Client/server application, 6, 7
CMP (container-managed persistence), 508, 509, 514, 515
Collect Orders application, 584-591
Combo boxes, 90, 91
Comment interface, 478, 479
Comments
    HTML, 66, 67
    JSP, 126, 127
    XML, 468, 469
Compile-time includes, 188, 189
Compiling servlets, 148, 149
Compressed files, 458, 459
Configuration
    SSL, 404-407
    Tomcat, 30, 31
Connecting to a database, 336, 337
Connection pooling, 356, 357
    installing, 358, 359
    using, 360, 361
Connection request header, 443
Connections
    https, 412, 413
    secure, 398, 399
Container-managed persistence, *see CMP*
Containers
    EJB, 504, 505
    Servlet and JSP, 12, 13
Container-managed security, 418, 419
Content type, 144-147
Content-disposition header, 447, 460, 461
Content-length header, 447, 448
Content-type header, 447
Context initialization parameters, 192-195
Controller, 174, 175
Controls, 82, 83
    tab order, 94, 95
Cookie class, 218, 219
Cookies, 204, 205, 216-221
    creating, 218, 219
    deleting, 220, 221
    enabling and disabling, 212, 213
    per-session, 212, 213
    persistent, 212, 213, 216-221
    request headers, 443
    retrieving, 220, 221
    setting age, 218, 219
    using, 218, 219
CookieUtil class, 224, 225
CREATE DATABASE statement, 316, 317
CREATE TABLE command, 318, 319

Custom error handling, 198, 199
Custom error pages, 134, 135
Custom tags, 268-300
    with attributes, 278-283
    with bodies, 274, 275
    BodyContent class, 288, 289, 300, 301
    BodyTagSupport class, 286-289, 298, 299
    conditional body, 274-277
    doStartTag method, 272, 273
    EVAL_BODY_AGAIN constant, 288, 289, 298, 299
    EVAL_BODY_BUFFERED constant, 286-289, 298, 299
    EVAL_BODY_INCLUDE constant, 276, 277, 294, 295
    EVAL_PAGE constant, 294, 295, 298, 299
    PageContext class, 272, 273, 288, 289
    reiterating, 284-289
    scripting variables, 290-293
    simple, 268, 269, 272, 273
    SKIP_BODY constant, 272, 273, 294, 295, 298, 299
    SKIP_PAGE constant, 294, 295, 298, 299
    tag handler class, 270-273
    Tag interface, 272, 273
    TagExtraInfo class, 292, 293
    TagSupport class, 272, 273, 294, 295
    TEI, 290-293
    TLD, 270, 271
    VariableInfo class, 292, 293
CuteFTP, 24, 25

D

Data access, 20, 21
Data Definition Language, *see DDL*
Data Manipulation Language, *see DML*
Data types with JavaBeans, 254, 255
Data validation, 178-185
    with servlets, 182-185
Database drivers (installing), 334, 335
Database management system, *see DBMS*
Database servers, 312, 313
Databases
    connecting to, 336, 337
    connection pooling, 356-361
    creating, 316, 317
    deleting, 316, 317
    deleting data, 342, 343
    drivers, 334, 335
    EJBs, 510, 511, 516, 517
    foreign key, 318, 319
    inserting data, 342, 343
    JDBC, 334-345
    joins, 326, 327
    meta data, 354, 355
    primary key, 318, 319
    queries, 324, 328, 329

relational, 318, 319
result sets, 324, 325, 338-341
for security restrictions, 424, 425
tables for authentication, 426, 427
updating data, 342, 343
viewing, 316, 317
DbConnectionBroker class, 358, 359
DBMS (database management system), 6, 7, 18, 19
DDL (Data Definition Language), 324
Debugging
JSPs, 132, 133
servlets, 158-161
Declarations
JSP, 128, 129
XML, 468, 469
DELETE statement, 328, 329
Deployment, 24, 25, 50
with SSL, 412
Deployment descriptor, 54, 55
for EJBs, 510, 511
destroy method (servlets), 152, 153
Development platforms, 18, 19
Digest authentication, 418, 419
Digital secure certificates, 400-403
Directives (JSP), 124, 125
Disabling cookies, 212, 213
DML (Data Manipulation Language), 324
doAfterBody method (custom tags), 298, 299
Document interface, 478, 479
Document Object Model, *see DOM*
Document Type Definition, *see DTD*
Document (XML), 466, 467, 480, 481
doEndTag method (custom tags), 294, 295, 298, 299
doGet method (servlets), 144-147, 152, 153
doInitBody method (custom tags), 298, 299
DOM (Document Object Model), 474-477
adding nodes, 482, 483
creating a DOM tree, 480, 481
hierarchy, 478, 479
interfaces, 478, 479
modifying nodes, 490, 491
reading a DOM tree, 486-489
writing to a file, 484, 485
Domain names, 24
doPost method (servlets), 146, 147, 152, 153
doStartTag method (custom tags), 272, 273, 294, 295, 298, 299
Download application, 230-239
code, 230, 233-239
file structure, 230, 232
user interface, 230-231
Downloading files, 460, 461
Drivers (JDBC), 334-337
DROP DATABASE statement, 316, 317
Drop down lists, 90, 91

DROP TABLE command, 318, 319
DTD (Document Type Definition), 472, 473, 486, 487
Dynamic web page, 10, 11

E

Editing code, 22, 23
EJB container provider, 506, 507
EJB Query Language, 508
EJB server, 504, 505
EJBHome interface, 510-513
EJBRemote interface, 510-513
EJBs (Enterprise JavaBeans), 12, 13, 504-519
bean implementation class, 514, 515
BMP (bean-managed persistence), 516, 517
callback methods, 514, 515
CMP (container-managed persistence), 508, 509, 514, 515
compared to JavaBeans, 244, 245
components, 510, 511
containers, 12, 13, 504, 505
creating and accessing, 518, 519
databases, 510, 511, 516, 517
entity beans, 508, 509
implementing, 510, 511
interfaces, 510, 511
persistence, 506-509
pros and cons, 506, 507
servers, 12, 13
session beans, 508, 509
types, 508, 509
using, 518, 519
Element interface (XML), 478, 479
Elements (XML), 190, 191, 468, 469
Email, *see JavaMail*
Email List application, 104-107, 142-145
database version, 362-369
with JavaBeans, 258-263
Model 2 approach (MVC), 168-171
user interface, 102, 103, 142, 143
XML version, 492-497
EmailServlet class, 144, 145
Enabling cookies, 212, 213
encodeURL method (HttpResponse), 214, 215
Encryption, 398, 399
Enterprise Java Beans, *see EJBs*
Entity bean implementation class, 510, 511, 514, 515
Entity beans
implementing, 510, 511
types, 508, 509
EntityBean interface, 510, 511, 514, 515
EntityContext object, 514-517
Environment variables (JAVA_HOME), 34, 35
Error handling, 198, 199
Error pages, 134, 135

errorPage directive, 134, 135
Errors
    404 HTTP error , 46, 47, 132, 133
    500 HTTP error, 132, 133
    in JSPs, 132, 133
    page cannot be displayed error, 46, 47
    in servlets, 158-161
EVAL_BODY_AGAIN constant, 288, 289, 298, 299
EVAL_BODY_BUFFERED constant, 286-289, 298, 299
EVAL_BODY_INCLUDE constant, 276, 277, 294, 295
EVAL_PAGE constant, 294, 295, 298, 299
Excel spreadsheets, 456, 457
Exception object, 134, 135
Expressions (JSP), 106, 107
Extensible Markup Language, *see XML*
External style sheets, 80, 81

F

File Download dialog box, 460, 461
File Transfer Protocol, *see FTP*
Files (downloading), 460, 461
Foreign key, 318, 319
Form-based authentication, 418, 419, 430-433
Forms, 82, 83
Forwarding requests and responses, 176, 177
FTP (File Transfer Protocol), 24

G

GenericServlet class, 146
Get method (HTTP), 104, 105, 114-117, 144, 145
getAttribute method (HttpSession), 208, 209
getAttributeNames method (HttpSession), 210, 211
getID method (HttpSession), 210, 211
getParameter method (HttpRequest), 108-111
getParameterNames method (HttpRequest), 110, 111
getParameterValues method (HttpRequest), 110, 111
getProperty tag (JavaBeans), 250, 251
getRequestDispatcher method (ServletContext), 176, 177
getServletContext (HttpServlet), 176, 177
getSession method (HttpSession), 208, 209
getWriter method (servlets), 146, 147
GIF (Graphic Interchange Format), 78, 79
GZIP compression, 458, 459
GZIPOutputStream class, 459

H

Headers (HTTP), 438, 439
    request, 442, 443
    response, 446, 447
Hidden fields, 84, 85, 228, 229
Home interface, 510-513
HomeSite, 22, 23, 62, 63

Host request header, 443
Hosts, 24, 25, 42, 43
Href tag (HTML), 72, 73
HTML, 8, 9, 62, 63
    anchor tags, 72, 73
    buttons, 86-89
    checkboxes, 88, 89
    coding, 66, 67
    combo boxes, 90, 91
    comments, 66, 67, 126, 127
    controlling tab order, 94, 95
    documents and pages, 64, 65
    form-based authentication, 430-433
    form tags, 114, 115
    forms, 82, 83
    Get method, 114-117
    hidden fields, 84, 85, 228, 229
    href tag, 72, 73
    hypertext links, 72, 73
    images, 78, 79
    includes, 186, 187
    links, 72, 73
    list boxes, 90, 91
    password boxes, 84, 85
    Post method, 116, 117
    radio buttons, 88, 89
    requesting servlets, 150, 151
    saving, 68, 69
    style sheets, 80, 81
    submit buttons, 82, 83
    tables, 74-77
    tags, 64-67
    text areas, 92, 93
    text boxes, 84, 85
    text controls, 84, 85
    URL rewriting, 226, 227
    viewing, 70, 71
HTTP, 8, 9, 438-461
    404 error, 132, 133
    500 error, 132, 133
    cache-control, 456, 457
    Get method in servlets, 104, 105, 144-147
    headers, 438, 439, 448, 449
    methods, 116, 117
    MIME types, 440, 441
    Post method, 146, 147, 228, 229
    protocols, 42, 43
    request headers, 442, 443, 448-451
    requests, 8, 9, 438, 439
    response headers, 446, 447, 454, 455
    responses, 8, 9, 438, 439
    returning excel spreadsheets, 456, 457
    sessions, 204, 205
    status codes, 198, 199, 444, 445
    status errors, 46, 47

URLs, 42, 43
XML, 498, 499
HTTP 1.1 specification, 438, 439
https, 398, 399, 410, 411
HttpServlet class, 16, 17, 146, 147, 152, 153, 176, 177
HttpServletRequest interface, 146, 147, 448, 449
HttpServletResponse interface, 146, 147, 455
HttpSession class, 208, 209
Hypertext links, 72, 73
Hypertext Markup Language, *see HTML*
Hypertext Transfer Protocol, *see HTTP*

I

IDEs (Integrated Development Environments), 22
   HomeSite, 62, 63
IllegalStateException class, 210, 211
Images, 78, 79
IMAP (Internet Message Access Protocol), 376, 377
Implicit JSP objects
   exception, 134, 135
   request, 106, 107
Importing classes in JSP, 124, 125
Include action, 188, 189
Include directive, 188, 189
Include files, 186-189
Init method, 152-155, 194, 195
Initialization parameters, 192-195
Inline DTD, 472, 473
Inner joins, 326, 327
INSERT statement, 320, 321, 328, 329
Inserting data in database, 320, 321, 342, 343
Installing
   JavaMail, 378, 379
   JSSE, 404, 405
   MySQL, 312
   Security, 418, 419
   SSL, 404-407
   Tomcat, 30, 31
Instance variables
   in JSPs, 128, 129
   in servlets, 154, 155
Integrated Development Environments, *see IDEs*
Interfaces
   for EJBs, 510, 511
   with JavaBeans, 256, 257
   SingleThreadModel, 156, 157
   tagging, 156, 157
Internal Server Error, 444, 445
Internet, 4-7, 18, 19
Internet Explorer (request headers), 452, 453
Internet Message Access Protocol, *see IMAP*
Internet Service Provider, *see ISP*
invalidate method (HttpSession), 210, 211
Invisible JavaBeans, 244, 245

IP address, 24
isNew method (HttpSession), 210, 211
ISP (Internet Service Provider), 24, 25

J

J2EE (Java 2 Platform Enterprise Edition), 12, 13, 504, 505
J2SE (Java 2 Platform Standard Edition), 12, 13
JAF (JavaBeans Activation Framework), 378, 379
Jakarta-Tomcat, *see Tomcat*
JAR files, 52, 53
   with Tomcat, 30-34
Java
   applets, 12
   JDBC, 334-345
   packages, 52, 53
   web programming, 12, 13
Java 2 Platform, Enterprise Edition, *see J2EE*
Java 2 Platform, Standard Edition, *see J2SE*
Java classes, 120, 121
Java Database Connectivity, *see JDBC*
JAVA_HOME environment variable, 34, 35
Java Runtime Environment, *see JRE*
Java Secure Socket Extension, *see JSSE*
Java Software Development Kit, *see SDK*
JavaBeans, 20, 21, 244-263
   abstract classes, 256, 257
   converting data types, 254, 255
   enterprise, 504-519
   getProperty tag, 250, 251
   interfaces, 256, 257
   invisible, 244, 245
   with Model 1 architecture, 172, 173
   properties, 244, 245, 252, 253
   request parameters, 252, 253
   scope, 248, 249
   setProperty tag, 250, 251
   useBean tag, 248, 249
   using in JSPs, 246, 247
JavaBeans Activation Framework API, *see JAF*
JavaExchange.com, 358, 359
JavaMail, 375-393
   addressing a message, 386, 387
   creating a message, 382-385
   installing, 377-379
   mail client/server, 376, 377
   protocols, 376, 377
   sending a message, 388, 389
JavaScript
   buttons, 86, 87
   functions, 178, 179
   validating data, 178-181
JavaServer Pages, *see JSP*
JBoss, 505

JDBC, 334-345
    connecting to a database, 336, 337
    connection pooling, 356-361
    database drivers, 334, 335
    deleting data, 342, 343
    inserting data, 342, 343
    prepared statements, 344, 345
    result sets, 338-341
    security restrictions, 424-427
    updating data, 342, 343
JDBC-ODBC bridge driver, 334, 335
JDBC realm, 424-427
Joins, 326, 327
JPG (Joint Photographic Experts Group), 78, 79
JRE, 12, 13
JSP, 14, 15
    accessing headers, 450, 451
    accessing HTML control values, 110, 111
    comments, 126, 127
    compile-time includes, 188, 189
    custom tags, 268, 269
    declarations, 128, 129
    deploying, 24, 25
    development platforms, 18, 19
    directives, 124, 125
    editors, 62, 63
    error pages, 134, 135
    errors, 132, 133
    exception object, 134, 135
    expressions, 106-109
    how they work, 136, 137
    IDEs, 62, 63
    importing classes, 124, 125
    include actions, 188, 189
    include directives, 188, 189
    include files, 186-189
    instance variables, 128, 129
    JavaBeans, 246, 247
    methods, 128, 129
    page directives, 124, 125
    reiterating custom tags, 283, 284
    request object, 110, 111
    requesting, 114, 115
    request-time includes, 188, 189
    saving, 112, 113
    scriptlets, 106-109
    servlet code, 136, 137
    session object, 208, 209
    summary of tags, 125
    syntax, 108, 109
    taglib directive, 268, 269
    tags, 106, 107, 124, 125
    thread-safe code, 128, 129
    tools for writing, 22, 23
    translation-time includes, 188, 189
    using Java classes, 118-123

JSSE (Java Secure Socket Extension), 404, 405

K

Keystore file, 406, 407
Keywords
    form, 86
    synchronized, 118, 119, 154, 155
    this, 86, 154, 155
    transient, 514, 515

L

LAN (Local Area Network), 6, 18, 19
Last-modified header, 447
Left outer join, 326, 327
Lifecycle of a servlet, 152, 153
Linked style sheets, 80, 81
Links (HTML), 72, 73
List boxes, 90, 91
Load command, 320, 321
Local Area Network, *see LAN*
Location header, 447
Log files, 162, 163
Login page, 430, 431

M

Macromedia HomeSite, *see HomeSite*
Mail, *see also JavaMail*
    client/server, 376, 377
    sessions, 382, 383
MailUtil class, 390, 391
Memory realm, 424, 425
Memory settings, 36, 37, 40, 41
Meta data, 354, 355
Methods
    in JSPs, 128, 129
    synchronizing, 156, 157
MIME types, 376, 377, 440, 441
    checking, 449
    excel spreadsheets, 456, 457
    setting, 454, 455
    XML, 498, 499
MimeMessage class, 384, 385
Model, 174, 175
Model 1 architecture, 172, 173
Model 2 architecture, 174, 175
Model-View-Controller pattern, *see MVC*
Multipurpose Internet Message Extension, *see MIME*
MurachPool class, 358, 359
Music Store web site
    class diagrams for business objects, 532, 533
    class diagrams for data access classes, 540, 541
    database diagrams, 536, 537
    directory structure, 530, 531

SQL scripts, 536, 538, 539
structure, 528, 529
user interface, 524, 525
MVC (Model-View-Controller pattern), 174, 175
my.cnf file, 322, 323
MySQL, 6, 7, 308-323
configuring, 322, 323
connecting to, 336, 337
creating a database, 316, 317
creating tables, 318, 319
database drivers, 334, 335
database server, 312, 313
deleting a database, 316, 317
deleting tables, 318, 319
foreign key, 318, 319
inserting data, 320, 321
installing, 312, 313
Load command, 320, 321
my.cnf file, 322, 323
mysql program, 314-317, 322, 323
primary key, 318, 319
pros and cons, 308, 309
scripts, 318-321
starting and stopping, 312, 313
using, 310, 311
viewing all databases, 316, 317

N

Native protocol all Java driver, 334, 335
Native protocol partly Java driver, 334, 335
Net protocol all Java driver, 334, 335
Netscape (request headers), 452, 453
Node interface, 478, 479
Node types, 476, 477
NodeList interface, 488, 489
Nodes, 476, 477
adding, 482, 483, 490, 491
child, 476, 477
deleting, 490, 491
hierarchy, 478, 479
inserting, 490, 491
modifying, 490, 491
parent, 476, 477
reading, 488, 489
sibling, 476, 477

O

Object pooling, 506, 507
onClick attribute, 86, 87
Oracle, 6, 7, 336, 337
Out of environment space error, 36, 37, 40, 41
Outer joins, 326, 327

P

Packages, 52, 53
Page cannot be displayed error, 46, 47
Page directives, 124, 125
Page Not Found error, 444, 445
PageContext class, 272, 273, 288, 289, 296, 297
Parameters, 104, 105
with Get and Post methods, 116, 117
with JSPs, 114, 115
with servlets, 150, 151
Parsing XML, 474, 475
Password boxes, 84, 85
Passwords, 424-427
Patterns, 174
PDF (Portable Document Format), 460, 461
Per-session cookies, 212, 213
Persistence, 505-509, 514, 515
Persistent cookies, 212, 213, 216, 217
Persistent data storage, 172, 173
Platforms, 18, 19
POP (Post Office Protocol), 376, 377
Portable Document Format, *see PDF*
Ports, 42, 43, 48, 49
Post method (HTTP), 116, 117, 228, 229
Post Office Protocol, *see POP*
Pragma header, 447
Prepared statements, 344, 345
Presentation layer, 20, 21
Primary key, 318, 319
PrintWriter object (servlets), 146, 147
Problems with Tomcat, 46, 47
Properties of JavaBeans, 244, 245, 252, 253
Protocols
HTTP, 42, 43, 438-461
mail, 376, 377
SSL, 398, 399
stateful, 204
stateless, 204, 205

Q

Queries, 324, 328, 329

R

Radio buttons, 88, 89
RA (Registration Authority), 402, 403
RDBMS (Relational database management system), 308
Realms, 424-427
Redirecting requests and responses, 176, 177
Referer request header, 443
Refresh header, 447
Registration authority, 402, 403
Reiterating custom tags, 284-289

Relational database management system, *see RDBMS*
Relational database, 20, 21, 318, 319
Relative URLs, 72, 73
release method (custom tags), 294, 295, 298, 299
Remote interface, 510-513
removeAttribute method (HttpSession), 208, 209
Reports application, 592-597
Request headers, 438, 439, 442, 443
    accessing, 449
    methods, 448, 449
    reading from JSP, 450, 451
Request line, 438, 439
Request object
    implicit, 106, 107
    in JSPs, 106, 107
    methods, 110, 111, 449
    in servlets, 144-147
Request parameters
    and JavaBeans, 252, 253
    reading in JSP, 110, 111
    in a URL, 114, 115
Request-time includes, 188, 189
RequestDispatcher class, 176, 177
Requesting servlets, 150, 151
Requests
    forwarding, 176, 177
    in HTML, 70, 71
    redirecting, 176, 177
Reset button, 86, 87
Response body, 438, 439
Response entity, 438, 439
Response headers, 438, 439, 446, 447, 454, 455
Response object, 144-147
Responses
    forwarding, 176, 177
    GZIP compression, 458, 459
    HTTP, 8, 9
    redirecting, 176, 177
    XML content, 498, 499
Restricted access, 418, 419
Result sets, 324, 325, 338-341
Right outer join, 326, 327
Roles, 424-427
Root directory, 52
Root element, 190, 191
    XML, 468, 469
Running servlets, 150, 151

S

Saving
    JSPs, 112, 113
    servlets, 148, 149
SAX (Simple API for XML), 474, 475
Schema languages, 472, 473

Scope
    application, 248, 249
    JavaBeans, 248, 249
    page, 248, 249
    pageContext, 296, 297
    request, 248, 249
    scripting variables, 292, 293
    session, 248, 249
Scripting variables, 290-293
Scriptlets, 106, 107
Scripts, 318-321
SDK (Java 2 Platform Standard Development Kit), 13, 14
Secure certificates, 400-403
Secure connections, 398, 399, 410-411
Secure Sockets Layer, *see SSL*
Security constraints, 418, 419, 422, 423
    passwords, 424-427
    realms, 424, 425
    roles, 424-427
    usernames, 424-427
Security (container-managed), 418, 419
SELECT statements, 324-327
sendRedirect method (HttpResponse), 176, 177
Server authentication, 400, 401
Server
    EJB, 12, 13, 504, 505
    web, 6, 7
Server.xml file, 38, 39
    with JDBC realm, 424-427
Service method, 152, 153
Servlet and JSP container, 12, 13
Servlet and JSP engine, 12, 13
Servlet code for JSPs, 136, 137
Servlet initialization parameters, 192-195
Servlet mapping, 196, 197
Servlet reloading, 38, 39
Servlet.jar file, 30, 31
ServletContext interface, 176, 177
Servlets, 16, 17
    coding, 146, 147
    content type, 144-147
    cookies, 204, 205, 216-221
    data validation, 182, 185
    debugging 158-161
    deploying, 24, 25
    destroy method, 152, 153
    development platform, 18, 19
    doGet method, 144, 145, 152, 153
    doPost method, 152, 153
    error handling, 198, 199
    GenericServlet class, 146
    Get method, 144, 145
    getWriter method, 146, 147
    how they work, 152, 153
    HttpServletRequest object, 146, 147

HttpServletResponse object, 146, 147
init method, 152-155
instance variables, 154, 155
lifecycle, 152, 153
log files, 162, 163
mail applications, 392, 393
methods, 152, 153
println statements, 144, 145
PrintWriter object, 146, 147
problems, 158, 159
reading initialization parameters, 194, 195
request object, 144, 145
requesting, 150, 151
response object, 144, 145
saving and compiling 148, 149
service method, 152, 153
servlet mapping, 196, 197
session tracking, 204, 205
sessions, 208, 209
SingleThreadModel interface, 156, 157
structure, 146, 147
synchronizing, 154-157
thread-safe code, 156, 157
tools for writing, 22, 23
URL encoding, 204, 205, 214, 215
working with parameters, 150, 151
Session beans, 508-511
Session ID, 204, 205, 214, 215
Session object, 204, 205, 208-211
Session tracking, 204, 205
SessionBean class, 510, 511
Sessions, 204, 205, 208, 209
create, 210, 211
invalidate, 210, 211
mail, 382, 283
scope, 248, 249
session ID, 214, 215
set age, 210, 211
URL encoding, 214, 215
setAttribute method (HttpSession), 208, 209
setContentType method (servlets), 146, 147
setDomain method (Cookie), 222, 223
setMaxInactiveInterval method (HttpSession), 210, 211
setPath method (Cookie), 222, 223
setProperty tag (JavaBeans), 250, 251
setSecure method (Cookie), 222, 223
setVersion method (Cookie), 222, 223
Shopping Cart application, 207, 208,
Shopping Cart application (Music Store web site), 558-577
structure, 562, 563
user interface, 558-561
Sibling nodes, 476, 477
Simple API for XML, *see SAX*
Simple Mail Transfer Protocol, *see SMTP*
SingleThreadModel interface, 156, 157

Singleton class, 358, 359
SKIP_BODY constant (custom tags), 272, 273, 294, 295, 298, 299
SKIP_PAGE constant, 294, 295, 298, 299
SMTP (Simple Mail Transfer Protocol), 376, 377
Software Development Kit, *see SDK*
Sound files (downloading), 460, 461
SQL, 308, 309
DDL, 324
DELETE statement, 328, 329
deleting data, 342, 343
DML, 324
INSERT statement, 328, 329
inserting data, 342, 343
joins, 326, 327
meta data, 354, 355
queries, 324, 325
result sets, 324, 325
scripts, 318-321
SELECT statements, 324-327
statements, 318, 319, 324-329
UPDATE statement, 328, 329
updating data, 342, 343
SQL Gateway application, 346-355
SQLGatewayServlet class, 350-353
SQLUtil class, 354, 355
SSL, 398-413
authentication, 400, 401
CA (Certificate authority), 402, 403
client authentication, 400, 401
configuration, 404-407
connections, 412, 413
deployment, 412
keystore file, 406, 407
RA (Registration authority), 402, 403
requesting secure connections, 410, 411
with restricted access, 418, 419
secure certificates, 400-403
self signed certificates, 404-407
server authentication, 400, 401
strength, 402, 403
testing environment, 404, 405
testing, 408, 409
Stack trace, 162, 163
Stand-alone development, 18, 19
State, 508
Stateful protocol, 204
Stateful session beans, 508, 509
Stateless protocol, 204, 205
Stateless session beans, 508, 509
Static web pages, 8, 9
Status codes, 439, 444, 445, 454, 455
Status line, 438, 439
Strength (SSL), 402, 403
Structured Query Language, *see SQL*

Style sheets, 80, 81
Submit buttons, 82, 83, 86, 87
Synchronizing threads, 128, 129
Synchronized code, 154-157
Synchronized keyword, 118, 119
System administrator, 506, 507

T

Tab-delimited files, 456, 457
Tab order, 94, 95
Tables
    foreign key, 318, 319
    in HTML, 74-77
    inserting data, 320, 321
    joins, 326, 327
    MySQL, 318, 319
    primary key, 318, 319
    SELECT statements, 324-327
Tag Extra Information class, *see TEI*
Tag handler class, 270-273
    with attributes, 282, 283
Tag interface, 272, 273
Tag library, 270, 271
Tag Library Descriptor, *see TLD*
TagExtraInfo class, 292, 293
Tagging interfaces, 156, 157
Taglib directive, 268, 269
Tags
    check boxes, 88, 89
    combo boxes, 90, 91
    custom, *see custom tags*
    form, 82, 83, 114, 115
    getProperty, 250, 251
    HTML, 64-67
    JavaBeans, 246, 247
    JSP, 106, 107
    list boxes, 90, 91
    radio buttons, 88, 89
    setProperty, 250, 251
    tables, 76, 77
    text areas, 92, 93
    useBean, 248, 249
    XML, 190, 191, 466, 467
TagSupport class, 272, 273, 294, 295
TEI (tag extra information class), 290-193
Text areas, 92, 93
Text boxes, 84, 85
Text controls, 84, 85
Text interface, 478, 479
TextPad, 22, 23
this keyword, 86, 154, 155
Threads
    in JSPs, 128, 129
    in servlets, 156, 157

Thread-safe code, 128, 129, 156, 157
TLD (tag library descriptor), 268, 269
    and attributes, 280, 281
    for body tags, 276, 277
    coding, 270, 271
    saving, 270, 271
TLS (Transport Layer Security), 398, 399
Tomcat, 12, 13
    authentication, 418, 419
    debugging servlets, 160-163
    deployment descriptor, 54, 55
    directories and files, 32, 33
    document root directory, 52
    error handling, 198, 199
    executing servlets, 152, 153
    implementing basic authentication, 428, 429
    implementing form-based authentication, 430-433
    installing, 30, 31
    installing database drivers, 334, 335
    JAR files, 52, 53
    JDBC realm, 424-427
    log files, 162, 163
    memory realm, 424, 425
    ports, 42, 43, 48, 49
    request parameters, 114, 115
    requesting JSPs, 114, 115
    requesting servlets, 152, 153
    saving and compiling Java classes, 120, 121
    saving and compiling servlets, 148, 149
    saving JSPs, 112, 113
    security constraints, 422, 423
    servlet code for JSPs, 136, 137
    setting initialization parameters, 192, 193
    SSL, 404-409
    starting and stopping, 40, 41
    TLD files, 270, 271
    troubleshooting, 46, 47
    using, 40-45
    viewing HTML pages, 70, 71
    WEB-INF directory, 52, 53
    web.xml file, 54, 55, 190-191, 422, 423
Transactions, 506, 507
Transforming DOM, 484, 485
Transient keyword, 514, 515
Translation-time includes, 188, 189
Transport Layer Security, *see TLS*
Troubleshooting (Tomcat), 46, 47

U

Unauthorized error, 445
Uniform Resource Locator, *see URL*
UPDATE statement, 328, 329
Updating data in database, 342, 343
URL encoding, 204, 205, 214, 215

URL rewriting, 226, 227
URLs, 42, 43
    absolute, 72, 73
    https, 398, 399
    relative, 72, 73
    requesting JSPs, 114, 115
    requesting servlets, 150, 151
    secure connections, 408-411
    and servlet mapping, 196, 197
    URL rewriting, 226, 227
useBean tag, 248, 249
User-agent request header, 443
User bean class, 244, 245
User interface layer, 20
UserDB class, 366-369
Usernames, 424-427
UTF-8, 469

V

Validating data
    with JavaScript, 178-181
    with servlets, 182-185
Validation (XML), 486, 487
VariableInfo class, 292, 293
View, 174, 175

W

Web applications, 4-7
    architecture, 20, 21
    components, 12, 13
    cookies, 204, 205
    deploying, 50
    in Java, 12, 13
    Model 1 architecture, 172, 173
    Model 2 architecture, 174, 175
    Model-View-Controller patter, 174, 175
    root directory, 52
    running, 50, 51
    session tracking, 204, 205
    structure, 52, 53
Web browsers, 6, 7, 42, 43
Web hosts, 24, 25
Web pages
    dynamic, 10, 11
    static, 8, 9
    viewing, 42, 43
Web programming with Java, 12, 13
Web resources (restricted), 418, 419
Web servers, 6, 7
Web.xml file, 54, 55, 190, 191
    context initialization parameters, 192, 193
    error handling, 198, 199

implementing basic authentication, 428, 429
    initialization parameters, 192, 193
    security constraints, 422, 423
    servlet mapping, 196, 197
    WEB-INF directory, 52, 53
WEB-INF directory, 52, 53, 190, 191
www-authenticate header, 447

X

XML, 20, 21, 466-499
    attributes, 470, 471
    child elements, 468, 469
    comments, 468, 469
    content, 469
    declarations, 468, 469
    DOM, 474, 475
    DOM tree, 476, 477
    DTD, 472, 473
    elements, 468, 469
    Java APIs, 474, 475
    nodes, 476, 477
    parent elements, 468, 469
    returning to browser, 498, 499
    root element, 468, 469
    SAX, 474, 475
    schema languages, 472, 473
    tags, *see XML tags*
    uses, 466, 467
XML document, 466, 467
XML Schema Definition, *see XSD*
XML tags, 466, 467
    child elements, 190, 191
    elements, 190, 191
    root element, 190, 191
    with web.xml, 190, 191
XMLUtil class, 492, 493
XSD (XML Schema Definition), 472, 473

For more on Murach products, visit us at
www.murach.com

For professional programmers

Murach's Beginning Java 2	$49.50
Murach's Java Servlets and JSP	49.50
Murach's Structured COBOL	$62.50
Murach's CICS for the COBOL Programmer	54.00
Murach's CICS Desk Reference	49.50
Murach's OS/390 and z/OS JCL	62.50
DB2 for the COBOL Programmer, Part 1 (Second Edition)	45.00
DB2 for the COBOL Programmer, Part 2 (Second Edition)	45.00
Murach's Beginning Visual Basic .NET	$49.50
Murach's VB.NET Database Programming with ADO.NET	49.50
Murach's ASP.NET Web Programming with VB.NET	49.50
Murach's SQL for SQL Server	49.50

Coming soon

Murach's C#

*Prices and availability are subject to change. Please visit our web site or call for current information.

Our unlimited guarantee...when you order directly from us

You must be satisfied with our books. If they aren't better than any other programming books you've ever used...both for training and reference....you can send them back for a full refund. No questions asked!

Your opinions count

If you have any comments on this book, I'm eager to get them. Thanks for your feedback!

Mike Murach

To comment by
E-mail:　　murachbooks@murach.com
Web:　　　www.murach.com
Postal mail:　Mike Murach & Associates, Inc.
　　　　　　3484 W. Gettysburg, Suite 101
　　　　　　Fresno, California 93722-7801

To order now,

Web: www.murach.com

Call toll-free:
1-800-221-5528
(Weekdays, 8 am to 5 pm Pacific Time)

Fax: 1-559-440-0963

Mike Murach & Associates, Inc.
Professional programming books

What the CD contains

- The Java™ 2 Software Development Kit (SDK), Standard Edition, version 1.4
- Tomcat 4.0, a popular servlet and JSP engine
- MySQL 3.23, a popular open-source database
- The source code for the applications presented in this book
- The SQL scripts for creating the databases used by the applications in this book
- A trial version of TextPad 4.5, a text editor that makes it easier for you to enter, edit, compile, and test Java code
- A trial version of HomeSite 5, a text editor that makes it easier for you to enter, edit, and save HTML pages

How to install the SDK

- Navigate to the directory on the CD named WindowsSDK, run the exe file, and respond to the resulting dialog boxes. Then, add the SDK's bin directory to the Windows command path. For more information, see figures A-1 and A-3 on pages 600 and 604.

How to install Tomcat

- Navigate to the Tomcat 4.0 directory on the CD and unzip the ZIP file onto your C drive. Next, copy the servlet.jar file from Tomcat's common\lib directory to the SDK's jre\lib\ext directory. And then, edit the catalina.bat file that's stored in Tomcat's bin directory so the JAVA_HOME variable points to the home directory for the SDK. For more information, see figures 2-1 and 2-3 on pages 31 and 35.
- For information about installing newer versions of Tomcat, such as Tomcat 4.1 or 5.0, visit our web site *(www.murach.com)*, go to the main page for this book, and click on the FAQs link.

How to install MySQL

- Navigate to the directory on the CD named MySQL, run the Setup.exe file, and respond to the resulting dialog boxes. Then, copy the JAR file from the MySQL_Driver directory on the CD to Tomcat's common\lib directory. For more information, see figure A-2 on page 602.

How to install the applications for this book

- Navigate to the root directory on the CD and double-click on the file named Install.exe. This creates a directory named C:\murach and copies all application files to this directory.
- To install the sample applications, copy the murach and musicStore subdirectories from the C:\murach\webapps directory to Tomcat's webapps directory.
- To create the databases for these applications, use MySQL to run the SQL scripts stored in the murach and musicStore subdirectories of the C:\murach\webapps directory.
- For more information, see figure A-5 on page 608.